Also by the Authors

THE ONLY JOB HUNTING GUIDE YOU'LL EVER NEED

JOBS '90

JOBS '91

JOBS '92

The Only
RETIREMENT
GUIDE
You'll Ever Need

KATHRYN & ROSS PETRAS

A FIRESIDE BOOK
Published by Simon & Schuster
New York London Toronto Sydney Tokyo Singapore

FIRESIDE
Simon & Schuster Building
Rockefeller Center
1230 Avenue of the Americas
New York, New York 10020

Copyright © 1991 by Kathryn and Ross Petras

All rights reserved including the right of reproduction
in whole or in part in any form.

First Fireside Edition 1995

FIRESIDE and colophon are registered trademarks of Simon & Schuster Inc.

Manufactured in the United States of America

10 9 8 7 6

Library of Congress Cataloging in Publication Data

Petras, Kathryn.
The only retirement guide you'll ever need / Kathryn & Ross
Petras.
p. cm.
Includes index.
1. Retirees—United States—Finance, Personal—Handbooks, manuals,
etc.   2. Retirement income—United States—Planning—Handbooks,
manuals, etc.   3. Retirement—United States—Planning—Handbooks,
manuals, etc.   I. Petras, Ross.   II. Title.
HG179.P448   1991
332.024'01—dc20   91-25536
                                                                CIP
ISBN: 0-671-70060-X

Note: This book reflects a great deal of research as well as the input of
experts on a wide range of technical subjects. In all cases, the authors
have tried to be accurate and up to date. Because of the timely nature of
the subjects covered, changing legislation, and the like, however, inac-
curacies may occur. Also, the inclusion of any specific source or the mention of any specific tactic or strategy does not necessarily constitute a
recommendation. Any recommendation the authors do make is based
upon their research and the data available to them—the reader must do
further research on his or her own to determine if a source or tactic is
the right choice. In those cases where legal or other professional advice is
required, the authors recommend that the reader seek the appropriate
assistance.

ACKNOWLEDGMENTS

A book of this breadth, depth, and complexity would have been impossible without the help of many friends and acquaintances— too many to be named here without adding another hundred or so pages.

But briefly, we would like to thank Robert Withers, for expert editing and needed suggestions, Elaine Pfefferblit for calmly shepherding the manuscript through various incarnations, Laura Demanski for always being helpful, Karolina Harris for being patient, and, of course, Ann Patty for everything else; John Russell of John A. Russell Associates; Shawn M. Foley, MSW; Maggie O'Donovan, Ginny Sakell, and particularly Craig A. Rosin of the accounting firm Coopers & Lybrand for their contributions—and a special thank you for expert insight and financial advice to Jonathan Brecht, financial consultant at Merrill Lynch, New York.

CONTENTS

Part II. Estate Planning and Legal Considerations 279

Introduction

WHAT IS RETIREMENT?

If you're reading this book, you're thinking about retiring—in the near future or even the not-so-near future. But what is it that you're visualizing? What does retiring mean to you?

It used to be simple. In the past, retirement was looked at as an ending—an end to regular work, an end to your so-called productive years. The rules were clear—when you reached a certain age, you retired from your job, collected your gold watch, your pension, and your Social Security benefits, and that was that.

It's not that simple anymore. The rules have changed. And the first rule is that there are no rules. In other words, *retirement in the 1990s can be anything you want it to be.*

Do you want to leave your job and move to a condo in Florida the minute you turn 65? Or do you want to leave your job the minute you turn *45?* Either way, you're retiring.

What if you don't want a traditional retirement? Perhaps you're forced into retirement by company policy before you're ready to take it easy. That's fine, too. You can opt for a new career or start your own business.

Or maybe instead you are looking forward to some time away from work. Retirement time means you finally have a chance to do things you've dreamed of. Traveling. Devoting time to your hobbies, your family, yourself.

These are all options you face. They're all different ways of retiring.

▶ **Who are today's retirees? Just as retiring can take many different forms, so today's retirees can be many different kinds of people.**

13

Retirees can be 35, 45, 65, or 75. Retirement isn't an age. It's a change in lifestyle. And you're the one who decides what you want that change to be and how to go about it.

Although retirement is now a very individual thing, there are a few remarkable facts about retiring in the '90s.

- *There are more retirees than ever before.* One reason is that nowadays there are more people living to the traditional retirement age—65 or older—than in previous times. And the number is going to keep growing. In 1990, one out of every five Americans was 65 or older. By 2025, it will be one out of every three.

- *Many people nearing retirement today are starting off with a big plus—few money worries.* Between robust Social Security benefits, employer-provided pensions and health insurance, the birth of such personal retirement plans as IRAs, and rising home values, the current crop of retirees and soon-to-be retirees are more comfortably off than any others in the past. People who are already retired or are nearing the typical retirement age of 65 control most of the money in the country—77% of financial assets of all U.S. households are currently held by people 50 or over, and 75% of all people over 65 own their own house.

- *Retirees in the 1990s and beyond can expect a long, healthy retirement.* We're all living longer. Our life expectancy is increasing. Where in years past, average life expectancy was 70 for men and 75 for women, now we can expect to live well into our 80s and 90s. And we can look forward to active senior years as well. Most of today's retirees are leading full, vibrant lives—unhampered, to a great degree, by poor health or frailty. According to a Census Bureau survey, about 80% of people over 65 say their health is good or excellent. With the aging of the population and the attention being paid to geriatric medicine and other health specialties, we can be assured that this trend will continue.

What does all this mean?

You can expect to face more years of happy, healthy retirement than ever before. If you're currently in your 50s and plan to retire at age 65, it's reasonable to assume your retirement will last 25 years or more.

Twenty-five years. That's quite an amount of time—time you can fill however you want. Perhaps you'll travel, see the world as you've always wanted to. Or you'll finally be able to pursue your hobbies. Or maybe you'll just relax a bit, kick back and take it easy after years in the rat race.

Remember: Retirement today is a beginning—the beginning of a new life.

The key, of course, is beginning that new life secure in the knowledge that you are well provided for, that you will live comfortably and enjoy your retirement years.

And the only way to do this is by planning.

HOW TO GET READY FOR RETIREMENT

Emotional Factors: Are You Ready to Retire?

▶ **As with any change in life, you have to be emotionally ready for retirement.**

To retire successfully, you need to have addressed the psychological side of things. You will have to be sure you have an idea of what retirement will be for you—what type of lifestyle you want, where you will live, and so on.

This is an aspect of retirement planning that, unfortunately, is all too often overlooked or bypassed. People often idealize retirement and fail to take major emotional factors into account at the outset. They picture themselves having a wonderful time, finally away from the pressures of work, the hassles of nine-to-five, and stop there. They don't actually think about what they will be doing with their newly found free time. Then retirement time rolls around and they find themselves with time on their hands and no idea of how to spend it. They wind up unstimulated, bored, or simply unhappy.

▶ **What about you? Have you thought about what retirement will mean for you?**

Or is it just a word—something you know is coming up but haven't seriously thought about. "I'll adjust when the time comes," you assume. Of course, the danger with this approach is that, when the time comes, you might not adjust as quickly as you thought. It can be a rough transition—switching from the old comfortable routines to something completely new. And if you haven't prepared, you might not make the transition smoothly.

The bottom line, then, is clear: Just as you must start preparing financially for retirement, you must also start preparing mentally. And the time to begin this is *now!*

Start by thinking about the following questions. Obviously there are no right or wrong answers. These questions are intended to give you insight into the psychological side of retirement and clue you in as to how ready for retirement you are.

- *Do I have interests outside of my job?* Studies show that retirees with active interests beyond their work adjust the best to retirement. They don't fall prey to the "I'm old, I have nothing to look forward to, I'm unfulfilled" trap that some older people find themselves caught in. If you linger at work, if you socialize almost exclusively with coworkers, if you bring work home at night and on weekends, you may be so tied up in work that retirement will be a rude shock. Try to gradually break away now. Start weaning yourself from the job and the people on the job. One of the best ways to do this is to scale back your hours at work as you get closer to retirement. This will ease the transition.

- *Am I involved in a range of activities and pursuits—in different areas?* A happy retiree tends to be a well-balanced one—a person with active interest in all sides of life, from the artistic to the athletic to the educational. Remember, retirement brings with it newly found free time. And most retirees discover that they want to fill that time with different activities, not the same one day in and day out. If you're not involved in different pursuits, start thinking about this now. Maybe there is something new that intrigues you. Or perhaps you can rediscover the interests you had years ago, but pushed aside for lack of time.

- *Am I willing to try new things?* Retirement is a time of adjustment— and it's a time of establishing new routines. If you're flexible you can make the move into retirement more easily. A good rule of thumb: If you've gotten involved in new activities (anything from taking courses at your community school to joining a health club) within the past five or so years, it's a sign that you are open to new experiences.

- *Am I at wit's end when I don't have a set schedule?* Come retirement time, you'll be responsible for your own routines. No more buses to catch, bosses to please, or meetings to attend. You won't have anyone or anything determining your day. If you are already happy filling in your free time with activities you have chosen, then retirement will come easily.

- *Do my spouse and I have separate interests? Do we give each other private time?* You and your spouse may be under the same roof for more hours than ever before. And regardless of how well you get along, it's also important for the two of you to have some privacy.

- *Have I discussed retirement with my spouse or companion?* Retirees who plan with their spouse are the ones who adjust well. Remember, retirement isn't a solo act—it includes you and your loved ones. Perhaps you will retire and your spouse will keep working for a while. Or perhaps you'll both be home, or traveling together. Whatever the specific case, if you keep your loved ones involved every step of the way, from the very beginning, you can be sure your retirement will fit in with their needs and routines.

- *How have I coped with major changes in my life up to this point?* How you handled moving to a new state, changing jobs, children's moving or marrying can clue you in to how you will handle the change of lifestyle that retirement brings.

- *Do I view retirement positively?* This is a vital question and one with far-reaching repercussions. If you are looking forward to retirement, if you view it as a welcome change in your life, a new adventure, then you probably will find it so. By the same token, if you consider retirement a necessary evil, something you don't really want to do but are forced to do, you might find your worst fears confirmed. Ideally, you should try for a positive outlook. Recognize that retirement isn't the end of the road, it's a fork in the road. You don't have to sit in a rocking chair. You can consider a nontraditional retirement. For example, look into a second career or starting your own business—something to keep you fulfilled.

- *Most important, do I have a clear idea of what I want from retirement?* What your retirement entails is entirely up to you. Satisfied retirees are those who know themselves and know what they need to make them happy and fulfilled. To make retirement work *for you*, you must first take into account your needs, your temperament, and your personality. Then visualize (and plan) a retirement that suits you.

Remember—the sooner you begin thinking about retirement and what you want from it, the more likely you are to reach your goals. Changing your lifestyle, as you will when you retire, can be a positive challenge . . . if you prepare.

If you focus on the emotional aspects of changing your life, the time you spend *now* will mean better times *later*.

The Practical Side: Taking the First Steps to Retirement Planning

▶ **A good part of assuring a successful and happy retirement is taking action—analyzing your current lifestyle, deciding what you want your retirement to be, then figuring out how to go about creating it.**

Stripped to the basics, that's really what retirement planning is. It's making decisions—*educated* decisions—about the future. What do you want? How much money will you need to maintain the lifestyle you'd like? How much money can you count on—from pensions, Social Security, and your present investments? And how can you raise the money you'll need to make up the difference?

This can be simple enough, if you take it step by step.

- *Start planning—NOW!* This first step is the most basic of all. Ideally, you should begin planning your retirement at least 5 to 10 years before your intended retirement, or even earlier. This will give you ample time to build up retirement finances, make the necessary emotional adjustments, and make all the legal and administrative arrangements retiring entails. If your retirement is closer than that, it's still not too late. Planning late is better than not planning at all. (For helpful hints designed for late starters, see Appendix: Late Starters, page 510.)

- *Be prepared to go with the flow.* Whatever you plan today may need to be changed tomorrow. These days you can't predict what will happen with the economy. Inflation rates go up and down. Taxes rise and . . . rise! Be prepared to change your plan as the times dictate, to take advantage of rising interest rates or to cash in on a stock market development.

- *Coordinate all aspects of retirement planning.* Your insurance, your investments, your tax picture, and your company savings plans are interrelated, and any retirement planning should be done considering the whole, not just the one piece you're looking at. A cohesive retirement plan works best.

- *Keep to the middle of the road.* Boring advice, perhaps, but sound nonetheless. Speculation is all well and good if you have money to burn, but in general, when you're planning for retirement, slow and steady wins the race.

- *Think about what you are working toward.* Having clear goals and a definite idea of why you are doing things (saving money, investing, etc.) helps you keep moving steadily along. You may want to set up incremental goals—ones you can reach at different points as you get closer to retirement. This way you can clearly see how well your plan is working.

- *Keep communicating*—with your spouse, your financial advisors, your family, your friends. Open lines of communication always help.

GETTING STARTED: HOW TO USE THIS BOOK

▶ *The Only Retirement Guide You'll Ever Need* **is designed to take you step by step through each aspect of your retirement planning.**

This book is divided into five sections, each focusing on a different element in planning for a successful retirement.

- *Part I, Financing Your Retirement* focuses on the financial side of retirement planning. It opens with a chapter on financial goals and planning, which tells you how to set savings and investment goals, how to figure out how much money you will need to live comfortably through your retirement, and what financial planners can do for you. It includes chapters on the different sources of retirement income—Social Security, pensions, IRAs, Keoghs and other retirement savings plans, and investments—and explains how each source of income fits into your retirement plan. It also includes a chapter on insurance, which tells you what insurance you will need during your retirement years, how Medicare can help cover *some* health-care costs, and what other insurance needs you will face. Part I considers the subject of investments in detail. It tells how to create a balanced retirement portfolio, how to choose a financial advisor, such as a broker, and how to invest in mutual funds. It also takes a detailed look at most of the major investments you'll make over the years— from money market funds to stocks and bonds to real estate.

- *Part II, Estate Planning and Legal Considerations* leads you through the basics of estate planning, including a discussion of wills, how to avoid probate, and how to pass more on to your heirs by avoiding high estate taxes through the use of trusts. In addition, it looks at some of the legal questions that may arise in your senior years, such as how and when to set up a power of attorney and how to cope with the death of a loved one.

- *Part III, Retirement Lifestyles: Getting the Most Out of Your Retirement* takes you through the next steps in retirement planning—with chapters on the important issues. The chapter on housing options looks at how to decide whether to stay in your current home or move, compares condos and houses, compares buying and renting, and includes an in-depth look at the different retirement communities available to you. The chapter on financing your new home with your old tells you the different ways you can sell your current home. The chapter on picking the perfect retirement spot considers how to choose the right locale in which to spend your retirement years, with lists and descriptions of popular retirement spots and some not-so-well-known gems.

- *Part IV, Healthstyles* focuses on an often-overlooked aspect of a successful retirement—your health. It includes advice on nutrition, exercise, common age-related diseases, health problems (including extensive sources), and medical care.

- *Part V, Active Retirement for the 1990s* takes a look at how you can make your retirement as fulfilling as possible. The chapter on working after retirement covers the different options open to you—from staying at your current company to starting a new business to doing volunteer work. A chapter on travel and leisure focuses on different ways for you to fill your free time, and includes discussions of special options open to retirees.

▶ **To make the book even more helpful to you, hundreds of sources are listed throughout.**

A large part of successful retirement planning is knowing where to go for information. So we've done some of the work for you and listed special sources that will help you in different aspects of retirement planning, including associations, newsletters, magazines, videotapes, and books. These sources appear in every section.

In addition, there are several excellent general sources that can help you plan your retirement—or can help enhance your retirement years. These are listed in the Appendix. Listings of government agencies, including special state agencies on aging, which can give you information on special programs and services available in your local area, also appear in the Appendix.

TIP: **Special mention should be made of the American Association for Retired Persons (AARP). This association boasts a membership of over 40 million people and offers a wide range of special programs and services for people over age 50. Some of their many services and pamphlets are referred to throughout the book. For membership information, see Appendix C.**

▶ *The Only Retirement Guide You'll Ever Need* **is designed to help you regardless of your age or your assets.**

It will give you the detailed information you need about different elements of retirement planning. It will answer the inevitable questions that will arise. And above all, it will enable you to design the retirement plan that will give you the quality of life you want—and deserve.

If you're in your 50s or 60s, you are probably looking at retirement 5 to 10 years in the future and are faced with a dizzying new array of retirement benefits and options. Use *The Only Retirement Guide* to help you make your way through the maze of investment strategies and to coordinate your current savings and retirement plans.

If you're in your 30s or 40s, you surely need to build a retirement nest egg. Current trends all point to one thing: From here on in, you're going to have to provide more of your retirement income yourself. The financial honeymoon retirees have been enjoying is coming to an end. Social Security benefits are being threatened. Employers are cutting back—and eliminating—their generous pension plans. Health benefits to retirees are often falling by the wayside. Use this book to help set up a self-directed retirement plan based upon careful and clever savings and investments that won't be affected by government or corporate cutbacks.

And whatever age you are, use this book to help design a personalized retirement plan—a plan that will lead you to a happy, successful retirement.

One final word: You are planning for what can be the most exciting, fulfilling time of your life. Enjoy!

▶

Financing
Your Retirement

PART I

Chapter 1

FINANCIAL GOALS AND PLANNING

INTRODUCTION

▶ **Planning for a secure financial future is not as simple as it used to be in the days before the wide swings in interest rates, housing prices, inflation, and the economy in general.**

Rock solid Social Security, rock solid bonds, and blue-chip stocks are all not quite as solid today.

But with a little bit of preparation, a little bit of thinking and planning, your financial future in retirement can be assured.

▶ **What is financial planning?**

The purpose of financial planning for retirement is simple—to ensure that you have a financially comfortable retirement. But of course, making these plans isn't necessarily easy.

Financial planning is not an exact science—no matter what some planners may suggest. You're dealing with uncertainty. No one knows what the future will bring. No one knows if inflation will increase to 10% a year, or if, instead, *deflation* might set in. But there are two things you can do in the face of this un-certainty.

1. *You can make reasonable and educated estimates of what will happen in the future,* and invest some money and make some plans accordingly.

That's obvious. It's reasonable to assume the stock market will increase in value over the long run, so it's reasonable for retirees to buy high-quality stocks or mutual funds. To go a step further, it's reasonable to assume a high-rated, highly recommended mutual fund, with a good record of investing, low fees, and a strong current portfolio of stocks, bonds, or money market funds, will continue to do well over the long run.

But what if . . .? What if those assumptions were wrong? Or what if *some* of the assumptions were wrong? What if the economy turns out to be completely different from what you (and the experts) anticipated? What if that fund declines in value?

You *can* do something to guard against uncertainties. You can directly address the issue, as does every good financial plan.

2. *You can be flexible.* You can change your plan to meet changing times, and you can make reasonable provisions for as many "what ifs" as you like. You can *diversify* investments the right way—some short term, some long term. You can buy the right types and amount of insurance, read the right financial magazines and try to anticipate events. In short, you can strategically plan for retirement contingencies.

That's the essence of financial planning, except for your role—setting your own financial objectives.

STEP ONE: DETERMINE YOUR RETIREMENT FINANCIAL GOAL

▶ **What will you need—and want—in retirement? What kind of income will sustain you?**

To answer the question, you might want to first answer another, a lifestyle question. How do you view your retirement? As a peaceful, resting time in your own home? Or as an active, busy phase of your life, involving travel, study, or new undertakings? This is where you must make your first major assumption. What percentage of your current income do you think will sustain you? Don't factor in inflation—that will be factored in later.

Most American retirees live on anything from 60% to 80% of their income just before retirement. The figure is less because working expenses, such as commuting, are cut, and mortgages and taxes tend to be lower.

In most cases, it's far better to assume you'll need an income at the high end of the range—80%. In this way, you allow yourself a cushion, should your plans become more ambitious or should your investments not work out as well as you hoped.

So, to find your target yearly income for retirement, simply multiply your current salary by 80% (or 0.8). That's the major goal of financial planning, to give yourself that comfortable level of income during your retirement.

STEP TWO: IDENTIFY YOUR RESOURCES

▶ **If you're like many retirees, you'll be relying on the so-called "three-legged stool": That is, you will fund your retirement primarily through three main sources of retirement income:**

- *Social Security*—which will pay you a percentage of your annual income based on how much you made over your lifetime. If you had a relatively low income, Social Security will pay benefits equaling up to 70% of your preretirement pay. If you had a relatively high income, you'll get about 28%. On the average, people get about 42% of what they made before they retired. (For more, see Chapter 2.)

- *Pension* (provided by your company)—which generally will replace about 50% to 75% of your current annual salary. Normally, your pension is a percentage of your final pay (a good plan will pay 1% to 1.5%) multiplied by your years at the company. (For more, see Chapter 3.)

- *Savings*—which will be as much (or as little) as you have saved during your working years. Some of these savings may come from such company-sponsored plans as 401(k)s, the rest may come from any saving and investing you've done on your own. This is the aspect of your retirement fund that you have the most control over. It's up to you to determine where you want your savings to go—which is why this is also the element of your retirement income that requires the most thought. (See Chapters 6 and 7.)

But it's not always that cut and dried.

If you're like many other retirees—estimated to be upward of 50% of the current working population—you may be missing a pension. Either you don't have one (perhaps you're self-employed or work freelance), or you've changed jobs often and it is far too small. Or your savings level may be too low right now to sustain you and your spouse through retirement.

This is where careful financial planning comes in.

The purpose of a strong financial plan is to address these problems and to make the third source, savings and investment, make up for deficiencies in the other two.

▶ **How can you get an accurate picture of where you stand—and how can you start planning what to do?**

The way to begin is to get a more exact target figure—a rough estimate of how much savings you'll need to retire and how much you'll need to save annually to reach this goal. By arriving at this estimate, you will also begin to see how much you must aim to earn on your investments.

Begin by completing Worksheets 1 and 2 on pages 30–34. Variations of these worksheets are used by financial planners. In most cases, theirs are more complex and more precise. These worksheets are designed to give you a *rough* idea of where you stand in terms of retirement financing. They are starting points.

Worksheet 1, What Will Your Retirement Cost? will give you a basis for estimating how much you'll need to save for retirement. You do this by estimating your expenses—what you're paying now and what you probably will be paying during your retirement. You'll notice a column of notes that will give you hints as to what your projected expenses may be.

Worksheet 2, How Much Will You Need to Save? (designed with data and assistance from Craig A. Rosin, from the accounting firm Coopers & Lybrand—Baltimore office) takes you to the next step— the amount you need to begin saving now to meet your retirement needs.

TIP: While Worksheet 2 gives you specific inflation and investment growth rates, it makes sense to try different scenarios—higher inflation (or lower), higher growth

rates (or lower). And if you're mathematically inclined or a spreadsheet whiz, you may want to take things a step further and flow through rates we haven't supplied— much higher inflation, or even _deflation,_ unheard of since the Depression, but possible in the future.

After going through the worksheet and filling in your numbers, you'll get some basic answers: the total amount of capital you'll need by retirement age to finance your retirement and the amount you should save annually to reach that number.

WORKSHEET 1: WHAT WILL YOUR RETIREMENT COST?

You will probably need from 60 to 80% of your current gross income to maintain your current lifestyle once you retire. This worksheet will help you estimate more precisely what you will need to retire comfortably and meet your expenses.

TYPE OF EXPENSE	CURRENT COSTS	EST. COST RETIREMENT	NOTES
1. Housing:			Most retirees see a decline of about 25% to 50% in basic housing costs—since mortgages are usually paid up, home improvements already made, and so on. If you plan to "trade down"—sell your present home and move into a smaller, less expensive one—expect even more savings. On the other hand, your utilities costs may rise, since you aren't working and will be spending more time at home.
Rent/Mortgage	_____	_____	
Maintenance	_____	_____	
Property taxes	_____	_____	
Utilities and telephone	_____	_____	
2. Food	_____	_____	Food costs generally remain roughly the same.
3. Clothing	_____	_____	Clothing costs often drop 20% to 35% because there is no longer a need to buy and maintain business clothing.
4. Personal Care: Health club, hair care, other grooming	_____	_____	Personal care costs often rise slightly after retirement.
5. Transportation: Car payments, maintenance, repairs, parking, gas, and other commuting costs	_____	_____	Commuting costs generally drop. However, if you are planning recreational car travel, transportation costs may actually rise.

6. Leisure and recreation:

Hobbies, movies, theater, cable TV, video rentals, dining out, etc. _____ _____

Travel _____ _____

If you're planning to travel or enjoy more recreational activities with your newfound free times, increase expenses by 20% or more, depending upon your lifestyle.

7. Taxes:

Federal income taxes _____ _____

State & local taxes _____ _____

Social Security/self-employment tax _____ _____

Taxes often drop for retirees—if they aren't working, they no longer have to pay Social Security or self-employment taxes; they pay no federal tax on at least half of their Social Security benefits; they may have moved to a new area with lower taxes or a state offering tax breaks for senior citizens. But if you're in a higher tax bracket (as many retirees are), taxes may stay the same or increase.

8. Medical/dental (including drugs) _____ _____

Medical expenses generally increase a minimum of 45%. Costs may actually rise up to _three times_ what you are currently paying.

9. Education _____ _____

Education expenses usually drop precipitously—often to zero, since by retirement time, most children have gone through school. But if you're planning on filling time with school or educational programs, factor the cost in.

10. Insurance: _____ _____

Life _____ _____

Medical/dental _____ _____

Liability _____ _____

Property _____ _____

Auto _____ _____

Where insurance costs are concerned, usually it's a mixed bag. Most retirees drop life insurance or scale it down by at least 50%. As for health insurance, while Medicare will cover most health insurance costs, you will probably be buying medigap insurance. Other insurance costs will probably remain relatively unchanged.

11. Loan/debt repayment _____ _____

Most retirees aim for _zero_ obligations for loans or debts upon retirement.

12. Gifts/charitable contributions _____ _____

Gift giving and charitable contributions often remain unchanged for retirees. However, your gift giving may increase if you want to distribute assets from your estate as gifts to family members, and so help keep down your estate taxes.

13. Family support _____ _____

Family support may decrease if you no longer have dependents. However, keep in mind that many retirees support older parents and—in tough financial times—offer help to children.

14. Savings & investments:
IRAs, Keoghs, company 401 (k) plans, etc.; all other savings and investments _____ _____

Savings and investment activity usually decreases—retirees no longer are contributing to a company plan; they've already amassed their retirement nest egg. However, it's wise to maintain about a 10% savings rate to hedge against inflation.

TOTAL EXPENSES _____ _____

Divide total expenses by current gross income to arrive at the entry on the final line.

CURRENT GROSS INCOME _____
Percentage of current income needed for retirement _____

WORKSHEET 2: HOW MUCH WILL YOU NEED TO SAVE?

Step 1: *What retirement benefits can you count on?*
ADD:

1. Estimated Pension Benefits (if any) _____ Only include defined benefit pension plans received as an annuity (not 401(k)s, ESOPs, etc.). See page 75 to estimate the amount or ask your pension manager for an estimate of the worth of the pension upon retirement.

2. Estimated Social Security Benefits + _____ See page 61 for information on how to estimate Social Security.

3. TOTAL: = _____ This total represents the guaranteed retirement benefits that you'll be receiving annually.

Step 2: *Is there a gap between what you need and what you will be getting?*
SUBTRACT

4. Annual income needed for retirement – _____ Dollar amount arrived at through worksheet 1 or 60–80% of current income.

5. TOTAL: Income Shortfall at retirement = _____ This is the amount of retirement expenses that your guaranteed benefits won't cover. Your savings and investments will have to make this amount up.

Step 3: *How much will you need at retirement time to bridge the gap and to keep in step with inflation?*
MULTIPLY line 5 by:

6. Factor A × _____ Factor A (from table on page 35) is based on the years you have until retirement and estimated inflation rate.

TOTAL:

7. Inflation-adjusted income needed = _____ This figure represents the amount of income you need in future dollar value at retirement.

MULTIPLY line 7 by:

8. 17.94% × 17.94% This figure assumes your retirement will cover 25 years—reasonable given average life expectancies.

TOTAL:

9. Capital needed for shortfall = _____ This is the capital you will need at retirement to make up for the income shortfall on line 7.

MULTIPLY:

10a. Pension amount (line 1) _____ Enter the amount on line 1.

10b. Factor B × _____ Factor B (from table on page 35) is based on inflation and years to retirement.

10c. Additional capital needed = _____ This figure represents the additional capital you will need to keep your pension up with inflation.

ADD: line 9 and line 10 for = _____ This is the total capital you will need upon retirement.
11. Total capital needed

Step 4:   What will your savings and investments be worth at retirement time?
ADD:.
12. Current savings & investments:
  a. IRAs and Keoghs _____

  b. Employer plans (SEPs, 401(k)s, + _____ This should be the total amount of any company plans (excluding your pension plan) that you're enrolled in.
      profit sharing, ESOPs)

  c. All other investments (stocks, + _____
      bonds, etc.)

  d. Total Savings/Investments = _____

MULTIPLY line 12d by:
13. Factor C × _____ Factor C (from table on page 35) is figured by estimating the years until retirement and the estimated growth rate of your investments.

TOTAL:
14. Savings/investments at retirement = _____ This total is the estimated worth of your savings and investments upon retirement.

Step 5:   How much capital will you need at retirement to meet your projected expenses?
SUBTRACT: line 14 from line 11
15. Net capital needed at retirement = _____ This is the net amount you will need when you retire to fund your retirement (in future dollars)

DIVIDE: line 15 by:
16. Factor D − _____ Factor D is from table on page 35.

17. Capital in today's dollars needed for = _____ This is the amount in today's dollars you'll need to save or earn to meet the expenses you've projected for retirement.
     retirment

FACTORS

The factors below are based upon an estimated average inflation rate of 4% and a return on investment of 7%.

Years to Retirement	10	15	20	25	30
Factor A:	1.48	1.80	2.19	2.67	3.24
Factor B:	5.59	6.80	8.28	10.09	12.25
Factor C:	1.97	2.76	3.87	5.43	7.61
Factor D:	16.80	32.95	57.59	94.54	149.16

Courtesy: Craig A. Rosin, Coopers & Lybrand—Baltimore

▶ **There is one very important number in Worksheet 2: the extra capital you must have to give yourself your target retirement income.**

Chances are this number was surprisingly large and daunting. Worse yet, it possibly should be even larger—in case the 4% inflation figure was too conservative, or if Social Security should become overburdened (by government borrowing against Social Security reserves) and payout decrease for certain categories of retirees.

But even without these considerations, the number probably seems high. There are two main reasons for this.

1. Your income must keep coming to you every year of your retirement—and the worksheet assumes that (like the average retiree) you'll live a minimum of 25 years after retirement.

2. The worksheet factors in a reasonable rate of inflation, and inflation eats into your capital or retirement nest egg in many ways. For example, during retirement, it forces you to withdraw more money from your savings to keep up with rising living costs. This reduces the amount of your investment (your principal). With a smaller principal, your earnings, which are based on the total amount of principal, are less. And so on. So you need a larger principal to make up for the erosion of inflation.

Nevertheless, there are some comforting aspects as well. First of all, the closer you are to retirement, the lower the odds that Social Security will reduce payout or your pension will be eroded by inflation. In short, the closer you are to retirement, the more you can rely on the government or your company plan.

But there's also some good news for those with a large or relatively large amount of time before retirement. The farther you are from retirement, the *easier* it will be to generate large amounts of money, through the power of compound interest, through the power of tax-deferred savings, and through prudent investing. For example, if retirement is 20 years away, by putting only $2,000 aside every year for 20 years at 8% interest, you'll have a nest egg of $98,845.

One final note. You may have looked for a line on the worksheet on which to place the approximate market value of your house. To be sure, home ownership has been the single best investment the average individual has made. And it has financed many a retirement. However, *prudent* investment planning dictates you do not count on your home to finance your retirement. For one thing, the price may fluctuate. For another, you may have difficulty selling it. Finally, you may use a substantial portion of any proceeds from the sale to finance another home—your retirement home. (For more on your home and how to use it as a source of retirement income and retirement housing, see Chapter 11.)

STEP THREE: DETERMINE HOW YOU'LL GET WHAT YOU NEED

▶ **Between now and your retirement date, you should aim to save and invest so that you get to the approximate amount on page 34.**

Savings and investment work in tandem. Your savings accumulate. You invest your savings. Your investments build up over the years, you keep on adding savings, and eventually you meet or exceed your targeted retirement nest egg.

▶ **Begin with savings—start saving now.**

Begin a graduated savings plan today, if you haven't already done it. Depending on your needs (as illustrated in the worksheet), the exact amount will vary. But in general, as much as is reasonably possible of your yearly salary should go into a retirement fund. The optimal *minimum* is:

5% of your yearly income in your 30s.

10% of your yearly income in your 40s.

15% or more in your 50s.

That is, every year during your 40s, you should aim at putting 10% of your annual salary into a retirement account. That account should be seen as inviolable—separate it from savings accounts for children's education or for vacations. And to repeat a point: If possible, save more. Due to the power of compounding, you will have a much greater amount later.

TIP: **Habits are hard to break, and the more frequently you indulge a habit, the harder it is to break it. Make saving that type of habit. The easiest way is to take a weekly amount out of your paycheck. If you save on a quarterly basis or an annual basis, it is easier to skip a period.**

Many preretirees aren't saving enough. According to a recent study by the investment firm Merrill Lynch, preretirees between the ages of 45 and 64 currently put about 14% of their yearly income into some sort of retirement fund. That might sound impressive, but 12% of all preretirees save nothing, another 22% save less than 10% (and, of course, another 16% don't know). And a wise or lucky 18% save over 20% per year.

▶ **Invest your savings.**

Creating a nest egg means investing your money—putting your savings in places where you'll earn a good return. And there are many ways of investing. You can even create your own self-directed pension plan.

But a major problem with most preretirees is that while they may *save,* they don't *invest.* According to a Merrill Lynch study, over half of all preretirees (53%) preferred to put their savings into savings accounts. These people could be *losing* money: With inflation recently at 7%, and with passbook savings at 5.25% (a bit more in certain types of accounts), these savers are watching the *real* value of their principal shrink at the rate of 1.75%. Because inflation is uneven (some items go up more than others), the real effect of inflation may be ignored. Also, unsophisticated investors look at their balances and as long as they see that the principal is increasing they don't worry. But remind yourself of the obvious: *Your principal must increase above the rate of inflation for you to make money.* Otherwise, each year the real value of your retirement nest egg will shrink.

The only way to assure that this doesn't happen is to invest your money. And that means accepting some risk. But it's even riskier *not* to invest—inflation can devour your savings, and your income after retirement.

Reading this book will give you the specific information you'll need to follow these three basic steps. You'll learn what the compounds of your financial plan are and how you can put together the best possible retirement plan that will meet the necessary criteria. Chapter 6, page 157, goes into detail on investing to meet your retirement objectives; Chapter 7, page 181, tells you what are the best investments to make. (Note: For specific assistance for early retirees, see Appendix: Early Retirement; for late starters, see Appendix: Late Starters.)

FINANCIAL PLANNERS

▶ **Some of you may want to consider working with a professional financial planner to devise a workable retirement plan.**

Financial planners can help you through the complexities of planning for retirement. Many corporations now offer financial planning services to their employees, to help explain pension and retirement plans. You may find an independent financial planner helpful. However, it is important to pick the right one—one who shares your general investment philosophy and is an ethical, competent member of the profession.

There are two basic types of financial planner: fee-only and commission planners. (There are also other professionals who may help with your financial planning: See pages 43–44.)

Commission planners used to dominate the field almost completely, but this has been changing. These are the "traditional" planners, who usually offer comprehensive financial plans and make most of their money selling you investments, for which they earn a commission. They may not charge any up-front fees, or charge fees that are credited toward commissions. Because of rapid changes in the financial world, some planners now shy away from overly comprehensive plans and instead register as money managers and manage clients' assets for a percentage charge. The key problem with these

TABLE 1.1: IMPORTANT AGES IN RETIREMENT PLANNING

Age	What It Affects	What Happens
55	401(k) and 403(b) plans, profit-sharing, Keoghs	If you retire at age 55, quit, or are otherwise "separated" from work, you can receive your money from 401(k)s, profit-sharing plans, or Keoghs *without* paying the 10% early withdrawal penalty.
	Your house	If you sell your house at age 55 or later, you may be eligible for a tax-free profit of up to $125,000.
59½	IRAs, Keoghs	This is the age at which you can withdraw money from your IRA or Keogh without paying the 10% early withdrawal penalty.
	Pension plans	You can receive a lump-sum pension plan distribution and take advantage of forward averaging (explained on page 87), a tax-saving technique.
62	Company pension plans	If you retire at age 62, some companies will allow you to receive full pension benefits. Check with your personnel department or pension administrator.
	Social Security	You can begin receiving Social Security benefits—but keep in mind that monthly benefits will be lower than if you wait until you are 65.
65	Medicare	At 65, you are eligible for Medicare coverage.
	Social Security	If you have signed up, you can start receiving full Social Security benefits.
	Pensions	Since this is the "typical" retirement age, you usually receive full company pension benefits at this point.
70½	IRAs, Keoghs, other tax-deferred savings plans	You *must* begin making withdrawals from IRAs and other plans at this age.

planners is lack of objectivity. With commission-based products to sell, they may advise you to spend more money than is necessary. Whenever employing commission planners, do not act on their investment recommendations immediately. Instead, compare them with other vehicles. For example, if a certain load (up-front commission) mutual fund is recommended, compare it with others of the same investment type.

Fee-only planners are, in most cases, a better bet for retirement advice. Instead of charging you commissions on investments, fee-only planners charge fees, either hourly or daily, and help you with specific investment problems, or help you put together your own retirement portfolio. Key advantage: with no commissions to earn, they tend to be more objective. Fees vary widely: from $50 to $200 an hour, or from $1,000 to $3,000 for six months of detailed planning.

SOURCE: For a list of fee-only planners, write: **National Association of Personal Financial Advisors,** 1130 Lake Cook Road, Suite 105, Buffalo Grove, IL 60089 (or call 800-366-2732).

What Planners Do

You can go to a financial planner for specific help—for example, to determine the benefits and costs of an early retirement package. Or you can go for more comprehensive help in setting up a personal retirement plan. Both options are becoming more common as financial complexities increase.

Typically, a financial planner reviews your financial goals and helps you prepare a net worth statement reflecting your assets and liabilities. From the two, he or she calculates your net worth (the difference between what you own and what you owe), establishes your current savings rate, your projected pension, your tax situation—and comes up with a series of recommendations. Where and how should you save and invest your money? This is probably the most frequently asked question, and like most, it has no definite answer. Working closely with you, a good financial planner will assess your risk profile and the rate of savings growth you need to meet your retirement goals, and will recommend investments and a savings program.

How to Pick a Good Planner

Be careful. The profession is currently changing. There is a law pending (supported by such groups as AARP) that seeks to standardize training and increase regulation. But currently there can be risks in choosing a financial planner, since virtually anyone can hang out a shingle and call him- or herself one. You should be aware of the potential for fraud or simply for poor advice. However, there are various accrediting agencies, some requiring tests for certification, others merely requiring adherence to a set of ethics.

The best way to choose a planner is to shop around until you find someone who both meets your needs and is professionally competent. Look for credentials, but look also for expertise and experience in your areas of need.

Key: *Ask questions.* Many planning professionals are shocked at how few clients ask about credentials, experience, and investment philosophy. Some important questions to ask:

1. *What are the financial planner's credentials?*
You're best off with a financial planner with legitimate credentials—certification from a professional organization, proper training, and so forth. The credentials to look for (and the associations, if you want listings of planners in your area to contact):

- *Certified Financial Planner (CFP):* Planners with a CFP after their names must follow a study program, pass an examination, and meet requirements for experience. For more information, contact: Institute of Certified Financial Planners, Denver Highlands, 10065 East Harvard Avenue, Denver, CO 80231, or call 800-282-PLAN.

- *Chartered Financial Consultant (ChFC):* Offered by the American College in Bryn Mawr, Pennsylvania. Planners here must pass 10 sections of study and two exams. For more information, contact: American Society of CLU and ChFC, 270 Bryn Mawr Ave., Bryn Mawr, PA, 19010.

- *Accredited Personal Financial Specialist (APFS):* This is offered by the American Institute of Certified Public Accountants. (For more, see CPAs, pages 43–44.)

These three titles are generally respected as offering certification based on training, which of course does not guarantee competence, but does provide some reassurance. There is also a professional association of planners that has no training requirements, but does maintain a registry of members, and will tell you which members are ChFCs, APFSs and CFPs:

- *International Association for Financial Planning (IAFP):* Planners here must simply join and agree to follow the code of ethics.

Members of the group's Registry of Financial Planning Practitioners have agreed to provide detailed disclosure of experience and training—which you should of course ask to see. Contact: IAFP Registry, Two Concourse Parkway, Suite 800, Atlanta, GA 30328 (or call 404-395-1605).

2. *Is the planner registered with the Securities and Exchange Commission (SEC)?*
Not a requirement for legitimacy nor a guarantee of competence, but it is one more check you may want to do.

3. *Is the planner a fee-based planner or one who gets a commission?*
As explained earlier, in most cases you are better off with a fee-based planner for objective advice.

4. *What products is the financial planner recommending or offering?*
Take a good, hard, clear-headed look at the products the planner is recommending, if a fee-based planner, or selling, if a commission planner. Never act immediately on advice. Check around first. Are the products considered prudent investments? Are they legitimate? How have they been rated by investment newsletters or experts? Are the products the best use for your money—or is the financial planner just gunning for a commission? Is the financial planner pushing products from one company in particular? Don't let a planner buy products for you. Do your own buying.

5. *What services does the financial planner offer?*
What areas can he or she handle for you? Among a few you might be interested in: tax planning, investment planning, estate planning, cash management, insurance. Make sure that the financial planner will cover the things you need.

6. *Who are the financial planner's other clients—and can you speak with them?*
One of the best ways to get real insight into how a financial planner works—and whether he or she will work well with you—is to speak with other clients.

7. *Along the same lines—can you see samples of the plans that the financial planner has prepared for other clients?*
This is also a great way of checking on how well the financial planner works and whether you agree with his or her suggestions.

Seeing sample plans in black and white will help you understand the kind of service the planner provides.

8. *Will the planner give you a written analysis?*

Having an analysis of your finances and recommendations of actions to take on paper is a real asset. Find out ahead of time if you can expect this. If you get a written analysis, you can study recommendations, take time before deciding, and gain a closer understanding of your finances.

9. *Has the planner ever been sued by clients?*

Do guard against the growing number of fraudulent "planners" passing themselves off as professionals. Don't just rely on the word of the planner. Check with the Better Business Bureau, professional associations, and so forth. If the answer is yes, go a step further and find out what the complaints were and what the outcome of the suit was.

10. *Does the planner deal with other professionals—lawyers, CPAs, and so forth?*

A good financial planner turns to professionals for assistance.

11. *Have disciplinary actions been taken against the planner—by the SEC, the state securities office, or such professional organizations as the National Association of Securities Dealers?*

Clearly if there have been actions taken against the planner, you might be better off going to another. This can be a tip-off to a planner who deals in unscrupulous money-making methods or fraud. You can get this information from the planner himself, or better yet, from your state securities office.

SOURCE: For a free guide on how to select a financial planner, plus a list of Certified Financial Planners in your area, call the **Institute of Certified Financial Planners** at 800-282-PLAN, or write them at: **Institute of Certified Financial Planners,** 2 Denver Highlands, 10065 East Harvard Avenue, Denver, CO 80231.

Other Professionals

▶ **CPAs (Certified Public Accountants), insurance agents, stockbrokers, attorneys, and bankers have all joined the planning bandwagon. Some may offer useful financial advice on retirement.**

CPAs: As professional members of the American Institute of Certified Public Accountants, CPAs are trained professionals in the nuts and bolts of finance. They can be particularly valuable in addressing tax problems in retirement planning, possibly the most complex and important (and confusing) area of retirement planning. Moreover, most tax considerations are highly individual, and an advisor familiar with your special circumstances can be a life-saver. One other plus: As these are certified members of a profession that is also licensed and regulated by state boards, the odds of unprofessional or fraudulent advice are lower. Only a small minority of CPAs specialize in retirement finance. For more information, contact: American Institute of Certified Public Accountants (AICPA), Personal Financial Planner Division, 1211 Avenue of the Americas, New York, NY 10036.

Insurance Agents: Insurance agents are probably the best people to advise you on the complexities of certain insurance investments, such as annuities. Problem: As salespeople, their prime objective is to *sell* you these same investments. Solution: Never buy anything immediately. Rather, go to several agents and compare similar products, check investment ratings in Best's, Standard & Poor's, or Moody's Insurance Reviews, available at your local library and only consider A-plus ratings. Also, read Annuities (page 258), and look at insurance only as part of a larger investment picture. A good bet: Go over insurance plans with your attorney.

Stockbrokers: A good broker can help you plan an investment portfolio that meets your retirement goals. Problem: As a salesperson (even if called a financial consultant) a broker wants to sell you products. Solutions: Seek a broker you have trusted for years—many people maintain strong relationships with brokers over decades—and check broker recommendations with outside sources, investment books, and so forth. Look for steady, conservative brokers.

THE BASIC GOALS OF FINANCIAL PLANNING

▶ **Whether you use a financial planner or not, there are certain key elements to planning your retirement finances. Let's summarize.**

To plan your retirement successfully, you need to know the answers to the following six questions. Page numbers where you can find answers, worksheets, or information that will help you are listed beside each question.

1. *How much will you need for a comfortable retirement?* You need to prepare an estimate of your expenses, including housing, health, insurance, and more. (Use the worksheet on pages 33–34.)

2. *How much can you expect as a guaranteed retirement income?* You need to estimate the income you will get from Social Security and from private pension plans. (See Chapters 2 and 3.)

3. *How can you build a retirement nest egg now—and how can you keep it growing?* You need to know how different self-directed savings and investment plans can earn you the retirement income you will need to bridge the gap between your guaranteed benefits and your probable expenses. (See Chapters 4, 6, and 7.)

4. *What type of investment portfolio will serve you best—and how will the specific investment vehicles fit into your retirement plan?* You need to know the different ways to invest your money and devise specific investment strategies for different points of your retirement plan. (See Chapters 6 and 7.)

5. *What insurance will you need?* You need to learn what Medicare will cover and what it won't, and to determine whether you should buy medigap insurance or long-term care insurance. In addition, you will need to determine your other insurance needs. (See Chapter 5.)

6. *What are the assets of your estate and how should they be distributed?* You need to estimate the value of your estate and devise an estate plan that avoids lengthy probate procedures as much as possible—and an excessive estate tax bite. (See Chapter 8.)

COUNTDOWN TO RETIREMENT

▶ **You won't be able to meet all these goals at once. Here's a breakout of what to do and when to do it.**

20 Years Before Retirement

▶ **This is the ideal time to lay a foundation for a retirement plan and begin long-range retirement planning.**

Problem is, it's also a time when most people aren't really thinking long-term. There are so many other draws on your time—raising children, meeting mortgage payments, simply making ends meet while you put aside money for the kids' college or other expenses. Nevertheless, those of you who are thinking about retirement 20 years in the future will be best off starting to plan for that retirement.

Here are some points to keep in mind.

- *Start saving and investing with an eye to the long term*—even putting away a hundred or so a month is an excellent start, and it can pan out later when retirement rolls around. When investing, think long-term growth. Put as much of your money as you feel comfortable with into such growth-oriented investments as stocks or stock mutual funds—keeping some, of course, in cash reserves and in income investments for balance and diversification. Develop an investment plan and begin investing money regularly. If you're in a high tax bracket, consider tax-exempt municipal bonds or bond funds. Look at purchasing some long-term zero-coupon bonds for your IRA for long-term growth. Smaller investors in particular can begin with U.S. Savings Bonds. (For more, see Chapter 7.)

- *Take advantage of 401(k) company plans* for a relatively painless way of beginning to build a nest egg. The pluses: Contributions are tax-free; earnings are tax-deferred; the company may match a portion of your contributions. (For more information, see page 115.)

- *If you are self-employed, consider opening a Keogh or SEP*—this will provide you with a pension upon retirement, a real help, since your other sources of retirement income will be limited to Social Security and savings. (For more information, see page 105–112.)

- *Be sure your family is covered in the event of your death or disability.* This early on, you can't afford to have your estate and finances drained by disability or death. Be sure you have enough life insurance to maintain your family's lifestyle. This is the stage of life when your life insurance needs are highest. (See page 121 for specific information.)

- *Draw up a will*—it's definitely not too early. While many people put this off, writing a will is a good idea at this stage of your life. (Even though you will be changing the will as you grow closer to retirement and as your financial situation changes.) Also, do such related things as choosing an executor and, especially if you own a family business, setting up an estate plan.

10 Years Before Retirement

▶ **Now is the time to start actively building up a retirement nest egg.**

Your financial needs are fewer—your children have grown, tuition has been paid, your house is probably paid up. There are several things you should do at this stage.

- *Track your cash flow to get an idea of how well your retirement savings program is working.* You can do this on your own, or fill in a prepared cash flow worksheet (these are available through financial consultants or planners—for example, Merrill Lynch puts out a Retirement Builder handbook with charts to fill in). This will help you determine if you are putting enough aside for retirement—and if not, can give you ideas of where to cut expenses.

- *If you will be receiving a company pension, speak with the pension administrator or personnel office about your plan*—how much you can expect, how the payment will be made (in a lump sum or as an annuity). You will need this information to determine how much you will need from your own savings and investments to contribute to a financially comfortable retirement. (For more information, see Chapter 3.)

- *Learn what your estimated Social Security benefits will be*—by completing a PEBS (Personal Earnings and Benefit Estimate Statement) form. Contact your local Social Security office or call

800-937-2000, ask for the form, fill it out and send it in. You will receive a report back from the Social Security Administration telling you your earnings history, how much you've contributed to Social Security, and most important, what benefits you can expect to receive on reaching 65. This will help you figure how much you will need in savings and investment. Also, if there are any errors in your report, you can correct them now. (For more information, see Chapter 2.)

- *Begin paying off all debts and loans.* You want to be able to retire debt-free, if possible. So now is the time to pay off any outstanding loans.

- *Examine your investment portfolio and begin making adjustments.* Assuming you'll be spending about 70% to 80% of your income during retirement, and taking inflation into account, assess whether your investments will give you the income you will need during retirement.

    Keep emphasizing growth-oriented investments—particularly if you foresee a shortfall—and put maybe 40% to 60% of your assets into stocks or stock funds. With 10 years, you still have time to build a large nest egg, and you still have time to take some risks.

    If you haven't begun a regular investment program, start immediately, particularly now that expenses are presumably down. Go on a savings blitz and put extra dollars into retirement investments. If you're in a high income tax bracket, keep on sheltering your earnings income in tax-free municipal bonds or deferred annuities, as well as IRAs and Keoghs. (For more, see Chapters 6 and 7.)

- *Contribute as much as possible to company savings plans*—such as 401(k)s. These will help you build your retirement fund quickly and fairly effortlessly. (For information on how these work, see page 115.)

- *If you have a large estate or intend to make financial gifts to children or relatives, now is the time to begin.* This will help you shift your estate over to heirs and help them avoid high estate taxes.

- *If you have a large estate (from $200,000 to over $1 million) and are in your 50s, start shopping around for long-term care insurance.* If you wait much longer, premiums will increase dramatically. Long-term care insurance will play the same role in retirement that disability insurance played in your preretirement—it's a safeguard against having your assets drained by long-term health costs. (For more information, see page 148.)

- *Start planning the lifestyle aspect of your retirement.* Think about what retirement will mean to you and what you want out of it. Set time aside to go over your retirement desires with your spouse. Be sure both of you are involved in the planning.

Five Years Before Retirement

▶ **At this point, you should move into high gear in retirement preparations—both financial and living.**

This is the time for double-checking on retirement goals and how your savings match your estimated retirement needs.
There are a number of actions to take at this time.

- *Determine as precisely as possible what your retirement expenses will be*—a vital step to take at this point, since you have only five years to raise the capital you will need to meet those expenses. One way of doing this is to pay all your expenses by check. This will allow you to track your cost of living and pinpoint probable retirement expenditures.

- *Start moving toward more conservative investments.* Reanalyze your income needs during retirement. Plan on purchasing more fixed income investments in the next five years and shifting in general to more conservative investments. But be sure to keep some of your money in growth investments such as stocks or stock mutual funds. (See page 200.)

- *Assess your retirement options and make a basic decision: Will you have to sell your house to finance part of your retirement?* You may *have* to sell your house, or you may just *want* to—now is the time to make that decision. The actual sale may take place any time between now and retirement. Of course, you want to postpone the sale until you are 55 or older to take advantage of the one-time $125,000 tax exclusion. (See page 361.)

- *If you are planning to sell your house, make the renovations and improvements it needs*—or those that will help it sell.

- *If you are planning to stay in your current home, make necessary changes for comfortable senior citizen living now,* instead of waiting until the last minute. (For specific suggestions, see page 330–31.)

- *If you are planning to move to a retirement community, start selecting one now*—many popular ones fill up quickly. Get your name on a waiting list so you can make your move upon retirement. (See page 345.)

- *If you intend to move to a new area, start researching and visiting the places you're considering*—get a feel for the locales that interest you so you can make an educated choice. (For more, see Chapter 12.)

- *It's a good time to begin thinking about hobbies, second careers, and other retirement activities,* instead of waiting until you are actually retired. Start pursuing hobbies, or thinking about the type of activity you will want to pursue. Look into the availability of educational courses, special groups, associations, and the like that can help you.

- *Start talking about your retirement with your family*—not just your spouse, but your children also. This will help the entire family make a smooth adjustment to the change in lifestyle that retirement brings. Discuss what you hope to do in retirement, your hopes, your plans.

One Year Before Retirement

▶ **This is the true countdown time—and the point at which you must do some careful double-checking of all your plans and preparations.**

You want to be sure to catch any potential problems before they develop into full-scale troubles upon retirement.

- *Determine the specific date for your retirement.* In some cases, the date of your retirement can mean an extra year added to (or lost from) your pension plan and other company retirement benefits. Speak to your pension plan administrator.

- *Analyze your tax situation,* to be sure you won't be hit with heavy taxes upon retirement. Be sure to factor in such things as selling your house and cashing in IRAs and other tax-deferred plans. If the tax picture looks grim, consider seeing a financial planner or accountant for help in redistributing your finances.

- *Check and recheck all of your financial information.* Get a Social Security estimate of benefits again; get the most current, updated information on your company pension plans and other savings plans.

- *Along those lines, find out if you have any options as to how your pension plan will be distributed*—lump sum, or annuity—and compare these options. Consider which one is better for your situation. (See page 80.)

- *Recheck your investments and income needs*—is your investment portfolio set for retirement? Will your bonds and other investments give you enough income in addition to your pension and Social Security? If not, consider buying an immediate annuity, or analyze other investments. A good idea: Project your income and expenses from now until age 90. Be sure to factor in inflation. Accelerate deductions and take capital losses now, if you foresee yourself in a lower tax bracket at retirement. If you are not sure how to do this on your own, speak to your financial planner or broker. Most carry specialized computer programs that will do the work for you.

- *If you are concerned you don't have enough to retire on after all, or if it seems that money will be tight, now's the time to look into part-time employment or freelance work.* Again, it's unwise to wait until the last minute. If you're concerned about a gap between your retirement savings and your retirement expenses, start exploring employment options. (But do keep in mind that excessive earnings can cut your Social Security benefits—see page 64 for more.)

- *If you're planning a move upon retirement, start housecleaning.* Decide what you want to keep, what you want to give away, and what you want to get rid of. Remember—most of you will probably be moving to smaller quarters. Much of what you've amassed over the years in your current home won't be necessary in your new home—or simply won't fit. This is also a good time to inventory your possessions and make decisions about bequests.

- *Check your will and update it, if necessary,* to reflect any changes in your estate, in your heirs, and so forth.

Six to Three Months Before Retirement

▶ The final months before you retire are important ones. You'll be taking care of last-minute details to assure a smooth transition into retirement.

Since you will be leaving your company soon, it's the best time to be absolutely sure you have everything you need for it (both information and paperwork). The steps you take now are the ones that will lead you directly into retirement.

- *Drop or dramatically reduce life insurance coverage,* if you haven't done so already. If you cash in your life insurance, you can invest the proceeds—and thus contribute more to your retirement nest egg. One proviso: If you have a large estate, instead of cashing in your policy, you may want to scale it down and keep just enough coverage to pay estate taxes and administrative costs upon your death.

- *Before you leave your job, get company records and other paperwork you may need,* such as earnings statements, any written material on your retirement health benefits or any other benefits. (Note: This is especially important if your employer has promised you something verbally—GET IT IN WRITING!) Also check any special deals the company might offer to retirees.

- *If you are expecting pension income from employers other than your current one, contact them now, in writing.* Give them six months' notification of your pending retirement, so they can do all the necessary paperwork.

- *Sign up for Social Security benefits and Medicare benefits.* (Full instructions on what you need and how to sign up are on page 63.)

- *While you and your spouse are still covered by company health insurance, get a complete physical.* This is a moneysaver. In addition, you can find out if there are any health problems you will be facing in the near future and so prepare for them.

- *Begin shopping around for a good medigap insurance package,* to fill in the gap that Medicare will leave. Because finding the best insurance policy takes a little time, it's wise to do this before you actually will need it.

- *If you are moving after retirement, make the initial preparations about one month before the move*—filling out change of address cards (so your mail service won't be interrupted), canceling utilities, finding a new bank and opening an account, and so forth.

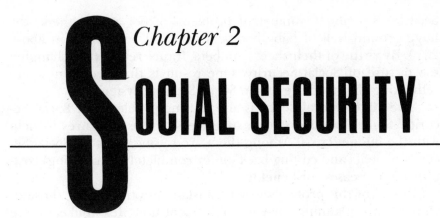

Chapter 2
SOCIAL SECURITY

INTRODUCTION

▶ **If you're like most potential retirees, Social Security is one of the first things that come to mind when you think about your retirement income.**

You may not be counting on it to provide a substantial amount of money—but you are counting on it.

This chapter will tell you how you can figure out just how much to count on. It will give you information on calculating Social Security benefits, how to get more specific information on the government, and how (and when) to apply for Social Security.

THE OUTLOOK ON SOCIAL SECURITY

▶ **Social Security is alive and well . . . so far.**

The troubles and controversy swirling around Social Security have been well documented in the press. To put it bluntly, Social

Security is facing a number of problems. Chief among them: the huge groundswell of baby boomers who will be retiring in about 2010. By virtue of their sheer numbers, future retirees are changing the picture of Social Security. One result is that people now are rethinking the structure of the Social Security system.

The huge federal deficit is also causing problems for Social Security. Some lawmakers have suggested various measures to help with the budget crisis. Among them are raising taxes on Social Security benefits and cutting back on (or completely eliminating) cost-of-living increases for benefits.

But all of this probably won't translate into trouble for those of you who are planning for your retirement now. It's unlikely there will be any cutbacks in benefits in the near future, especially as senior citizens flex their political muscle.

In the long term, however, it's wise to stay aware of developments with Social Security. Should any changes occur, they will affect your retirement planning.

SOURCE: For information on Social Security, contact your local Social Security office and request their retirement booklet. In addition, you can get an excellent fact sheet on Social Security from: **Women's Equity Action League,** Suite 305, 1250 I Street NW, Washington, DC 20005 (202-898-1588).

▶ **Social Security oversees three programs: retirement benefits, disability benefits, and most often overlooked, survivors' benefits, as well as the Supplemental Security Income program.**

Retirement benefits are what most people think of when they think of Social Security. More than 27.5 million people (workers and their dependent spouses and children) receive monthly retirement benefits from Social Security.

Disability benefits are designed to assist workers *under* the age of 65 who are disabled. (In some cases benefits go to eligible family members.)

Survivors' benefits are meant to help widows or widowers of workers who were eligible for Social Security.

The *Supplemental Security Income (SSI)* program is designed to help people with limited income or resources who are 65 or older, disabled, or blind.

This section will primarily deal with retirement benefits.

▶ **One point to keep in mind: Where retirement income is concerned, Social Security is designed to be an** *additional* **source of income for retirees, not the sole source.**

In other words, don't overrely on Social Security. (This is especially true if you're in your 30s. The way things are going, who knows how much Social Security you'll be getting in 30 years—or how much it will be worth?)

Social Security was designed to be one leg of the so-called three-legged stool for retirement—the other legs being private pensions and personal savings.

Many Americans are counting more heavily on Social Security than they should. According to recent government data, 62% of the more than 22 million Americans who are 65 or older depend on Social Security for half or more of their income.

Our advice—split it out more. If you plan *now,* think ahead, invest wisely, and save, you won't be caught depending on Social Security more than you should.

HOW SOCIAL SECURITY WORKS

How You Earn Your Retirement Benefit

▶ **Social Security is designed to work on a "pay as you go" basis— you contribute a percentage of earnings now; when you retire, you get a percentage of lifetime earnings back.**

As you work, you contribute to the Social Security fund. Each year, you get credits from Social Security based upon your gross income—up to a maximum of four credits per year. Because you get a credit for only a minimal amount of earnings, if you work full-time, you can be assured that you'll earn four credits a year.

As an example: In 1990, you received one credit for each $520 of gross income you made that year, up to a maximum of four— regardless of how much greater than $2,080 your gross income was. This amount will continue increasing automatically each year as wages increase.

Moreover, each year you contribute a percentage of your salary to Social Security, and your employer matches it. For example, in 1991, you contribute 7.65% of your salary up to a $53,400 cap to Social Security; your employer chips in an equivalent 7.65%. If you're self-employed, you underwrite the entire contribution yourself.

All these contributions are tracked by the Social Security Administration. While you don't make the amount you contributed back, you do receive benefits when you retire because of your participation in the system. The combination of the number of years you worked (and credits you've earned) and the amount you've contributed to Social Security determine the benefits you receive.

▶ **On average, to be eligible for full Social Security retirement benefits, you need to have worked for a minimum of 10 years and earned 40 credits.**

If you turn 62 in 1991 or later, you need to have earned 40 credits to be fully insured by Social Security.

If, however, you turned 62 before 1990, you need to have earned fewer credits (specifically, if you reached the age of 62 in 1986, you need 35 credits; in 1987, 36; in 1988, 37; in 1989, 38; in 1990, 39).

Do keep in mind: the number of credits you earn only determines your eligibility for Social Security payments. It *doesn't* determine the amount of money you get from Social Security.

▶ **Your retirement benefit is based on an average of your lifetime earnings.**

Social Security figures out the benefit you will receive by averaging your income. One thing in your favor—your five lowest average working years of earnings aren't included.

Benefits are adjusted to be in sync with cost-of-living increases, indexed with the Consumer Price Index. Each year, your benefits will rise the same percentage that the cost of living does.

TIP: Keep an eye out for news stories and developments involving Cost of Living Adjustments (COLA). This is one Social Security benefit that has been questioned. To help cut the deficit, some legislators have suggested cutting COLA increases. It's a good idea to keep abreast of this.

SOURCE: The **National Council of Senior Citizens,** a nonprofit organization of clubs, councils, and other groups, is an advocate for senior citizens. It distributes information on Social Security legislation, as well as other areas of interest to senior citizens. For information, contact: **National Council of Senior Citizens, 925 15th Street NW, Washington, DC 20005** (phone 202-347-8800).

The percentage of your annual income that Social Security replaces clearly depends upon how much you made over your lifetime. Those with low incomes can receive benefits worth as much as 70% of their preretirement pay; those in the upper brackets—who have earned more than the maximum covered by Social Security ($53,400 in 1990)—get about 28%. The higher your income, the lower the percentage. On average, people make about 42% of what they made before they retired.

When You Receive Benefits

▶ **When you start to receive retirement benefits is largely up to you: You can get them as early as age 62, or you can wait. Rule of thumb: The longer the wait, the bigger the benefits.**

Obviously the first proviso is that you can't begin receiving benefits until you retire. Beyond that, however, it's fairly open.

If you choose, you can begin getting Social Security benefits when you turn 62. But by doing this, you permanently reduce the amount of your monthly benefits by 20%. If you retire at 63, your benefit is reduced by 13.5%; at 64, by 6.66%.

You receive full retirement benefits when you retire at the "normal retirement age" determined by the Social Security Administration. These ages vary depending upon when you were born, as follows:

Year of Birth	When You Receive Full Retirement Benefits
1937 or earlier	65
1938	65 and 2 months
1939	65 and 4 months
1940	65 and 6 months
1941	65 and 8 months
1942	65 and 10 months
1943–1954	66
1955	66 and 2 months
1956	66 and 4 months
1957	66 and 6 months
1958	66 and 8 months
1959	66 and 10 months
1960 and later	67

▶ **Waiting to collect your retirement benefits—putting it off until after you reach your "normal" retirement age—pays. And it pays well.**

You earn special credits—delayed retirement credits—for each month past your normal retirement age that you delay receiving benefits. These credits raise the amount of the retirement benefit you'll receive once you retire. You can keep accruing these credits until you reach age 70.

The rate of delayed retirement credits depends on the year of your birth, as follows:

When You Reach 65	Monthly	Yearly %
Before 1982	$1/12$ of 1%	1.0%
1982–1989	$1/4$ of 1%	3.0%
1990–1991	$7/24$ of 1%	3.5%
1992–1993	$1/3$ of 1%	4.0%
1994–1995	$3/8$ of 1%	4.5%
1996–1997	$5/12$ of 1%	5.0%
1998–1999	$11/24$ of 1%	5.5%
2000–2001	$1/2$ of 1%	6.0%
2002–2003	$13/24$ of 1%	6.5%
2004–2005	$7/12$ of 1%	7.0%
2006–2007	$5/8$ of 1%	7.5%
2008–or later	$2/3$ of 1%	8.0%

TABLE 2.1: WHAT YOU'LL BE GETTING FROM SOCIAL SECURITY—APPROXIMATE MONTHLY RETIREMENT BENEFITS

(if worker retires at normal retirement age and has had steady earnings)

Worker's Age in 1990	Worker's Family	Retired Worker's Earnings in 1989								
		$10,000	$15,000	$20,000	$25,000	$30,000	$35,000	$40,000	$45,000	$48,000 or More[1]
25	Retired worker only	$648	$830	$1,013	$1,196	$1,296	$1,381	$1,467	$1,553	$1,604
	Worker and spouse[2]	972	1,245	1,519	1,794	1,944	2,071	2,200	2,329	2,406
	Final year earnings[3]	13,700	20,550	27,400	34,250	41,100	47,950	54,800	61,650	65,760
	Replacement rate[4]	57%	48%	44%	42%	38%	35%	32%	30%	29%
35	Retired worker only	599	767	935	1,098	1,199	1,289	1,357	1,436	1,484
	Worker and spouse[2]	898	1,150	1,402	1,647	1,798	1,933	2,035	2,154	2,226
	Final year earnings[3]	12,700	19,050	25,400	31,750	38,100	44,450	50,800	57,150	60,960
	Replacement rate[4]	57%	48%	44%	41%	38%	35%	32%	30%	29%
45	Retired worker only	547	700	852	1,006	1,101	1,168	1,234	1,296	1,332
	Worker and spouse[2]	820	1,050	1,278	1,509	1,651	1,752	1,851	1,944	1,998
	Final year earnings[3]	11,700	17,550	23,400	29,250	35,100	40,950	46,800	52,650	56,160
	Replacement rate[4]	56%	48%	44%	41%	38%	34%	32%	30%	28%
55	Retired worker only	496	632	771	906	986	1,027	1,071	1,107	1,126
	Worker and spouse[2]	744	948	1,156	1,359	1,479	1,540	1,606	1,661	1,689
	Final year earnings[3]	10,700	16,050	21,400	26,750	32,100	37,450	42,800	48,150	51,350
	Replacement rate[4]	56%	47%	43%	41%	37%	33%	30%	28%	26%
65	Retired worker only	456	582	708	832	896	925	946	965	975
	Worker and spouse[2]	684	873	1,062	1,248	1,344	1,387	1,419	1,447	1,463
	Final year earnings[3]	10,000	15,000	20,000	25,000	30,000	35,000	40,000	45,000	48,000
	Replacement rate[4]	55%	47%	42%	40%	36%	32%	28%	26%	24%

[1]Earnings equal the Social Security wage base from age 22 through 1989.
[2]Spouse is assumed to be the same age as the worker. Spouse may qualify for a higher retirement benefit based on his or her own work record.
[3]Worker's earnings in the year before retirement.
[4]Replacement rates are shown for retired worker only.
Note: The accuracy of these estimates depends on the pattern of the worker's actual past earnings, and on his or her earnings in the future. It is assumed that there are no future benefit increases after January 1990 and no average wage increases after 1988. Estimated benefits are adjusted upwards by 1 percent for each year that the year of initial eligibility exceeds 1990, to reflect expected real wage gains.
Source: Social Security Administration.

Similarly, if you return to work after you start receiving retirement benefits, your added earnings may result in higher benefits. Your earnings will be credited to your earnings record and Social Security will refigure your benefit.

▶ **Your family members can also get Social Security benefits if you're receiving retirement benefits.**

In certain cases, spouses or children are also eligible for monthly Social Security benefits.

Your children will receive benefits if they are:

- Unmarried and under 18 (or under 19 and a full-time elementary or high school student).

- Unmarried, over 18, and severely disabled before age 22 with a continuing disability.

Your spouse will receive benefits if he or she is:

- 62 or older.

- Under 62 and caring for a child under 16 or disabled who is also receiving a Social Security benefit based upon your record.

In most cases, your marriage must have lasted at least a year before family members are eligible for monthly benefits under your Social Security retirement record. Nonworking or lower-benefit spouses receive about 37% of the full worker's retirement benefit at age 62; about 41% at age 63; about 46% at age 64; and 50% at age 65 (unless they receive a federal, state, or municipal government pension or are eligible for Social Security benefits equal to over 50% of their spouses' benefits).

▶ *Survivors' benefits* **are similar to straight retirement benefits for dependent spouses.**

If you're a widow or widower of a worker eligible for Social Security, you can receive survivors' benefits based upon your spouse's benefits. You receive full benefits at age 65 or older, partial benefits as early as age 60.

If you're divorced, and your ex-spouse dies, you're also covered by the Social Security Survivors program, provided the marriage lasted at least 10 years and you didn't remarry before you reached age 60.

If you're taking care of a child under age 16 or one disabled before age 22, however, the length-of-marriage rule does not apply.

If you're disabled, you're eligible for survivors' benefits at age 50 to 59—about 72% of your spouse's benefits.

▶ **When a Social Security recipient dies, the surviving spouse (or children if there is no spouse) receives a lump-sum death benefit ($255 in 1991).**

STEPS TO TAKE BEFORE YOU RETIRE

Finding Out About Your Benefits

▶ **Before you reach retirement age, check with the Social Security Administration to find out your projected Social Security benefits. The earlier, the better.**

Do this for two good reasons.

Reason 1: You can plan your retirement better when you factor in your expected Social Security benefits.

Reason 2: The Social Security Administration, like any bureaucracy, makes mistakes—mistakes like overlooking a few years of your earnings. It's not all that common (the Social Security Administration says less than 1% of eligible wages slip past them and don't get counted), but it does happen.

This is why the Social Security Administration advises that you check their records of your earnings every three years or so. Remember—you've been paying into Social Security. You should get every penny that is due you.

TIP: Don't be conned by people or companies or official-sounding "agencies" offering to send you your Social Security information for a fee. (At last check, most were charging about $15.) You can get the information yourself—free.

▶ **You can get an estimate of your Social Security retirement benefit by contacting Social Security and asking for a Personal Earnings and Benefits Estimate Statement (PEBS) request form.**

Visit your local Social Security office or call Social Security at 800-234-5772 to get your PEBS request form. The form asks for very basic information: name, address, birth date, last year's actual earnings, this year's estimated earnings, the date you expect to retire, and an estimate of your future average yearly earnings (typically the same or slightly more than this year's estimated earnings). That's it.

Once you've mailed it in, you can expect a report back in about four weeks. This will include:

- A breakout of your earnings and Social Security contributions each year.

- How much you can expect from Social Security upon retiring—given for retirement age 62, age 65, and age 70.

- The amount you would receive if you become disabled.

- The amount your spouse would receive should you die.

▶ **If there's a mistake in your recorded earnings, be sure to get it changed as soon as possible.**

Mistakes do happen. Sometimes—in fact, usually—people don't catch them until they reach retirement. If you do realize that some of your eligible earnings are missing from the PEBS, get it corrected quickly. Any gap in your earnings will affect the amount of Social Security benefits you receive upon retirement, because benefits are calculated by averaging your earnings in the 35 years you were paid the most. If your account doesn't show earnings from certain high years, your average will be pulled down—and your benefits will be substantially lower.

It's not difficult to get errors corrected. You do, however, have to show proof that there was a mistake made by the Social Security Administration in accounting your earnings. To do this, you need evidence of your earnings for the disputed period of time—a W-2 form or, if you're self-employed, a copy of the pertinent income tax return (especially the form SS, which shows the amount you paid for Social Security).

TIP: **If you have any trouble or disputes regarding your Social Security benefits or earnings, you have recourse. First, call your Social Security office and ask them to reconsider. If you disagree with this decision, you can get a hearing with an administrative law judge. If you are still dissatisfied, you may request a review by the appeals council, and then may take your case to the federal courts.**

For legal advice, information or assistance, you may want to contact: National Senior Citizens Law Center, Suite 400, 2025 M Street NW, Washington, DC 20036 (202-887-5280). This is a public interest law firm specializing in the legal problems facing senior citizens—including problems with Social Security.

Applying for and Receiving Social Security Benefits

▶ **Apply for Social Security *three months* before you retire. This way you can be sure that you'll begin receiving checks the month you do actually retire.**

It's a simple process. Call your Social Security office to find out the best time to come in. In some cases, you'll be able to apply over the phone.

TIP: **Don't call the Social Security office on the first week of the month, or Mondays and Tuesdays of other weeks. Those are their busiest times. It's best to call Wednesday through Friday—and if possible, call either early in the morning or late in the afternoon.**

If you can't apply over the phone, when you go to the Social Security office, bring the following with you:

• Your Social Security card.

• Your birth certificate or other record of your age, such as a baptismal certificate.

• Proof of recent earnings (the past two years' W-2 forms or, if you're self-employed, your SE income tax returns).

If your spouse is eligible for benefits on your record, he or she should bring the same material. It's also a good idea to bring your marriage certificate.

TIP: **If you're applying for survivors' benefits, also bring your spouse's Social Security number, proof of your marriage, a death certificate or other evidence of your spouse's death, and if you are supporting children, proof of that.**

If you want your Social Security checks to be directly deposited in your checking or savings account, bring along your checkbook, passbook, or written proof of your account, such as a bank statement with your name and account number on it.

TIP: **This is a good time to apply for Medicare benefits as well, since you should apply for both three months before retiring and can apply for both at the same office. (See page 138 for more on Medicare.)**

▶ **You'll receive your Social Security benefits check on the third day of each month.**

The monthly check you receive covers the benefits you are due for the *previous* month. It is mailed so you will get it in the mail on the third day of each month. When that day is a weekend or a holiday, the check is mailed earlier.

If you've opted for direct deposit instead, the money will be automatically deposited in your account and available to you on the third of the month. In general, this is a quicker, hassle-free way of getting your benefits. A plus: Since the money is already in your account on the third, you save the time you would have had to spend depositing the check yourself.

WORKING AFTER RETIREMENT: HOW IT AFFECTS SOCIAL SECURITY

▶ **If you work after you've retired, you might wind up losing all or part of your Social Security coverage during the time that you work.**

It depends on how much you earn. Social Security has set up "annual exempt amounts"—the amount of income you can earn and still keep full retirement benefits. If you earn more than the annual exempt amount, you earn less in retirement benefits.

The breakdown is by age (the figures given are for 1990):

- *If you're under 65,* you may earn up to $6,840. Earn more than that and Social Security will withhold one dollar in benefits for every two dollars you earn above that limit.

- *If you're 65 to 69,* you may earn up to $9,360. Earn more than that and Social Security will withhold one dollar in benefits for every three dollars you earn above the limit.

- *If you're 70 or older,* you may earn any amount and face no benefits reduction.

The only time this doesn't apply is in the first year you retire. In that first year, your income is measured monthly. In other words, as long as your income doesn't exceed the *monthly* income limit (in 1990, $780 if you're 65 to 69, $570 if you're under 65), and as long as you don't perform "substantial" services in self-employment (45 or more hours a month), you can receive your full benefit for that month regardless of whether your earnings, added up, exceed the yearly limit.

▶ **All income from employment—including self-employment— counts.**

What doesn't count? All other income—anything from lottery winnings to savings, pensions to investments, rental income to insurance.

TAX CONSIDERATIONS

▶ **Depending upon your total income, your Social Security benefits may be taxable.**

The more you make, the more likely you'll be in for a tax bite. A portion of your benefits will be subject to taxes if your adjusted gross income, plus nontaxable interest income and one-half of your Social Security benefits, exceeds the allowable base amounts. If you are:

- An individual with a total income over $25,000,

- A couple filing jointly with a total income over $32,000,

- A couple filing separately but living together for *any* part of the year (note: In this case, there is *no* base income at all; any income is taxable),

you will owe taxes on the lesser of:

- one-half of your benefits, or

- one-half of the amount of your combined income (adjusted gross income plus nontaxable interest income and 50% of your total Social Security benefits).

At the end of each year, you'll receive by mail a Social Security Benefit Statement (Form SSA-1099) showing what you received as benefits. If any of your benefits are subject to tax as outlined above, you will use this statement to complete your federal income tax form.

SOURCE: For more information on taxation and Social Security, contact your local Internal Revenue office and request the following publications: Publication 554, *Tax Benefits for Older Americans* and Publication 915, *Tax Information on Social Security.*

SPECIAL SITUATIONS

▶ **You are divorced, but your former spouse is eligible for Social Security benefits.**

If your marriage lasted at least 10 years and you have been divorced at least two years, you can apply for and begin receiving family benefits once you reach age 62, even if your former spouse isn't receiving his or her retirement benefits yet. (The length-of-marriage rule doesn't apply if you are caring for a child under 16 or disabled who gets benefits.)

The only criteria are that your former spouse be at least 62 and be eligible for Social Security benefits.

▶ **You are divorced and your former spouse has died—and neither of you remarried.**

As with the above situation, you are eligible for family benefits. The criteria in this case are that you must have been married at least 10 years (unless you are caring for a child under 16 or disabled who gets benefits), and you must not have remarried before age 60. You can begin receiving reduced benefits once you reach 60—or wait until you turn 65 for full survivors' benefits.

▶ **You receive a pension from work not covered by Social Security (for example, from the federal civil service system or from state or local systems).**

In this situation, Social Security uses a different formula to figure your retirement benefit. The result? You'll receive a lower benefit from Social Security than if you weren't covered by the pension.

For information on this, call your local Social Security office and ask for the pamphlets *A Pension from Work Not Covered by Social Security* or (for government employees) *Government Pension Offset.*

SUPPLEMENTAL SECURITY INCOME

▶ **If you're 65 or older with limited income or financial resources, you may be eligible for Supplemental Security Income (SSI).**

This program, run by the Social Security Administration, pays monthly checks to certain low-income people. If you're disabled, blind, or 65 or older and living on a very low income, you can apply for SSI.

To be eligible, you must have resources (which includes bank accounts, cash on hand, and investments) of $2,000 or less if you're single, $3,000 or less for a couple. Your maximum allowable income (which includes Social Security benefits, pensions, and earnings as well as noncash items you receive, such as food or shelter) varies from state to state.

Generally, however, you are probably eligible for SSI if:

• You don't work and your monthly income is $406 or less if you're single, or $599 or less if for a couple.

• You do work, and your monthly income is no more than $857 for one person or $1,234 for a couple.

▶ **The amount you receive for SSI varies.**

In 1991, the basic monthly check was $407 for one person, $610 for two. But the actual amount you receive may differ—if you have other means of income, you may get less.

Your check may also fluctuate from month to month, depending upon the specifics of your situation, such as your income and your living arrangements.

SSI payments are adjusted to rise with the cost of living.

▶ **To apply for SSI, just contact your local Social Security office.**

It's a fairly simple process. Call your local Social Security office or call the main number (800-2345-SSA) to set up an appointment. A representative will tell you what to bring with you to the appointment to help determine your income and resources.

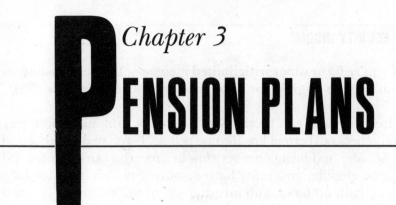

Chapter 3

PENSION PLANS

INTRODUCTION

▶ **For many retirees, pension plans are a crucial source of retirement income. As mentioned earlier, they are generally considered one of the three main sources of retirement income.**

You may be covered by a pension plan through the company you're currently working for. If you're in the civil service, the government will provide you with a pension. If you're self-employed, you may have set up your own pension plan—a Simplified Employee Pension (SEP)—to take care of a portion of your retirement needs. (Note: Since a SEP is a type of IRA, you can read about SEPs and how they fit into a retirement savings plan in Chapter 4, IRAs, Keoghs, and Other Retirement Savings Plans.)

Whatever your situation, it is important for you to understand your particular pension plan, how it works, how you'll be receiving your pension income upon retirement, and how you can best manage your pension income to avoid a tax bite when you can least afford it.

This chapter is designed to give you an idea of how different pension plans work. In its look at private pension plans, it explains the different types of pension plans you may receive from your company—*defined-benefit* plans, *defined-contribution* plans, and *Supplementary Employee Retirement Plans*—the differences between the different types, how they work, and the advantages and disadvantages of each. You can learn how to estimate your pension—which will help you determine how much you can count on upon retirement, and how much you will need to earn from your personal savings and investments.

This chapter also gives an overview of the pensions offered by federal, state, and local governments, and explains how benefits are determined.

Finally, this chapter explains the different ways you may be receiving your pension payouts upon retirement—as an annuity or as a lump sum distribution—and how to best handle the money you receive.

OUTLOOK

▶ **First, a question many people have been asking: Are pension plans still safe?**

While historically, pension plans have been considered one of the three main sources of retirement income, lately their role in retirement planning has come under scrutiny.

With ups and downs in the economy, troubled times, and corporate cutbacks, many people nearing retirement have become concerned about the state of their pension plans, and, in fact, about the stability of the pension system in general.

First, the good news: The pension system is still alive and relatively well—in spite of reports of potential pension shortfalls.

Now the bad: The potential shortfalls do still exist. For example, in May 1990, the Pension Benefit Guaranty Corporation, a federal agency, reported that the pension funds of 50 leading corporations were *each* at least $440 million short of the money needed to meet their pension obligations. One reason for this situation: Companies have been mining pension funds for assets used in the rush of mergers, acquisitions, and takeovers of the late 1980s. As a result, many companies are changing over to pension plans that are less costly to them and less beneficial to employees. (On page 90, we discuss the different strategies companies are using to shut down current pension plans.) Another piece of bad news: Pensions haven't been keeping up with inflation, according to recent U.S. government data.

▶ **The bottom line on private pension plans: While most experts still consider pension plans a crucial aspect of retirement income, they're not as valuable as they used to be.**

With companies switching from defined-benefit to defined-contribution plans (both of which are explained at length in this chapter), the importance of pension plans in most people's retirement planning is shrinking.

A good rule of thumb: Those of you born before 1946 will likely find pensions a more important part of retirement financing than those born after 1946. If you fall in the latter group, your pension will probably represent only a minor part of your retirement income. To finance your retirement, you'll be relying more on personal investments and savvy money management. (For detailed information on investing, see Chapters 6 and 7.)

▶ **Government and military pension plans will probably continue strong.**

It's an old rule of thumb: You might not get the highest salaries for government work, but you get security. And a key part of that security lies in the pension you receive for government or military service.

For example, if you joined the military before August 1, 1986, you can retire after 20 years of service and receive a monthly pension of 50% of your basic pay—regardless of your age on retirement. If you serve for 10 more years, you receive 75% of your pay as a pension. Military pensions also include automatic cost-of-living (COLA) increases.

Government pensions are similarly generous: After 30 years of service, most state and local civil servants receive 50% of their basic pay. Federal civil servants receive more—about 56% of pay based on averaging the three highest-income years. And about 50% of all government workers get COLA increases.

(For more detailed information on military pensions, see page 76; on civil service pensions, see page 77.)

PENSION PLANS FOR THE SELF-EMPLOYED

▶ **If you're self-employed or if your employer doesn't offer a pension plan, you have several options.**

In these cases, it's up to you to set up some sort of personal pension plan. The best move? Look into SEPs, which are pension plans specifically designed for the self-employed. As such, they fill the gap in your retirement plan by providing you with guaranteed pension income. (For specifics on SEPs, see page 110.) In addition, you may want to explore setting up other self-directed retirement plans, such as Keoghs (explained on page 105) and IRAs (page 94).

PRIVATE PENSION PLANS

▶ **Pension plans are designed to offer employees a theoretical "payback" for their years of company service.**

Of course, at the same time, employers deduct contributions they make to pension plans—making their altruism a tax-saver for them.

Normally, your pension is determined as a percentage of your final pay (or, in some cases, your *average* pay) multiplied by the number of years you work at the company. A good plan is 1.0% to 1.5% of your last salary multiplied by the number of years you have worked. Some pension plans allow you to borrow against the amount you have vested, with certain restrictions.

A very few plans (fewer than 5%) also include *cost of living adjustments* (COLAs) as part of the arrangement, which helps keep pension payments in sync with inflation. While this is a great feature, don't count on it. Most companies have eliminated this practice.

▶ *Vesting schedules* **spell out the years of service you have to put in before you are entitled to a pension—either a full pension or a percentage of that pension.**

Vesting periods determine when you own your share of the pension plan. The terms for vesting are determined by the Employee Retirement Income Security Act (ERISA). Under this, the following rules apply:

- *Full or Cliff vesting:* In the past, employees had to work for up to 10 years until they were fully vested. Now the length of service you need to put in has been cut to 5 years. But if you leave before 5 years of service, you forfeit your claim to any pension money.

- *Partial vesting:* New rules put into effect in 1989 set up the following vesting schedules. After 3 years of service, you get 20% pension vesting; after 4 years, 40%; 5 years 60%, after 6 years 80%; after 7 years 100%. (Note: If you work under a union contract approved before March 1, 1986, this may not apply to you until your contract expires.)

SOURCE: A good source of information on pensions is the **Pension Rights Center.** Among their publications: *Can You Count on Getting a Pension?* Contact: Pension Rights Center, 1918 16th Street, Washington, DC 20006.

▶ **If you're covered by a private pension plan at your company, it will be one of two types: a defined-benefit or a defined-contribution plan—and those with higher incomes may encounter another variation: a SERP.**

Defined-Benefit Plans

This type of plan used to be the most commonly offered private pension plan, but this is changing. More than 38 million people are covered by defined-benefit plans, but as corporate costs for defined-benefit plans rise, the number of such plans will shrink. Already there has been a decline: In 1975, 39% of U.S. workers were covered by corporate defined-benefit plans; the number fell to 31% by 1988.

How it works: With a defined-benefit plan, you receive a *guaranteed* amount of money upon retirement based on your years of service, your salary level, and other factors. This amount is predetermined and is not affected by how the company pension fund is performing, how much the company has contributed, the economic situation, and so forth. The amount of money the company contributes to the pension fund can vary. The only set figure is your benefits. Because of this, you can easily estimate how much you will get on retirement.

Pros: Defined-benefit plans are federally insured, which means that regardless of what happens to your company or to the economy, you are guaranteed a fixed monthly payment from the plan. This allows for easier retirement planning, as you can be sure of your pension income.

Cons: You have no say in how and where your money is invested. Also, defined-benefit plans are usually not portable—that is, if you change jobs, you cannot switch your pension over to your new company.

Defined-Contribution Plans

Defined-contribution plans are becoming more popular among corporations. In 1975, about 6% of U.S. wage earners were covered by defined-contribution plans. This number skyrocketed to about 15% by 1988, and this trend will probably continue.

How it works: Under a defined-contribution plan, the company contributes a set amount to the company pension fund in your name—typically a percentage of your salary. You may be responsible for choosing what you want your contributions invested in—options range from company stock to other stocks to fixed-income securities. The amount you will receive upon retirement is not guaranteed and depends on how well the fund was invested, the state of the economy at the time you retire, and so forth. The only definite figure in this sort of plan is the amount of money *invested*, not the amount of money you will receive. With a defined-contribution plan, you receive periodic statements about your pension—what the holdings are, how much you have as of the last quarter of the last year. Keep in mind: The statement *doesn't* tell you how much you will have on retirement. You will find that out only when you actually retire.

The most common defined-contribution plans offered are *profit sharing, 401(k)s, thrift plans* (also called savings plans), and *employee stock ownership plans* (ESOPs). (For information on these, see Chapter 4.)

Pros: These plans are usually portable. If you switch jobs, you may be able to take your account with you and roll it over into your new employer's 401(k) or into an IRA. Another plus, particularly if you're a savvy money manager, is that you can opt for a growth-oriented investment and make more money.

Cons: You don't have the same degree of safety offered by a defined-benefit plan, since your pension money is only as safe as what it is invested in. For example, if the market crashes the day you retire, your pension nest egg will crash along with it—and there's absolutely nothing you can do about it.

SOURCE: To help you understand your particular pension plan, send away for AARP's free booklet: *A Guide to Understanding Your Pension Plan.* Write to: AARP Fulfillment Center, 1909 K Street, NW, Washington, DC 20049.

SERPs—Supplementary Employee Retirement Plans

SERPs are growing in use as employees who earn the most find their pension protection decreasing.

How it works: A SERP is a retirement plan designed to supplement the retirement benefits of higher-paid employees—typically those upper-level managers who earn over $200,000. A key difference between SERPs and regular pensions is that, with a regular pension, the company pays your pension benefits from a specific pension fund to which it has been contributing pension money in your name. With a SERP, the company pays your retirement benefits out of its general operating profits. There is no prefunding. In addition, because a SERP isn't a standard qualified pension plan, you don't get the guarantees you get under other pensions. For example, if the company goes bankrupt, you don't automatically receive your pension money. You would have to file a claim like other creditors. Similarly, if the company is taken over, new management technically could decide not to pay you. Regular vesting schedules don't apply—this, again, because SERPs aren't qualified pension plans.

However, SERPs do have a positive side—particularly because they enable higher-income professionals to receive a larger amount of pension money on retirement. Under a qualified pension plan, the federal government sets a cap on benefits ($102,582 in 1990). Any retirement benefits above the cap would have to come from another source—a SERP.

TIP: Because SERPs can be risky, find out if much of your pension is coming from a SERP. If yes, find out if your company has set up a trust to secure it. Trusts protect the money in the SERP.

Pros: If you're in an upper income bracket, SERPs enable you to get the money you can't from a qualified pension.

Cons: As mentioned, SERPs aren't guaranteed, prefunded, or bound by government regulations—you could lose your entire benefit amount if the company runs into trouble, or if you leave.

CALCULATING YOUR PENSION

▶ **Calculating your pension doesn't have to be an exact science. For most of you, a simple rough estimate of your pension will be enough for you to get ahead with your retirement planning.**

Follow this basic rule of thumb: Your pension benefits will generally equal 50% to 70% of your last year's salary.

That's the simplest way of determining pension and Social Security income. However, if you want to calculate your pension more precisely, you should ask your plan administrator or human resources staffer for specific information on your pension—exact terms, conditions, and the formula used to figure pension benefits.

▶ **While there are a number of different formulas used to figure pension benefits, chances are your company will use one of the two following formulas—*percentage of earnings per year of service* or the *integrated formula*.**

Percentage of Earnings per Year of Service

How it works: This formula is straightforward. Benefits are figured by multiplying a percentage of your salary (usually between 1% to 2%) by the number of years you worked at your company. The salary upon which the formula is based is usually your final year's pay or the average of your highest-paid three to five years. (A few companies average your salary over all of your years at the company—which works out badly if you worked your way up—but this version is not all that common.)

EXAMPLE: You earn $50,000 a year and have been with the company for 25 years. Your company bases its pensions on 1.5% and final year's pay. Your pension calculation would be: $50,000 times .015 times 25, making your annual pension benefit $18,750.

Integrated Formula

How it works: This formula is actually a way for your employer to reduce your pension benefits, because your employer figures your pension by taking into account the Social Security benefits you'll be receiving. With *defined-benefit plans,* the employer reduces your monthly pension benefits by a percentage of the monthly amount you receive from Social Security. If it's 50% integrated, the employer deducts 50% of the Social Security benefits.

EXAMPLE: Your monthly pension benefits amount to $1,562. Your monthly Social Security benefits are $975. Under a plan with 50% integration, you'll receive $1,075 in pension benefits, plus your Social Security benefits.

With *defined-contribution plans,* it gets more complicated. When making contributions into your pension account, the employer may include those Social Security contributions that are part of your retirement benefits (old age, survivor, and disability insurance—OASDI) as a portion of the set amount. In other words, if under your defined-contribution plan, 12% of your salary is to be contributed, your employer can include his OASDI contribution as part of that 12%.

GOVERNMENT PENSION PLANS

Military Pension Plans

▶ **Military pension plans offer generous benefits for service in the armed forces.**

Military pensions are high—substantially higher than the average private pension. Another big plus—when you're in the military, you can retire after 20 years of active, uniformed service *regardless* of your age.

How they work: Your pension benefit depends upon when you entered service as a regular or reserve member of the armed forces. If you entered:

- *Before August 1, 1986:* You can retire after 20 years of service with 50% pay. Each year thereafter up to 10, the amount you receive increases until it reaches a cap of 75% of your basic pay.

- *After August 1986:* You get 40% base pay when you retire after 20 years of service; 75% after 30 years of service.

Military pensions also pay survivors' benefits to surviving spouses if they were married to the military retiree for at least one year, and to the mother of the retiree's children. In these cases, the survivor will receive 55% of the pension.

Divorced spouses are also eligible for benefits. However, the rules are more stringent: To collect a pension benefit they must have been married to the military retiree for a minimum of 10 years, and this while he or she was on active duty; they must file a court order to collect pension benefits.

Pros: Automatic cost-of-living increases; healthy payments.

Cons: Military pension money is subject to federal income tax and sometimes to state income tax. (It is partially exempt in 25 states, completely exempt in 6 states.)

Civil Service Pension Plans

▶ **Pensions for federal government workers are second only to military pensions in terms of benefits.**

When you work for the federal government, you're usually well rewarded when it comes to retirement money. For example, if you've put in a long stint as a federal employee, you can expect to make about 60% of your final salary through your pension. Add to that the automatic cost-of-living increases and you can look forward to a well-funded retirement. State and local government pensions may vary in terms of both payouts and safety, a particular concern in today's budget-cutting era. You'll have to check on your own.

How they work: Federal civil service pensions are determined by averaging the pay you received during your three highest years of income—or High 3 Years—and factoring in how many years you worked. Multiply your average high pay by 1.5% for your first 5 years of service; by 1.75% for the second 5; and by 2% for each year over 10. This will be your basic yearly pension.

EXAMPLE: You are retiring from the government after 25 years of service. Your "High 3" salary averages out to $45,000. You figure your annual pension as follows:

$45,000 × 1.50% × 5 years = $ 3,375.00
$45,000 × 1.75% × 5 years =   3,937.50
$45,000 × 2.00% × 15 years = 13,500.00
Your pension = $20,812.50

As for vesting, the schedule is as follows: To collect your pension at age 55, you need 30 years of service; at age 60, 20 years of service; and at age 62, only 5 years of service.

If you participate in the Federal Employees' Retirement System

(FERS), you can make contributions—up to 7% of salary—which are matched by the government agency you work for.

Survivors are covered under government pension plans. If you die after a minimum of 18 months of civil service, your spouse or children under 18 receive 55% of your benefit under the formula used for disability payments (disability pays about 40% of your average High 3 years). The proviso: You must have been married at least one year or have children together.

Pros: Benefits are higher than in the private sector; COLA increases keep benefits high.

Cons: Pension benefits are taxable; the budget deficit is causing legislators to think about cutting benefits.

TEN QUESTIONS TO ASK ABOUT YOUR PENSION PLAN

▶ **Knowing that you're getting a pension isn't enough. You should know as much as you can about your pension *before* you decide to retire or leave your present job.**

Picking and assessing a pension plan is a key consideration in early preretirement planning. There are a number of questions you should ask about your pension. Some are very basic—but you'd be surprised at how many people don't know the basics about their pension plan. Remember: It's *your* money. The more you know about the money you'll be receiving, how and when you'll get it, and how much you can expect, the better you can plan for a financially secure retirement.

1. *What type of pension plan does my company offer?* A simple question, but one that makes a difference. Do you have a defined-benefit plan? If so, you can make a rough estimate of the amount of money you'll receive when you retire. Is it a defined-contribution plan? If so, speak to your pension manager for general estimates.

2. *When do I begin participating in the plan?* At some companies, you'll have to wait a period of time before you are allowed to begin participating in the company pension plan—often at least three months after being hired; sometimes as much as one year.

Knowing when you become a plan participant will help you keep track of retirement earnings.

3. *What is the vesting schedule? When am I partially vested? Fully vested?* Clearly, this is important to know—especially if you are planning early retirement or changing jobs.

4. *Once I'm vested, what happens to my money if I leave my job?* If you quit, can you take the money with you and roll it over into another plan? Under some plans, you are entitled to the lump sum accrued in your pension plan. Under others, your money will be kept for you until you reach retirement age—typically 65. In this case, you have to find out what (if anything) you must do to receive your benefits on your retirement. Are there forms to file, people to contact, steps you'll have to take?

5. *What about early retirement—am I covered under this plan?* Some pension plans are designed to begin payment not on retirement, but on your reaching age 62 or 65. This is an important factor in planning an early retirement, as your pension benefits will probably play a fairly major role in financing your retirement. Other pension plans, "sweetened" pensions, are designed to *encourage* early retirement. Under a common early retirement arrangement, employees add five years to their service record and five years to their age on their pension. Typically, you'll wind up with about 50% of what you're currently making.

6. *What is the plan invested in?* Investment vehicles can vary widely in risk, yield, and so forth. While you may not be able to do anything about what your company pension plan is invested in, it makes sense to know. You can then make your own assessment of the plan's stability and how important your outside investments will be.

7. *Do I have any say in how my money is invested?* Some pension plans allow you to give suggestions on investing.

8. *What happens to my pension if I choose to work past retirement age?* Will you lose benefits? Keep gaining? Companies are not bound to continue making contributions to your pension plan once you pass 65, but some do. Others allow your pension amount to continue accruing interest—which means that once you do retire, your benefits have grown, sometimes substantially.

9. *Does the plan include disability benefits? Death benefits?* This differs from plan to plan, especially as companies try to cut back on their benefits and pension costs.

10. *What is the financial condition of the plan?* This question has (unfortunately) become more important. Ask also if the plan administrator believes there may be future difficulty in paying benefits.

SOURCE: If you are concerned about the health of your pension plan, ask your employer for a copy of government **Form 5500**—which will tell you about the plan's investments, how many investment managers there have been, and so forth. Also helpful is the six-dollar guide, ***Protecting Your Pension Money.*** Contact: **Pension Rights Center,** 918 16th St. NW, Suite 704, Washington, DC 20006.

RECEIVING YOUR PENSION: HOW SHOULD YOU COLLECT YOUR BENEFITS?

▶ **Collecting your benefits should be simple . . . but it isn't.**

Receiving pension distributions seems straightforward: Once you turn 59½, you get the money in your pension plan, free and clear. If you want your money before you reach 59½, you face a 10% penalty. However, there are several exceptions—cases in which the penalty is waived. Among them:

• If you become disabled, and thus unable to work, the penalty is waived.

• If you are at least 55 and retire or otherwise leave the company (called "separation from service" by the IRS).

• If you have quit, retired, or otherwise left the company, and receive your pension payout in a series of scheduled payments over your life expectancy (or the joint expectancy of you and your designated survivor). You can determine the amount of the payments by checking a life expectancy table (such as the IRS table in Publication 575, available at your local IRS office). These payments must be roughly equal and must be paid at least annually. You must receive these payments for at least five years. If you change the schedule so that it doesn't qualify for the exception or switch to get a lump sum distribution, you'll have to pay a "recapture tax."

(Note: These exceptions also apply to other retirement plans, including Keoghs, 401(k) plans, and profit-sharing plans.)

▶ **If you wait until you are age 59½ to get your pension payout, you may have two options.**

Some companies allow you to choose how you want to receive your money. In these cases, you can get your payout either as an annuity—a monthly check for life—or as a lump sum.

The trick, of course, is knowing which type of payout method works best for you. Following are explanations of both ways of getting your payout and the pros and cons of each.

Annuities

▶ **The big plus with annuities: You are guaranteed monthly income for life.**

Because you aren't receiving one lump sum, but guaranteed monthly payments, you are safer—you can't lose your entire pension benefit through poor investments or unwise spending.

On the downside: If inflation continues, fixed monthly benefits will erode in terms of purchasing power as time goes on. And some annuities are unsafe, overpriced, or overly complicated. For more considerations, see page 258.

There are several different types of annuities:

1. *Straight life or single-life annuity*

How it works: This method is perhaps the simplest: All payments go to one person—the pension holder. Period. Nothing more, nothing less.

Pros: This method pays more than any other pension payment method.

Cons: Payments go only to the pension holder. Upon his or her death, the pension is finished.

Best for: Single retirees; couples in which one partner is independently wealthy; couples in which one partner has a short life expectancy.

TIP: **Couples electing this method may choose to take the higher payment and invest some of it in a life insurance policy for the pension holder. This will provide an annuity for the surviving spouse.**

2. *Joint and Survivor Option or Joint and Survivor Annuity*

How it works: With this method, both pension holder and spouse receive pension payments. The pension holder gets monthly payments until he or she dies, at which point the "designated survivor" (typically the spouse) gets a percentage of pension payments. This percentage can be as little as 50% or as much as 100% (rare, but possible). Companies by law automatically offer this option with at least a 50% annuity to the surviving spouse to married employees. It is up to the employee to decide, with the permission of his or her spouse, against this.

Pros: This method, popular with married couples, guarantees income for a surviving spouse.

Cons: Joint pensions pay less than single pensions—usually about 10% less—so be sure to determine whether you can afford to live on the smaller payments. If the pension holder *outlives* the spouse, any benefits of this method are negated: The pension holder has received less money than if he or she had opted for a single pension.

Best for: Couples, especially those with a wide age difference; couples who have other good sources of retirement income.

TIP: **Experts say that the safest survivor benefit is *at least* 75%. One thing to keep in mind, however: With a high survivor's percentage, you get a higher percentage taken out of the pension holder's payments.**

3. *Period certain annuity*

How it works: This is a variation on the joint and survivor method. With a period certain annuity, the pension holder receives payments. Upon his or her death, the designated survivor receives an annuity for a specified period of time, usually 5 or 10 years.

Pros: Like the joint and survivor annuity option, a period certain annuity provides for a survivor, without cutting as much into the monthly payments of the pension holder.

Cons: Because the survivor payments are not for the lifetime of the survivor, this doesn't provide long-term support.

Best for: People who want a sum of money for short-term support of a survivor—for example, a college-age child could pay tuition with the benefit; newlyweds could use the benefit for a down payment on a house.

▶ **A variation on joint and survivor annuities is called** *pension maximization*—**and it's something to be on the lookout for.**

Pension maximization (or pension max) is something that financial planners, insurance agents, and others may offer you. Women in particular should be aware of this, as some professionals will insist that this will leave more money for the surviving spouse (given life expectancies, usually the wife) to live on. In simple English, pension maximization means that the pension payments increase—or are maximized—by having the pension holder (with written agreement from his or her spouse) arrange for pension payments to cover his or her lifetime only—that is, choose the single-life annuity.

In this way, a husband and wife receive larger payments than in other pension arrangements (such as joint and survivor option). With this extra money, they invest in a life insurance policy on the pension holder to provide for the spouse if the pension holder dies first. Theoretically, by doing this, either spouse benefits: If the pension holder survives, he or she continues receiving the larger pension check; if the spouse outlives the holder, he or she will receive life insurance money to replace the pension. Either way, the survivor makes out.

At least that's what it's *supposed* to mean. But often—in fact, usually—it doesn't work out that way. The common problems?

• The insurance company investments don't pay as well as predicted, which means the insurance policy *won't* provide as much as promised for the survivor. In this case, you'll be forced to accept the lower coverage (which may mean that your spouse isn't well protected), increase the amount of the life insurance coverage (which may cost a great deal), or drop the policy.

• The spouse loses survivor's rights to the pension—which means he or she also loses cost-of-living adjustments (if any) and, possibly, health insurance.

The best bet? Don't get lured into "pension maximization." You're better off sticking with the pension as is.

Lump Sum Distributions

▶ **With lump sum distributions, you get all the pros and cons of having a large sum of money immediately on hand.**

Unlike an annuity payout, with a lump sum distribution you can't count on a regular income over your lifetime. However, also unlike an annuity payout, the option allows you to invest your money and so assure that it keeps its purchasing power.

While lump sum distribution is not a common option, it is popular with employees. According to a recent survey, while fewer than 50% of employers surveyed offered this option, *over* 50% of the employees at these companies chose lump sum distribution.

How it works: A lump sum distribution is exactly what it sounds like: The pension holder receives the retirement benefit in one lump sum upon retirement. The pension plan administrator determines the lump sum by projecting your life expectancy (per actuarial tables), totaling the amount the plan would have paid you monthly over your life, and factoring in the interest rate the plan administrator predicts it would earn.

TIP: Generally, the higher the interest rate, the lower the lump sum you receive. This is an important consideration when deciding between lump sum and annuity payouts.

Pros: Since you receive the money at once, you can invest the money—and get tax breaks.

Cons: You have to have an investment plan or your money will quickly disappear. One of the biggest drawbacks if you *don't* plan:

taxes. (For detailed information on this aspect of lump sum distribution and on how to deal with high taxation, see Taxes and Your Pension, below.)

Best for: People going for early retirement; people with other sources of income; people with money management skills; people who need the capital (to start a business or buy a house, for example); people in poor health.

▶ **A final note about lump sum distributions: Don't be tempted into making rash investment decisions.**

If you receive a sizable lump sum distribution and are thinking about investing it, our advice is simple—Wait. When you first get a large sum of money, you might not be thinking as clearly as usual—which may lead to unwise investment decisions. So instead of immediately plunging into a major investment, stop and think. Opt for something conservative and safe to park your money in for a short period—perhaps a CD or Treasury securities—and *then* come up with an investment plan.

TAXES AND YOUR PENSION

▶ **Depending on how large a pension payout you'll be receiving, you may get hit with a very healthy tax bite.**

Blame the 1986 tax law, which imposed stiffer taxes on pensions. If you're looking forward to a generous pension payout, be prepared for the 15% excise tax now required on amounts above certain limits. You are liable for this 15% excise tax if:

- The combined payout of *all* of your retirement plans (including qualified pension plans, profit-sharing plans, IRAs, and Keoghs) is over $150,000 a year.

- You receive a one-time lump sum distribution of your retirement plans equaling over $750,000.

The 15% penalty is applied to the total amount over the limit. But there *is* a loophole. According to federal law, if you have accumulated at least $562,000 in retirement benefits *before August 1986,* you can "grandfather" those funds. This allows you to receive a lump sum payment that won't be subject to the excise tax. However, you must have already made this election on your 1988 income tax return, Form 5329. (Note: If you would rather receive your payments annually, instead of in a lump sum, you can still get around the 15% tax—but it requires careful planning, following formulas, and the like. Your best bet in this situation? Talk to your accountant or financial planner.)

▶ **Since you will have to pay taxes on your pension money once you begin receiving it, it's important for you to understand your options.**

Naturally your tax situation will depend on the way you receive your pension money—as an annuity or as a lump sum distribution.

If you're getting your pension money as an annuity, your tax picture is fairly straightforward. You just have to take into account the amount you'll be getting and include that in your regular tax planning.

However, if you're getting your pension money as a lump sum distribution, it gets a little more complicated. Remember: *All of the money you have received as a lump sum pension distribution is taxable* (except for any after-tax contributions you made). Because you're receiving a large amount of money in one lump sum, you have to protect it from the equally large tax bite that can follow if you don't plan. What you should do to protect the money, however, depends upon your specific situation.

▶ **If you've received a lump sum distribution, but don't need the money immediately, open an IRA.**

This is the best move to make if you won't need your pension money for three or more years. You can roll your pension distribution into an IRA if:

- the money represents at least 50% of your total pension benefits

- You are receiving all of the distribution in a single tax year

- the distribution is being paid because the pension holder retired, quit, became disabled, or died.

Most experts advise rolling your pension money into an IRA within 60 days of receiving it. This way, you don't have to pay any taxes at all on that money until you withdraw it. Since you aren't required by law to withdraw any money from an IRA until you reach age 70½, this can add up to substantial tax savings.

▶ **What if you need the money immediately, so can't roll it into an IRA? If you're eligible,** *five-year forward averaging* **may be your best bet.**

Forward averaging allows you to act as if your distribution is the only income you received for the year—and was spread over a five-year period. You pay the entire tax on the sum in one year, but the tax will be at a lower rate than if it were taxed like your regular income.

You can use five-year forward averaging if:

- You have been a participant of the pension plan for at least five years.

- The lump sum distribution you've received is from a qualified retirement plan—pension, profit sharing, or stock bonus—and it represents 100% of your money in the plan.

- The money will be paid within a single tax year.

- You are 59½ or over. (Note: There is an exception to this rule for people who were 50 or over on January 1, 1986. If you were born before 1932 you can use five-year forward averaging with no penalty. If you were born between 1932 and 1935, you also can use forward averaging, but you must pay a 10% penalty on the total.)

If you meet all of the above criteria, forward averaging can save you a sizable tax chunk. Here's how it works.

The formula: Take 20% of the lump sum you receive, *add* the standard deduction, then (acting as if that amount were your sole income) check the tax tables for the tax on that income. Multiply that amount by five. The total is the tax you'll pay on your lump sum—and it will be substantially lower than the tax you'd pay on the lump sum as a single year's income.

If the lump sum is under $70,000, you'll get another break. The "minimum distribution allowance" makes a portion of the money tax-free—up to a maximum of $10,000. As such, if you receive from $10,000 to $20,000, 50% of the distribution won't be liable for taxes.

There's less of a tax-free portion on distributions ranging from $20,000 to $70,000. To determine how much is tax-free: take 20%

of the amount of your distribution that is over $20,000. Subtract this figure from the maximum allowance of $10,000. The resulting figure is the tax-free portion of your distribution. For example, if your pension distribution is $50,000, first, you would multiply $30,000 (the amount over $20,000) by 20%. Then you would subtract the resulting figure—$6,000—from $10,000. The result—$4,000—is the tax-free portion on $50,000.

A special note: If you were born in or before 1935 and so turned 50 before January 1, 1986, you can still take advantage of *10-year forward averaging.* You treat your lump sum pension distribution as sole income received over a 10-year period and pay taxes on it accordingly, based on 1986 tax rates. Figure out the taxes on one-tenth of the lump sum. Multiply that amount by 10—and that is the entire tax.

For either method you must file an IRS Form 4972, which includes instructions.

Keep in mind: According to IRS rules, you can only opt for averaging *once.* This means that, if you switch jobs, receive a lump sum distribution from the pension plan at your first company, and decide to forward average it, you *can't* average the lump sum distribution you'll receive as pension payment from your new job.

Which method will save you more money—an IRA or forward averaging—really depends upon your specific situation. The best thing you can do is sit down and try "what-if" scenarios—projecting your taxes and income into the future and determining on paper which method will result in the best tax picture for you.

There are, however, some rules of thumb that may give you a broad idea of which will work best for you. Here is a quick rundown of characteristics:

WHICH IS FOR YOU: A BRIEF CHECKLIST

IRA ROLLOVER	FIVE-YEAR AVERAGING
High income	Low income
No need for immediate cash	Need for immediate cash
Lump sum over $50,000	Lump sum under $50,000
Want to build estate	No immediate plans for estate building
Savvy money manager	Poor money manager

One final word of warning: as of late 1991, the government was strongly considering the elimination of five-year forward averaging. Ten-year forward averaging looked safer. Keep abreast of any developments in pension legislation.

▶ *If you're receiving your pension before you reach age 59½,* **your tax situation is slightly different.**

As mentioned before, when you get your pension money before the "average" retirement age—that is, 59½ or older—you may be hit with a *10% early withdrawal penalty.* If your company has a special "retirement at 55" option, this penalty is waived. And if you receive an annuity, you can avoid this penalty. However, if you receive a lump sum distribution of your pension benefits before age 59½, you are liable for the 10% penalty.

To avoid the double whammy of taxes *and* the penalty choose one of the following two options. Both will keep you from paying the 10% penalty. The first will keep you from paying taxes until later. The second will keep the tax bite smaller than it would be if you took the entire amount.

1) First, you could *transfer the money you've received into a "segregated IRA"*—an IRA that you set up separate from any other IRA, solely intended for "preretirement distribution." You can't transfer this IRA into another; you can't contribute to this IRA. It is set up for your pension distribution *only.* Why is this a good move? Because your segregated IRA gives you a certain degree of flexibility—you can either keep the IRA until you retire or roll the amount in the IRA into another pension plan. Either way, you win at tax time. This method is a good choice if you want to keep your pension money as a retirement nest egg.

2) Second, you could *annuitize the distribution*—that is, set up a payment plan for yourself based upon your life expectancy as shown on a life expectancy table (IRS Form 575, or a life insurance table). This way, you pay yourself the same amount each year for at least five years. This method is a good choice if you *don't* need the money for retirement, but instead want to keep up your cash flow now.

SPECIAL SITUATIONS

▶ **What if your company pension plan is discontinued?**

This is something that, unfortunately, is happening more often nowadays. More companies are focusing on cost cutting, and one area they're cutting back in is pension plans. At the same time, many companies are being taken over by other companies. Acquiring companies often will take excess (uncommitted) monies from pension plans, discontinue the plans, and pay only those benefits earned under the original company. Often acquiring companies are paying employees their benefits by buying them annuities, which means employees lose the cost-of-living increases (if any) they may have gotten through pension payments. This practice of taking money from pension plans, called "reversion," is increasing. By the end of the 1980s, more than 2,000 companies had applied for pension reversions with the IRS.

The result—more people aren't getting the pension plan they expected. According to the federal government, over 60% of the workers whose pension plan is terminated get *lesser or no replacement retirement benefits.*

So what can you do if your pension plan is discontinued? The hard truth—not much. More specifically, you can do the following things:

If you're already retired and your company shuts down its pension plan, you'll be switched to a fixed-rate annuity. Protect yourself and your now-static income by beefing up investment of nonpension money. (For more information, see Chapters 6 and 7.)

If you're still employed by the company, your action depends upon the particular action your company takes to replace the pension plan. Among the most common:

- The company sets up *a new pension plan.* In this case, there's little for you to do. In fact, it's probably the best option you can hope for. The company keeps on doing all the work; you reap the benefits. The possible drawback: New plans often pay less.

- The company *covers current employees under the present plan, while separating retirees from it.* This situation is often called a "spin-off." Possible drawback: a loss in cost-of-living increases, if any.

- The company switches from defined-benefit to *defined-contribution plans.* In this case, you must take on more responsibility for financing your retirement, because the pension benefits are no longer set in advance, and because you may be making choices about where your pension money is invested. Many companies switching to defined-contribution plans are also offering their employees preretirement planning to help them make the right decisions. Possible drawback: Your pension money is only as safe as what it is invested in. For more information on defined-contribution plans, see page 73.

- The company *doesn't replace the abolished pension plan.* This is the worst-case scenario—and it happens about 25% of the time. If it happens to you, all you get are the benefits you already earned under the old plan. Your best move should you find yourself in this situation: Set up your own "replacement plan" by investing in IRAs, annuities, and the like.

One more point: if you find yourself in a bad situation due to a pension plan change, you and your fellow employees may consider fighting back in the courts—you may win. There have been successful suits recently.

▶ What if your company goes bankrupt?

Again, this happens more often than it used to. The seriousness of the situation depends upon your particular pension plan. More specifically:

- If you've been under a *defined-benefit plan,* don't worry. Defined-benefit plans are insured by the Pension Benefit Guaranty Corporation, a federal agency. This means that all monies accrued under a defined-benefit plan will be paid as promised. The only problem is that, while the majority of employees in this situation will get 100% of what they are entitled to, some individuals who were promised special benefits (executive benefits, early retirement benefits, and so forth) may not get these, and will instead receive a lower amount than anticipated.

- If you've been under a *defined-contribution plan,* your plan is *not* federally insured. In this case, your employer has only been responsible for contributing to the plan—not for the amount of benefits you will receive. Your pension has been funded by a separate trust set up by the company. And you'll receive whatever is in it at the time. Clearly, if a portion (or all) of your plan was invested in your corporation's stock, that part will be worthless.

▶ What if you are widowed, and your husband (or wife) is the pension holder?

Under the general rule of thumb, if your spouse dies before the age of 55, you will begin receiving benefits the year that your spouse would have turned 65.

Check with the pension fund administrator for specific information regarding survivor's benefits.

▶ What if you are divorced?

When you divorce a pension holder, you can still be a participant in your former spouse's pension plan if you were dependent on your spouse's earnings during your marriage and if you ask for pension benefits as part of your divorce settlement. In this situation, you are a complete—but separate—pension plan participant. That is, you can begin collecting spousal pension benefits once your former spouse qualifies for early retirement (usually age 55), even if he or she still works. Similarly, you can also receive survivor's benefits upon your former spouse's death if he or she dies before retirement age.

SOURCE: An excellent source of information that can help you in this situation is *Your Pension Rights at Divorce: What Women Need to Know.* It's $14.50 and can be ordered from Pension Publications, 918 16th St., NW, Suite 704, Washington, DC 20006.

▶ What if you continue working after age 65?

This depends upon your company—companies aren't required to continue contributing to pensions once you pass 65, but some do. A common compromise: The company ceases making contributions, but allows your portion of the pension fund to continue accruing interest income.

Chapter 4

IRAS, KEOGHS, AND OTHER RETIREMENT SAVINGS PLANS

INTRODUCTION

▶ **There are other kinds of retirement savings besides pension plans that you can count on to provide income for you when you reach retirement.**

Pension plans and Social Security are, obviously, not enough to finance your retirement. You have other options open to you to help you build your retirement nest egg—options that are relatively simple and, in the case of company-sponsored plans, such as 401(k)s, almost painless to participate in.

Of course, the savings plans you choose depend upon your specific situation. This chapter is designed to give you the information you'll need to make the right choices. It takes a look at the different options open to you: IRAs and Keoghs, which you can set up on your own, and savings plans set up by your company—such as profit-sharing plans, 401(k)s, and ESOPs. (Some of these company-sponsored plans may be part of your pension plan. In this case, the information in this chapter will help you better understand what you can expect from your pension.) Some of the plans discussed offer you limited choices of how your money will be invested—these are often useful if you aren't money-savvy. Others give you the opportunity to choose investment vehicles—allowing you to opt for higher-risk and higher-yield investments or slow and steady conservative ones.

▶ **This chapter is especially important if, like an increasing number of retirees, you *aren't* covered by a pension plan through your company, or if you are self-employed.**

In this case, you will be relying on your own self-directed plans to provide you with a pension income. This chapter takes a look at the two savings plans especially designed for the self-employed (and for employees of small companies): Keoghs and SEPs (Simplified Employee Pensions). It explains how you can set these plans up, how much you can contribute to them, and how you can receive retirement income from them.

One final note: When reading this section and planning a course of savings, keep your goals in mind when selecting different savings plans. Often a combination of savings plans is the most effective way of keeping your retirement nest egg growing—and shielding it from tax bites.

IRAS

▶ **IRAs (Individual Retirement Accounts) are the most common form of personal retirement planning.**

Perhaps you, like many people, already have an IRA. About one in five American taxpayers are regular IRA contributors.

In the 1980s IRAs were hailed as an almost perfect investment vehicle for retirement planning—a sure-fire way of accumulating retirement money and avoiding high taxes. Then came tax reform, and the tax laws changed. Where IRAs were once fully tax-deductible, they became only partially so—more designed for low- and middle-income earners, or for people without a pension plan.

But IRAs aren't the be-all and end-all many assume they are. They might fit into your retirement plan—but don't make the mistake of thinking you *must* open an IRA.

How it works: IRAs are simply savings accounts that are specifically designed for retirement purposes. Each year, you can invest up to $2,000 in an IRA if you're single or if you're married and maintaining an IRA separate from your spouse. If you work and your spouse doesn't, you can contribute up to $2,250 into separate IRAs, called "spousal accounts."

The money you contribute annually can be deducted from your taxable gross income either entirely or partially, depending upon your income (for specifics, see pages 96–97).

You can invest your IRA money in anything from stocks to bank CDs to money funds to zero-coupon bonds and switch investments as you please. However, you *cannot* invest in "collectibles"—art, coins, gems, or stamps. Many people opt for more than one IRA—perhaps one that is invested in a stable mutual fund and another in a more risky investment. Others start out by putting their IRA money in riskier investments, then gradually switch to safer, lower-yielding investments as they approach retirement. Generally speaking, you're best off putting bonds and cash investments in your IRAs to defer taxes on income. (With stocks, you don't pay on gains until you sell.) And avoid putting tax-free investments (like municipal bonds) into an IRA.

TIP: **To save account fees on several IRAs—which can range from about $10 to $50— consolidate your IRAs into one. A bonus: This makes keeping track of your money easier.**

TIP: **Don't put more than you should in your IRA. Contributing more than the maximum is easier to do than you might think—especially if you're participating in a company plan. Keep close tabs on your contributions to 401(k)s, company-sponsored savings plans, and the like. If you do contribute more you'll pay the IRS a 10% yearly penalty on the excess plus any interest or earnings it has accrued, until you withdraw the excess money. In addition, when you withdraw the excess and you are under 59½, you'll pay an additional 10% tax on the withdrawal.**

Here are the penalties and rules for IRAs.

- In most cases, if you take money out of your IRA before you reach 59½, you pay a 10% penalty. In addition, the money you take out becomes part of your taxable income.

- The money you invest in an IRA must be *earned income*—this means salaries, self-employment income, commissions, tips, and the like. It doesn't include income the IRS considers unearned— rent, interest, dividends, pension distributions, Social Security payments, and so on.

- You cannot borrow from your IRA or borrow against it, using it as collateral for any sort of loan.

Pros: IRAs are a fairly painless way of saving toward retirement. If you can deduct a high proportion of your IRA you're saving on your taxes. Your tax-deferred IRA should grow faster than other non-IRA investments. Depending upon the sort of investment you choose, you can build a healthy nest egg by the time you reach 59½. However, you can contribute as little as you want each year, depending upon your financial state at the time. IRAs are easy to open, fairly easy to keep track of, and readily available. A big plus is their flexibility. You can transfer your IRA from place to place, change investments, and so on, depending upon your needs and the economic climate.

Cons: Your money is, in effect, untouchable until you reach retirement age—unless, of course, you pay a 10% penalty for premature withdrawal. Younger people who need liquidity might find IRAs too rigid an investment vehicle. In addition, those of you in the higher income brackets who don't get a tax break by investing in an IRA might do better investing in something else. Another drawback: You can't borrow against your IRA if you find yourself in a financial pinch, regardless of how much money you have saved in it.

▶ **The key reason so many people still choose to invest in IRAs is taxes.**

Under the 1987 tax law, IRA contributions are *fully deductible* if:

- You are not participating in an employer-sponsored plan, such as a pension, profit-sharing, or other plan that gives you tax breaks.

- You are in such a plan, but have an adjusted gross income of less than $25,000 for singles, less than $40,000 for couples.

They are *partially deductible* if:

- You are single, are covered by a plan, and have an adjusted gross income of $25,000 to $35,000.

- You are married, you or your spouse is covered by a plan, and you have a combined adjusted gross income of $40,000 to $50,000 on a joint tax return.

They are *not deductible* if:

- You (or your spouse) are covered by a plan and your adjusted gross income is over $35,000 if single, over $50,000 if married.

TIP: **You must keep track of your nondeductible and deductible IRA contributions by filing IRS Form 8606. You also must be sure to keep each year's copy of this form, as they will be used to calculate your tax when you begin making withdrawals.**

▶ **With tax deferral, your IRA contributions can grow (theoretically) faster than most other investments.**

This is why so many people jumped on the IRA bandwagon back when they were first introduced and why conventional wisdom still dictates investing in IRAs. It's a matter of simple arithmetic.

You deposit money in an IRA. Each year it earns interest. And each year what the IRA has earned is untaxed and is added to the principal, which means that in the following years you'll be earning interest on a larger sum of money. Of course, the real plus is that you won't be paying taxes on your IRA earnings—a big difference from other investments and savings accounts.

Of course, the amount you earn depends on your tax bracket. If you're in a lower tax bracket, you can save more and therefore earn more. In a higher bracket, you'll save, and therefore earn, less. By the same token, your earnings also depend on your IRA interest rates.

For example, if you deposited the maximum $2,000 each year in IRAs with varying interest rates, here's what your investment would be worth after the indicated number of years, given 6 percent, 8 percent, or 10 percent interest rates:

YEARS	6% INTEREST	8% INTEREST	10% INTEREST
5	$11,950	$12,671	$13,431
10	27,943	31,290	35,062
15	49,345	58,648	69,899
20	77,985	98,845	126,005
25	116,312	157,908	216,363
30	167,603	244,691	361,886
35	236,241	372,204	596,253

And you could make even more if you invest your IRA in something with a higher yield, such as stocks or bonds. Of course, you could also make less. Again, it's a question how you invest your IRA, whether you opt for a conservative investment with slower growth or a riskier investment with the potential for high growth. Also, you'll earn more if your IRA is with an institution that compounds interest *daily* as opposed to yearly.

But generally speaking, the bottom line is clear: Tax-deferred compounding of your IRA can add up to a sizable nest egg, if you can afford to leave your money in the IRA for a number of years—preferably at least 10.

▶ **While the big advantage of IRAs is deferring taxes, for younger people currently planning their retirement, this may not be as big a plus as you think.**

If you're 35 or younger, IRAs may not be the best choice for your nest egg.

According to a late 1989 National Center for Policy Analysis study, about 60% of the workforce will probably be paying higher taxes when they retire than they are now. In other words, while you're saving 15% tax on your IRA money now, you may be paying a lot more—perhaps 50% to 60% tax—when you're 65. This could offset all the gains from tax deferral over all those years. Not to mention that you had your money tied up and were unable to use it, without paying a penalty, for any needs that might have arisen during those years. Our suggestion: Consider other avenues for savings and investment. Keep an eye on tax rates. Don't automatically think an IRA is the right move to make. (See Chapters 6 and 7 for specific information on different investment strategies.)

How to Open and Maintain an IRA

▶ **You can open IRAs at a wide range of places—from banks to brokerage houses to insurance companies to credit unions.**

Generally, you should choose *where* you open your IRA depending upon *how* you want your money invested. For example, if you're thinking about investing in stocks, you're probably best off at a brokerage house; if you want only bank CDs, open your account at the bank that offers the best rates. Shop around before you open an IRA.

Find out who's offering the services you want, check their fees, and so on. Some institutions charge a start-up fee—usually about $25—and most impose an annual maintenance fee—usually $25 or less.

Once you've made a decision and you're ready to open your IRA, you'll find that it's a very simple process. Once you have contacted a financial institution, you'll fill out an IRA application—a basic form that asks your name, address, birth date, Social Security number, beneficiary, and the type of investment you're interested in. That's it. Nice and simple.

▶ **At brokerage houses and at other financial institutions, you have a choice—a** *self-directed* **or a** *professionally managed* **IRA.**

The difference between the two is obvious. With a *self-directed IRA,* you call the shots—what to invest in, when to buy and sell, and so forth. Usually, with self-directed IRAs, you invest in stocks and bonds, follow the market, and play the odds like an ordinary investor.

With a *professionally managed* IRA, your money is invested for you. The normal way to obtain professional management for your IRA is to put your IRA money into a mutual fund. The mutual fund managers choose investments according to the fund's basic strategy. All you have to do is sit back and collect the profits—or accept the losses. Of course, you can switch into and out of a fund at any time. (For more on buying the right mutual fund for your IRA, see Mutual Funds, page 200.)

▶ **At some point, you may want to reinvest your IRA—by transferring it to another financial institution.**

Transferring your IRA—from one bank to another bank, from a bank to a brokerage house, and so forth—is a fairly common, fairly hassle-free procedure.

It's an all-paper transaction. You don't touch your money, you don't physically withdraw it, you do nothing but notify the financial institutions involved to transfer your IRA funds from one to the other. An example: Sylvia L. has an IRA at her local bank, invested in CDs paying 10% interest. She learns that a national bank is paying 11% on CDs. She goes to the national bank, fills out an application to open an IRA, then fills out a transfer form asking that the money from the local bank be transferred to the national bank. The national bank then sends the form to the local bank. Once she has filled out the application and the transfer form, Sylvia does nothing but wait for the national bank to notify her that the transfer has been made. An extremely simple procedure.

In addition to the ease with which you can transfer your IRA, there's another plus: You can make as many transfers as you want each year. One hitch: In some cases, such as switching your IRA money into and out of certain mutual funds, you may wind up paying up-front "load" fees that reduce your yield.

TIP: **Before you actually transfer an IRA from one financial institution to another, be sure to ask how long the transfer will take. Sometimes there's quite a time lag between your request and the actual transfer. You might be better off withdrawing the money and rolling it over yourself.**

▶ **You can also transfer your IRA yourself—bypassing the paperwork by withdrawing the cash from your IRA and depositing in a new IRA. This is a *rollover*.**

With a rollover you *physically take the money* from your IRA to transfer it from one retirement program to another. In effect, it's a withdrawal, but one which isn't penalized because you're putting the money back into an IRA. Remember, if you transfer your account and don't touch the money, it's a simple transfer—not a rollover.

When you roll over your IRA, you have 60 days in which you can transfer your IRA from one place to another. *If you don't complete the transfer within 60 days, it will count as a withdrawal,* and you'll have to pay a 10% penalty.

You can roll over your IRA only once in a 12-month period. Because of this regulation, you're best off transferring your IRA whenever possible.

▶ **You can "borrow" from your IRA *as long as you redeposit the money within 60 days.***

This is a relatively new development with IRAs, made possible by legislation in 1990. Under the new law, you are allowed to withdraw money—all or part—from your IRA for any purpose. You will pay no penalty for the withdrawal if you redeposit the money in the IRA within 60 days.

IRA Withdrawals—When and How to Make Them

▶ **The rules governing IRA distribution payments are straight-forward.**

- You can begin making distribution payments from your IRA when you reach age 59½.

- You *must* begin making distributions when you reach 70½.

- In most cases, should you decide to withdraw funds from your IRA before the age of 59½, you face a 10% penalty.

▶ **There are ways around the 59½ cut-off point.**

People can withdraw money from an IRA before age 59½ *with no penalty* if the IRA holder:

- Dies.

- Becomes disabled and is unable to work.

- Redeposits the money in the IRA within 60 days.

- Annuitizes the withdrawal—that is, sets up a scheduled series of payments based on his or her life expectancy.

The last instance—made possible under the new tax law—is the one you should be aware of. Unfortunately, too many of us have been brainwashed into thinking that, once our money is in an IRA, it's there until we hit 59½. But by doing this, we may be missing out. In fact, we might be losing money by waiting.

▶ **Sometimes the wisest move is *not* to wait until you're 65 to start tapping your IRAs.**

The rule of thumb has long been: Keep your money in your IRAs as long as you possibly can—if you can hold out until you're 70½, so much the better.

But that rule of thumb has changed.

If you're in your 50s or 60s and you've accumulated a healthy sum of money in IRAs, your best bet might be to start making withdrawals now.

Why? A variety of reasons—all of them related to taxes. First, most experts predict that taxes will rise. By beginning IRA withdrawals early and paying current taxes on the monies you receive, you can avoid paying the higher taxes ahead in the long term. Second, if you have a large amount of money in your IRA, remember that distributions of over $150,000 are subject to a 15% excise tax. Yet again, by beginning withdrawals early, you avoid an onerous tax. Third, keep in mind that income taxes are lower than estate taxes. If you have a large amount in your IRA and it stays untouched until you're older, it may wind up as part of your estate—and your heirs will be faced with a large tax.

One other reason to consider early withdrawal—and a very legitimate one: You need the money *now,* not when you're 65½. Maybe you've opted for early retirement, maybe you want the money for other reasons. Whatever the case, do remember that you *can* begin tapping your IRA.

▶ **To begin making withdrawals from your IRA before the age of 59½ while avoiding the 10% penalty, you have to take it step by step.**

The key is making your IRA withdrawals in an organized and orderly way. Keep in mind that if you don't follow the requirements listed in the tax law, you will have to pay the 10% penalty.

Here are the steps to take:

First, study actuarial tables to find out what your life expectancy is. Your best bet is to get IRS Publication 575—Pension and Annuity Income—which includes life expectancy tables.

Next, amortize your account over your projected life expectancy, using a reasonable rate of interest (typically 8%). Then set up a payment schedule, giving you a distribution from your IRA each year.

Key points to keep in mind:

- *Your payments must be relatively equal.* For example, you can't take out a large sum the first year, then smaller amounts in subsequent years just to meet a debt.

- *At the least, you must make yearly distributions.* If you want, you can make the payments more frequent—say, every six months. But your schedule should arrange for you to receive at least an annual payment.

- *The payment schedule must be in effect for at least five years and until you reach age 59½.* If you discontinue or change your schedule, you face a retroactive penalty.

▶ **From age 59½ to age 70½, you can withdraw as much or as little as you want from your IRA—with no penalties, restrictions, or other hassles.**

How much or how little you withdraw each year is up to you. As with a pension, electing a lump sum distribution has its definite drawbacks—namely, high taxes. Of course, if you need the money immediately, clearly a lump sum distribution is a logical choice. However, when possible, you are better off taking less. Not only do you save on taxes, but the more you can keep in your IRA (or other tax-sheltered account), the more the balance can compound tax-free.

▶ **When you are 70½, even if you are still working, you _must_ begin withdrawing money from your IRA (and other tax-sheltered accounts, including Keoghs, 401(k)s, and profit-sharing plans).**

Waiting until the last minute to break open your IRAs and other accounts means you must follow the strict guidelines the IRS has established and withdraw a set minimum per year. The IRS has drawn up timetables to determine how much money you must take out each year based upon your life expectancy.

As when making an early withdrawal from your IRA, you must set up a payment schedule for yourself based upon your life expectancy or the life expectancy of you and your beneficiary. (You can find the life expectancy tables you'll need in IRS Publication 575, available from the IRS.) The amount of the withdrawal you must make is based upon your age when you are making the withdrawal and the amount of your IRA. You divide the amount of your IRA by the number given for your age on the life expectancy table. The figure you get is the _minimum_ amount you must withdraw from your IRA.

TIP: If you want as much money as possible to stay in the IRA for as long as possible, you should seek the highest possible life expectancy. One way of doing this is to choose a beneficiary who is younger than you. Your joint life expectancy will be lower than your life expectancy on your own. One catch: You're only allowed a 10-year difference between your age and your beneficiary's even if there actually is more of a difference in years.

TABLE 4.1: JOINT AND LAST SURVIVOR LIFE EXPECTANCY
(FOR YOU AND A BENEFICIARY
USED FOR IRA DISTRIBUTIONS AFTER YOU REACH 70½)

YOUR AGE	65	66	67	68	69	70	71	72	73	74
	Your Joint Life Expectancy is:									
70	23.1	22.5	22.0	21.5	21.1	20.6	20.2	19.8	19.4	19.1
71	22.8	22.2	21.7	21.2	20.7	20.2	19.8	19.4	19.0	18.6
72	22.5	21.9	21.3	20.8	20.3	19.8	19.4	18.9	18.5	18.2
73	22.2	21.6	21.0	20.5	20.0	19.4	19.0	18.5	18.1	17.7
74	22.0	21.4	20.8	20.2	19.6	19.1	18.6	18.2	17.7	17.3
75	21.8	21.1	20.5	19.9	19.3	18.8	18.3	17.8	17.3	16.9
76	21.6	20.9	20.3	19.7	19.1	18.5	18.0	17.5	17.0	16.5
77	21.4	20.7	20.1	19.4	18.8	18.3	17.7	17.2	16.7	16.2
78	21.2	20.5	19.9	19.2	18.6	18.0	17.5	16.9	16.4	15.9
79	21.1	20.4	19.7	19.0	18.4	17.8	17.2	16.7	16.1	15.6
80	21.0	20.2	19.5	18.9	18.2	17.6	17.0	16.4	15.9	15.4

Source: Internal Revenue Service.

Once you have set up a payment schedule, you must stick to that schedule. If you underwithdraw, you face a penalty of 50% of the difference between what you actually withdrew and what you were supposed to withdraw.

(Note: These payment rules are the same ones that apply to other retirement plans—including pension plans, 401(k)s, and profit-sharing plans. The difference? The company determines the payouts; you don't have to.)

▶ **The popular rule of thumb: if you *don't* withdraw your IRA money early, your best bet is to hold off as long as possible— preferably until you reach age 70½.**

By waiting, you continue reaping the benefits of tax-deferred savings, interest, and growth.

Do keep in mind, though, that you *must* begin withdrawing money from your IRA by April 1 of the year you reach age 70½. If you don't begin making withdrawals, you face a steep penalty— 50% of the difference between what you actually withdrew and what you should have withdrawn.

▶ **One final note: Be on the lookout for a new kind of IRA.**

A new "Super IRA" may be coming—with advantages for almost everybody. It would be fully deductible. Early, tax-free withdrawals would be allowed for first homes, major illnesses, or college tuition for children. In short, the Super IRA would restore most of the advantages that were lost with the tax reform of 1986.

KEOGH PLANS: SAVINGS PLANS FOR THE SELF-EMPLOYED

▶ **If you're on your own where work is concerned (as is anyone from a doctor or a lawyer to a writer or an actor), you can set up your own answer to a company pension—a Keogh plan.**

Keoghs are, in effect, pensions for the self-employed (or company pensions for employees of small businesses). Even if you hold a regular job and moonlight as a freelancer, you can open a Keogh plan. Keep in mind that sometimes people who don't think they're self-employed are eligible for a Keogh. The key question to ask yourself: Did I earn *any* money away from my regular place of employment? If the answer is yes, you might want to look into Keoghs. They're a good addition to any other plans you may already be contributing to. The big plus? Even if you're contributing the maximum $2,000 to an IRA, you can still contribute to a Keogh. That means more tax deferrals—and more retirement income. Two other advantages Keoghs have over IRAs: You can continue contributing to a Keogh *after* age 70½, and if you take a lump sum distribution, you can use five-year averaging to ease the taxes.

As with typical company-sponsored plans, a Keogh gives you an opportunity to defer taxes on contributions to the plan. And the contributions can be quite large. Depending on your particular circumstances and the Keogh you set up, you can contribute as much as 25% of your earned income—up to a maximum of $30,000 a year. As with an IRA, taxes on interest and other income earned by the Keogh are also deferred. There are two types of Keoghs—*defined-contribution*—which can be either profit-sharing or money-purchase pension plans—and *defined-benefit*. With either type of Keogh, the ultimate goal is simple: to gain retirement income. You are setting up your own pension plan to guarantee yourself an income when you turn 59½—the age at which you can begin withdrawing Keogh money without penalty.

SOURCE: Most brokers and financial planners offer literature on Keoghs. For example, you can get a booklet on setting up a Keogh and the various options from your local broker at Merrill Lynch or many other brokerages. For the federal guidelines on Keoghs, contact your local **IRS** office and ask for **Publication 560**.

▶ *Defined-contribution Keoghs* **are the most common type of Keogh plan.**

How it works: A defined-contribution Keogh can be either a *profit-sharing* or a *money-purchase* plan.

With a *profit-sharing plan,* you can contribute as much or as little as you want to your Keogh each year. In good years, you may want to contribute the maximum, which is about 15% of your earned income if you're an "employee-owner" or, if self-employed, about 13.043% of your net income up to $30,000 of your earned income. In the leaner years, you can choose to contribute nothing at all.

With a *money-purchase plan,* you contribute a set percentage of your income each year (which can be higher than 15%). You determine the percentage of your earnings you want to contribute—and *you must meet this percentage each year*—regardless of how much or how little you made that year. If you don't make the proper payment, the IRS will fine you 5% of the amount you underfunded. You'll have 90 days to make up the difference or pay a penalty equaling 100% of the amount you owed. The minimum you can contribute is 3% of your earned income, the maximum is 25%—20% if you are self-employed.

Another option is a combined *profit-sharing/money-purchase* Keogh. With this, you can contribute 15% to profit sharing and 10% to money purchase—determined by subtracting the contribution from your income, then applying the percentage to the remainder.

An important financial note: the IRS has different guidelines for Keogh contributions for self-employed people, for employees, and for business owners.

• Employees of a small company can make the straight contribution. That's 15% of their compensation for a profit-sharing plan, 25% for a money-purchase plan.

• If you're self-employed, your contributions are based upon your earned income, which is defined by Congress as your net self-employment earnings *minus* the deduction allowed for 50% of your self-employment tax *minus* any contributions to a qualified retirement plan.

- To come up with the specific contribution you can make to your plan, here's the formula: Multiply net earnings (minus the deduction allowed for 50% of your self-employment tax) by contribution percentage; divide the result by 1 plus contribution percentage. This is your maximum contribution.

- If you're a business owner and you establish a Keogh, you determine contributions based upon your net income—that is, income of receipts minus expenses. When you post a loss, you can't contribute to the Keogh that year.

Who should use which type of plan? In general, profit-sharing Keoghs are good bets if you can't count on regular profits from year to year or if you aren't sure how much money you'll be willing to commit to a Keogh each year and don't want to be tied to a specific schedule. They're usually best for entrepreneurs, people in their 30s who are focusing on building their business. Money-purchase pension plans might work better for you if your level of income—and profits—is predictable, and if you want to take advantage of the higher contribution rate (25% or 20% depending upon your employment status). The other—and possibly best—choice is to set up a combined plan. In this case, you get the best of both worlds. You have the ability to contribute the maximum amount to the plan, plus the flexibility to contribute *less* in the less-than-great years.

Pros: Defined-contribution Keoghs are relatively flexible in that you can either handle your own investments or have a money manager do it for you. This is an asset if you're interested in hands-on investing, or on the other hand, if you would rather have an expert do the work. Either way, you can determine how much risk you want to assume. Another plus is that you can contribute to your Keogh up to any age (although you do have to start making withdrawals by age 70½). Unlike IRAs, Keoghs permit forward averaging when you withdraw.

Cons: As with IRAs or any other investment vehicle or savings plan that restricts you from touching your money until you reach retirement age, Keoghs do tie up your money, and there is a penalty for early withdrawal. This may be a drawback for people who need liquidity, or for young people who may face a bigger tax bite later.

▶ *Defined-benefit Keoghs* **are more complicated than defined-contribution Keoghs—and less popular.**

How it works: With defined-benefit Keoghs, you decide what your annual pension amount will be by averaging your income from your "High 3" years—that is, your highest pay in three consecutive years, up to a maximum amount. This maximum changes yearly to keep up with inflation. In 1990, the maximum pension amount was $102,582.

Once you have decided how large you want your pension to be, you must figure out how much you must contribute each year to meet your goal. To do this, you'll have to consult an actuary, according to IRS rules. Obviously the earlier you start contributing to your defined-benefit plan, the lower your contributions will be.

TIP: **Because contributions are based on meeting a set pension goal,** *not* **on percentage of income, defined-benefit Keoghs are a good way to build a pension quickly— but only if you're pulling in a fairly healthy salary. One note: If you're self-employed and you incorporate your business, you can't set up a Keogh for yourself at the company. Why? Because as the owner of an incorporated business, you are now an executive earning a salary, not self-employment income.**

Pros: You can raise a hefty amount of money and can contribute up to *100%* of your self-employment income.

Cons: These plans can give you bookkeeping headaches—each year you must submit an actuary-prepared report about your plan to the IRS—which also can cost quite a bit. In addition, if you're a business owner with full-time employees who have worked for you for three years or more, you *must* include them in your defined-benefit plan. Furthermore, your benefits can't be higher than the "percentages of compensation going to employees."

How to Set Up, Maintain, and Withdraw from a Keogh

▶ **Anyone who advises you "just go to the bank and set up a Keogh" is a fool.**

Setting up a Keogh is a relatively simple process—in many ways like setting up an IRA. In other ways, however, it is far more complex.

This is why you should do a little research first.

You can open Keoghs at banks, brokerage houses, and other financial institutions. Our recommendation—get written material from the institutions you're considering and *read it carefully*.

Decide what type of Keogh you want—defined-contribution or defined-benefit? Most of you will (and should) choose defined-contribution Keoghs. If you do, do you want the profit-sharing or money-purchase version? Clearly there are choices to be made—choices that shouldn't be made lightly.

Talk to experts—your lawyer, accountant, or tax advisor—to make sure you meet the legal requirements and see how your benefits will fit into your retirement plan.

Once you've made up your mind, it becomes a straightforward process: Contact the financial institution with which you've decided to open your Keogh, fill out the application, and that's it. Some institutions may require a minimum opening balance, but there is no federal requirement for this.

TIP: **It sounds simple, but many people forget this point. If you want your Keogh to qualify for tax deductions in the year in which you set it up, you must set up your Keogh by December 31, *not* April 15, which is the deadline for contributing to IRAs.**

▶ **Opening and maintaining a Keogh requires a great deal of paperwork.**

The year you open your Keogh and every third year after that you are required by the IRS to file Form 5500-C—a questionnaire about your Keogh. It is due on July 31 (or the last day of the seventh month following the close of your fiscal year) and is extremely time consuming to fill out. Late filings bring steep penalties. Your best bet is to have an accountant or your Keogh administrator do the form for you. It may cost, but it will save you time and aggravation.

In the intervening years, you file a simpler form—a 5500-R or a 5500-EZ.

▶ **Keogh withdrawals are similar to IRA withdrawals.**

As with IRAs, you can begin withdrawing from your Keogh account without penalty after you reach 59½—and you must begin making withdrawals by 70½. You can opt for a lump sum distribution, a payment schedule (described on page 103), or a combination of the two.

You can make *early* withdrawals from your Keogh without paying the 10% penalty in certain circumstances—the same ones that apply to company pension plans. Among them: you become disabled; you are at least 55 and are "separated from service" (you retire, resign, or are fired); and you set up a series of scheduled payments based on your life expectancy. (For more details, see Chapter 3.)

▶ **Keoghs have one big advantage over IRAs: When you withdraw money from them (after age 59½), you can use forward averaging to ease the tax bite.**

Using forward averaging to spread your distribution payments over a five-year period keeps your tax burden down but your cash flow up. (For information on forward averaging, see Chapter 3.)

Some other positive aspects of Keoghs to keep in mind:

- Having a Keogh doesn't rule out having other retirement savings—particularly IRAs. With a Keogh, you can still contribute up to another $2,000 each year to your IRA. The tax deductibility, of course, depends on your tax bracket and earnings.

- If you are self-employed and own 10% or less of a business, you can borrow up to $50,000 from a Keogh.

- You can continue to contribute to your Keogh up to any age— even after age 70½. This can be a big tax break for older retirees.

SEPS

▶ **If you're self-employed, you should also look into SEPs.**

SEPs—Simplified Employee Pensions—can be useful savings vehicles for the self-employed. They are retirement plans designed specifically for small businesses and the self-employed.

How it works: Essentially SEPs are IRAs funded by employers or by a self-employed individual. As with IRAs, you face a penalty for withdrawing money before you reach age 59½ (unless you meet certain requirements—see page 101). Unlike IRAs, SEPs permit you to contribute more than $2,000 a year—much more. As with an IRA, you can open a SEP at banks and other financial institutions. You can choose what you want your SEP invested in—stocks, mutual funds, and so on.

When you have a SEP at a company: Employers can make annual contributions to the SEP of 15% of the employee's yearly salary or $30,000, whichever is less. Employees can also contribute by deferring a portion of their salaries, but the amount they contribute is then deducted from the employer's allowable maximum contribution. Contributions you make to the SEP are deducted from your gross income. In many cases, companies offer SEPs *in addition* to defined-benefit pension plans. When you can participate in a SEP in addition to another pension plan, employer contributions for all plans together are limited to 25% of the total amount in the plans or the minimum-funding standard of the defined-benefit plans. It is very important to keep track of this—because the IRS will. If your total plans have excess contributions, you must withdraw the excess amount before you file your tax return. This amount must be reported as income, or you face a penalty.

If you're self-employed, it's the same—you can contribute the lesser of 15% of your compensation or $30,000. However, compensation for the self-employed equals *earned* income—that is, net self-employment income *minus* SEP contributions. A big plus for the self-employed: unlike Keoghs, SEPs can be opened at any time before April 15. This is especially helpful for self-employed people who find themselves making more money than they had expected—a great last-minute tax shelter. But also unlike Keoghs, if you take your money in a lump sum, you can't use forward averaging to cut taxes.

Distribution of a SEP is just like distribution of an IRA—in most cases, you face a penalty for making withdrawals before age 59½; you *must* begin making withdrawals by age 70½; and you can take your money in a lump sum or by setting up an annuitized payment schedule (see page 103 for details).

Pros: In effect, SEPs are pension plans without the drawbacks. Because SEPs are IRAs, they are taxed as such. SEPs offer a large degree of flexibility—you (or an employer) design the plan, including such options as salary deductions, which are a way of deferring taxes; you can vary the amount you contribute from year to year, or not contribute at all one year. SEPs are portable (you can roll them into another plan or into an IRA should you change jobs); they're easy to open and maintain—you don't have to worry about excessive paperwork and you don't have to file paperwork to the IRS each year (as with a Keogh). Also, as mentioned above, you can open a SEP after December 31—a very big plus for the self-employed who find themselves needing to reduce their tax bite at the last minute.

Cons: As with IRAs, your money is effectively tied up until you reach retirement—at which point you receive your money and are faced with the (probably) higher taxes. Because of this, SEPs might not be as cost-effective as they appear to be, if you are currently in your 30s.

SOURCE: A helpful free brochure is *An Employer's Guide to Understanding SEPs.* Contact: Investor Information, The Vanguard Group, Vanguard Financial Center, P.O. Box 2600, Valley Forge, PA 19482 (800-662-7447).

BUILDING YOUR NEST EGG ON COMPANY TIME—AND MONEY: PROFIT SHARING, 401(k)s, 403(b)s, THRIFT PLANS, ESOPs

▶ **One of the best ways of adding to your retirement fund is by taking advantage of company plans.**

If you work for a company, you probably have a variety of plans open to you—all of which can help you save money toward retirement.

You're often given a choice as to which plans you want to participate in. The most common plans are profit sharing, 401(k)s, thrift or stock plans, employee stock ownership plans (ESOPs), and (for smaller businesses) Simplified Employee Pension plans. (Note: In many cases, these plans are used as *defined-contribution plans,* serving as your pension plan—see page 73.)

The big advantages of company plans are that, in most cases, they're easy to participate in, and most are fairly simple to understand and follow. You should get a report on your plans each year, with an explanation of the funds, where they're invested, and how much money you have in your name. Some companies even go a step further and project earnings over a few years—a definite help if you're close to retirement. Another—possibly the biggest—advantage is that most qualified company retirement plans are tax-deferred. Your money can grow over the years undisturbed.

The downside, however, is lack of access to the money in these employer-sponsored tax-deferred plans. Usually you can't receive your money until you either retire or resign. At that point, you'll receive a lump sum distribution, or, less commonly, an annuity. (For the tax consequences for each method, see Chapter 3.)

As with other tax-deferred plans, such as pension plans, or Keoghs, if you make withdrawals from your company-sponsored plan before age 59½, you face a 10% penalty, unless you meet one of the following criteria:

- You are 55 or older and take early retirement or are otherwise "separated from service," as the IRS terms it—that is, you resign or are fired.

- You set up a series of annuitized payments based on your life expectancy or the joint life expectancies of you and your designated beneficiary. (For more on this, see IRAs, page 102.)

- You switch to another company and roll the money you receive from the first company into a tax-deferred retirement plan at the second company, or roll the money over into an IRA.

- You are disabled or need the money for medical expenses that are greater than 7.5% of your adjusted gross income. (For more detailed information regarding nonpenalized hardship withdrawals from a 401(k), see page 116.)

As with most other tax-deferred plans, you *must* begin making taxable withdrawals (that is, begin receiving your payments) when you reach age 70½.

Another disadvantage to keep in mind is the excess distribution penalty mentioned on page 85. This is the 15% excise tax levied if you receive more than the limit from pensions, other company retirement plans, IRA, Keoghs, etc. If you make contributions to a number of company plans, and also hold IRAs and the like, it is easier than you may think to wind up with an amount over the limit. For this reason, you should be sure to keep on top of your plans and be aware of the amounts in each plan.

Following are brief looks at the different types of plans and how they work.

Profit-Sharing Plans

▶ With *profit-sharing plans,* your company annually puts a portion of its profits into a fund for employees, which is invested.

Your company probably offers this—it's a very common form of plan, with nearly half a million companies offering profit sharing to their employees.

How it works: It's very easy to understand. The company simply contributes a percentage of profits to a fund. This fund can be invested in one or a number of ways. Generally, you can choose how you want your profit-sharing money invested. The common options are company stock, a diversified stock account, or a fixed-income account.

The amount of money the company contributes annually can vary. The *maximum* contribution per employee is $30,000 (up to 15% of the employee's salary). The minimum contribution is zero. If the company posts a weak performance it may contribute *nothing at all* to profit sharing. The bottom line, then: Profit-sharing plans are as stable as the company. If a company is managed well, you'll probably see a healthy profit-sharing amount when you retire or resign.

You're fully vested in a company profit-sharing plan after three to seven years with a company, or between your third and seventh year with the company, and can receive your profit-sharing money at any point after that should you quit or retire. You also can receive your profit-sharing money if you become disabled. In all cases, however, you'll receive your profit-sharing money as a lump sum distribution—a one-time payment.

Pros: Profit-sharing plans require nothing from you—no personal contributions, no salary deferments, and so on—which makes this a painless way of earning money. It's all your company's money. You can just sit back and reap the benefits. As with some pension plans, you may be able to borrow from the vested amount in your profit-sharing plan.

Cons: Nothing major. However, if profit sharing is your sole pension plan, do be aware that, as with other defined-contribution pension plans, you won't be able to estimate your retirement nest egg as you go along. Moreover, the amount you will receive depends on how well the fund was managed.

TIP: **A word of caution: Should you quit your job, you'll probably receive a lump sum distribution of your profit sharing. If so, *be careful!* According to a number of surveys, most people spend their profit-sharing money within the first year of receiving it. The better move for retirement planning is to reinvest it in CDs,**

Treasury issues, or your stock portfolio. (For specific investing suggestions, see Chapter 7.)

401(k) Plans

▶ *401(k)s* **have been the fastest-growing type of employee plan for the past few years, and they are still growing in popularity.**

On the average, about 62% of the employees in a company elect to participate in their company's 401(k). This has become a very popular way of saving—and earning—money. You contribute a portion of your salary, your company contributes a percentage of your contribution, and the combined monies are invested.

How it works: A 401(k) is a *salary-reduction plan*. You contribute a portion of your salary to the plan up to a maximum amount. This maximum changes yearly to keep in tune with inflation rates. In 1990, the maximum was $7,979. Your employer can match your contribution—paying anything from a percentage to the full amount you have paid. The most common matching amount is 50%. You don't pay taxes on any of the money—neither on the salary you save in the account nor on the amount your company contributes nor on the money earned through investments—until you withdraw it at age 59½.

In most cases, your company will offer you investment options (usually three options, but sometimes as many as seven). Then you decide where and how you want your 401(k) invested. The three most common investment options are stock funds, bond funds, and Guaranteed Investment Contracts (GICs).

- *Stock funds:* The company invests the money in stock mutual funds. In some cases, you'll be able to choose between different stock portfolios—conservative to more risky. This may be a good choice for you if you don't have other high-growth investments. One plus: Stocks tend to do better than the other two options in the long term.

- *Bond funds:* The company invests your 401(k) in bond funds—typically stable high-grade corporate and Treasury issues. These are usually less risky than stock funds, and this is a good choice if you have other non-401(k) growth investments and want a fairly low-risk 401(k).

- *Guaranteed Investment Contracts (GICs):* Very popular (well over half of employees choose this option), GICs are insurance company–sponsored fixed-income investments. You are guaranteed interest and return of principal. This has historically been a good choice if you want a safe, stable plan and aren't looking for high growth in your 401(k). However, recent problems with insurance companies may make this riskier than in the past.

TIP: In many cases, you'll also be given the option of investing in your own company— getting company stock for your 401(k). Experts suggest that the most you should invest in your own company's stock is 10%. Lower than that is even better. With corporate ups and downs and an uncertain economy, you're better off not tying your retirement fortunes to your company's stock performance.

Pros: Most experts consider 401(k)s definite best bets. Why? You save in taxes; your employer typically matches your contributions, which further increases your nest egg; the plans are portable and can be rolled into other plans or into an IRA.

Cons: As with an IRA, your money is essentially tied up until you hit age 59½—which might make investing in a 401(k) a bad move if you are in your 30s and want to avoid a hefty tax bite in the future. Another disappointing trend: Because 401(k)s are so popular, some employers are easing back on matching contributions, figuring that employees don't need them as incentives to participate.

▶ **Although usually your money stays in a 401(k) until you reach age 59½, there are ways of withdrawing early.**

The trick, of course, is meeting the requirements. And, frankly, this isn't all that simple.

Unlike IRAs, to make an early withdrawal from a 401(k), you *must* meet both of these two requirements: You must have an immediate and heavy financial need, and you must have no other resources "reasonably available" to meet the need. In other words, you must be in dire straits.

Meeting the first requirement is fairly straightforward. The following situations are examples of financial circumstances that will allow you a 401(k) hardship withdrawal:

- You have medical expenses.

- You are buying a principal residence.

- You have tuition expenses (for postsecondary school) for your-self, your spouse, your children, or your other dependents.

- You need money to avoid being evicted from or to meet mortgage payments on your principal residence.

As for the second requirement, showing that you have no other resources available to help you meet your financial need, it's a little more difficult. Generally speaking, you fulfill the requirements for a hardship withdrawal in the following circumstances:

- You already receive all the distributions (excluding hardship distributions) and *all nontaxable loans* possible from all of your company plans.

- You wait 12 months from the time you receive the hardship distribution before making any new contributions—either deferrals or nondeductible contributions—to the 401(k).

- Once the 12-month suspension is over, you cut back on your 401(k) contributions for the remainder of the year—by subtracting any amounts you contributed the prior year.

- Also keep in mind that you will owe a 10% early withdrawal penalty unless you meet the exceptions (separation from service, deductible medical expenses over 7.5% of your adjusted gross income, etc.) listed on page 113. You can also avoid paying an early withdrawal penalty if you roll your 401(k) money into an IRA within 60 days.

403(b) Plans

▶ **403(b) plans are 401(k)s for employees of public schools, hospitals, and other nonprofit organizations.**

How it works: 403(b)s are 401(k)s for public-sector employees. Under a salary reduction program, you contribute a set amount to the program—up to a maximum $9,925 each year. (The maximum amount rises in step with inflation.) With a regular 403(b), your money is invested in tax-sheltered annuities; with a 403(b)(7), the investment vehicles also include mutual funds. The money in your account is tax-free until you pull it out at age 59½.

Pros: The same as for 401(k)s. You get tax savings; if you change jobs, you can roll your 403(b) into other plans or into an IRA; you have some degree of autonomy where investing is concerned.

Cons: Also the same as for 401(k)s—namely, lack of liquidity. Your money is essentially tied up until you hit age 59½. However, all things considered, the pros far outweigh the cons.

Thrift Plans

▶ *Thrift* or *savings plans* **are similar to 401(k)s.**

Company thrift or savings plans are related to profit-sharing plans. However, in their setup, they are most like 401(k)s. As with 401(k)s, your employer matches your contribution to the plan. Unlike 401(k)s, with thrift plans you are contributing *after-tax* pay.

How it works: You contribute a percentage of your after-tax pay to the plan—usually between 2% and 6%. The company contributes a matching amount—usually from 25% to 50% of your contribution, but it can match the full amount. This money goes into a fund, which is invested most often in stock mutual funds, sometimes in blue-chip stocks or company stock. Your contributions to the plan aren't tax-deductible, but earnings on the investments are tax-deferred, so your money is compounding.

As with other company plans, when you retire or resign, you receive your money—in this case, in a lump sum distribution. Because the amount you contributed was from your after-tax pay, *you pay no taxes on that amount.* However, you will owe taxes on the rest—the investment earnings *and* the employer's contribution. As for early withdrawal penalties, to some degree the same rules that apply to other employer-sponsored retirement plans apply to thrift-plans—that is, you face a 10% penalty for early withdrawals from the plan, unless you meet the criteria outlined earlier. However, this penalty does *not* apply to your savings in the plan, only to the employer contributions and the earnings.

Pros: You can make a decent amount, especially if the company matches a healthy percentage. In addition, all earnings on your account are tax-deferred, so you can save and avoid a tax bite. Many companies allow you to borrow from your *vested benefits* in a savings plan *penalty-free*.

Cons: Relatively few. You have little to lose in savings or thrift plans.

Employee Stock Ownership Plans (ESOPs)

▶ *ESOPs* **are similar to profit-sharing plans. But the company gives you shares of company stock instead of shares of company profits.**

ESOPs are becoming more evident in corporate America, especially as companies use them in an effort to fight takeover bids. They're also credited with improving company morale and productivity in some cases—the theory being that employees will work harder if they own a piece of the company.

How it works: You are given shares of stock in the company. The number of shares you receive is based on your salary. Typically, you can get shares equaling anything from 5% to 25% of your annual salary, up to a maximum of $60,000. You usually don't have to pay taxes on the stock you own until you leave the company (either by retiring or by switching jobs) or sell them. When you reach age 55, the company must offer you a choice of other investments for a portion of your account balance.

Pros: Like profit sharing, ESOPs require nothing from you. All you have to do is work for the company and receive the stock. And, should your company be performing well, that stock can add up to quite a bit over the years you're there.

Cons: Nothing truly major—you won't lose anything of your own, but do keep in mind that company stock can fall as well as rise. This means that a sizable chunk of stock that's worth a lot today may be worth a lot *less* tomorrow, when you retire. In other words, ESOPs are nice to be involved in, but don't count on them too much for retirement financing.

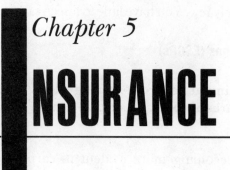

Chapter 5

INSURANCE

INTRODUCTION

▶ **Retirement planning must include your total financial picture to be as effective as possible. And part of that picture is insurance—*all* types of insurance.**

Many people planning retirement think about life insurance and health insurance and forget other forms of insurance. They might be making a very costly mistake.

This chapter covers the different forms of insurance you'll need to consider when you plan for retirement: life insurance, health insurance (including Medicare), long-term care insurance, disability income insurance, auto insurance, and homeowner's insurance. Some insurance may be already available to you through Social Security or your company. For the rest, you'll need to rely on your own investments and savings.

LIFE INSURANCE

How Life Insurance Fits into Your Retirement Plan

▶ **Life insurance plays different roles when you're planning a retirement.**

Very early in your retirement planning—usually when you're in your 30s or 40s—life insurance acts as a safety net in the event of your death. It assures you that your dependents will manage without you, that the children can go to college, the house can be paid off, and so on. This is the time when you'll be buying term life insurance, universal, or other policies that act as protection against your death.

Later, when you get more involved in intensive retirement planning and building up a retirement nest egg, you can use life insurance to generate income. This is the time when you can look at life insurance both as a safety net *and* as cash accumulator.

At this point, some of you may prefer to drop term life insurance (which gets more expensive the older you are) and opt for a cash-value policy, such as variable life (in which you can choose the investment vehicles you want your cash reserves invested in). However, if you're a strong financial manager with a good investment track record, you may be better off sticking with term life and investing your money on your own. With a strong investment portfolio, the earnings on your investments can well make up for the increased cost of the term life.

▶ **How much coverage do you need until you reach age 65? It depends upon your income, your age, and other variables.**

The old rule of thumb is that your life insurance coverage should equal 7 to 10 times your annual salary. That's fine for a very broad-brush approach, but you also have to look at your very specific situation. Do you have dependents? Are you paying college costs? Mortgages? Does your spouse work?

WORKSHEET 3: HOW MUCH LIFE INSURANCE DO YOU NEED?

Step 1: How much in immediate or fixed expenses should your policy cover?

ADD:

1. Projected Fixed Expenses

    a. Funeral and death expenses   _____

    b. Estate taxes   _____

    c. Mortgage/other debts (if applicable)   _____

    d. College savings/tuition (if applicable)   _____

    Other expenses (such as elder care)   + _____

2. Total fixed expenses to be covered   = _____

Step 2: How much will your family need for living expenses?

3. Your current annual household expenses   _____

SUBTRACT:

4. Costs incurred by you (food, clothing, etc.)   − _____

5. Subtotal   = _____

SUBTRACT:

6. Income   − _____

    (Social Security benefits spouse's take home pay, survivors pension benefits, etc.)

7. TOTAL: Your family's annual expenses   = _____

MULTIPLY:

8. Line 7 by the number of years you want your family covered   × _____

9. TOTAL: Family living expenses to be covered   = _____

Step 3: How much life insurance will meet your family's needs?

ADD:

10. a. Line 2   _____

     b. Line 9   + _____

     c. Total Expenses   = _____

SUBTRACT:

11. Cash value of investments   − _____

SUBTRACT:

12. Lump sum payments payable upon your death (death benefits, retirement plan distributions, etc)   − _____

13. TOTAL ESTIMATED INSURANCE COVERAGE NEEDED   = _____

▶ **When it's time to retire, it's also time to get rid of your life insurance—or at least scale it down dramatically.**

When you are a retiree, life insurance becomes much less important than it was in the past. You don't have a growing family to take care of, you're older, you're not trying to build cash reserves—now's the time to live off the money you've been (theoretically) saving.

That's why for most of you retirement time is the right time to drop your current whole life insurance policy or convert it into a low-value policy that is paid up.

To put it bluntly, the money you're spending on insurance premiums can be more wisely used elsewhere.

When you hit retirement age, you have some choices.

- *You can cash in your policy.* A good strategy for savvy investors. By doing this, you get a lump sum of cash that you can invest as you wish.

- *You can switch to a paid-up policy.* This is the most prudent move of all. By doing this, you get the best of both worlds: You get a lesser-value policy that will cover your funeral expenses, debts, etc. Plus you can use the money you once spent on premiums for investing.

- *You can convert your policy to an annuity*—that is, turn the cash value of your policy to an annuity that gives you a lifetime income. This is what many people automatically do—often because the minute they turn 65, their insurance agents start pushing the insurance company's investment vehicles. Frankly, while it's an easy move to make, it isn't a recommended option; there are other investments that may serve you better. (For more information, see Chapters 6 and 7.)

There is one instance when you should consider *keeping* your life insurance policy once you retire. If *you have a substantial estate—in excess of $600,000—that you want to pass to heirs.*

When you have a sizable estate, life insurance can be put in trust. It can cover estate taxes, probate fees, inheritance taxes, legal fees, and the like. By doing this, you keep the estate intact for your heirs. (You'll want to consult an attorney for details.) If you are not in this situation, though, strongly consider dropping your life insurance coverage upon retirement.

▶ **There are two basic, common types of life insurance—*term* and *whole life*.**

The differences between the two types are simple: Term life insurance policies pay a death benefit upon the policyholder's death; whole life insurance policies pay a death benefit, but also offer a "cash value"—that is, you get a tax-deferred savings account of money that is invested and grows over the life of your policy. You can borrow against this "cash value" account, and it is transferred tax-free to your beneficiaries upon your death.

It sounds great, which is why, in the past, most people automatically opted for whole life policies because of the advantage of tax-deferred savings. However, there is now more debate about the wisdom of paying the higher premiums demanded by whole life policies for the lesser amount of insurance coverage. In addition, there are rising concerns about the stability of many insurance companies, about their investment choices, and more.

What should the savvy preretiree do? To a great degree, it depends upon your confidence in yourself as a financial manager and your specific needs. If you are confident in your investing ability, you may be best off opting for lower-cost term life insurance. In this way, you can get more coverage at the same time that you invest the money you would have spent on whole life in your own choice of investment vehicles.

However, if you plan to hold the insurance policy for *15 to 20 years minimum,* opting for whole life may be the better deal, chiefly because of the advantages of tax-deferred growth of assets.

As for those of you who are already retired or will be retiring shortly, as mentioned earlier, you are best off steering clear of an expensive life insurance policy completely.

Term Life Insurance

How it works: Term life insurance covers you for a set period, a term, which can be anything from one year to 20 years or more. Most companies stop offering death benefits after you reach age 75 (some even earlier than that).

Annual renewable term is the most common type of term life. As the name suggests, each year you have the option to renew the insurance. You pay an annual premium, which will increase with your age. *Decreasing term* allows you to pay the same premium for the term of the policy, but benefits decrease as you grow older.

Convertible term allows you to convert your term insurance to a permanent whole life or universal life policy without having to take another medical examination.

Pros: Premiums are low relative to the coverage you receive; if you're fairly young and have a growing family, term life serves as an "instant estate" should you die.

Cons: Premiums keep rising as you renew the terms and as you get older—by the time you reach retirement age, you may be paying a great deal.

Best for: People in their 30s and 40s or people with growing families. Savvy money managers who believe they can make up for the rising cost of term insurance with strong investments.

TIP: **One way to make term insurance fit into your retirement planning is to buy decreasing term insurance that stops when you hit retirement age. This way, you and your family are covered should you die before retirement, and you've saved money that you could have spent on more expensive whole life. You can use that money for self-directed investments or for retirement savings.**

Whole Life Insurance

How it works: Relative to term life, whole life is initially more expensive, but as you grow older, it becomes less so. There are several different types of whole life insurance.

Traditional whole life covers you for your entire life for one set premium and pays a fixed death benefit. You can pay premiums every month, three months, six months, or year. The premiums you pay at the beginning of your policy are more expensive than comparable term insurance, but these higher premiums go toward the cash value of your policy. The cash value keeps building tax-free during the life of the policy, according to the policy schedule. This allows you to borrow against the cash value or easily cash in the policy for its value should you need quick cash. This type of whole life insurance works best for middle-aged people with nonworking spouses or other dependents who want permanent insurance and the certainty of regularly scheduled premiums.

Single-premium whole life is the simplest of the policies—you pay one lump sum payment at the outset. That's it. For the one sum, you receive lifetime coverage—and, because you have paid up the policy at once, you get much more insurance coverage than the amount of the premium. Some policies are designed to pay a fixed return, so are low-risk investments; others give you a choice of investment vehicles, so hold more risk but have more earning potential. This is best for people who want or need life insurance, and who want a safe parking place for a large amount of money.

Universal life is a popular form of life insurance combining typical life insurance with a tax-favored cash accumulation plan, but one which has run into problems lately—because of changing interest rates. It is designed primarily for people interested in building an estate while maintaining death protection. This type of policy gives you a certain amount of flexibility: You pay a premium and choose how much should go toward insurance and how much toward cash accumulation; you can change your death benefit, increasing or decreasing it depending on your needs; you can change your premium—both the amount you pay and when you pay it. It is usually less expensive than traditional whole life policies. But the flexibility has a drawback: Just as you can change the premiums you pay, so the insurance company can change the coverage you get for those premiums. Typically, when interest rates plunge, your premiums increase if you want to maintain the coverage you initially had. If you don't want to pay higher premiums, you face other negatives— the cash value decreases, your death benefit decreases, or your coverage is canceled. The bottom line? Be cautious when shopping for this form of life insurance. Drawbacks aside, this type of policy usually works best for younger people—in their 30s or 40s—who seek lower-cost insurance protection at the same time they begin building up an estate.

Survivorship whole life (or joint and last survivor, or second to die) covers two people, but the death benefit is paid after the death of the second person. It's best used when you want to protect your estate. For example, if you own a business and want to pass the business to your survivors, survivorship whole life will take care of estate taxes after both insured parties die and leave the business untouched. Usually this form of whole life is less expensive than comparable policies covering only one person—often you can get survivorship whole life for the same annual premium as traditional whole life.

This is best for people in their 40s or 50s, especially those with estates worth over $1 million that they want to pass on to children.

With *variable life,* your cash reserves are invested in your choice of investment vehicles—from stocks and bonds to money market portfolios to zero-coupon bonds and other Treasury offerings. Although the cash value of your policy guarantees a minimum death benefit, the value of the policy will vary according to the specific investments and their performance. As with traditional whole life policies, you pay your premiums on a regular schedule that you determine—every three months, six months, or year. This is best if you are interested in combining the stability of a regular life insurance policy (with scheduled payments and so forth) with a degree of flexibility where investments are concerned.

Pros: One of the above forms of whole life is a logical choice if you want death protection benefits to protect your survivors (spouse, children, etc.) and want to begin building cash reserves at the same time. You can borrow against whole life; your cash reserves build up tax-free.

Cons: A substantial amount of money is tied up in a life insurance policy; once you've reached a certain age, you are probably better off taking the money than keeping it in a policy.

Best for: People with nonworking spouses; people interested in protecting their estate and leaving a sizable estate for spouse, children, or other dependents—since whole life pays transfer costs (estate taxes, inheritance taxes, funeral costs, probate and other legal fees, etc.).

TIP: **If you have a risky medical history, or if you're having trouble getting life insurance because of your age, consider using an independent insurance agent specializing in "impaired risk" placements. These agents are experts at obtaining life insurance coverage for people with health problems. For names of such agents, call your state insurance office or send for *Insurance & Alternatives for Uninsurables* by Roger Kessinger, P.O. Box 8933, Boise, ID 83707 ($27.95).**

The Before-Death Option

▶ **As public concern about long-term health care keeps rising, life insurance companies have responded by developing new options for life insurance policies that will help people pay for nursing home stays, medical treatment, and the like.**

The *before-death option* (also called living insurance, living needs benefits, and accelerated death benefits) is a new feature available with many life insurance policies, designed to help people with long-term care.

How it works: This feature is specifically designed to replace long-term care insurance. With this type of policy, you have a regular whole life policy that accumulates cash, but you, the policyholder, can collect a portion of the death benefit yourself. Of course, this means your survivors receive less upon your death. But for most people, it's a good choice. One drawback is the price. (Note: Check your state's laws regarding the legality of receiving accelerated death benefits. Some states don't allow it.) Living insurance policies can cost anything from 5% to 30% more than a corresponding regular insurance policy.

Different insurance companies offer different types of policies that cover different things. One common form of the before-death option pays benefits when you need long-term care and enter a nursing home. With this type of policy, you usually receive a monthly payment worth about 2% of the policy's cash value for each month you need long-term care.

Another type pays benefits when you have certain medical conditions (among those commonly covered are heart attack, terminal cancer, stroke, and liver failure). With this type of policy, you usually receive a lump sum payment of 20% to 30% of your policy. And typically it's up to you what to do with the benefit—use it for nursing home care, home nursing, anything.

Another type of accelerated death benefit policy actually pays the death benefit if the policyholder is either terminally ill or permanently confined to a nursing home. For example, a Prudential policy offers these terms: If they are terminally ill, policyholders may submit a doctor's certificate stating they have six months to live. Then they receive a lump sum payment of their death benefit. If they have been in a nursing home for a minimum of six months and will not be released, policyholders can receive either a lump sum payment or monthly payments of the death benefit. In either case, the benefit is paid in full—but the interest Prudential would have earned on the money over the six months is deducted. With this type of policy, survivors receive no benefits upon the policyholder's death.

Pros: Like long-term care insurance the before-death policy gives the policyholder the ability to meet the often crippling costs of long-term care and allows the terminally ill to maintain financial quality of life without dipping into family savings that are intended for a survivor. Policies are often flexible as to how money can be spent—in some cases money can be used for whatever the policyholder wants, even nonmedical items.

Cons: Because they're relatively new, policies can be costly. Coverage also varies widely—you have to be sure such diseases as Alzheimer's are covered. State regulations may vary. Survivors receive substantially less of a benefit upon policyholder's death and, in some cases, receive no benefit at all. Another problem: Benefits may be taxable—the IRS hasn't ruled on whether accelerated death benefits are tax-free.

Best for: People in their late 50s who want life insurance coverage and the added benefit of long-term care coverage.

TIP: **Before you buy this option, compare prices with a standard long-term care policy. When you reach retirement age, you might be better off cashing in this policy, buying a standard long-term care policy and investing the rest of the money. Another option: Find out whether you could get the same amount of money by borrowing against the cash value of your existing life insurance policy.**

Buying Life Insurance

▶ **If you're still years away from retirement and you're planning to buy life insurance—because you need to increase your coverage or because you haven't been covered at all—here is a brief refresher on the steps to take.**

A few hints on insurance buying:

- *Be sure the insurance company you deal with is rated highly* by at least two of the three companies that rate insurance companies—A or better by Best & Company, BBB or better by Standard & Poor's, and Baa or better by Moody's. (You can check insurance ratings in their respective directories, available at your local library.) Firms with lower ratings may be cheaper, but they are less stable. This isn't the time to stint. A good rule of thumb: You want to deal with an insurance company that will be in business 15 to 20 years from now—that is, when you're beginning to get your payments, or when your survivors are.

- *One of the best ways of getting an insurance agent or broker is by asking family, friends, or colleagues for recommendations.* If they're satisfied with their agent or broker, chances are you will be too.

- *Check your agent's or broker's credentials.* Also, if you want special services, such as financial planning, find out if your agent is certified. (For more on this, see Financial Planners, page 38.)

- *Keep in mind: You have an out if you discover you* don't *want the life insurance policy you've bought.* You can cancel your life insurance policy within 10 days of delivery and pay *no penalty.*

TIP: Watch out for fraud. It's not overly common in the insurance industry, but it does occur. Some warning signs: an agent or broker who asks you to write a check to him or her personally, asks for cash, or doesn't tell you his or her credentials. Always pay by check or money order made out to the insurance company.

- *To save money, consider buying low-load policies directly from a life insurance company.* Because you won't be paying an agent's commission, you'll pay substantially less in initial costs.

SOURCE: If you have any questions or problems, the insurance industry runs a **no-fee hotline.** Call 800-942-4242, weekdays from 8:30 A.M. to 8:00 P.M.

- *If you're buying term life insurance,* ask about special offers. Many companies offer special arrangements and discounts that aren't advertised or widely known. Ask agents and brokers if there are any special offers you can take advantage of. One common offer is a discount if you pay at least one year's premiums in advance. Similarly, check to see if there are any discounts offered if you buy more insurance. Often, the more you buy, the less you pay.

SOURCE: Certain companies offer information and recommendations on low-cost term life insurance policies. **InsuranceQuote** (based in Chandler, Arizona) and **SelectQuote** (based in San Francisco) charge no fee for recommendations. Call InsuranceQuote, 800-972-1104, or SelectQuote, 800-343-1985. Another company, **Insurance Information,** charges $50, but will refund the amount if you don't save at least that much on your first year's premium compared to your current policy. Their number is 800-472-5800.

- *If you're buying whole life:* be extra careful in evaluating policies. Always try to compare policies to see if you're getting the best possible deal. The simplest way is to use cost indexes, available from the insurance companies. One is a surrender-cost index that shows you what your policy would be worth if you canceled it in 10 years; the other is an interest-adjusted payment index that shows you the average premium for $1,000 in coverage. Also check the performance of the policy's investment funds.

- *If you have health problems and are having difficulties finding a life insurance company that will cover you, or one that will offer a policy that isn't prohibitively expensive, you have several options.* A good bet: Work with an independent insurance agent who specializes in impaired risks (people with health problems). For assistance in locating such an agent, contact your state Insurance Department (listed in your local telephone directory) or check the Yellow Pages. Many insurance agents will list their specialty.

HEALTH INSURANCE: MEDICARE, MEDIGAP, AND OTHER FORMS OF HEALTH INSURANCE

▶ **Two general points to keep in mind as you plan your retirement: Health care costs will account for a large chunk of your retirement money—and they'll keep rising.**

It's not a pretty picture.

Over the past few years the cost of health care has been skyrocketing. By 1995, the average 62-year-old retiree will be paying about $4,700 per year in health costs, including insurance premiums and general expenses; the average 65-year-old will be paying $3,400. By 2000, costs will be even higher—about $5,500 per year for a 65-year-old, $7,500 for a 62-year-old.

Add to this the fact that Medicare benefits have been getting lower and you have a rather convincing argument for thinking ahead about your retirement health insurance coverage.

▶ **The first step to take: Understand the different types of health insurance available to you and the times when you might need them.**

You'll probably find yourself relying on more than one type of health insurance over the course of your retirement. No one type of policy covers everything. So to get the proper coverage—either before the age of 65 or after—you need to put together a package of policies that will cover your medical and health needs.

The insurance you need also depends upon your age. After you hit 65, you can factor in federally funded Medicare to help defray mounting health costs. Before 65, it's up to you.

Briefly, here's an outline of the insurance available to you.

If you retire before you reach 65, you will have three main choices for health cost planning.

- *You can opt for employer-provided health insurance,* which will continue your coverage after you're retired, until Medicare kicks in. These group plans cost you less than an individual policy does. Typical group plans often include basic hospital/medical coverage for a relatively low cost.

- *You can choose a private insurance plan.* Depending upon the degree of coverage you want, this can be a high-cost or a low-cost option. Generally, if you want an individual policy similar to the type of group policy you probably had at work—comprehensive major medical insurance—you'll be paying a higher amount than participants in a group plan. But if you don't want to pay the high premiums—and you don't need the coverage— you can ask for a high deductible. The higher the deductible, the lower your premiums. To pay even less, buy a catastrophic policy, designed solely for coverage of a major illness or accident.

TIP: **If you have few medical needs, consider opting for a low-cost high-deductible medical insurance policy *only*. While this will take care of your bills if you're hit with a major illness or catastrophic accident, it won't eat up your retirement funds. You can put the money you save into investing instead.**

- *You can join a Health Management Organization* (HMO) or *Preferred Provider Organization (PPO).* While an HMO or PPO is not a form of insurance per se, it is a viable way of keeping down health costs. With an HMO, you pay a set monthly fee and receive medical services with HMO-associated doctors and hospitals. With a PPO, you pay a low copayment to receive discounted services from "preferred" doctors and hospitals. (For more information on HMOs and PPOs, see Chapter 14.)

TIP: **Don't become overinsured. Many people make the mistake of having overlapping policies. Think and compare before you buy.**

After you reach 65, you will rely primarily on two different types of health insurance.

- *Medicare kicks in to become the backbone of your health insurance coverage.* Federally funded Medicare covers inpatient hospital care, home health care, hospice care, medical services—including surgery, anesthesia, diagnostic tests, and physical therapy—and 80% of general medical care (up to approved Medicare limits). In effect, Medicare replaces private hospital/medical insurance. (Medicare is dependent on your involvement with the Social Security system, or with a government pension.)

- *You'll probably need medigap insurance.* This specially designed supplemental health insurance covers what Medicare won't pay for, such as eye care and hearing aids. You'll need to pay for this type of insurance.

TABLE 5.1: DIFFERENT TYPES OF HEALTH INSURANCE PLANS AND WHAT THEY COVER

Group or individual health plans can consist of one or a combination of the following:

Basic Hospital covers all or most hospital charges—including semiprivate room, nursing care, minor supplies, and meals—for two months, sometimes more, and may cover other medical services, such as X-rays, lab tests, anesthesia, medication, and operating room charges.

Basic Medical covers most (usually 80% to 85%) doctors' charges incurred while at the hospital—including room visits, surgery, radiology, lab tests, and other services not included in the basic hospital plan.

(Note: The above two policies are the type offered by companies such as Blue Cross/Blue Shield.)

Major Medical covers general medical expenses, including doctors' services (office visits, in-hospital and outpatient treatment, etc.), specialists' services (consultations, treatment, etc.), radiology services (X-rays, lab testing, etc.), anesthesia, private nursing, prescription drugs. Coverage is not complete. You pay a deductible, and you pay a copayment. In other words, the insurance company picks up a percentage (usually about 80%) of the costs above the deductible; you pay the remaining percentage—the copayment.

Catastrophic is designed to cover the high cost of care in the event of a major illness, such as cancer. This covers the *entire* cost of medical bills after they add up to a certain amount beyond the deductible. (Until the bills mount up, you usually are responsible for a copayment of 20% or so.) Some catastrophic policies will pay set amounts for major expenses such as hospital care and surgery, but will cover minor expenses, such as office visits, only after you reach a predetermined level of costs—usually a high one.

Dental (often included as part of a major medical plan) covers dental care and services, including office visits, treatment, periodontal services, etc. This can be set up as a regular insurance policy with deductible and copayment arrangement, or as a scheduled-benefits plan, which sets a determined coverage cost for different procedures.

Generally, a retiree before the age of 65 should have some combination of the above to avoid being wiped out by the high cost of health care.

▶ **Whatever age you are, start saving now with an eye to paying for medical insurance down the road. As with most retirement planning, the earlier the better.**

If you're planning an early retirement, this is especially important. You can't count on Medicare at all until you reach 65. So you may be caught in a bind: Your former employer may very well cut your health benefits, or not offer them at all, and you won't have the Medicare coverage to help you out.

There are a few steps you can take immediately.

Get information *now.* Learn about Medicare—what you can expect, what it will cover, and what it won't. Find out about the insurance you have at work. Is there a way to continue its coverage after retirement? If so, what is entailed?

Start saving *now.* Make health costs an integral part of your retirement planning. Factor in the higher costs and higher incidence of medical problems you'll probably encounter.

TIP: If you can afford it, put away about $2,000 a year earmarked solely for health insurance once you've retired. You might put the money into a tax-deferred annuity, a 401(k), or any interest-earning vehicle—and in this case, you're best off putting it into a plan that won't let you tap the money until you reach retirement. That way you won't be tempted to dip in. By the time you reach retirement, you'll have enough to get a good policy and to cover premiums without any trouble.

Following is an in-depth explanation of the different forms of health insurance—Medicare, medigap, and private insurance—what they cover, and how they can fit into your retirement plan.

Employer-Provided and Individual Health Insurance: Coverage Before Medicare

▶ **In many cases when you're retiring, the best possible move is to keep employer-provided health insurance—*especially if you are retiring before the age of 65 (which means before Medicare coverage begins).***

Employer-provided health insurance is a great stopgap between the time you retire and the time you receive Medicare. It's usually cheaper than going out on your own and buying a similar private policy, and you're already covered by the policy so you don't have to get a physical check-up.

Problem is, it's getting harder to keep. High costs are forcing many employers to cut back on insurance coverage. One of the first areas that gets the axe is coverage of retired employees.

Still, it's not yet time to write off this avenue for health insurance. Many people can—and do—retire with some health care coverage provided by their former employers.

In fact, according to a 1990 National Center for Health Services Research report, 49% of the 22 million retired people 55 or older had some form of health care insurance through their former employers in 1987.

In general, present retirees don't have to worry too much. Most companies that have offered their employees health benefits upon retirement will continue that coverage. But if you're a recent hiree or if your retirement is a few years down the road, then you might have something to be concerned about. If you won't be covered by your company plan upon retirement, look into private health insurance—especially if you're retiring early.

▶ **Check and double-check what your company's policy is concerning health insurance benefits for retirees.**

The rules keep changing. What you were told when you were hired might not hold true anymore.

A few things to be sure you know:

- *Will the retirement health benefits cover my dependents?* Your company may limit coverage of dependents, or may not cover dependents at all. This is becoming more common. Under many retiree health plans, coverage of dependents is strictly limited, with stringent eligibility rules. Other plans don't cover dependents at all—coverage is limited to the former employee alone. Or the company may require that you pay for coverage.

- *If my spouse is employed by another company, does my company policy cover him or her?* Coverage of a working spouse (who can get health insurance through his or her employer) is one area many companies are cutting back on.

• *What happens to my coverage if I take a full-time job after I retire?* Many companies will stop covering you with their employer-provided health insurance if you work full-time for another company. Their reasoning: If you're working somewhere else, why should they be picking up your insurance costs?

• *Does coverage vary according to how many years I worked here?* It's an increasingly common practice for companies to provide coverage in line with your years of service. For example, if you were with your company for 20 years, you may receive 80% coverage; if only 10 years, 20%; if over 25, 90% and so on. If you've been recently hired and have worked for your company for only a few years, you may not be eligible for any coverage after retirement.

• *If insurance rates go up, will the company cover the cost increases, or will I?* Some companies will pay only a set amount for insurance. When premiums go up, you pay the difference.

• *Will the company policy cover me only if I go to an approved doctor, HMO, or PPO?* This is another way for companies to keep a cap on costs. To receive insurance coverage for an office visit, medical services, or treatment, you must go to a company-specified HMO or PPO.

• *Is there a "maximum benefit limit"?* An increasing number of employer-provided health insurance policies set a limit to the dollar amount of claims. Once you reach the limit, you no longer are covered by the policy.

• *What about premiums? Copayments? Deductibles?* Chances are, if you haven't been responsible for paying for one or all of the above in the past, you will be now or in the future. Or, if you were paying one or all in the past, chances are the amount you'll be paying will go up. Many companies are shifting more of the costs to you, the employee—which translates into higher premium payments, copayments, or deductibles. They're either increasing your share of costs or imposing employee costs where they hadn't before.

TIP: Keep abreast of any and all changes in your company policy. Even something that looks inconsequential—say, a small increase in your premium—is important. It may signal the intent to change other, more important parts of your policy. *Keep informed!*

▶ **A coming trend is prepaid retirement health coverage.**

If you are currently working at a company, check to see if this type of plan is available.

It is a relatively new plan that many companies are introducing to help defray the high costs of health benefits and still enable employees to retain employer coverage upon retirement.

With prepaid coverage, you make a monthly contribution to the company retirement plan. The amount is usually determined by your age. After a certain period—usually 10 years—you are eligible to receive full health benefits upon retirement. If you leave the company before you retire, you receive the full amount you have contributed plus any interest it has earned.

▶ **Another trend: Companies are setting up their own medical centers for employees and retirees.**

These corporate medical centers are growing in popularity. They are cost-savers for the corporation and might be a cost saver for you. With this sort of program, you are covered by employer insurance as long as you seek treatment at the company clinic.

▶ **In today's cost-conscious corporate environment, be prepared for your company to eliminate coverage of retirees entirely.**

This is something to be on the lookout for. It's an unfortunate trend—and being caught unaware might cost you money.

Start by finding out the specifics. Is everyone affected or just those hired within the last year or so? As mentioned before, often companies aren't covering new employees, but they will continue retirement coverage for their present employees—particularly those with tenure in the company.

Next, take a look at the written policy. Does the policy state that the company reserves the right to terminate or change the plan? If it doesn't, you might be legally entitled to the coverage as previously set forth.

Finally, speak to an attorney, one with experience in this area. Often you won't have to go further. The company may rethink its policy when it hears from an attorney.

▶ **Sometimes you're better off with private health insurance.**

Too many people automatically assume that sticking with a company policy is the best route, but this is not necessarily true. Depending upon your needs, you might be better off with a lower-cost, no-frills private health insurance policy.

This depends on such variables as the coverage your employer-provided plan provides, the cost to you, and the type of medical coverage you need or feel comfortable with. Often, if you shop around, you will find that a private plan may actually save you money compared to the group employer plan you are eligible for.

▶ **Another option: Keep your employer-provided plan and buy supplemental insurance as well.**

This move makes sense if your company plan doesn't cover such things as eye care, dental care, prescription drugs, or outpatient care.

▶ **In many cases, a temporary stopgap insurance plan is the best bet.**

If you're retiring before you reach 65—and before Medicare kicks in—consider buying a temporary health insurance policy specially designed to fill the period between your actual retirement and your eligibility to receive Medicare. For a fixed, one-time premium, you are covered until you receive Medicare. This is often a good choice if you are unable to keep your employer-provided plan.

Medicare: How It Works, What Is Covered—and What Isn't

▶ **The big question on a lot of people's minds: How much less will Medicare cover by the time they retire?**

It's a problem that has been developing for the past few years. Medicare spending has been going up, coverage is going down—and people are beginning to get worried. And rightly so.

The facts: As our population gets older, Medicare spending keeps increasing. It's already over $70 billion—and it's still going up. At the same time, the government has been cutting back on the amount Medicare covers.

Keep your eyes peeled and your ears open for news stories and legislation concerning Medicare. Remember—any changes made in Medicare will affect your retirement lifestyle. If there are cutbacks, you're the one who'll have to pay—by paying for your own medical insurance.

▶ **Despite the less-than-positive outlook, you can probably still count on Medicare to ease *some* of your medical expenses.**

How it works: Virtually everyone is eligible for Medicare once they turn 65. The basic rule is that you need to have worked for 10 years or be the spouse of an eligible person. The technical requirements are that you must be 65 or older, eligible for (or receiving) Social Security benefits, or a former government employee (with certain limitations) or the spouse of such a person.

To get Medicare when you're under 65, usually you must have been receiving Social Security disability benefits for over two years, although there are exceptions made for government employees.

Three months before your 65th birthday, you should apply for Medicare. Contact your local Social Security office for information on what is involved. Usually there's little if anything for you to do. If you've applied already for Social Security benefits, you'll automatically receive a Medicare card in the mail. All you have to do is follow the instructions on the card. However, if you haven't applied for Social Security benefits, you'll have to file an application to receive Medicare.

There are two parts to Medicare: Part A, which is premium-free hospital insurance, and Part B, medical insurance, which requires payment of monthly premiums.

Medicare Part A helps you pay for inpatient hospital care, some inpatient care in a skilled nursing facility, home health care, and hospice care. Most beneficiaries pay no monthly premium. But there are exceptions. If you don't have 10 years of work credits, you *buy* Medicare Part A and pay a $175 a month Part A premium. If you enroll late, the premium may even be higher.

Medicare Part B helps you pay for doctors' services, outpatient hospital services, durable medical equipment (such as wheelchairs, in-home oxygen equipment, and other equipment prescribed by a doctor for your in-home use), and other supplies not covered by Medicare Part A—prosthetic devices, certain vaccines and drugs, and more. It covers all of these as long as the cost does not exceed "approved amounts"—based on Medicare estimates of reasonable costs.

For Part B coverage, you must pay premiums ($31.90 a month), deductibles ($75) and coinsurance or copayments (the 20% the plan doesn't cover) yourself—or through another insurance plan.

(The table on pages 141–42 gives you a quick reference of what services are covered under each plan, what Medicare pays, and what you pay.)

TIP: The federal government puts out a free *Medicare Handbook* each year, outlining benefits, services, what to do when you have problems, and so on. You can find this handbook at your local Social Security office.

Pros: Medicare is easy to receive and it does help ease up on some of your health care costs. The bottom line: You would be crazy *not* to sign up for Medicare.

Cons: It isn't a cure-all by any means—Medicare-approved amounts are often lower than actual charges; many hospitals, doctors, and other medical practitioners charge higher rates because of Medicare reimbursement; there are large gaps in coverage.

▶ **Be aware of various legal—but unfair—practices your doctor might use to get as much Medicare money as possible.**

It's an unfortunate reality of the Medicare system: Doctors can legally take advantage of the millions of dollars worth of Medicare money—and, although the government foots the bill, it winds up costing you money.

Look out for:

- *Unnecessary tests or appointments:* These are among the most common ways for doctors to increase their Medicare income. Be wary if your doctor orders test after test on you—especially the same or similar tests—to confirm an original test, or if your doctor has you come in for repeated office visits that seem unnecessary— perhaps you could have phoned in the information he or she needs, or mailed it.

- *Unbundling:* Instead of being charged one overall fee for medical services connected with one treatment, you are billed for each separate service.

- *Drop-in hospital visits:* When you're in the hospital under the care of a specialist, your general practitioner drops in to say hello and

TABLE 5.2: WHAT MEDICARE COVERS
MEDICARE (PART A): HOSPITAL INSURANCE-COVERED SERVICES PER BENEFIT PERIOD[1]

SERVICES	BENEFIT	MEDICARE PAYS†	YOU PAY†
HOSPITALIZATION Semiprivate room and board, general nursing and miscellaneous hospital services and supplies	First 60 days	All but $592	$592
	61st to 90th day	All but $148 a day	$148 a day
	91st to 150th day	All but $296 a day	$296 a day
	Beyond 150 days	Nothing	All costs
POSTHOSPITAL SKILLED NURSING FACILITY CARE . . . In a facility approved by Medicare. You must have been in a hospital for at least 3 days and enter the facility within 30 days after hospital discharge.[2]	First 20 days	100% of approved amount	Nothing
	Additional 80 days	All but $74 a day	$74 a day
	Beyond 100 days	Nothing	All costs
HOME HEALTH CARE	Visits limited to medically necessary skilled care	Full cost of services 80% of approved amount for durable medical equipment	Nothing for services 20% of approved amount for durable medical equipment
HOSPICE CARE Available to terminally ill	Up to 210 days if doctor certifies need	All but limited costs for outpatient drugs and inpatient respite care.	Limited cost sharing for outpatient drugs and inpatient respite care.
BLOOD	Blood	All but first 3 pints per calendar year	For first 3 pints‡

* 60 Reserve Days may be used only once; days used are not renewable.

† These figures are for 1990 and are subject to change each year.

‡ To the extent the blood deductible is met under one part of Medicare during the calendar year, it does not have to be met under the other part.

[1] A Benefit Period begins on the first day you receive service as an inpatient in a hospital and ends after you have been out of the hospital or skilled nursing facility for 60 days in a row.

[2] Medicare and private insurance will not pay for most nursing home care. You pay for custodial care and most care in a nursing home.

MEDICARE (PART B): MEDICAL INSURANCE-COVERED SERVICES PER CALENDAR YEAR

SERVICES	BENEFIT	MEDICARE PAYS	YOU PAY
MEDICAL EXPENSE Physician's services, in-patient and outpatient medical services and supplies, physical and speech therapy, ambulance, etc.	Medicare pays for medical services in or out of the hospital	80% of approved amount (after $75 deductible)	$75 deductible* plus 20% of approved amount (plus any charge above approved amount)†
HOME HEALTH CARE	Visits limited to medically necessary care	Full cost of services 80% of approved amount for durable medical equipment (after $75 deductible)	Nothing for services 20% of approved amount for durable medical equipment (after $75 deductible)
OUTPATIENT HOSPITAL TREATMENT	Unlimited if medically necessary	80% of approved charges (after $75 deductible)	Subject to deductible plus 20% of approved amount
BLOOD	Blood	80% of approved amount (after $75 deductible and starting with 4th pint)	First 3 pints plus 20% of approved amount (after $75 deductible)‡

* Once you have had $75 of expense for covered services in 1990, the Part B deductible does not apply to any further covered services you receive for the rest of the year.

† You pay for charges higher than the amount approved by Medicare unless the doctor or supplier agrees to accept Medicare's approved amount as the total charge for services rendered.

‡ To the extent the blood deductible is met under one part of Medicare during the calendar year, it does not have to be met under the other part.

Source: U.S. Department of Health and Human Services.
Note: These are 1990 figures.

see how you are. You think it's a friendly visit, but it's not. Weeks later, you receive a bill.

- *Expensive or unnecessary treatments:* To make the most money possible, the doctor orders the most expensive treatment possible—or orders a procedure done that isn't necessary, when, for example, diet, lifestyle modification, or medication would be as effective as surgery.

- *Waived copayments:* When the doctor waives the 20% Medicare copayment charge, watch out. It looks like you're saving money—after all, you aren't paying the usual 20% uncovered by Medicare. But think again. Often doctors try to make up the 20% elsewhere—typically by overcharging for services.

The best rules of thumb to keep medical costs down and prevent any rude surprise:

- Ask your doctor what you'll be charged before you accept treatment. If the cost seems unreasonably high, try negotiating with the doctor. If you still can't reach what you consider a reasonable fee, consider looking elsewhere for medical care—either to other doctors or to HMOs. Get referrals from friends, colleagues, associations, and so forth. Call different doctors and find out what they charge for the procedure you need.

- Talk to your doctor. Ask questions about your treatment, the medication you're receiving, the procedure the doctor has recommended. Keep abreast of medical developments.

SOURCE: To report suspected Medicare fraud, call the toll-free hotline at the **Office of the Inspector General of the Department of Health and Human Services:** 800-368-5779. (Use this number *only* to report such fraud.)

▶ **When you retire, you can't assume Medicare will take care of most of your needs. The reason? There are large gaps in Medicare coverage.**

Yes, Medicare is (for Part A, at least) free. But it's far from perfect—and far from all-encompassing where payment for coverage is concerned. You pay the deductibles, copayments, the difference between the Medicare-approved amount and any higher amount charged by a hospital, doctor, or other health care worker; you even pay the total amount of many operations, treatments, medications, and other nonapproved health costs.

You'll also run into costs that aren't immediately apparent. Medicare payments are based upon Medicare's estimates of "reasonable charges" for the medical services you receive. Unfortunately, Medicare estimates are sometimes lower than the norm. Who pays the difference? You will.

And there are the hidden expenses you might get hit with. For approved facilities. The problem is, only about a third of the nursing home beds in America are in Medicare-approved facilities.

These are some of the reasons you should be sure you have supplementary health insurance—"medigap" insurance (see below).

Medicaid

▶ **Medicaid is a federal- and state-funded health insurance program for people who need financial aid for medical expenses.**

To be eligible for Medicaid, you must have an annual income *below* the poverty level—below $5,440 for singles; below $6,870 for families. Medicaid will pay for Medicare premiums, for copayments and deductibles, and for nursing home care. (For more on Medicaid, see Long-Term Care Insurance, pages 150–51.)

Veteran's Health Benefits

▶ **The federal government also provides veteran's health benefits.**

Veteran's benefits include hospitalization, outpatient care, dental care, mental health care, nursing home care, prosthetic devices, special care for the blind, and other special programs. These services are provided by Veterans Administration hospitals and staff members.

You're eligible for these benefits if you are a veteran with an honorable or general discharge and have a service-connected disability or are disabled by age or disease. You are also eligible if you are the surviving unmarried spouse or disabled child of a veteran who had a service-connected disability.

SOURCE: For more information on veteran's benefits, contact the Veterans Administration and ask for the publication *Federal Benefits for Veterans and Dependents.* Contact: Veterans Administration, Office of Public Affairs, 810 Vermont Avenue NW, Washington, DC 20420 (202-233-2843). Or you can send for the free booklet *Federal Benefits for Veterans,* from Consumer Information Center, P.O. Box 100, Pueblo, CO 81009.

Medigap Insurance: What It Covers, How to Choose

▶ *Medigap insurance* **is designed to pick up the difference between what health services, hospitals, and doctors actually cost and what Medicare will actually pay.**

Over three-quarters of the people covered by Medicare also have their own health insurance, and the vast majority of them plan to continue renewing it. You should be one of them.

Since Medicare won't cover such things as the first day in a hospital and countless other inevitables you'll come upon at some point during your lifetime, medigap insurance can make a difference.

In addition, many medigap plans will pick up the cost of eye care, dental care, outpatient doctors' care, and prescription drugs. Prices for policies range from about $550 to $1,400 a year.

What it covers: Medigap insurance is offered by most major insurance companies. It is supplementary health insurance created specifically to fill in the holes left by Medicare. In 1991, the National Association of Insurance Commissioners made plans to streamline the medigap policies offered to the public. The result—they designed 10 standard medigap policies intended for introduction in early '92. Different states may choose to offer only a few.

All of the 10 will cover a "core" package of benefits. These benefits are:

- Payment of 20% of Medicare-approved fees for doctors' services.

- Payment of the patient's required per-day contribution to the hospital bills for the 61st to the 90th day of a hospital stay ($157 daily in 1991).

- Payment of all patient's charges for blood.

- Partial coverage for long-term hospital stays (over 90 days).

Beyond these core packages, the 10 standard policies differ. A brief rundown: Nine of the 10 policies offer payment of the entire Medicare hospital deductible ($658 in 1991) and cover treatment for medical emergencies that occur during travel overseas. Eight of the policies pay for the per-day contribution skilled nursing home care ($78.50 in 1991) from the 20th day through the 100th day of the stay. Three cover the $100 Medicare deductible for doctors' bills. Three cover *all* doctors' charges not covered by Medicare; another one covers 80% of such charges. Two cover preventative health care services (including shots for influenza, booster shots for tetanus and diphtheria, and tests for colo-rectal cancer, hearing disorders, diabetes, and thyroid problems). Two policies offer a prescription drug benefit up to a maximum of $1,250 in 1991. One policy offers an extended drug benefit—paying up to a maximum $3,000 in 1991.

TABLE 5.3: MEDICARE SUPPLEMENT STANDARDS

Here are the 10 different policies, labeled A to J, which were to be introduced in 1992. The core package is included with all options.

	A	B	C	D	E	F	G	H	I	J
Core	✓	✓	✓	✓	✓	✓	✓	✓	✓	✓
Skilled nursing home			✓	✓	✓	✓	✓	✓	✓	✓
Hospital deductible		✓	✓	✓	✓	✓	✓	✓	✓	✓
Doctor deductible			✓					✓		✓
Excess doctor charges						80%		100%	100%	100%
Foreign travel			✓	✓	✓	✓	✓	✓	✓	✓
At-home recovery				✓		✓			✓	✓
Prescription drugs					Basic				Basic	Ext.*
Preventive screening							✓			✓

NOTE: The core package includes payment of the patient's 20% share of coverage for doctors' services; the patient's $157-per-day contribution to hospital bills for the 61st through 90th day; the patient's contribution for blood; and some coverage for hospital stays beyond 90 days.
*Extended
Source: National Association of Insurance Commissioners

Pros: Once you're receiving Medicare, medigap insurance is the logical way to plug the holes; it's generally a good idea to get a medigap policy.

Cons: Cost can be high; coverage offered does not usually give you 100% protection.

▶ **As medigap insurance has become a virtual necessity, rates have gone up.**

The General Accounting Office recently noted that the average annual cost to senior citizen policyholders was about $840 a year in 1990—up from $702 in 1989. That's a 20% increase. And it's probably going to keep going up.

So what can you do to assure yourself that your retirement money won't be eaten up by hospital or medical bills? Obviously, your best bet is finding medigap insurance that covers the most—and costs the least for that coverage.

Select insurance companies that have gotten a high rating from two of the three companies that rate insurance companies. Check your local library for A. M. Best's, Moody's, and Standard & Poor's insurance reports. Call the different companies and ask them to send you *written* information on their medigap coverage. Don't let brokers or agents get away with verbal explanations. You'll want to sit down and do a policy-to-policy comparison.

Compare prices for the different plans. Obviously you're looking for the specific amount of coverage you need for the lowest price.

TIP: **Look into group plans—like the American Association of Retired Persons' Group Health Insurance Program—to keep costs down. Group health plans are often quite a bit cheaper than individual health plans. If you belong to any special associations or organizations check to see if they have a group plan you can buy into.**

Once you've narrowed your choices, *ask for a second opinion.* Even if the policies are from the most reputable of insurance companies, you want to be perfectly sure of your decision. Be sure you understand the policy completely before you sign on the dotted line. And *always ask to see the written policy.*

TIP: **You can have your medigap insurance policy analyzed by a computer program— the Medigap Check-Up Program—to be sure that your coverage is adequate and right for you. Call or write: United Seniors Health Cooperative, 1334 G Street, NW, Suite 500, Washington, DC 20005 (202-393-6222).**

SOURCE: **The Council of Better Business Bureaus** puts out a pamphlet of helpful tips on medigap insurance, what to look for in a policy—and what to look out for. For this, send $1.00 and a self-addressed stamped envelope to: The Council of Better Business Bureaus, Department 023, Washington, DC 20042-0023.

Another source of information is the **Guide to Health Insurance for People with Medicare.** This free booklet is put out by the federal government. Check for it at your local Social Security office or order it from: Consumer Information Center, Department 59, Pueblo, CO 81009.

▶ **If you are turned down for a medigap policy, you can still get coverage.**

There's no need to get overly concerned if your application for medigap insurance is rejected. Contact your state Blue Cross/Blue Shield and ask them about their open-enrollment period. This is a designated time during which all applicants will be accepted.

LONG-TERM CARE INSURANCE

▶ **Long-term care insurance covers nursing home stays and other forms of long-term health care.**

It's one of the newer forms of health-related insurance specifically aimed at our aging population. Insurance companies have been jumping on the long-term care bandwagon, offering a wide range of policies with widely varying costs and coverage.

With life expectancies getting longer, more people are facing the often prohibitive costs of long-term care. Nursing home care costs an average of $30,000 a year and, in some parts of the country, the cost can shoot up to nearly $100,000. Home health care on a long-term basis is equally costly—with average in-home charges of $8 to $10 an hour. Medicare will not cover most of these costs.

And the costs keep mounting. According to a recent survey of actuaries, nearly half believe that retirees will need from $50,000 to $200,000 in savings for long-term care in the year 2000.

This is where long-term care insurance comes in. By paying premiums now, you avoid that cash outlay later—when you're on a fixed income and can ill afford heavy expenditure.

How it works: There are no hard and fast rules governing long-term care insurance. Prices and coverage vary widely. Some policies cover one-year stays at a nursing home, some cover longer periods. Some policies require that you pay for the first month of care, others the first three months. Most require that you become ill or injured before payment begins—if you are admitted to a nursing home for no reason but frailty, your stay won't be covered.

Care coverage can be split into three areas: *skilled care* (intensive health/medical care), *intermediate care* (less specialized or intensive care, such as rehabilitative therapy), and *custodial care* (practical nursing care, such as help in eating, getting dressed, and walking). Most policies cover all three types of care, but benefits may vary for each. In addition, some policies cover home care, elder care centers, or "respite care" (sporadic short-term nursing home stays), while others cover only nursing home care (and some of these cover only skilled nursing home care, others both skilled and custodial nursing home care).

Most policies pay set, fixed daily costs—"indemnity benefits"—averaging about $85 a day.

With most policies, you decide how long you want the waiting period to be before benefits begin. There is usually a choice between immediate coverage (also called first-dollar coverage) or a wait of 20, 30, 90, or 100 days. You also may decide how much time the benefits will cover—usually two to six years.

Costs vary according to coverage, but range from about $400 annually for policyholders in their 50s up to the low $3,000s for policyholders in their 70s.

Pros: Fills in the gap left by Medicare, which only picks up the tab for stays at skilled nursing homes after a hospital stay; the combination of the high cost of long-term care and longer life expectancies make long-term care insurance a prudent hedge for many middle-income people.

Cons: The wide variety of policies, types of coverage offered, price, and so forth makes it easy for you to get confused or scammed; cost is generally high; benefits often don't keep pace with rising costs—by the time you use your insurance, nursing home costs may be well over the daily indemnity benefit your policy pays.

TIP: **With certain life insurance policies, you can get the benefits of long-term care insurance without the high cost. Check to see if your life insurance policy has a *before-death option*. With this option, the insurance company will pay out the death benefit before the policyholder has died—to cover nursing home or long-term care. The cost? Only an annual charge of about $50 to $100 added to your regular insurance costs, which is substantially less than most long-term care insurance policy premiums. (See page 127 for more information on this provision.)**

▶ **The best time to buy long-term care insurance is when you're in late middle age.**

If you're in your 30s, 40s, or early 50s, don't waste your money buying long-term care insurance. You probably won't need long-term care for a number of years yet; by the time you do need it, you'll have spent quite a bit in insurance premiums.

If you're in your 70s or older, you'll be socked with extremely high prices, because you're in an age group more likely to be admitted for nursing home care.

The bottom line? Buy long-term care insurance when you're in your late 50s or early 60s. It's the wisest move for your money: Premiums don't start soaring until you reach 65, so you won't face prohibitively high premiums. Moreover, you're entering an age group that is statistically more likely to need long-term care—the odds of your having to go into a nursing home after the age of 65 are two out of five. Buying the insurance is a good way of avoiding a cash drain in your retirement years.

▶ **Don't assume you should buy long-term care insurance merely because it's popular or you're getting older.**

Yes, long-term care insurance is a good choice for many retirees. But it's certainly not right for everyone. You should *avoid* long-term care insurance if:

- *You are in your 30s or early 40s.* You're better off investing the money you would spend on insurance premiums. This way you can earn the money you might have to spend on nursing home care.

- *You can count on an informal support network to take care of you should you need long-term care.* Family, friends, and neighbors may provide you with the care you need. Also explore what community services are available to you. Church groups, meals programs, and local senior centers, for example, may offer the type of assistance you need—anything from visiting nurses to house-cleaning to elder day-care centers.

- *Your medical background is such that it's unlikely you'll need long-term care.* If your family medical history and your own medical profile point to a low probability that you will need long-term care, don't spend the money on insurance. But do check with your doctor first to get a professional opinion.

- *Your income is lower than $15,000 and you have less than $50,000 in assets* and thus may be eligible for Medicaid. Getting insurance may prevent you from getting Medicaid. Check to see what eligibility requirements your state has, by calling your state Medicaid number (listed under "State" in your local telephone directory).

▶ **Nursing home care is the aspect of Medicaid most useful to retirees. And under 1988 legislation, a married couple can use Medicaid to cover nursing home care costs *without* having to go broke.**

The Medicare Catastrophic Coverage Act of 1988 included Spousal Impoverishment Protection. Under this, a person entering a nursing home can go on Medicaid while his or her spouse keeps a house, assets (the dollar amount varies from state to state; as an example, in 1989 New York State allowed the spouse to keep up to $60,000 in assets), and an annual income (again, the dollar amount varies from state to state).

▶ **If you have more than the state limit in assets or if you are a widow or widower and want to protect your estate, you can still manage to qualify for Medicaid payment of nursing home care (not for home health or hospital care).**

The trick, of course, is protecting your assets—and to do this, you have to plan well in advance, because under the law, Medicaid can claim any assets you hold within *30 months* before applying. So you must protect your assets 30 months in advance. It's tricky—and some people consider it unethical. Proponents of this maneuvering, however, say it's just like knowing the ins and outs of the tax laws to get the best possible break on your taxes. Because of the complexity of this issue, you should seek qualified legal advice when planning to protect your assets. Here, however, is a brief rundown of the different steps you could take.

- Transfer the deed of your house to your children, but set up a *life estate*—which allows you to live there until you die.

- Transfer your money to exempt assets—in other words, spend it. Buy household goods, set up a funeral and burial plot fund, pay for household improvements.

- Transfer money to your children or others as gifts.

- Begin paying your children for services (driving, housecleaning, and any other service they provide you).

- Set up irrevocable trust funds. (For information on trust funds, see pages 291–92.)

SOURCE: An excellent book on how to qualify for Medicaid and have it pay for nursing home care is *Avoiding the Medicaid Trap,* by Arnold D. Budish (Henry Holt). Check for it at your local bookstore or call the publisher at 800-247-3912.

▶ **If you decide to buy long-term care insurance, take the following steps.**

First, be sure the insurance company is financially sound. Choose a company that has been rated highly by two of the following: A− or better by A. M. Best & Company, BBB or better by Standard & Poor's, or Baa or better by Moody's. To get ratings, ask your agent or check each company's insurance review at your local library.

Next, take the time to get the best policy possible. You choose the length of time before benefits begin (the waiting period or the deductible, depending upon the language of the policy), and you choose the length of time the benefits will cover.

For an adequate policy, you should choose:

A waiting period (or deductible) of no less than 20 days but no more than 90 days. The rule of thumb is that premiums go down as waiting periods go up. So if you choose less than 20 days, you'll be paying a great deal more, more than 90, and you'll be paying too much out of your own pocket. Furthermore, according to medical experts, most skilled care is not needed for more than 100 days. If your policy doesn't begin paying until after that, the premiums may indeed be low, but the benefits may never be paid out.

A benefit period of at least two years. This is the minimum length of time recommended by experts. Less than two years isn't worth your money.

TIP: **Check into group insurance plans such as AARP. Premium costs will be lower than those for individual plans, sometimes substantially lower—with savings of up to 30% reported.**

▶ **With so many different policies and different sorts of coverage, you have to be careful. To be sure you are getting the best coverage, look for the following provisions and clauses.**

It is difficult to wade through all the verbiage, sales talk, and polished sales packages put out by insurance companies. Nevertheless, bull through it all. You must be sure you're getting what you want—the best coverage for the least money.

The following features *aren't* available in every long-term care insurance policy, but they should be. The best policy for you should contain a number of things:

- *Coverage of all three levels of care:* Don't get a policy that omits one or more types of long-term care. You want coverage of skilled, intermediate, and custodial—in other words, complete, comprehensive coverage.

- *Guaranteed renewability:* With this provision, the policy can't be canceled as long as you meet your premium payments. Furthermore, the rate can't be increased unless the state okays across-the-board increases for all policyholders with the same coverage. (If you live in a state that follows the voluntary rules set by the National Association of Insurance Commissioners, this clause will be in the policy as a matter of course.)

- *Inflation-adjusted benefits:* This keeps benefits in sync with rising costs. While this feature may cost you quite a bit more, it's worth it. Since you're probably not going to be using your long-term care insurance for a number of years, this provision is a virtual necessity. By the time you need the insurance to cover nursing home costs, those costs will have ballooned. If possible, choose a policy with an inflation-adjustment formula that compounds the benefit from the previous adjusted amount (like inflation itself), not one that bases the increase on the original benefit, or one that allows for periodic inflation adjustment. And watch out—some policies offer "inflation-protection riders" that are not compounded but merely increase the benefit 5% to 6%. For this, your premium charge can go up 30% or more.

- *Home care provision:* This covers you for long-term health care in your home. Be careful—while many policies do have this provision as a regular benefit, others carry it as a rider, which means you pay an extra premium for home care coverage. As with policies in general, the dollar amount of coverage varies, but usually pays about half of the nursing home benefit—or about $40 daily on average.

- *Alzheimer's disease/Parkinson's disease coverage:* Get it in writing! Some policies don't cover Alzheimer's, Parkinson's, or stroke-induced dementia, which are the leading reasons people need nursing home care. Even if there's a clause containing the words "organically related disorder" (the industry term covering these diseases), be sure the policy *specifically* states that it covers Alzheimer's, Parkinson's, and dementia.

- *No prior hospitalization requirement:* Under many policies—some experts estimate up to 75%—you don't get covered for nursing home benefits unless your nursing home admission follows hospitalization (typically the requirement is nursing home admission within 30 days of a hospital or skilled nursing home stay of at least three consecutive days). Look for a policy without this exclusion—and avoid the policies that require a premium to waive the prior hospitalization requirement. What you want is a policy with *no* prior hospitalization required at no extra cost. (As with the guaranteed renewability provision, this provision will be in policies sold in states adhering to the NAIC recommendations.)

- *No exclusions for preexisting conditions:* Some policies won't give you coverage for a preexisting medical condition—that is, a condition for which you were given medical advice or treatment within six months before buying the policy. Avoid these and opt for a policy with no such exclusions.

- *Coverage in any health-care setting:* Be sure the policy doesn't just pay for stays at Medicare-certified nursing homes. Many are so limited. You're better off with flexibility and choice.

▶ **Finally—***read the fine print carefully!*

An obvious step, but one that many don't take. Horror stories abound about people who didn't receive the benefits they were led to believe they were due. A recent *New York Times* article mentioned a few cases: One woman in the hospital with Parkinson's disease and a severe lung infection had her claim turned down because she had not been in the acute-care section of the hospital—even though the hospital said she received acute-care treatment. Another woman had her policy canceled because she was hospitalized when she bought the policy and the insurance company explained that it didn't cover patients who were hospitalized when they bought the policy—even though the insurance agent collected the first premium payment in the woman's hospital room.

Remember: Don't get sidetracked by sales patter. And don't be falsely reassured by a company name. (For related information on long-term care, see Continuing Care Retirement Communities, page 350.)

SOURCE: The Health Insurance Association of America puts out a helpful free booklet, ***The Consumer's Guide to Long-Term Care Insurance.*** Write: Health Insurance Association of America, PO Box 41455, Washington, DC 20018.
Also useful is ***Long Term Care: A Dollars & Sense Guide*** (price, $6.95):

United Senior Health Cooperative, 1334 G Street, NW, Washington, DC 20055.

A good book on the topic is *Elder Care: Choosing & Financing Long-Term Care* (Nolo Press), by Joseph Matthews.

DISABILITY INCOME INSURANCE

▶ **Disability income insurance fits into retirement planning** *before* **you retire—chiefly to prevent you from having your retirement savings wiped out.**

It's one of the most overlooked types of insurance. But if you don't have disability insurance, you can find yourself without the retirement nest egg you've carefully saved. According to statistics, one in three people aged 30 to 65 become disabled for at least three months. The bottom line? Without disability insurance to cover the income you lose when you can't work, you'll be digging into your pockets and using retirement savings.

This is why disability should be part of your insurance package before you retire. Once you retire, disability becomes a less important aspect, since Medicare or your other health insurance will cover your medical expenses.

How it works: Disability income insurance covers unexpected injury or illness that prevents you from working. Most employees have some sort of disability coverage through their employer-provided insurance package. The typical disability plan pays a percentage of your salary—up to about 60%, up to a set monthly limit of $5,000 to $10,000. There are also individual and supplemental policies available, usually designed for people who are self-employed or for those who earn a high salary and want to augment their company plan. Even these plans don't provide full salary benefits, capping instead at about 70% to 80% of total salary. (Although you don't get full salary benefits with either group or individual disability, compare it with Social Security disability, which pays only about 25% of the maximum salary covered, $51,300.)

Costs and benefits vary from policy to policy. Among the factors affecting cost are the waiting period before payments start (as with long-term care insurance, the longer the waiting period, the lower the premiums); the length of benefits coverage (common lengths include coverage until you reach 65 or lifetime coverage).

There are special features that also affect cost, such as a residual-benefits clause, with which you get partial benefits for partial injuries, or an inflation protection (or cost-of-living adjustment) clause.

Pros: It makes sense to keep disability coverage if it's employer-provided. If you have very meager retirement savings, lifetime disability benefits may help you out.

Cons: If you are self-employed, you face high costs.

▶ **If you count on your employer to provide you with disability insurance, double-check the specifics of the insurance when you near your retirement time.**

For how long after you turn 65 or after you retire will you be covered by the disability insurance? *If you are retiring after you turn 65, it is very important to find this out.* Many plans—both employer-provided *and* private—automatically stop covering you after your 65th birthday.

Also check the stability of the disability income insurance plan. As with other forms of health insurance, more employers are cutting back or even terminating disability coverage. If this happens to you, consider buying private disability to carry you over to retirement. Again, you don't want to have to dip into your retirement savings to tide you through a period when you can't work.

▶ **If you intend to work part-time after you retire, also check the availability of employer-provided disability insurance.**

AUTO INSURANCE

▶ **When you're thinking about retirement or actually retired, one of the things you should be trying to do is scale back your expenses. One place you can do this is auto insurance.**

If you're like most people, you won't be driving as much after retirement. You won't be going to work every day, so you won't be relying on your car or following the same driving patterns you used to. This means you're not as much at risk for a car accident—which also means it might be a good idea to increase your auto insurance deductible. The higher your deductible, the lower your premium costs.

Another way to reduce auto insurance costs is to cut back or discontinue, if possible, your medical-payments coverage (which is voluntary coverage in no-fault states). This aspect of auto insurance covers necessary medical payments if you, others on your policy, or someone in your car is hurt in a car accident, or if you are injured in someone else's car. Again, since most retirees are driving less, they're less likely to be involved in a car accident—which means they won't be as likely to need this sort of coverage. Furthermore, your health insurance or Medicare and the health insurance of your passengers should cover the medical expenses incurred in an accident. (Note: There is one drawback to canceling medical-payments coverage. Uninsured passengers injured in your car will have to sue you to get coverage.)

Also see if you can drop uninsured motorist coverage. While this is mandatory in some states, in others it is voluntary. Uninsured motorist coverage covers you and your passengers if you are involved in an accident with an uninsured driver. As with the above, your health insurance or Medicare will probably take care of your medical expenses if this happens to you.

TIP: **Check about Senior Discounts. Many insurance companies offer 10% to 20% discounts for drivers over age 50. Also ask your insurance agent about other discounts offered—for nonsmokers, women, and so forth.**

HOMEOWNER'S INSURANCE

▶ **Because retirees live on fixed incomes, homeowner's insurance can make the difference between being able to replace your house and possessions when disaster strikes—and losing it all. Further, your house is probably a major asset—and you'll want to protect its value in case you need or want to sell.**

This is an often overlooked area of retirement planning, chiefly because most homeowners have their insurance and don't think about it except when they're paying their bills.

How it works: Depending upon the specific policy, homeowner's insurance can cover damage to your house or other personal residence, as well as damage to other structures on the property; damage to personal property; liability incurred when someone is injured on your property as a result of your negligence; your living expenses when your personal residence is left uninhabitable by a disaster covered in your policy (fire, hurricane, tornado, and so forth).

There are two common types of homeowner's insurance: *HO-3 (or "Special Form")* is the most popular, covering loss or damage to your house for all risks (except those specifically excluded, such as normal wear and tear and war), but covering little if any loss or damage to house contents. *HO-5 (or "All Risk")* is more comprehensive, covering both the house itself and the contents of the house from all risks (except, as with the other type of insurance, those risks specifically excluded).

TIP: **If you opt for the first type of insurance, HO-3, you can get a personal articles floater added to your policy for an additional premium. This floater will cover valuables you designate (jewelry, collectibles, and so forth) up to a set dollar amount. The added cost varies according to the appraised value of the items you're insuring.**

▶ **Shortly before you retire, go over your policy. This might be a good time to reassess what you have.**

Start by having your residence appraised. This will give you and your insurer a good idea of the base worth of your home. Next, go through your home and make an inventory of your possessions— this can be a written list, photographs, or videotape. Be sure to keep one copy of this inventory away from your residence, perhaps with your attorney or in a bank safe deposit box. This way, should your home be destroyed, you still have documentation of what you owned.

TIP: **If you have any special possessions—collectibles, antiques, artwork, or the like— have them appraised by an expert. You want to be sure you cover their worth.**

The type of policy you choose—or decide to keep—depends on how much money you want to spend, as well as how much you have to protect. Ask about special discounts or rates that are offered in specific cases. For example, nonsmokers often get discounts because risk of fire is substantially lower.

TIP: **Often if you install a burglar alarm, you can receive lower rates. Check it out. The initial investment for the alarm may pay off in lower premiums.**

Chapter 6

INVESTMENT: THE BASICS

INTRODUCTION

▶ **Now that you've evaluated your potential Social Security and pension benefits and your insurance needs and costs, you may be even more aware of the importance of investments in your retirement planning.**

For most of us, pensions and Social Security simply won't cover all our retirement costs. We must *invest* our savings to create a nest egg that will supplement our pensions and Social Security when we retire.

But how do we invest? What do we invest in? Once it was easy. Buy a few "blue chips"—stocks or bonds of a rock-solid U.S. corporation like U.S. Steel—and then sit back and collect the dividends or interest.

Times have changed, for better and for worse. First the good news. There are more ways of making money today than ever before. You can buy a stock or a bond, but you can also buy a mutual fund—a collection of stocks or bonds managed for you by professionals.

Or you can buy a "Ginnie Mae"—a different sort of bond that is made up of bits and pieces of thousands of mortgages. You can even buy options that allow you to bet on the performance of the stock market. And so on and on.

And now for the bad news. All of these new means of making money can make things very confusing for the average investor. And in today's uncertain markets, it can be tricky deciding which investment to pick. Maybe all you want to do is sit back and let others do the worrying for you. In this case, a mutual fund is probably your best bet. But which mutual fund? There are thousands. How can you tell the good from the bad?

▶ **This chapter and the following chapter are designed to cut through the jargon and help you decide the best possible investment plan for *your* retirement.**

This chapter covers investing *basics*—including such topics as investment planning, how to build a strong portfolio that meets your very specific needs, and how to find a stockbroker. Chapter 7 covers investing *specifics* and takes a look at the major investment vehicles— from money market accounts all the way to stocks, bonds, and tax-free municipals.

These two chapters will give you the ammunition you need to devise an investment strategy that will assure you the retirement funds you will need.

YOUR RETIREMENT AND INVESTMENT GOALS

▶ **The problem most investors face: They don't have a carefully considered investment plan.**

Maybe they buy what their broker recommends, or what the latest issue of *Money* magazine says is hot. They don't ask themselves: What am I doing? Where does this fit in with my investment plans? In other words, many investors make their investments without a long-term plan. This is haphazard investing. It usually leads to putting too much money into risky investments, or playing it too safe and overconcentrating in rock-solid but low-yielding investments. Either way these investors lose.

▶ **Take the time to develop an investment plan.**

Look before you leap into any new investment, and before you even consider buying anything—develop a plan. Work on creating a portfolio of investments that balances all your needs.

▶ **Developing a plan doesn't mean that you must master all the complexities of finance.**

It just means that you must take a commonsense look at your financial goals and spend a little time deciding how best to meet them. Even if you have very little money, you gain by developing an investment plan, one that gives you a greater return every year over the years. An extra percentage point or two on an investment, even a small one, adds up to a lot more money at retirement.

▶ **Planning your investments begins with goal setting.**

You may think your goals are obvious. You want enough money for retirement, period. But take a minute to reflect. As with most financial matters, people too often ignore the basics and then later get tripped up in the complexities. Starting simply is the best way of investing wisely.

As a retirement investor you actually have three interacting investment goals: preservation of principal, growth of principal, and income.

▶ **Goal 1:** *Preservation of principal*—**you want to keep and protect what money you've already got.**

It makes sense. And it sounds easy to do. Just stick your money into some sort of interest-bearing bank account or CD. There's a hitch, however. You've got to match or beat the inflation rate. Otherwise, perhaps slowly but always surely, the *value* of your principal will shrink and you won't meet your first goal. You'll actually lose some of your money in terms of buying power.

It's simple, it's obvious, but many people ignore this very basic idea—why else is there over $100 billion invested in low- or no-interest bank accounts?

EXAMPLE: Here's how inflation works against you. Assume inflation increases to 7% a year, and you have $1,000 invested in a CD paying 6% a year, compounded quarterly. After one year your $1,000 will have grown to $1,061.40. Sounds great. You've not only kept your $1,000, but you've made $61.40 more. But first there's inflation to consider. One year of 7% inflation means that to buy what $1,000 bought last year you'll need $1,070 this year. In other words, you'll have to add $70 to that $1,000 you invested, *just to keep even*. But at 6% compounded, you didn't. You added only $61.40. In real terms, in terms of buying power, you actually *lost* $8.60, the difference between $70 and $61.40. You lost almost 1 percent of the real value of your investment in one year.

Many people keep their savings in savings accounts for years. Losing 1 percent of your principal year after year adds up. And losing less than 1 percent also adds up. In either case it doesn't make sense. This section tells you how to avoid this all too common problem.

▶ **Goal 2:** *Growth of principal*—**or in other words, having your savings grow.**

Making your money grow is what investing is really all about. Chances are you don't have enough stashed away to live on during retirement. You don't want to just preserve what you've got, you want it to grow into a larger nest egg.

But how do you make your money grow? Should you put it in a CD? In a mutual fund? In stocks or bonds? In most cases, the best answer is to use all of them, as parts of a unified investment plan or, in other words, a balanced portfolio. The key to good investing is to diversify among various types of good investments, to create a mixed basket of investments, with some money in safer but lower-yielding instruments and some in higher-yielding but less safe investments. This section shows how to create such a diversified portfolio.

▶ **Goal 3:** *Income*—**whether from dividends, interest, or drawing down on your savings.**

After you retire, and sometimes before, you'll want a steady stream of money coming in from your investments to supplement your income from pensions, Social Security, and work. Here planning is extremely important, because the type of investment you pick now will determine how much income you will receive and how frequently you'll be getting a check. This section shows you how to choose among different income-yielding investments, and where they fit into your investment portfolio.

▶ **Mutual fund investors, like stock or bond market players, need to plan a balanced portfolio, just like everyone else.**

Mutual funds are one of the great financial inventions of the twentieth century. Instead of buying stocks or bonds one at a time, you buy shares of a mutual fund—a private corporation that buys and manages thousands or millions of shares. And you get a small piece of the profits it makes and the income it earns. No worrying over what stock to buy—the expert managers of the fund do most of the worrying for you. There's one problem, though. Many people seem to feel that buying one or two funds is all they should do for their retirement accounts. And they lose money because of this.

First of all, you should spread your money (and your risk) among several funds—and without a balanced plan you'll find it difficult to choose the right types of funds. Second, a plan allows you to *anticipate* what your fund should be doing and helps you get into the right funds and out of the wrong ones. Later in this chapter, several model portfolios show you how to balance the different types of funds in your fund portfolio. (Note: For a detailed look at funds and what to buy, see pages 200–213.)

▶ **Small investors, with only a few thousand dollars, need to plan a balanced portfolio as well.**

Too often, small investors just give up and leave their money rotting in a low- or no-yield bank account. If you've only got a little money now, don't make this mistake. If anything, you need planning *more* than does a well-to-do investor. But before jumping in:

- Like everyone else, make sure to keep a small nest egg handy in a bank account (a good rule of thumb is to try to keep up to three to six months' salary) or in some place where you can easily gain access to it in an emergency.

- With the rest of your money, create a balanced portfolio, as described in the next sections of this chapter. Don't worry if it's small—it will grow.

- Note that some investments work better for small investors than others. Many mutual funds accept investments as low as $500. So do banks—and savings bonds are another consideration. All of these are highlighted in Chapter 7.

HOW TO CREATE A BALANCED PORTFOLIO TO MEET YOUR RETIREMENT GOALS

▶ A *balanced* portfolio allows you to meet all your retirement goals—income, preservation of capital, and growth.

A portfolio is simply an itemized list of investments. A *balanced* portfolio is one that offsets riskier investments with safer ones, and offsets investments in one area with other investments in different areas. It's also balanced in terms of the goals mentioned above—with some investments oriented toward growth, some toward preservation, and some toward income. A balanced portfolio should keep some of your money in reserves for emergencies, and should keep some waiting for better opportunities. The mathematics of creating a near-ideal portfolio are daunting, but simple common sense and a few basic ideas can put you as close as you need to be. First, we'll look at the major balancing acts involved in portfolio building—and then we'll build retirement portfolios that meets your requirements. At the end of this section, we'll show three model portfolios—and show how you can adapt them to your own specific needs.

▶ Portfolios are balanced among the basic building blocks of finance.

These are the major investment instruments that will protect your money, yield you income, and give you growth in a balanced portfolio:

- *Stocks:* either as a collection of different stocks or in one or more stock mutual funds. Stocks usually make up the growth part of your portfolio, but such dividend-paying stocks as utilities can also give you income. Stocks are usually seen as riskier than other investments, but many "blue chips" are very safe.

- *Bonds:* either as a collection of individual bonds or in one or more bond funds or unit trusts. Bonds constitute the income part of your portfolio; as "fixed-income" investments they pay you a steady, predetermined income, year after year. Bonds are usually seen as safer than other investments, although interest rate fluctuations can hurt the value of your bond investments. Furthermore, some bonds, such as junk bonds, are highly risky.

- *Cash:* either in money market accounts or money market mutual funds. Usually, by placing your money in higher-yielding money market funds, you serve the main goal of keeping some liquid reserves and protecting your principal at rates above inflation. In this sense, keeping your money in these accounts is usually seen as very safe.

- *Other:* real estate, limited partnerships, gold, and precious metals. These specialized areas can vary widely in terms of risk and potential growth.

As you can see, all of these components serve your basic investment purposes to a greater or lesser degree. In most cases, they serve more than one purpose—a strong stock can give you growth *and* income, for example. Also, in most cases, the level of risk depends not just on the basic type of investment, but on the *specific* type as well. Government bonds are very safe, "junk" bonds usually aren't.

▶ Portfolios balance risk and reward.

There's a basic relationship between investment risks and rewards that usually holds: the more risk you are willing to accept, generally speaking, the greater your *potential* reward will be.

Obviously, you won't make a fortune sticking your money in a not-so-risky FDIC-backed bank CD (certificate of deposit) but you can make a bundle putting your money in the growth stock of a small company with a hot new product. Of course, if that product fails in the marketplace, the stock price could collapse and you could lose a bundle as well. There's an implicit risk in most investments that promise a better-than-average return.

▶ There are two main questions concerning risk: how much you can tolerate, and how much you need to accept.

Some investors are more risk-averse than others. You should know your own attitude toward risk—and know how much you can comfortably accept. If you're a nervous investor, be aware that to make your nest egg grow, you'll have to accept some risk, but you should lean toward safer investments. At the end of this section, we show a portfolio geared to risk-averse investors as well as one for moderate risk-takers. And in Chapter 7, we rate individual investments in terms of safety.

You should also realize that if you're far from your financial goals, you may have to accept more risk in order to increase your nest egg. However, in most cases, retirement investing should lean toward the conservative. In general:

- *Diversify your portfolio:* Don't buy only stocks, buy stocks *and* bonds. Don't buy only one specific bond, buy several. Don't buy one mutual fund, spread your risk among several. This makes sense. No matter how good one investment is, it can always collapse or just not earn you the returns you hoped for. Always put your eggs in more than one basket—always put your money in several different investments.

- *Reduce risk as you get closer to retirement:* The closer you get to retirement the less time you have to make up for losses from risky investments that fail.

- *Remember that the riskiest thing you can do is play it completely safe:* By sticking all or most of your investments in the safest—and usually lowest-yielding—investments (such as insured bank accounts), you miss out on growth. And, with inflation, you could actually lose money.

The chart on page 167 is a guideline of investment risk. Refer to it whenever you change or start an investment portfolio.

▶ **Before looking at the model portfolios, you must answer two final questions:**

First, *How much growth are you looking for?* Don't bother answering this question too specifically—just have a general idea. Remember, you should always think about growth, particularly if you're far away from retirement. But even *during* your retirement, inflation may heat up, or you may live much longer than expected, or your needs and expectations may change. In these cases, you'll need more money, which growth-oriented investing can provide. Best bet: Look at the moderate portfolio following and emphasize stocks, stock mutual funds, or stock and bond mutual funds. After checking the model portfolios below, also see more specific information on:

Stocks (page 213).

Mutual funds (page 200).

Growth stock funds (page 205).

TABLE 6.1: INVESTMENT PYRAMID

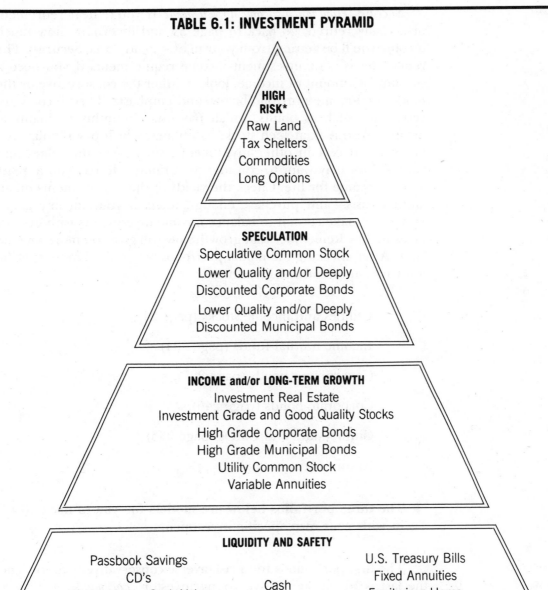

HIGH RISK*
Raw Land
Tax Shelters
Commodities
Long Options

SPECULATION
Speculative Common Stock
Lower Quality and/or Deeply
Discounted Corporate Bonds
Lower Quality and/or Deeply
Discounted Municipal Bonds

INCOME and/or LONG-TERM GROWTH
Investment Real Estate
Investment Grade and Good Quality Stocks
High Grade Corporate Bonds
High Grade Municipal Bonds
Utility Common Stock
Variable Annuities

LIQUIDITY AND SAFETY

Passbook Savings		U.S. Treasury Bills
CD's	Cash	Fixed Annuities
Life Insurance Cash Value		Equity in a Home
Money Market Funds		U.S. Government Notes and Bonds

*Financial risk is a function of uncertainty and price volatility. The distinction between high risk and speculation is one of increased uncertainty and price volatility. Deeply discounted bonds are speculative only in the sense that their prices will fluctuate. If held to maturity, deeply discounted bonds are securities for total return.

Source: Merrill Lynch

Second, *How much income do you need?* If you're near retirement or actually retired, go back to page 33 and determine how much income you'll be getting from your pension and Social Security. The remainder is your investment income requirement. If you need a substantial amount of income, look at either the conservative or the moderate income portfolio below, and emphasize fixed-income investments, such as bonds, which pay out a monthly or biannual income. Also look at such stocks as utilities, which pay regular dividends, and certain other investments, such as Ginnie Maes and CMOs. You may want to consider an annuity—to pay you a guaranteed income for life. Check the yields of these investments on an annual basis—and purchase enough to meet your income goals. However, make certain to balance income investments with growth investments. Remember that growth now will give you more income later. After checking the model portfolios below, read more specific information on income investments:

Utilities and income stocks (page 213).

Income mutual funds (page 204).

Government bonds (page 227).

Corporate bonds (page 246).

Ginnie Maes and CMOs (page 236).

Annuities (page 258).

▶ **The three portfolios below are models for you to use and fill in with your own specific investments.**

The first portfolio is for a risk-averse conservative investor, and the last is for an aggressive young investor. *The middle portfolio is recommended for most investors—it best balances growth, income, and safety.* Note that you need not necessarily use just one portfolio all the time—some investors follow a dynamic portfolio strategy, starting aggressively when young, leaning toward moderation during middle age, and ending with a conservative portfolio at retirement. Others argue that a middle strategy is best for most people of all ages. What's the best strategy? The one you're most comfortable with.

The portfolios are listed by goals, with the approximate mixes of investments that fit these goals. Page numbers show where to find more details about the specific types of investments.

A VERY CONSERVATIVE RETIREMENT PORTFOLIO

Principal goals:

To preserve capital and to provide income—but note that this portfolio also provides some growth. This is the sample portfolio with the least risk, least volatility, and lowest return.

Best for: those nearing retirement or in retirement (usually aged in their late 50s on up) and those who are already asset-rich and are also risk-averse.

Where to Put Your Investment Money

Put 20% to 40% in cash, money market funds, and related investments. Key goals: maintaining cash reserves and preserving capital, while earning some income. Go for the upper limit when markets look extremely vulnerable and experts are beginning to talk about recessions and layoffs. Concentrate on the safest funds that buy only U.S. Treasury securities; but for more yield you may want to consider putting some money in funds that invest in other money market instruments. And for complete ease of access in case of emergency, put some money into a local bank money market account. One major disadvantage with this much money tied up in cash: You lose out on potential growth.

For more information on this investment component, see:

Savings accounts (page 185).

Money market accounts (page 188).

Money market funds (page 190).

Short-term bond funds (page 233).

U.S. Treasury Bills (page 195).

CDs (page 197).

Put 20% to 40% in bonds or bond funds. Key goal: income, combined with preservation of capital. Go for the upper limit when it looks as if interest rates are falling to lock in current high rates. Go for the lower limit when it looks as if rates are rising; wait to buy more later. Smaller savers in particular should consider beginning with U.S. Savings Bonds, Bank Certificates of Deposit, and Treasury Bond mutual funds. A nice way of long-term saving is to buy a zero-coupon bond. Others may buy U.S. Treasury Bonds, notes, high-rated tax-free municipal bonds, and conservative corporate bond funds as well.

At retirement, to assure yourself a guaranteed income, you may also consider buying an immediate annuity. For more information on this investment component, see:

U.S. Savings Bonds (page 227).

U.S. Treasury Bonds (page 230).

GNMAs, etc. (page 236).

Zero-coupon bonds (page 242).

Corporate bonds (page 246).

Tax-free municipal bonds (page 250).

Annuities (page 258).

Put 25% to 35% in stocks or stock funds. Key goals: growth, income. Buy mostly utilities for dividend income and blue chips for steady growth. Aim for the upper limit when it looks as if stocks are poised for growth. For tax-deferred growth, you may wish to consider a deferred variable annuity investing in stock funds. For more information on this investment component, see:

Stocks (page 213).

Mutual funds (page 200).

Annuities (page 258).

Put 5% in precious metals or precious metal funds. Key goal: to "hedge" against the "what ifs" of a major stock market or money market collapse. For more, see:

Precious metals (page 272).

A MODERATE RETIREMENT PORTFOLIO

Principal goal:

Growth. Also seeks to balance growth with safer investments and provide income. This portfolio involves a bit more risk, more volatility, and higher returns.

Best for: those who want to emphasize relatively safe growth throughout their preretirement and retirement years, those with 10 years or more before retirement (usually under 55), and older preretirees with substantial sources of guaranteed income (pensions and so forth).

Where to Put Your Investment Money

Put 40% to 60% in stocks or stock funds. Key goals: growth, some income. Diversify among different types of stocks, including income foreign stocks or foreign stock funds in the portfolio. Look for growth stocks, particularly blue-chip (stalwarts in the market) growth stocks, income stocks, some speculative growth stocks. For tax-deferred growth, you may want to consider a deferred variable annuity investing in stock mutual funds. For more information on this investment component, see:

Stocks (page 213).

Mutual funds (page 200).

Annuities (page 258).

Put 20% to 30% in bonds or bond funds. Key goal: income. Same general strategy as with the more conservative portfolio. Go for the upper limit when it looks as if interest rates are falling to lock in current high rates. Go for the lower limit when it looks as if rates are rising; wait to buy more later. Smaller savers in particular should consider beginning with U.S. Savings Bonds, Bank Certificates of Deposit, and Treasury Bond mutual funds. For long-term savings consider buying a zero-coupon bond. Others may buy U.S. Treasury Bonds, notes, high-rated tax-free municipal bonds, and conservative corporate bond funds as well. Those in retirement may want to consider buying an immediate annuity to guarantee long-term income. For more information on this investment component, see:

U.S. Savings Bonds (page 227).

U.S. Treasury Bonds (page 230).

Ginnie Maes, etc. (page 236).

Tax-free municipal bonds (page 250).

Zero-coupon bonds (page 242).

Annuities (page 258).

Put 15% in cash and money market funds. Key goal: cash reserves, preservation of capital. For more information on this investment component, see:

Savings accounts and money market accounts (page 185).

CDs (page 197).

Zero-coupon bonds (page 242).

Annuities (page 258).

Put 5% to 10% in precious metals funds. This is your "hedge" portion. For more information on this investment component, see:

Precious metals (page 272).

Put 10% in real estate. Currently most real estate investments are in the doldrums. Nevertheless, some investments will continue to do well—and now might be the time to buy. For more information on this investment component, see:

Real estate (page 267).

AN AGGRESSIVE RETIREMENT PORTFOLIO

Principal goal:

Growth. Safety is not ignored, but this type of investor seeks safety in the knowledge that over the long term, principal will grow substantially. This portfolio has high risk, high volatility—and the highest potential returns.

Best for: those with 20 years or more before retirement who are not risk-averse and who will not need the money they invest, and for others with substantial assets elsewhere.

The aggressive investor will make decisions about the best way to allocate assets and will revise those decisions as the markets fluctuate. A speculative investor should be highly attuned to the current state of the investment markets and his or her investments and should know when and whether to switch among the various investment options.

Where to Put Your Investment Money

Put 25% in large growth stocks or stock funds. Key goal: growth. For more information on this investment component, see:

> Stocks (page 213).
>
> Mutual funds (page 200).

Put 25% in smaller growth stocks or stock funds. Key goal: growth. For more information on this investment component, see:

> Stocks (page 213).
>
> Mutual funds (page 200).

Put 25% in high-yield income securities. Key goals: high income, growth. Consider buying more volatile long-term bonds, some lower-rated (and higher-yielding) bonds, some intermediate-term bonds. You may aggressively trade bonds, including zero-coupons, for capital gains. For more information on this investment component, see:

> U.S. Treasury Bills and Bonds (pages 195, 230).
>
> Ginnie Maes, etc. (page 236).
>
> Tax-free municipal bonds (page 250).
>
> Annuities (page 258).
>
> Zero-coupon bonds (page 242).

Put 5% to 20% in cash money market. Key goal: capital preservation. Even aggressive portfolios should maintain at least this amount of cash or near cash equivalents. At the same time, a market timer might switch a large percentage—up to 80%—into cash if other markets seem headed for recession. For more information on this investment component, see:

Savings accounts and money market accounts (pages 185, 188).

CDs (page 197).

Zero-coupon bonds (page 242).

Put up to 10% in real estate. You may want to take some chances with real estate investment trusts, currently at low prices. For more information on this investment component, see:

Real estate (page 267).

Put 5% to 10% in precious metals. See:

Precious metals (page 272).

▶ **How to get a tailor-made retirement portfolio.**

If you're not comfortable doing it yourself, there are many experts only too glad to do one for you—usually for a fee.

Essentially, they'll ask you questions to determine your risk profile, get an idea of pension, Social Security, and other benefits to estimate your retirement income needs. They usually plug the numbers and the information into a computer program. Then they'll suggest specific investments and a buying strategy.

Most full-service brokers, many financial planners, many discount brokers, and major accounting firms can do this for you. For more on how to choose these financial planners, see Financial Planners (page 38) and the section on Stockbrokers below. The mutual fund T. Rowe Price has a detailed portfolio planner as well; for information, contact: T. Rowe Price, 100 East Pratt St., Baltimore, MD 21202-1090 (800-638-5609).

HOW TO BUY INVESTMENTS FOR YOUR PORTFOLIO

▶ **Once you've decided in general what kind of investments you want, you have many options as to where to purchase them.**

Once you simply went to your local stockbroker. Today, you have more of a choice. You can buy stocks, bonds, and other investment instruments via:

- *Some banks:* Now that the barriers of the Glass-Steagall Act are falling down, banks are allowed to sell bonds, stocks, and mutual funds to non–trust account customers. Key advantages: convenience, automatic movement of your money from a bank account into your brokerage account, fairly low rates (on a trade of $10,000, a bank broker will usually charge about 1%, versus the 2% a full-service broker charges). Note that bank *trust* departments, however, charge full-service rates. Key disadvantages: Banks are new to the business, services or research may be limited, and some banks are facing serious financial problems.

- *Some financial planners:* Not recommended as a means of buying investments. Key advantage: convenience. Disadvantages: financial planning is a little-regulated field—so you have to be careful in deciding whom to trust. Moreover, the planner may get commissions from brokers or funds for your investments, and may therefore be somewhat biased. One option: Get advice from a financial planner, but buy the investments on your own.

- *Mutual funds:* Recommended for retirement investing. This is the major starting point for many investors, who can buy a wide variety of funds, some specializing in money market, others in stocks, in bonds, in stocks *and* bonds, and in tax-free bonds. Investing is easy—usually you start by picking up the phone and calling the fund. Brokers and banks also sell funds. (For more on how to find and pick the right funds, see Mutual Funds on page 200.)

- *Stockbrokers:* Recommended for retirement investing. Brokers can sell you virtually any type of investment, including mutual funds and annuities, and of course individual stocks and bonds. There are many factors to consider when choosing a broker.

▶ **Not all brokers are alike. Here's how to pick the one for you.**

There are three basic types of brokers: full-service brokers, discount brokers, and deep-discount brokers. The basic differences between the three are cost and the range of services offered. Whatever the size of discount offered, reputable brokers are insured against losses by the Securities Investor Protection Corporation (SIPC) for $500,000 in cash and securities (but no more than $100,000 in cash), and often by other insurance as well. The SIPC also offers you limited protection against broker fraud. Here are some details to consider before deciding which type of broker to call.

Full-Service Brokers

These are usually the big names of finance—Merrill Lynch, Prudential, Dean Witter Reynolds. They charge the most but in return offer the most services, including investment advice, newsletters, personalized attention, and new investment products. Is the investment advice worth the cost? For those with honest, smart brokers it may very well be. The authors maintain an account with a top-notch full-service broker. On the other hand, full-service brokers are salespeople who earn a commission on what you buy and sell; their advice may be somewhat biased. They may encourage you to buy and sell more than you need to, or encourage you to buy more expensive investment products (with higher commissions).

Pros: *Personalized attention.* If you have a good broker, he or she can provide recommendations tailored precisely to your needs. *Expertise.* A good broker may know the market much better than you do and help you make a lot of money by his or her advice. *Research.* Full-service brokerages have in-house analysts, who recommend stocks for clients; brokers will send you specific research, as well as general investment newsletters and advice. *Convenience.* Large brokerages offer "one-stop" financial shopping—you can put all of your money in various investments (stocks, bonds, funds, IRA accounts, and so forth) under one umbrella; many full-service brokers have offices nationwide. *Range.* Most offer a very wide range of services and products. A final advantage for retirees: Many offer special services for elderly retirees. For example, Merrill Lynch has introduced a telephone buying system for the hearing-impaired; Shearson is training its brokers in the concerns of the elderly.

Cons: *Cost.* Much higher—usually twice that of a discount broker, four times that of a deep-discount broker. This can add up. In some cases, you will get biased advice. There's always the risk of a broker "churning" your account—buying and selling frequently so as to earn more commissions.

Where to find one: Virtually anywhere. The largest five retail brokers are:

Dean Witter

Paine Webber

Prudential Securities

Merrill Lynch

Shearson Lehman

Discount Brokers

They sell you stock at lower commissions—usually about 50% less than regular full-service brokerages. On a typical $10,000 stock trade, a discount broker will charge you about 1% or $100, whereas a full-service broker may charge you 2%, or $200, or more. Discount brokers are cheaper because they forgo in-house research and (usually) advice—normally they simply execute the trades you request on the telephone. Like full-service brokerages, they're insured and regulated by the SEC, so your money is as safe (although, as with regular brokers, expertise and business ethics may vary). Major discount brokers offer a wide range of services.

Pros: *Cost.* The savings add up the more trades you do. *Convenience.* Major discount brokers have offices around the country.

Cons: As with full-service brokers, there's usually a minimum commission charge (about $50), so if you're only making small trades, there's no real cost advantage. In addition, you may want the advice, analysts' research, and attention to your investments you can get from a *good* full-service broker—this can pay off in times of market trouble, such as the minicrash in 1987.

Where to find one: Here are three major discount brokers, with their central office phone numbers.

Fidelity Brokerage (800-544-7272).

Charles Schwab (415-627-7000).

Quick and Reilly (212-943-8772).

Deep-Discount Brokers

They charge you about one-half the rate of a discount broker, one quarter the rate of a full-service broker on most trades. On a $10,000 stock transaction, for example, expect to pay half a percent, or $50. Deep discounters vary greatly in size; some maintain many offices in various regions, others are one-office firms. But they buy and sell stocks on the same electronic systems used by full-service and discount brokers. They are also insured by the SIPC. Deep discounters are often used by stock market pros, who know what they want and don't want or need advice.

Pros: *Cost.* Usually about one-quarter the standard rate. According to one expert some deep discounters, because they deal frequently with skilled traders, are particularly good at getting you the best trades.

Cons: As with discount brokers above. Also, they offer a more limited range of services.

Where to find one: Mercer, Inc., publishes a listing of discount brokers, along with the fees they charge for various typical services. Write or call: Mercer Inc., 80 Fifth Avenue, New York, NY 10011 (212-807-6800).

SOURCE: *Investing at a Discount: Saving on Commissions, Management Fees and Costs,* by Mark Coler, president of Mercer, Inc.

▶ **Just in case: Where to go if you have a problem with your broker.**

If you're having trouble with your broker, take action! First speak to the supervisor, and if you don't get satisfaction, complain to: Office of Consumer Affairs, Securities and Exchange Commission, 450 Fifth Street NW, Washington, DC 20549 (202-272-7440).

Disputes in the stock market are usually arbitrated. In most cases, you don't go to court, you go to the Arbitration Department, National Association of Securities Dealers, 33 Whitehall Street, New York, NY 10004 (212-858-4488). Or you can go to the arbitrator associated with the market where your stock is traded. *For the New York Stock Exchange,* contact the Arbitration Director, New York Stock Exchange, 11 Wall Street, New York, NY 10006. *For the American Stock Exchange,* contact the Arbitrations Hearings Department,

American Stock Exchange, 86 Trinity Place, New York, NY 10006.

Just recently, the New York State Court of Appeals ruled that if you have a dispute with a broker, you may now go to the *American Arbitration Association* (generally considered the most objective for small investors) if:

- Your contract is governed by New York state law.

- Your contract does not say that arbitration must start with a stock exchange arbitrator or that of the NASD.

SOURCE: *Lies Your Broker Tells You,* by Thomas Saler, a former stockbroker (Walker, $19.95), helps you cut through the sales hype.

Newsletters

▶ **Many people look to mutual fund and stock market newsletters to help them pick the right fund or stock for the right time.**

This is not necessarily a bad idea—but be careful. Think about it before jumping in.

Newsletter writers are (fallible) human beings. Many are wrong. Many are wrong frequently.

Be aware that many people find newsletters addicting, and wind up subscribing to three or more and following three or more conflicting investment strategies.

The better way to approach newsletter investing: Pick the one with your investment philosophy and stick with it, at least for a while. On the positive side, there are some top-rated newsletters out there that deliver streetwise, top-notch advice. But how can you pick the right one out of the hundreds out there?

First decide what kind of investor you are or want to be. As a retiree you probably don't intend to invest superaggressively. So you'll be looking at conservative or relatively conservative publications.

Now you'll have to pick a newsletter. One way is to first check *The Hulbert Guide to Financial Newsletters* (316 Commerce Street, Alexandria, VA 22314, 800-443-0100, ext. 459, monthly, $135 for 12 issues). This is a centralized guide to newsletters. It lists 120 major newsletters and tracks their performance. Pick the one that matches your risk and investment philosophies with your performance expectations.

If the newsletter is new and has no long-term track record, you can track its stock or bond picks on your own—and match its recommendations against their performance on the market for a number of months.

Take out a trial subscription—you can often get one for a low price. Or write or call and ask for a back issue as a prospective subscriber. Most newsletters will send you a free back issue or two— check the issue to see if you're getting what you need: sound, good, clear advice.

TABLE 6.2: TWELVE RULES OF INVESTING

Investing can't be summed up in 10 pages—or 500—but the basics are fairly simple. Most people go wrong when they ignore them. Below are a few more basic rules of solid investing. Keep them in mind and you should do well.

Rule 1

Invest holistically. Take a combined approach to investing—include all your assets when making investment decisions. For example, if you have a guaranteed government pension, take this into account when determining the amount of risk you can afford to take.

Rule 2

Diversify: Don't put all your eggs into one basket. It's obvious: If one investment lags behind the rest, you're not stuck making less; if one investment collapses, you won't have lost everything. Don't put all your stock market money into one stock or one category of stock. With mutual funds, spread your money among several different types of funds. Not diversifying is a common failing of investors.

Rule 3

Shelter your investments. Don't pay taxes when you don't have to. Put investments earning high income into tax-deferred accounts, such as 401(k) plans or IRAs. By deferring taxes and reinvesting, you'll increase your retirement nest egg much faster. For example, $2,000 invested yearly and compounded at 8% grows to $17,169 in 20 years—but with taxes deferred it can become almost $100,000. Note: Don't put your emergency cash reserves in sheltered accounts. You may need this money fast.

Rule 4

Don't squeeze investments for yield. A common mistake of pseudosophisticated investors is searching for that extra half-point of yield on an investment. Examples abound. A recent article in a major magazine spent several paragraphs telling readers how and where to get an extra half-point or point on their bank savings account—at the possible cost of less safety. If you've got $10,000 in your account, note that 0.5% of that is $50. Is an extra $50 a year worth the worry and hassle of moving your savings account to an unknown bank across the country?

Rule 5

Emphasize total return, not yield. Yield is the percentage return you receive as an investor, based on the amount you invested or the current market value of what you invested. Of course you should look for high-yielding investments, but not at the expense of something called total return—which is the increase in value of your investment (or market appreciation) plus any dividends or interest payments over a year or a period of years. For example, many very risky investments are currently very high yielding—but the odds on an adequate total return over the long run aren't good. In other words, you may lose your principal, see it shrink, or see other investments overtake yours.

Rule 6

Don't lose out on good returns in an effort to avoid risk. According to a recent survey, this is the most common mistake today's investors make. Afraid of the wide swings in the stock and bond markets, they play it safe and put all their money into supersafe money market funds. They violate rules 1 and 2; worse yet, as explained earlier, these investors usually see their principal whittled away by inflation.

Rule 7

Try dollar cost averaging. Put the same amount of money on a regular basis into the stock market or into mutual funds of stocks—regardless of price. For example, plan to invest $1,000 every quarter buying the same stocks, whether the market is up or down. Why does it work? You buy more shares of the stock with your $1,000 when the price is low, and when it rises, you've got more shares to produce a profit. And you keep on buying when it's high—because, for one thing, the stock could go still higher. According to Louis Engel in *How to Buy Stocks,* if you dollar cost averaged, "You could have made a profit of 90% on the stocks listed on the New York Stock Exchange over almost any period of four or five years you might want to pick in the last quarter century."

Rule 8

Watch your investments. Even if you've put all your money in excellently managed mutual funds, even if you have a full-time financial planner, it still pays to watch your money. Mutual fund managers change, financial planners can be wrong, and both can misjudge your financial goals.

Rule 9

If you don't understand it at all, you shouldn't invest in it. Though frequently ignored, this rule saves you money. This doesn't mean you have to be an expert, just enough of an informed layperson to know that maybe the high-yielding bond fund with safe-sounding Bb bonds is actually a junk bond fund and carries a great deal of risk. (Though it was in your school days, a B is not a high grade in the bond market.) If you don't know, do a little research before buying. Note that you can't escape this rule by buying mutual funds—even here you should know the fund's type, record, fee structure, and current strategy.

Rule 10

Don't overreact. Many people read the papers, panic, and sell everything—and lose more than if they had stayed in. This is particularly true for those with retirement accounts, who should be relatively conservatively invested anyway. For example, if you had a strong, blue-chip stock portfolio before the crash of 1987 and hadn't sold, you would have saved commissions, suffered a paper loss on Black Tuesday and a strong recovery by Thursday, and several months later your stocks would be at *higher* prices. *Volatility,* the ups and downs of the market, averages out in the long run. The odds that you'll lose money in the stock market go down the longer you hold stocks.

Rule 11

Don't overinvest. Many people overdiversify their investments: They buy a little of everything. In general, you are better off keeping your investments as limited as possible, given the right amount of diversification. This way, you will be able to keep on top of your investments. You will know what is happening—and when to get out. At the very least, you won't have to spend as much time mastering many different investments.

Rule 12

Don't assume the future will be like the past. Many investors assume current trends will continue unchanged. They are often wrong. For example, gold skyrocketed in the 1970s, giving a total return of 21% for the entire decade, far better than stocks or bonds. But in the 1980s, the same metal earned a total return of 2.8%, far worse than stocks or bonds.

Books

▶ **Many excellent books have been written on investing, and many are excellent sources for retirement investors.**

In general, the better the book, the less flashy the title. Avoid the "How to Make $1,000,000 with Stock Market Futures in One Year" type of book—generally, the author is the only one making the million, via book royalties. Some excellent general sources:

- *Marshall Loeb's 1991 Money Guide,* by Marshall Loeb, the managing editor of *Fortune* magazine (Little, Brown, 1990). A definitive guide to almost every aspect of personal money management. Highly recommended.

- *The Money Manual,* by Peter Passell, financial columnist for *The New York Times* (Prentice-Hall, 1991). A superb, concise, easy-to-read, and authoritative guide to investments, with useful tables, lists of the best funds and brokers, and savvy investment advice. Highly recommended.

- *Still the Only Investment Guide You'll Ever Need,* by Andrew Tobias (Bantam Books, 1987, $4.95). A modern classic, chatty, easy to read, yet authoritative. Perfect for a beginning investor, with a deceptively simple style; it's excellent for the sophisticated as well.

- *How to Buy Stocks,* by Louis Engel and Brendan Boyd (Bantam Books, 1983, $4.95). Another classic, first published in 1953 and updated since. Calm and authoritative, it gives you an outline of the stock market, explains the ins and outs of stock investing, and shows how slow, steady stock market investing is still the best way to go—even in the face of extraordinary volatility.

Chapter 7

INVESTMENT: THE SPECIFICS

INTRODUCTION

This chapter deals with the specific types of investment that may be part of your retirement portfolio.

In each case, we explain what the investment is, strategies for investment, and how and where to buy it. You can read this chapter all at once to get an overview of the different investment vehicles available to you, or you can use it like an encyclopedia, referring to the appropriate sections after your broker has recommended a particular investment vehicle.

Investments for the Cash Reserves Portion of Your Portfolio

▶ **Keep cash reserves for emergencies, and as a parking place for your money.**

Try to keep from three to six months' salary in an easily accessible account—just in case. Many times, however, you'll want to keep far more in these accounts. You may be waiting for the right time to invest in the stock market, you may be in retirement and drawing down the money, or you may just be a conservative investor. The investments below—savings and money market accounts, money market funds, and Treasury Bills—meet these needs.

Bank Certificates of Deposit are also included here, although they are not liquid like the other investments. However, you can maintain very short-term CDs as well as longer-term CDs: They're a good area for savings.

SAVINGS ACCOUNTS

▶ **Savings accounts were the starting place for most people planning retirement, and are a parking place for financial reserves.**

The first step in any retirement investment strategy is obvious—accumulating enough money to begin investing. And throughout your lifetime, it will always be essential to keep at least some of your money easily and immediately available and safe—a financial reserve to cover emergencies. Most people begin with a savings account. However, there are now higher-yielding alternatives to savings accounts, such as money market accounts and funds, and for some, short-term bond funds. These are all covered in this chapter.

What they are: *Savings accounts* are held in banks, savings and loan institutions (S&Ls), or credit unions. They are called "fixed-return" accounts; they offer a specified, fixed rate on the principal, or money you invest, as set by law. Recent rates were 5.5% for a passbook account, 5.1% for a NOW account, and a bit more at credit unions.

Banks, S&Ls, and credit unions offer regular statements on the money you deposit in savings accounts, easy deposits (sometimes with low minimums), and very easy withdrawals. Savings accounts in federally chartered banks, S&Ls, or credit unions are insured for up to $100,000 per individual per bank by the federal government through the Federal Deposit Insurance Corporation (FDIC) and other federal agencies (and more if you open separate accounts such as testamentary trusts).

Another type of account, called a *NOW* account, or *Negotiable Order of Withdrawal* account, allows you to earn interest on your checking account. Some people put their money in these instead of savings accounts. However, NOW accounts are usually so loaded with fees and restrictions that you're better off tying your savings account to your checking account and forgoing this option.

The newest wrinkle on savings accounts is *forced savings accounts*. These accounts offer you higher rates; in return you must agree to make regular deposits on a timetable.

Pros: Savings accounts are convenient and easy to set up. As long as the institution holding your account is federally insured, your money (up to $100,000) is safe.

Cons: Low rates. You can earn much higher returns on your money elsewhere. In fact, one of the most common mistakes retirees make is keeping overly large sums of money (or *all* of their money) in savings accounts and missing out on higher-yielding investments. If the inflation rate is near or above your savings account interest rate, you'll actually be *losing* money in terms of purchasing power.

Savings Account Investment Strategy

▶ **Savings accounts are a starting point for many investors.**

The money put in savings accounts falls in the most conservative cash portion of your portfolio. Use savings accounts for:

- *Initial investing:* Savings accounts are useful for very small investors because the minimum needed to open an account is usually very low (sometimes as low as several hundred dollars).

- *Reserve funds:* Always keep three to six months' salary in a safe, easily accessible place for emergencies. Money market accounts are better because the interest is higher—but some people prefer to keep a portion ($1,000 or so) in a savings account.

▶ **This said, remember that the low, fixed savings account rate works to your disadvantage if inflation is medium or high.**

Best bet: Look at money market accounts and money market funds. These offer higher interest.

How to Set Up a Savings Account

▶ **Setting up a savings account is easy.**

Over 90% of all investors in the United States have had a savings account, which is opened simply by going to your local bank, filling in the required forms, and depositing a minimum sum of money.

▶ **Be sure that the institution holding your savings account is federally insured.**

Your money in a federally insured bank is safe up to $100,000 *per person* in the event of a bank failure. You'll get your money back. Note that if you have $200,000 in two different accounts at the same bank you're only covered for $100,000 (unless this money is placed in a joint account or a testamentary trust—check with your banker or lawyer for details)—but if you have $100,000 in each of *two* different federally chartered banks, S&Ls, or credit unions you're fully covered.

The federal insurance to look for is:

- *For banks:* FDIC or Federal Deposit Insurance Corporation.

- *For savings and loan institutions (savings banks):* FSLIC or Federal Savings and Loan Insurance Corporation.

- *For credit unions:* National Credit Union Share Insurance Fund.

Some state-chartered banks and credit unions are insured by state agencies instead of these federal insurers. It's best to avoid these institutions, even though they may offer higher savings rates. Reason: it's less certain that state or other insurance will reimburse you if your bank defaults.

▶ **Check the financial health of your bank before depositing your money.**

Even though federal insurance guarantees your principal up to $100,000, you're better off placing your money in a strong bank. So far, depositors at failed banks have had to wait a maximum of three days to get their money; nevertheless, why take chances, particularly now with problems at many more banks? Here's how to check bank safety:

- *For banks:* Write to the Federal Deposit Insurance Corporation, Disclosure Group, 500 17th Street NW, Washington, DC 20429. Reports on each bank cost $2.50.

- *For savings and loan institutions (savings banks):* Write to OTS, Information Services Division, 1700 G Street NW, Washington, DC, 20552.

- *In both cases:* Don't just rely on the reports, since the government information could be out of date.

A quick way to check, for a fee, is to call one of several private bank rating services, including:

- *Veribanc:* 800-44BANKS. Cost is $10 for one bank, $3 for each additional bank.

- *Sheshunoff Information Services:* 800-456-2657.

- *Bauer Financial Reports:* 305-441-2062.

- *IDC Financial Publishing:* 800-544-5457.

TIP: **Many banks now offer special packages for senior citizens—which can mean people as young as 50. They may include higher interest rates on CDs or savings accounts, although requirements such as minimum balances may be stiff. Many banks also offer free checking for senior citizens without requirements.**

MONEY MARKET DEPOSIT ACCOUNTS

▶ **Money market accounts are an easy way of making more than you would with a savings account, without sacrificing safety.**

Many investors now make deposits in money market accounts instead of savings accounts. They're a better alternative for retirement (and other) accounts because your money earns more.

What they are: Money market deposit accounts are another type of bank deposit account you can open with a minimum balance, usually around $1,000. They're convenient: They allow you transfer and withdrawal privileges—although usually with certain limitations on the number of checks you may write, or with minimums on the amount. But instead of a fixed savings account rate of 5.5% or so per year, they pay you a fluctuating percentage based on the rate the banks earn by investing the pooled money in the money market (which is a financial market of short-term investments in bank, government, and corporate debt). Usually (but not necessarily) the rate you are paid is higher than a savings account rate, hovering under the six-month Treasury Bill rate. If your balance falls below the minimum, your rate drops to a lower passbook rate. If these accounts are held in federally insured banks, S&Ls, or credit unions, you will fall under the federal $100,000 insurance per individual depositor per bank.

Pros: A higher return than a fixed-rate savings account—but just as safe, providing the bank is insured. They are a good area for reserves, and like savings accounts, they're as convenient as walking to your local bank.

Cons: You can earn higher returns elsewhere. There are often minimum balance requirements.

Money Market Account Investment Strategy

▶ **Put your reserve money into a money market account instead of a savings account.**

In terms of safety and liquidity, money market accounts from federally insured banks are as good as savings accounts, and you can use them as both a reserve fund and a starting point for investing. Even though rates fluctuate, rates are almost always higher than savings account rates. And if they do fall, just take your money out.

How to Set Up a Money Market Account

▶ **Put your money in well-run federally insured banks.**

See *How to Set Up a Savings Account* on page 186 for more information.

The mechanics of setting up an account and finding a strong federally insured bank are the same as for savings accounts.

▶ **Money market account rates vary among banks.**

The highest money market rates being paid by regional and national banks are published in the financial section of most major newspapers. *Money* magazine also publishes a monthly listing. Nowadays there's no problem with opening an account at an out-of-state bank offering better rates. Look for consistency: Some banks "tease" by offering high opening rates, then dropping them several months later.

MONEY MARKET FUNDS

▶ **Many retirees now put some of their cash reserves into money market funds.**

Money market funds are private mutual funds that are a bit riskier—and higher yielding—than savings or money market accounts. Because so many retirees have shares of money market funds, this section will look at them in detail.

What they are: Money market funds are mutual funds that invest in money market instruments. (See Mutual Funds, page 200.) Instead of depositing your money in a bank, you buy shares of a mutual fund, which is privately managed. As with money market bank accounts, your money is pooled with that of other investors and put into the money market. The money market is a financial market for banks, corporations, government agencies, and funds, which buy and sell a wide variety of *short-term* government and corporate securities, such as U.S. Treasury Bills, commercial paper (short-term commercial debt), and longer-term bonds and notes that are about to mature. The fund pays you a rate based on the money it earns from these investments. Of course, because these money markets fluctuate, the rate you receive fluctuates as well. The funds charge a small management fee as well.

As with a normal bank account, you can write checks against the money you have in the fund (although there may be some limitations on the amount or number of checks you may write), your fund account is credited daily, and you can withdraw your money easily. Minimum investments may be higher than for bank accounts—usually $1,000 to $5,000 on up—but you get a higher rate. There's a hitch, of course—money market funds are not federally insured.

There is a wide variety of money market funds for you to choose from, and naturally some funds give you better returns than others. The differences are basically due to the fund manager's choices of investments. Some of the safest funds are invested only in U.S. government–guaranteed short-term securities: These are almost as safe as federally insured bank accounts. Other funds, which usually pay higher rates, invest in riskier securities.

There are also *tax-free money market funds,* which offer you tax-free income by investing in short maturity tax-free investments. They can be valuable to top-tax-bracket investors in high-tax states—in many cases they can buy a triple tax-free fund for that state, free of federal, state, and local taxes. These are riskier, however, since your money is less diversified.

Families of funds are many funds that are managed under one umbrella. The advantage: You can easily switch funds—from a money market fund to a stock fund, for example.

Pros: Higher returns than money market deposit accounts (usually from 1% to 3% higher), and usually more free services. In fund families, you can switch to other funds.

Cons: Not federally insured, but there are many highly regarded funds, and some that invest *only* in the safest U.S. Treasury issues, which makes them almost as safe as federally insured accounts. Rates *do* fluctuate—recently they were not much higher than savings account rates.

Money Market Fund Investment Strategy

▶ **Retirement investors should consider putting at least some of their cash into money market funds.**

Because money market funds usually pay 1% to 3% more than money market deposit accounts, they can keep you ahead of inflation better in today's (and probably tomorrow's) inflationary environment. Therefore, they're well-suited for the cash portion of your portfolio, meeting your goals of keeping liquid reserves and preserving your capital. Of course, be aware that rates fluctuate. In mid 1991, rates dropped to only one-quarter percent higher than savings accounts, prompting investors to consider other, better-yielding investments, like short-term bond funds for some of their money (see page 233).

But are they safe? No fund shareholder has ever lost money on *any* fund (as of early 1991). And there are funds that are extremely safe (see below). However, some riskier funds recently invested in certain money market securities that went sour. In these cases, the fund managers absorbed the losses and fund shareholders didn't lose a thing—the money market fund industry wants to preserve its reputation for safety.

▶ **Conservative investors should stick with the safest funds, called U.S. government money market funds—and more ag-**

gressive investors should also put at least a portion of their money in these funds.

Because funds are not government-insured, prudent retirement investing dictates putting a reserve of *at least* three to six months' salary into one of these safe funds (if you don't have that money in a government-insured savings or money market account). You'll lose a few tenths of a percent in average yields, but you'll gain in peace of mind.

These funds invest only in U.S. Treasury Bills and U.S. government–guaranteed short-term securities. Government backing means that if the securities default, the government guarantor will make good the loss, and you won't lose your money. It's almost as safe as FDIC insurance for your bank account. The absolute safest funds invest *only* in U.S. Treasury Bills or U.S. Treasury–backed securities; slightly riskier are funds that also invest in securities backed by other U.S. government agencies.

▶ **One final advantage: In most states, most of the income from U.S. government money market funds is exempt from state and local tax.**

In fact, for those in higher brackets in states with high state income taxes, the tax savings usually offset the slightly lower yields.

A few well-regarded U.S. government funds are listed below. However, there are many others; read the next section on how to buy funds before making any decisions.

Capital Preservation Fund, 800-472-3389 (invests only in super-safe Treasury Bills; generally seen as the safest money market fund).

Dreyfus U.S. Guaranteed, 800-782-6620.

Fidelity U.S. Treasury, 800-544-8888.

Vanguard U.S. Treasury, 800-662-7447 (invests only in Treasury-guaranteed short-term securities).

How to Buy a Money Market Fund

▶ **Pick safe, well-run funds with low expenses.**

Always remember that any expenses or fees the fund charges you reduce your yield. It's one thing to find a fund yielding, say, a percentage point above all the others—but then, if you read the fine print, you may find you're paying a lot extra for check writing, or high up-front fees. Results: a wash. Obviously, it's to your advantage to compare costs and yields carefully.

▶ You can find a money market fund almost anywhere.

Money market fund names, yields, and numbers are listed in newspapers and business magazines. *Money* magazine publishes a monthly list of the highest-yielding funds along with their phone numbers. *Kiplinger's Personal Finance Magazine* and *Money* both periodically list the safest money market funds, as well as their recommendations.

Call and request information before making your choice, of course. Look for safety and quality always.

Two other sources:

- *Standard & Poor's* maintains a listing and a rating of money market funds. The list is not all-inclusive, however, since some funds choose not to pay for a listing and a rating. Write: Standard & Poor's, Mutual Fund Ranking Group, 20th Floor, 25 Broadway, New York, NY 10004, or call 212-208-1882.

- *Donoghue's Report* lists asset size, average yield, average maturity, and current yield of hundreds of money market funds. Call Donoghue's Report: 800-343-5413.

Before investing in a fund, check it out. With all funds, look for:

- *Minimum investment required:* Before going any further, be sure you have enough money to invest in the fund. Funds have a minimum investment, which may range from $1,000 to many thousands.

- *Diversification:* Look for funds that are sufficiently diversified to withstand any problem with their investments. Rule of thumb: A fund should have no more than 1% of its assets with any one issuer (such as one corporation's commercial paper).

- *Large size:* A fund should be large enough to absorb problems with its individual investments. Rule of thumb: A fund should have more than $1 billion in assets.

- *Low management fees:* Don't pay more than you have to. Rule of thumb: A fund should have management fees of about 0.5% to 1%. The average in 1991 was about 0.7%. But double-check for other costs, such as charges for check writing.

- *A family of funds:* If your fund is part of a family of funds, chances are you'll be able to switch excess cash into higher-yielding funds via telephone, a convenient feature.

If you're interested in the technical issues, and particularly if you want to invest in higher-yielding funds, also check:

- *Maturity dates of investments:* All funds invest their money in short-term money market instruments. The question is how short. You'll find your fund's average maturity in many newspaper or magazine listings, right next to the fund's performance figures. Rule of thumb: Pick funds with shorter average maturities—up to 50 days. The longer the average maturities in the fund, the riskier, although yields are usually higher. Most funds have portfolios that mature in 31 to 40 days—though a few have maturities of under 10, and a few of over 70 days. (By law, average maturities can't be longer than 120 days.) Long maturities mean a fund won't keep up with changing interest rates. This is fine if rates are falling. You'll be getting a higher rate while others in shorter-maturity funds are not. But it's not so good if they are rising. Longer maturities are usually riskier.

- *Riskiness of investments:* Remember that higher yields come when funds assume more risk. They may buy more risky corporate debt (commercial paper), overseas CDs, anything that is paying more than the safest short-term rates. By law, a fund can invest only in high-rated issues (actually, the top two highest ratings)—however, the ratings can fall *after* the fund has bought them. Look for commercial paper investments of less than 25%, or the safest commercial paper investments, rated A-1 or better by Standard & Poor's.

▶ **The best bet for conservative investors is to keep things simple.**

Look for large, well-known, well-run funds with average maturities invested very safely. Major business and consumer magazines list, describe, and rate the best ones periodically. Let the pros worry about the extra yields. In most cases the difference won't amount to much. Two well-regarded money funds, in addition to the others mentioned earlier:

AARP Money Fund, 800-253-2277 (safer than many, since its commercial paper holdings are only in high grades).

Fidelity Spartan Money Market, 800-544-8888 (minimum investment of $20,000).

SOURCE: *Donoghue's Moneyletter* (P.O. Box 6640, Holliston, MA 01746, semimonthly, $99 a year), and *Income and Safety, Money Fund Safety Ratings* (monthly newsletter, 3471 North Federal Highway, Fort Lauderdale, FL 33306).

TIP: **Some money market funds waive up-front fees, which raises yields—and attracts new investors. Then after they've attracted enough, they increase fees and your yields drop.**

U.S. TREASURY BILLS

▶ **U.S. Treasury Bills are among the safest of all investments.**

Particularly if you're well-heeled, look at U.S. Treasury Bills as a convenient parking place for your money. If you haven't got the money or the inclination, stick with the money market funds described above and look at those that invest in Treasury Bills.

What they are: U.S. Treasury Bills (T-Bills) are short-term U.S. government debt instruments that mature (come due) in less than a year. There are various types: One type is issued every week, matures in three or six months, and comes in a minimum denomination of $10,000 and after that in multiples of $5,000. Other U.S. Treasury Bills are issued once a month and mature in a little under one year.

T-Bills are sold at a discount. This means that when you buy one, you pay less than the face value of the bond. You wait and then receive the full face value when the bill matures. The difference is the interest—the money you have earned on your initial investment.

T-Bill rates are usually a bit less than similar maturity bank CD rates, but unlike bank CDs, the interest you receive from your T-Bills is exempt from state and local taxes. T-Bills also usually yield less than longer-term U.S. Treasury notes or bonds.

Pros: *Supersafety.* T-Bills are backed by the full faith and credit of the U.S. government. They are *state and local income tax–free.* They are *liquid:* You can easily sell them if you need the money before maturity.

Cons: *Lower rates.* You can earn more elsewhere. There is a *relatively high minimum investment* of $10,000 (unless you buy a T-Bill fund).

T-Bill Investment Strategy

▶ **T-Bills are a supersafe parking place for your retirement reserves.**

For the cash portion of your portfolio, you can't get any safer than T-Bills, which are backed by the U.S. Treasury. And they're short-term, so you don't get locked into lower rates for long periods.

But remember that other investments pay more. In general, T-Bills are best for larger investors who are seeking a place to park a substantial amount of money, in particular for the short term, and who may need the tax advantages with state and local taxes.

▶ **Look at T-Bill money market funds for your retirement.**

Money market funds that invest only or partly in T-Bills can give you the tax advantages of T-Bills without some of the hassles, generally for a fairly small price, and usually for low minimum investments. Use them as holding places for the cash portion of your portfolio, as you would a savings or money market account. (See page 192 for names and numbers of some of these funds; you can find others listed in mutual fund directories.)

How to Buy U.S. Treasury Bills

▶ **You can buy individual Treasury Bills from your broker or direct from the U.S. Treasury.**

Buying a T-Bill is as easy as picking up the phone to your broker. Commission charges are generally small, about $50 a transaction. If you want to avoid paying this commission, you can call the U.S.

Treasury direct at 202-287-4091. Call 202-287-4113 if you want the latest T-Bill information.

▶ **Make certain you don't confuse the discount with your yield when you buy T-Bills.**

An easy mistake to make is to confuse discount with yield. Remember that these bills are issued at a *discount* from their face, or par, value. For example, if you buy a $10,000 bill at a 10 % discount, you'll pay $9,000 now and get $10,000 later. You'll have earned $1,000 in interest. And this means your effective yield is not 10%, but higher. Why?

Just do the mathematics. Divide the interest (in this case $1,000) by the amount of the bill (in this case, $9,000, *not* $10,000, since all you've really invested is $9,000): $1,000 divided by $9,000 is .111. Your yield in this case would be 11.1%

Of course, it usually gets more complicated—if you bought the bill from a broker, you'll be sold the bill at a discount different from the original; time may have elapsed between issuance and your purchase, and so forth. Best bet: Ask your broker for the current market value and yield to maturity if you're not buying direct.

BANK CERTIFICATES OF DEPOSIT (CDs)

▶ **Bank CDs are an easy, convenient parking place for your retirement savings—particularly IRAs.**

Bank Certificates of Deposit or CDs are convenient, easy to set up, flexible (you can lock up your money for a few months or for twenty years), and frequently used by retirement investors.

What they are: Certificates of Deposit (CDs) are time deposits at a bank or institution. The depositor agrees to leave his or her money at a bank or similar institution for a specified period of time for (usually) a specific rate of interest. Once deposited, the money can't be withdrawn until the period ends, or the depositor pays a penalty (usually three months' interest on CDs of up to a year, but penalties can be higher). Just recently, some banks began introducing "no-penalty" CDs, for which the bank agrees to waive early withdrawal penalties. In exchange they offer you less interest—so much less, in fact, that these no-penalty CDs are a poor deal.

CDs may be short term, measured in days, or long term, usually up to 12 years. CDs issued by government-insured banks are backed by $100,000 insurance per depositor (for all money in that bank, including other accounts).

There are different varieties of CDs besides the normal type described above. The other major types of CDs are described below:

Variable CDs: Here, the rate isn't fixed, it varies with short-term Treasury rates. These are not recommended—you're locking up your money just to have it float with market rates.

Zero-coupon CDs: These don't pay current interest, but are sold at a hefty discount. The interest accrues over the years, and at maturity you collect the face value. At current rates, you can double your money in approximately 5 or 6 years, or quadruple it in 11 or 12 years. These are best used for tax-deferred accounts—otherwise you'll wind up filing with the government for the "shadow" interest you're earning. (For more, see Zero-Coupon Bonds on page 242.)

Financial institution–insured bank CDs: Many major financial institutions, such as stockbrokerages, sell bank CDs. The advantage: They shop around for you and put your money in banks, maybe across the country, that pay the highest interest. Note that although they may place your money only in government-insured banks, this does not mean that the banks are necessarily sound banks. It does mean that you are insured for $100,000 per separate account at federally insured banks.

Nonbank CDs: Many other institutions offer CDs—they may be called "thrift certificates" or something similar. Avoid them—they won't have federal insurance, and you won't know the credit-worthiness of the borrower.

Pros: Little management is required, competitive interest rates are offered, you can lock in high rates, and you can choose how long you want your money earning money in the bank. Finally, as long as you buy your CD at a government-insured bank, up to $100,000 of your money is protected by government insurance.

Cons: CDs offer little liquidity—if you need the money before the CD matures you'll pay penalties.

CD Investment Strategy

▶ **CDs are a good option for your IRA money. They are easy to roll over, offer competitive interest rates, and can be very safe.**

CDs are good places for savings, such as money in your IRA, which presumably you won't be needing until retirement. You have two main considerations: How long? At what rate? It depends on how long you want to tie up your money. Just don't tie up any savings you may need for emergencies.

▶ Shop around for the best rate.

Rates vary between banks and over time, depending on what interest rates are doing. Read the economics pages of the paper and see what bank rates are doing, particularly the prime lending rate and the Treasury Bill rate. If rates are going up, it may pay to wait before locking up your money in a long-term CD.

While comparing rates, make sure you're not comparing apples and oranges. Banks *compound* interest on your money in your CDs— and it makes a difference how frequently they do it. Some do it daily, others weekly, others quarterly. The more frequently they compound your money, the more money you'll have at the end of the year—and the better the *effective annual yield*. When comparing banks' rates, always ask for effective annual yield—that way you're comparing true rates no matter what the compounding period.

TIP: Ladder your CD investments: Put some money in a 6-month CD, some in a year CD, some in a two-year CD, etc. This way you'll have money coming due if rates rise and you want to reinvest.

TIP: See if you can buy a CD during the holiday season. Because people are drawing down their bank accounts to buy gifts, banks are losing their reserves. They often add a point or so to their CD rates to attract customers.

How to Buy a CD

Many newspapers and business or money magazines (*Barron's, Money, Kiplinger's Personal Finance Magazine,* and so forth) publish listings of banks that offer CDs at the highest rates. Another source is *Banxquote Online,* which maintains a nationwide databank of CDs, ranked by yield and maturity (*not* by bank safety); for free quotes call 800-325-3242.

▶ Don't forget to look for bank safety.

Even with $100,000 deposit insurance, you'll want a strong bank—if the bank folds and is taken over, there is no obligation to pay you the same rate of interest. (See pages 187–88 for details on looking for a strong bank and for a listing of services, such as Veribanc, that give bank ratings.)

If you know how to read financial statements, you might want to check those of the banks you are investing in. Look for a solid earnings record, low levels of real estate investment (or for a savings and loan, strong real estate investment), and a high ratio of equity to liabilities.

TIP: **Beware of so-called "CD annuities" sold as CDs by some banks. These are not CDs at all, but annuities—and they are not federally insured like CDs. (For more, see Annuities on page 264.) Watch for other tricks by banks, such as offering high opening rates, which drop after a time, leaving you locked in a lower-yielding investment.**

Growth Investments for Your Portfolio

▶ **Mutual funds and stocks are investments that primarily fit into the growth portion of your portfolio.**

However, the Mutual Funds section also includes general information on other types of mutual funds. Later, when reviewing bond fund investments, refer to this section for tips on how to assess bond mutual funds. Mutual funds are one of the easiest ways to invest, so this section goes into detail. Stocks are the principal avenue of capital growth for all investors.

MUTUAL FUNDS (STOCKS)

▶ **Mutual funds are a convenient way of investing in stocks, bonds, or the money market without doing too much work.**

They're used by over 15% of all retirees, and for good reason. All you do is buy shares in a fund. The fund managers take your money, pool it with the money of thousands of others, and invest it for you. And you sit back and collect (or reinvest) the profits.

On the other hand, some mutual funds have lost money for their clients, and recently, many funds have done quite badly. In fact, the average mutual fund has increased less than the stock market as a whole, in terms of annual performance. That's not to say there aren't many winners, just that, as with all investing, there's no such thing as a free lunch.

What they are: Mutual funds are simply pools of assets—which can be stocks, bonds, cash, or a combination—that are managed by professionals for a fee, usually calculated as a percentage of the amount invested.

When you decide to buy open-end mutual funds, the managers issue you new shares in proportion to your investment, pool your money with that of the other shareholders, and invest it according to the fund's strategies. You get back a proportionate share of the returns the fund makes from its investments.

How do you make money from mutual funds?

- From a proportionate share of stock dividends earned on the stocks (if the fund is invested in stocks).

- From a proportionate share of interest on bonds or other debt instruments (if the fund has bought bonds or money market funds).

- From a proportionate share of the capital gains when the managers sell stocks, bonds, or other assets in the portfolio for a profit.

You can have this money automatically reinvested in the fund or you can take it as income.

Many mutual funds today belong to giant *fund families,* like Fidelity, T. Rowe Price, and Vanguard. Investors can switch from one mutual fund to another within these families, usually without any extra cost.

Most mutual fund shares (except for closed-end funds—see below) are sold on the basis of their net asset value—that is, on what all the investments in stocks, bonds, or whatever are worth at market values on the day you buy them. Similarly, if you decide to leave your fund, you sell your shares back to the fund on the basis of this net asset value.

Funds sometimes charge an up-front commission or load, expressed as a percentage of the amount invested (up to 8.5%). Many experts recommend that most investors look for *no-load* mutual funds, which charge no up-front commission. In addition, funds charge percentage management fees, sometimes percentage "marketing fees," and sometimes an exit fee for leaving a fund.

There are many different types of funds, and the usual way of classifying them is by investment strategy. They can range from a superconservative money market fund invested only in short-term U.S. Treasury Bills to an aggressive growth stock mutual fund invested only in small corporations. On a different scale, there are two basic types of mutual funds—regular or "open-end" mutual funds, which were described above, and closed-end funds, briefly described below.

Closed-end funds work a bit differently than open-end funds. They're closed because buyers are not issued new shares in proportion to their investment; instead buyers must go to the stock market and buy the shares of the fund just like a normal stock. The price is based on supply and demand—not on the value of the assets, as with an open-end mutual fund. And as with a stock, with a closed-end fund you earn capital gains if you sell shares of your fund for a profit. Recently, many closed-end funds were selling for a discount—in each case, the price on the closed-end fund in the stock market was less than the market value of all the stocks in its portfolio.

TIP: **Don't be tempted if your broker tells you about a *new* closed-end fund (a so-called IPO or initial public offering of a closed-end fund). With these, you'll have to pay an underwriting fee up front—and you'll automatically lose some of your yield. Best bet: Buy one already traded on an exchange—and first examine its track record.**

SOURCE: See ***A Close Look at Closed End Funds.*** Write: The Investment Company Institute, 1600 M Street NW, Washington, DC 20036.

Pros: *Expert management.* Experts do the stock and bond picking and worrying for you. Some managers have made a lot of money for shareholders. *Diversification.* Mutual funds are collections of many stocks and bonds—many more than all but the wealthiest investors could put together on their own. *Convenience.* Most funds are easy to get into and out of; most have telephone switching and regular statements; with most you can decide whether to reinvest your money or take it as income.

Cons: The risks of the financial markets are still there. Some funds do poorly, and the average fund doesn't beat stock market increases. Moreover, strong past performance is no guarantee of future performance. And for all the advantages of diversity, some specialized mutual funds, like those that invest in a single industry, are diversified by company but not by investment type. If you're not otherwise diversified, these can be dangerous.

Mutual Fund Investment Strategy

▶ **Since mutual funds vary according to investment strategy, you should spread your risk—and your money—among several different types.**

Particularly if you're planning to put most of your money into mutual funds, it pays to put your money into several funds with different investment strategies and a different mix of investments to keep your retirement portfolio balanced.

Below, we've listed the basic types of funds best suited for your retirement portfolio.

▶ **Investors should look first at *total return funds:* These funds are designed to obtain the highest yield possible given a low-risk strategy.**

They're tailor-made for retirement investment since they offer a conservative strategy that balances growth with safety. No super highs—but probably no super lows either. Total return funds vary by type, but basically, they buy stocks paying dividends (for income and growth) and often bonds and preferred stock (for income and security). Although strategies may overlap, there are three basic types to consider.

First, *balanced funds:* These buy common stocks and bonds or preferred stocks in a roughly equal balance—until recently, the typical mix was 60% stocks and 40% bonds. The stocks are often blue-chip stocks—those of the major U.S. corporations with strong earnings. Similarly, the bonds are usually a mixture of government and high-quality corporate bonds. They are for the most conservative, income-oriented investor. According to the rating company Lipper Analytical Services, the average balanced fund returned 78.5% over the past five years, the best returned 117.4%. Some strong performers in recent years:

Dodge & Cox Balanced, 415-981-1710.

Phoenix Balanced Series, 800-243-4361.

Wellington Fund, 800-662-7447.

Second, *equity income funds:* These tend to offer a bit more income and higher capital gains; here, fund managers pick a more variable mix of stocks and bonds. Often they concentrate on high-yielding (but conservative) stocks, such as utilities. Some recent top performers:

Financial Industrial Income, 800-525-8085.

Oppenheimer, 800-525-7048.

Third, *growth and income funds:* These are the premier blue-chip funds that tend to buy stocks with rising earnings and steady and rising dividends. They're very popular with investors and are a good starting point in mutual fund investing. According to Lipper, the average growth and income fund returned 91.8% for the past five years; the best, 132.0%. Some recent good performers were:

Dodge & Cox Stock Fund, 415-981-1710.

AIM Charter, 800-347-1919.

▶ **Also, for stability, look at *index funds*.**

The idea behind these conservative funds is "If you can't beat 'em, join 'em." Most mutual funds do *less* well than the stock market itself or the major stock market indexes—such as the Standard & Poor's 500. So index funds buy a basket of stocks, mostly blue chips, with the aim of matching the performance of a major stock index. When the index goes up—or down—so should your fund. Many index funds have done much better than other funds on a long-term basis. One potential problem for the 1990s: Small stocks may be the big gainers in the next 10 years. Most index funds concentrate on the big corporations, since small companies tend not to offer the slow, predictable growth desired, although some funds now include them.

Some major index funds, with the indexes they follow:

Vanguard Index Trust (S&P 500), 800-662-7447.

Vanguard Index Trust Extended Market (Wilshire 5,000 minus the S&P 500; a smaller-company fund), 800-662-7447.

Vanguard International Equity, 800-662-7477.

Dreyfus People's Index Fund (S&P 500), 800-645-6561.

▶ **Other less conservative funds can give you better than average growth—including growth funds and international funds.**

Growth funds are the centerpieces of the mutual fund industry—run by (sometimes famous) managers who carefully search the market for undervalued stocks from all areas and (sometimes) rack up impressive gains. Many of these funds are the largest in the industry, with many billions invested. These are for somewhat aggressive investors. The best tack to take for retirement investing is to put some money in one or more of these funds and balance it with a more conservative fund. Also, watch your timing; most growth funds fall steeply when the market drops—and this can be a good time to buy. Some of these funds specialize in smaller, aggressive companies; these "small-cap" stock funds are often risky—they go down harder and more quickly during market downturns—but often are very rewarding. According to Lipper Analytical Services, the average growth fund returned 90.7% for the five years ending in June 1990; the best returned 117.4%. Some top growth funds:

AIM Weingarten, 800-347-1919.

Twentieth Century Select, 800-345-2021.

Vanguard World-US Growth, 800-662-7447.

International funds are used by investors to hedge against U.S. economic problems and as a way of participating in world economic growth. These funds invest in foreign stocks that trade on foreign stock exchanges, usually in Europe and Asia. Many analysts expect high growth rates, particularly in Europe, as the economic unification of 1992 propels an economic renaissance. A similar fund type is the *global fund,* which invests in U.S. stocks as well as international stocks. A key advantage to both: more diversification, and protection from sharp rises in the dollar. According to Lipper, the average international fund returned 209.3% for the past five years, the best 281.8%. The average global fund returned 137.1%; the best 272.5%. Recently, however, these funds have done very poorly. Two major funds:

T. Rowe Price International Stock, 800-638-5660.

Kemper International, 800-621-1048.

▶ **There are other mutual funds that specialize in bonds or other debt instruments.**

The basic types are described here. But for more details, see the sections on money market funds and on bonds.

Money-market funds: These specialized funds invest in short-term money market debt. Most are lower yielding than other funds for a reason—most are safer. (See page 190 for details.)

Bond funds: These funds offer fixed-income investments that provide you income. Key: The longer the average maturity of bonds in the fund, the higher the yield, and the greater the risk. Most experts advise retirees to look for two criteria:

- Medium- to short-term maturities (less than 10 years).

- Investment in government securities, very high-grade corporate bonds, or high-rated tax-free municipal bonds. And see the balanced and income funds on pages 203–4 which include bonds.

(For more, see the bond fund sections under U.S. Treasury securities, page 233; GNMAs, etc., page 239; Tax-Free Municipals, page 253; Corporate Bonds, page 248.)

▶ **You can buy funds to fill in virtually any portion of your portfolio—or you can create a portfolio consisting completely of funds.**

The nice thing about mutual funds is their incredible diversity— there's a fund for almost every type of investment. Many investors diversify among funds for balance and to meet their different investment goals—a stock fund for growth, a bond fund for income, and a money market fund to hold income reserves safely. A sample retirement fund portfolio for a moderately conservative investor:

- 20% money market fund investing in U.S. Treasuries.

- 35% bond funds: 15% intermediate-term U.S. Treasury bond fund, 10% high-grade corporate bond fund, and 10% Ginnie Mae fund.

- 45% stock funds: 20% index funds or total return funds, 20% growth funds, and 5% international fund.

▶ *Fund families* **offer another convenience. When your investment strategy changes, you can switch funds, usually via the telephone, tailoring your fund strategy precisely.**

Mutual funds have been merging recently, and giant fund families are becoming more common. They offer advantages. For example, when the stock market begins to move, you can move money from a bond fund into a growth stock fund, then, when interest rates look right, move them back into a bond fund.

Some fund families do the switching for you. *Multifunds* are funds that invest in a portfolio of other funds from the family, depending on basic strategy and the state of the economy.

When investing in funds in a fund family, make certain to check the ratings of each individual fund: No fund family is all winners. Some major fund families that have shown fairly strong funds across the board:

Vanguard, 800-662-7447 (the king of the no-load, low-cost funds).

Kemper, 800-621-1048.

Dreyfus, 800-782-6620.

▶ **Don't get tripped on income taxes when your fund distributes your income.**

Here are a few notes on mutual funds and taxes—but remember to seek the help of a qualified accountant, since it can get complicated.

The money you earn from a fund is taxable—even if it is reinvested in the fund.

Mutual funds will send you an IRS Form 1099-DIV every year, which lists your total fund distributions for the year and breaks them down by type. Dividend income and interest from money market or bond funds is taxable as normal income. The form also lists net capital gain distributions for the year—the profits the fund gained from buying or selling stocks and bonds. These are taxed as capital gains.

It's not always easy to figure out the tax consequences of your fund distributions. There are several sources of confusion—below we've spelled out how to avoid making mistakes that many fund owners make.

First, if your fund declares dividends in the fourth quarter of, say, 1991, but doesn't pay them until January of 1992, you still owe taxes as if the dividends had been paid in 1991. Why? Don't ask.

Second, funds must distribute 98% of income and capital gains by December. This can create a tax problem if you buy shares late in the year—in this case you pay tax on profits the fund made before you bought the shares. For example, if you buy $20,000 worth of shares in December, and a week later receive an $800 distribution check, that $800 is taxable even though the share price may not have changed. What to do: Call the fund, find out when a distribution is due, and switch to another fund (such as a money market fund) for that month, then switch back after the distribution. If this results in a net gain, you'll pay tax only on the gain. If this results in a net loss, you can take a tax loss—if you follow IRS rules and wait 31 days before switching back to the first fund.

Third, if you sell shares of your mutual funds, you are of course taxed on the capital gains, or profits, you may have made by selling shares of the fund. And don't forget: If your fund offers check-writing services, every time you wrote a check you were technically selling shares, so you'll owe tax on the profits made from shares sold. In addition, if you transferred money from one fund to another you'll owe taxes on any profits made.

The IRS lets you use three methods of figuring out your tax bite when you sell stocks or shares of your mutual fund. Unless you specify otherwise, the IRS will assume you're using the first-in, first-out (FIFO) method, which means the first shares you bought will be recognized as the ones sold. If your fund isn't doing very well this can be good. Your first shares may have cost more than the last shares you bought, so your tax bite will be less—or you may get a tax loss. But if your fund share prices have risen, this means you'll be paying more in taxes. In this case, you may be better off using the average cost method (where you calculate the average cost of all the shares of your fund) or the specific identification method. With this last method you'll have to identify specifically which shares you're technically selling. Write to the fund, ask them to identify your exact shares by date of purchase. The idea is to lower your taxes by listing and selling the *highest*-price shares. Get written confirmation.

One final note: If you've sold all your shares in your mutual fund, and if you've followed a standard policy of reinvesting dividends, remember that those dividends were taxed before. Don't pay double tax on them now when figuring out your capital gains tax.

SOURCE: **IRS Publication 564** explains in detail taxes and mutual fund investing. For a free copy, call 800-424-3676. Or check various tax books.

How to Pick and Buy Mutual Funds

▶ **Once you know the general types of funds, you've got to pick specific funds for your portfolio.**

Transferring from one mutual fund family to another can be very time consuming, so it pays to research carefully before plunking down your money.

You'll have four main considerations:

- Investment philosophy.

- Performance—a strong record over the past 5 or 10 years.

- Quality of services.

- Cost.

▶ **It's fairly easy to find detailed data on mutual funds. But don't be deluged with or mesmerized by data.**

For example, you can easily find fund performance for last year, but how much does that matter? You need to evaluate consistency of performance, investment strategies, and more.

▶ **The rough and ready way to pick a fund is to read the major consumer and business magazines.**

Many do most of the work for you. *Money* and *Kiplinger's Personal Finance Magazine,* for example, publish current recommendations on mutual funds in most issues. They'll delineate safety concerns, give you historical performance figures, break out costs, give you phone numbers, and tell you about services. That's enough for some, but many people prefer to balance things out by doing a little research on their own.

▶ **You can also read listings by the major rating services and compare mutual fund performance and cost yourself.**

Many magazines, and most major newspapers, publish daily, weekly, and quarterly mutual fund results.

For example, *Barron's* runs a very detailed quarterly guide to mutual funds. The analysis is done by the professional rating firm of Lipper Analytical Services.

Most listings are broken down by fund type—according to investment strategy, with listings of total return by percent for the current quarter, for the year to date, for 1 year, 5 years, and 10 years. In addition, usually next to each fund listing is an NL, LL, or L, indicating whether the fund is a no-load, low-load (sales commission of less than 4.5%), or load fund (up to 8.5% commission). Some other sources:

- For a listing of hundreds of no-load mutual funds, write for the directory published by the No-Load Mutual Fund Directory, 11 Penn Plaza, Suite 2204, New York, NY 10001.

- Another listing can be found in *The Handbook for No-Load Investors* ($45). The same firm publishes the *No-Load Investor Newsletter*. Write No-Load Fund Investor, P.O. Box 283, Hastings-on-Hudson, NY 10706 (800-252-2042).

▶ **Get and read the *prospectuses* and annual reports from the mutual funds you like.**

These list the costs and explain the philosophy behind the fund's management. You can get them from the fund, or from your broker. Take the time to wade through. Ask the following questions.

- *What is the fund's investment objective?* Make certain the fund's objectives and risk are acceptable. Check out the investment strategies: Is the fund simply buying and selling stock, or is it taking more chances by hedging, shorting stock, and playing the options market? Also check back issues of *Money* magazine and others to see if they've rated the fund for safety. If you want to go further, ask for the fund's "Statement of Additional Information," which will list the stocks, bonds, and other instruments the fund is invested in. Look at the investment mix and give it your own rough rating on risk: Is the fund investing in blue chips or junk bonds? Finally, don't be put off by all the negative "boilerplate" that even the safest funds put in for legal reasons. All of them will tell you they're risky—your job is to read the ratings in magazines and figure out the *real* risk.

- *What are the fund's returns?* Funds are glad to show you how much they're making for you; but look at the fees and costs and subtract them from the returns. If you're paying a sales commission, that lowers your total return. Also subtract annual management fees and marketing fees. It's obvious, but many people forget. Don't look only at the highest-return funds; look also at high-return funds that offer a fairly high degree of safety in addition to good returns. One good way to get a quick fix on the effects of cost on returns is to check the mutual fund company's *expense ratio*, usually found in the tables of the prospectus. Compare it with others. A high ratio means the company is spending heavily on overhead—and that can sometimes mean lower returns for you, or a riskier strategy as the company attempts to offset its high costs by risky high-yield strategies. Rule of thumb: Look for 1% or under; over 1.5% is probably too high.

- *Are returns consistent?* No fund is perfectly consistent—in fact, in 1990 most funds did very poorly. Nevertheless, a good fund for retirement should be relatively less volatile than most, unless you intend to pursue a more speculative investment path. Look for strong, consistent returns over a five- or ten-year period.

- *Has management changed?* You might buy a fund with a great track record, only to find that the person responsible for this has left the fund's management.

- *How do you buy and redeem shares?* Is there a minimum investment? Is there a minimum redemption? Can you write checks against your balance? Can you switch to another fund over the phone? This can be important if you watch the market and want to make quick switches. Avoid funds with clauses *requiring* you to buy more shares on a regular basis: Not only do you lose flexibility, but if the fund does badly you may be stuck throwing good money after bad.

- *How much will it cost?* This is vital. Read the data up front. Many people make mistakes in this area—getting overcharged, paying fees they are told to ignore by fast-talking sales people. It pays to be careful and check costs for yourself. Weigh and balance the costs of funds. For more on costs, see below.

SOURCE: The *Guide to Mutual Funds* (**Investment Company Institute,** 1600 M Street NW, Suite 600, Washington DC 20036; call 202-775-9750) is a publication of the **National Association of Mutual Funds** and contains information on how to read and assess mutual fund prospectuses as well as listing thousands of funds—but without ranking them. Also ask for a copy of the institute's catalogue, which lists other mostly free publications.

▶ Cost is a vital feature with mutual funds.

The higher the cost of the fund, the less money you have working for you. The key consideration is "load" or sales commissions. However, some no-load funds load up on annual fees—marketing fees called 12b-1 fees as well as management fees. Naturally, annual fees can eat into your yields. Nevertheless, on average, load funds tend to charge roughly the same *annual* fees—which makes no-load funds usually cheaper.

When looking at costs, always take in the whole picture. Look for:

- *Sales commission:* Is it no-load or low-load, or is there a high sales fee? No-loads charge no sales commissions; low-loads charge up to 4.5%; load funds charge from 4.5% to 8.5%.

- *Management fee:* A yearly managing fee is charged to you as a percentage of the money you have invested in the fund. Watch for the rate—the median is 1.5%.

- *12b-1 fee:* This is a marketing fee of up to 1%, paid annually. Many no-load funds throw in a 12b-1 fee.

- *Redemption costs:* Some no-load funds make up for their lack of sales commission by getting you going out. These "back-end-loads" sometimes start at a high 5% or so, and decline yearly (as long as you hold shares) to nothing. Exit fees for withdrawing money also are sometimes charged, usually around 1% to 2%.

- *Reinvestment costs:* Some funds charge you commissions if you invest your dividends back into the fund—this can eat significantly into your long-term profits. Best bet: Avoid these funds.

▶ Where do you buy funds?

Many funds—including independent funds and fund families—are available directly to the public. Simply dial the phone number and follow the specific instructions from the fund.

Other funds are run by brokerage houses and banks—and in this case you should call the appropriate bank or brokerage house. Brokerage funds tend to be load funds, because your broker is making a commission selling them to you. But for some, there is an offsetting advantage of consolidating fund and nonfund investment activities under one umbrella. And one brokerage, Merrill Lynch, rated highest (along with Vanguard) in shareholder service among major fund families.

Bank funds are relatively new. Most banks offer six or fewer funds, and so far results have been variable. They're convenient for some: You can switch into and out of them via your checking account.

SOURCE: An association of no-load funds offers a mutual fund starter kit for $12.50 that includes an audio tape, a companion volume, and a directory of funds. Write or call: **The Mutual Fund Education Alliance,** 1900 Erie Street, Suite 120, Kansas City, MO 64116 (phone 816-471-1454).

STOCKS

▶ The best place for long-term money growth is the stock market.

The numbers say it all: Over the past 50 years the stock market has earned on average 9% compounded, more than any other investment. And although there have been downturns, crashes, and minicrashes, if an average investor had stayed invested in the market, buying and holding stocks, those stocks would have come out ahead of any other major investment. Conclusion: Most retirement accounts should include stocks, or stock mutual funds.

What they are: Stocks, or more correctly, shares of stocks, are shares of ownership in a corporation. When you buy a stock, you buy a very small piece of the corporation, along with various rights. As an owner of common stock you can vote on management (but usually own far too few shares to have any real impact), but most important, you make money in two different ways.

- *You can receive income, or dividends,* which are profits of the corporation. These are usually given out quarterly (if at all; some companies don't make a profit, others reinvest profit in the company).

- *You can get capital gains,* or profits from holding and then selling the stock for more than you paid for it, usually to other investors on one of the stock exchanges.

Most stocks are traded on exchanges, such as the New York Stock Exchange, the American Exchange, the various regional exchanges, the NASDQ, or the National Association of Security Dealers exchange for over-the-counter stocks. Some common stock market terms:

- *Common stocks* have been described in the preceding paragraphs.

- *Preferred stocks,* or convertible preferred stocks, give investors the safety advantage of a bond with the upside potential of a stock (although the preferred stock price doesn't usually rise in value as much as the price of common stock during good times for the corporation). Preferred stocks pay a fixed dividend (which must be paid before the common stock holders receive any profits).

- *Warrants* are the rights to buy a stock under predetermined conditions—at a certain price up to a certain date, after which the warrant expires and is worthless. They trade like stocks on the exchanges, but are far riskier, because there is no underlying ownership of a corporation.

- *Bull market and bear market* is Wall Street jargon for, respectively, markets with rising prices (and often volume) and markets with falling prices. The stock market tends to move in large cycles—climbing for several years of bull markets, peaking, then falling into a bear market. Of course, bull markets often have downturns and bear markets upturns; these terms refer to general trends.

TIP: Note that while bear markets may presage recessions, the market usually starts turning upward (getting bullish) midway through or six months before a recession's end. Often the very beginning of this new bull market is the best time to buy stocks. However, according to many experts, you shouldn't waste time predicting recessions and the like: Just concentrate on the long-term prospects of a company.

SOURCE: *How to Buy Stocks* by Louis Engel and Brendan Boyd (Bantam Books, $5.95), is a classic basic guide to the stock market—calm, authoritative, and extremely useful.

Pros: Buying stocks is one of the best ways to make money, in two ways: through dividends and through capital gains (upon sale of the stock). Stocks were, and are, one of the main routes to wealth and security in America. Over the long haul, they have earned the best rates, and they've beaten inflation. By holding on to good stocks, you can keep ahead of inflation and earn better than 9% *average* annual growth—with better returns for better stocks.

Cons: Investing in stocks isn't easy—and without the services of a trustworthy expert it can be easy to lose money. The market can be very risky—as investors holding stock during the 1987 crash learned. (But on the other hand, investors holding good stocks, such as Merck or Morgan Guaranty, didn't lose much at all—in fact, their stocks recovered and were at *higher* prices just months later.) Buying the *right* stock can be chancy—and your broker, as a salesman, will probably be far better at selling you stocks than at advising you about the right ones for you.

Investment Strategies

▶ **Follow the experts and adopt a *long-term* stock strategy: Pick your stocks carefully and hold most of them. Trade cautiously.**

This may not be the glamorous way, but it is the best way to make money. This does *not* mean you shouldn't buy or sell—only that you should resist the temptation to do so at every opportunity. Many losses on the market occur from *churning* stocks; an overeager and usually somewhat ignorant investor just buys and sells too often, racking up high commissions charges, few dividends, and small or nonexistent capital gains. The solution: Pick stocks carefully, research well, and keep calm.

While it is essential to read the financial pages, don't do what the typical amateur investor does and overreact to the news, good and bad. A bad investor follows the stock market adage in reverse: buying high (when the market is booming and friends are giving hot tips) and selling low (in a panic just when the market goes down and before it recovers).

▶ **Construct your stock portfolio carefully, in accordance with your long-range investment plans.**

Don't buy stocks on a whim. And never buy stocks on a hot tip—by the time you've heard it, so has everyone else on Wall Street. (And they're *selling* the stock to you, the poor dumb investor.)

A strong portfolio is *diversified,* balanced so that gains in one area will offset losses in another. This can't be done in a casual way. For example, one investor put all his money in what he knew: defense. Fine in the booming 1980s—but he lost quite a bit in the early 1990s. Another thought she had balanced the growth part of her portfolio with safe banking stocks. She lost on both in mid-1990.

▶ **The best way of building a strong stock portfolio is to diversify among various types of stocks—and keep some money out of the market entirely.**

There are many theories of stock investing. In general, though, the best approach is to follow three basic and extremely simple adages:

- Buy good value stocks—even if you take a lot of time to find them.

- Don't put all your eggs into the same basket.

- Don't overload your portfolio with too many stocks.

Simple, but many people don't do these things.

▶ **Diversify among stocks in different categories.**

A prominent investment strategist, Peter Lynch, former manager of the extremely profitable Fidelity Magellan Fund, author of *One Up on Wall Street,* listed three basic categories of stock that are good for most investors. They are listed (and modified) below. Note that these are not hard and fast categories, and they can overlap.

- *Growth stocks:* It seems that everyone uses this term nowadays. Make certain that the growth stocks in your portfolio are indeed growth stocks—stocks with above-average earnings expectations, based on your own research and that of your broker or planner. Some indicators: A substantial amount of profit should be plowed back into operations, and company revenues and earnings should exceed industry averages, as should past returns. Market behavior: Prices of these stocks tend to go up much more rapidly than average in bull markets. On the downside, prices may also fall more rapidly in bear markets.

- *Stalwarts:* These are primarily the large blue-chip stocks, like Bristol Myers, that pay a reasonably high dividend and are growing at a good and predictable rate. These companies averaged annual growth of 16% over the past decade. Market behavior: These stocks are steadier than growth stocks, losing less in downturns, recovering more quickly—but growing less quickly in bull markets.

- *Turnarounds:* This category includes special situations, such as changes in assets, that suggest you invest. It also includes *cyclical* stocks, those stocks whose prices fluctuate according to the state of the economy. A classic example is the auto industry. Stock market wisdom says buy Ford in a recession, when its price is down and its sales are down, hold it, then sell it a few years later when the economy is booming, car sales are booming, and the price is at its peak. Then wait for the next economic slowdown or recession to buy it again.

Also look at another category of stock, that could be included with the "stalwarts" but is best looked at separately by retirees or those nearing retirement.

- *High-dividend stocks:* This category includes such stocks as utility stocks, which have a record of steady, high dividend payments. They are good in slumps because dividends offset declines in stock prices. On the other hand, some stocks in this category, such as commercial banks, have recently been very weak. Best bet: Stick with the safe utilities.

▶ **In all cases, aim to diversify not only by category but also by industry.**

For example, you're obviously not diversified if you have stock in gas utilities, oil company corporate bonds, and turnaround oil and gas equipment lessors, even though they are distributed among different categories. And even though they may each be strong as individual investments, it's obvious that a downturn in oil and gas might affect them all. Most investment portfolios are not so obviously undiversified—nevertheless, it is a very common problem. People tend to buy what seems hot at the moment—and in many cases end up overconcentrated.

▶ Look for good *values* among stocks.

Value means that the stock is underpriced for its quality or its potential. Many people ask: If the stock market is so efficient, why are there *any* value stocks? Shouldn't they have already been scooped up by the experts?

The answers: The stock market isn't all that efficient, at least not in the short run. Also, stock analysts, like everyone else, tend to study more stocks that are big and that everyone knows about. They send their recommendations to stockbrokers, who go on and sell them to the public. Meanwhile, some boring but promising stocks, ignored by the analysts, sit and languish—until one day someone notices them and values start increasing. And then the value buyers make their money.

But be very careful when looking for value—sometimes low-priced stocks are low because they're dogs.

How and what to look for? First of all, remember the basic idea—low price, high value—and read on.

▶ The best way to find value stocks in the stock market is by buying stocks in your area of expertise.

The best place to put some of your money is in a field you already know. You have one up on all the stock market experts. They know the stock market or the finances of the industry, but you know the industry from the inside. You can spot trends before Wall Street has heard of them. *You may be ahead of the game.*

▶ Many investors study key corporate ratios to find value stocks.

One word before getting into corporate ratios. Ratios rely on reported numbers—and reported numbers were reported in the *past*. Don't forget that many, many times, the past can't predict the future. Many times it doesn't even come close. Example: U.S. Steel before it was USX had a great past, building on a great industry, steel, which also had a great past. The future didn't turn out so great—and U.S. Steel sold most of its steel and became USX. Here are some ratios in common use.

- *Price-earnings ratio (P/E):* This is a key ratio for determining whether to buy. P/E is price divided by net earnings per share of stock. For example, a $10 stock with earnings of $1 a share has a P/E of 10; if earnings go up to $2, its P/E is 5. Rule of thumb: Buy good stocks with low P/Es. Good values (the time to buy) tend to occur when a well-run company has a P/E below the industry average. Higher P/Es usually occur when the market already thinks a company is heading for fast growth—more investors have already bought the stock, which means it may be too late for you to make a good profit. But beware of a declining P/E; it could mean the company is in trouble and investors are bailing out. Also, P/Es aren't infallible—some low P/Es are low because the company and its stock are dogs. If you know how to analyze financial figures, look at the company's annual report and check its balance sheet carefully for financial health and growth prospects. Check Value Line or Standard & Poor's for P/E industry averages. Recent P/E averages were around 11. As a general rule, a P/E of 10 or under is good, but a lot depends on the industry averages and the market itself. The S&P 500 stock index tends to be around 10 in a bear (declining) market, 14 in a bull market.

- *Net worth:* This is stockholder's equity shown on a per-share basis. Investors look for rising net worth, because this indicates that the underlying value of the company is growing.

- *Dividend yields:* This is the percent of share price that is paid out annually in dividends. For example, if you buy a stock for $100, and it pays a $5 dividend per year, your yield is 5% (even if the price has risen in the meantime). Recently, the average was 4%. Historically, high-dividend stocks tend to produce better long-term total returns than low-dividend stocks—but don't use this criterion alone, since growing companies often reinvest dividends, which in turn increases growth.

▶ **Also look for high-quality stocks in your prime categories.**

What is high quality? The main criteria are profitability, growth, financial outlook, and corporate strategy.

- *Profitability:* Measured by return on equity (ROE), which is the profit earned by the corporation divided by the number of shares outstanding.

- *Growth:* Measured by the rate at which the corporation is raising its dividend and increasing its revenues, and by how fast (and steadily) its common stock price is rising.

- *Financial outlook:* Look for low debt levels. Rule of thumb: For most corporations, under 40%; for utilities, under 60%.

- *Corporate strategy:* What is top management doing, vis-à-vis its competitors? Assessing this involves research, but it can be the most valuable aspect of analysis.

▶ **Another good bet is to pick stocks in strong or growing industries.**

Some good industries for the 1990s (according to conventional wisdom, so be careful):

- *Environmental:* Estimates are that pollution control expenditures could rise from 1.7% of the GNP to 3%, which means strong growth for firms specializing in this area.

- *Pharmaceuticals:* A revolution in drugs and drug delivery, coupled with always strong demand, makes this a prime area. Many of the giants are buying innovative, undercapitalized biotechnology firms, further adding to potential long-term growth.

- *Computers:* A little riskier, but computers are ubiquitous tools, and should expand their markets overseas and vertically, as computers are integrated further into business and the home.

- *Telecommunications:* Everyone uses the phone, and now there are an increasing number of uses for it.

▶ **Particularly for people near or in retirement: Pick stocks in solid industries that can weather recessions and do well in bull markets.**

There is some overlap with other categories above. Generally, these industries include "all-weather" stocks. Make sure you pick strong companies in these fields.

- Utilities.

- Telephone.

- Food stocks.

- Pharmaceuticals.

- Energy.

▶ **Also check with outside sources that rate stocks and analyze corporate strategies.**

One note: Most analysts, and most brokers, go along with conventional wisdom—and conventional wisdom is often wrong. Conventional wisdom said Hitler wouldn't start a war in 1939, for example.

The stock market is not immune to disasters arising from conventional wisdom. Conventional wisdom did not predict the breadth and timing of the crash of 1987. If it had, most funds and individual portfolios would not have lost as much money as they did.

When reading an analyst's reports, weigh what is said very carefully. Look at the statistics, look at general economic news reported in the newspapers. Balance everything with your own knowledge. Some good sources:

- *Value Line Investment Survey* (711 Third Avenue, New York, NY 10017, $495 a year): Found in most libraries, this weekly survey service profiles almost 1,700 corporations, ranking them on safety and potential. It includes statistics and well-written profiles. They're excellent for giving you a "feel" for the company and its prime industries. *Value Line OTC Special Situations Service* (same address, $395) pinpoints over-the-counter stocks that look poised for growth. For subscriptions to either, call 800-633-2252.

- *Standard & Poor's Stock Guide* (Standard & Poor Corporation, 25 Broadway, New York, NY 10004): This manual gives pertinent data (high and low prices, assets, earnings, dividends) as well as quality ratings. It is issued monthly, and is available at libraries or via your broker. S&P publishes a wealth of other stock market material.

- *Moody's* (Moody's Investor Service, 99 Church Street, New York, NY 10007): Moody's publishes financial information on publicly traded stocks in massive volumes arranged by industry, as well as a yearly investment situations volume, and a weekly bulletin on over-the-counter industrial stocks. You can often find these at the library.

TIP: **Another excellent source is *Vicker's Weekly Insider Report* (available from your broker or library), which among other things tells you if company insiders are buying stocks of their company. If they are, they probably expect stock appreciation, which means it might be a good time for you to buy as well.**

▶ **Carefully *weed* your portfolio.**

Take out the duds, add strong new investments. But don't overdo it. Sometimes a corporation you purchased will go nowhere, and with research, you will realize it was a bad buy. Sell it if the price seems right. When recessions seem imminent, consider a *defensive* strategy, buying more recession-resistant investments such as power utilities and phone companies (even in downturns people need power and use phones), and trimming such vulnerable companies as retailers. Particularly at the onset of what seem to be severe recessions, many investors move out of stocks into cash or Treasuries, planning to get back into the market when prices drop further. Don't panic and dump stocks that may go down for a while, but will also rebound during a recovery. And remember, the best time to *buy* stocks is during a recession, when prices are unusually low and good values abound.

▶ **In summary: There many specialized strategies for investing in stocks, but the key for retirees is always to diversify and pick strong stocks.**

There are strategies different from those recommended above. For example, some investors buy companies for book value—hoping that in a break-up they'll get more out of the sale of a bankrupt company's assets per share than they paid for the stock. Most retirement investors shouldn't try this type of investing—for one thing, do you *really* know how to price a company's assets? With a leasing firm, can you deduce the market value of a drilling rig?

Many investors also play the options markets, betting on swings in stock price. Options can be used conservatively. "Protective puts," for example, can protect you from the consequences of a downswing in the price of your stock. But in most cases, you're best off avoiding them. Your goal should be steady growth. Just take a calm, value-oriented approach and the odds are you'll outperform many of the experts.

SOURCE: *Characteristics and Risks of Standardized Options* (available from most brokerage houses, or from the American, Chicago, New York, Philadelphia, and Pacific exchanges, as well as the **Options Clearing Corporation**) is a fairly complete explanation of options trading and the special requirements and risks involved.

Taxes and Your Stocks

▶ **Dividends are income, taxable as normal income.**

Make certain to include your broker's commissions and fees in your investment figures. And remember that capital gains are taxed at a different rate.

Capital gains or losses are the difference between what you paid for the stock and what you eventually sell the stock for. If the difference is positive—if you sell your stock for a profit—you have a capital gain. If the difference is negative—if you sell your stock for a loss—you have a capital loss.

If you've bought shares of stock over a period of time, and are now selling some, it may pay to specify *which* shares you're selling. Chances are you bought some shares high, and some of those shares may be down and have given you a capital loss. And if you specify it is those shares you are selling, you can show the loss on your tax return. But in general, when going over the tax consequences of your investments, seek the help of a qualified accountant.

How to Buy Stocks

▶ **Once you just went to a broker, but there are now many other ways as well.**

You may go to a full-service broker, or a discount broker, or now that the regulatory barriers are coming down, to your local bank. (For these options, see page 175.) You may also choose to let experts pick your stocks for you via a mutual fund (as described in the first half of this chapter).

Income Investments for Your Portfolio: Bonds

Most people understand the idea behind stocks, or equity investment. Not as many people are familiar with bonds, or debt investment. But master a few terms and ideas, and you'll be able to fit these into your portfolio—and not get scared away when your broker starts talking about "strips" or "Ginnie Maes."

▶ **Bonds are income investments.**

Bonds produce income for your retirement. Stock dividends can go down or be canceled, but buy a bond and every six months, you'll get a fixed amount of income as an interest payment. In addition, bonds offset other types of investments in a balanced retirement portfolio.

▶ **Someone who buys stock *owns* a piece of a company; someone who buys a bond *lends* money to a company.**

Bonds are *issued* by governments, by corporations, and by certain other organizations that need to borrow money. They are usually sold in chunks of $1,000 (or sometimes $5,000) as part of large multimillion-dollar issues. They have a stated *maturity* when they're issued—in other words, the bond issuer promises to pay back the entire face value of the bond (called par value) at a specified date in the future. In the meantime, bondholders are entitled to a specified rate of interest—usually paid twice a year.

▶ **When you buy a bond, you want to make certain you'll get your principal back in the end, and in the meantime, keep on getting your interest payments.**

The safer the bond, the greater the certainty that the bond issuer won't default. Fortunately, you have help in deciding which bonds look like safe investments. Bonds are rated for safety by various rating organizations. The three major services are:

- Fitch Investors Service.
- Moody's Investors Service.
- Standard & Poor's (S&P).

All three publish their ratings of thousands of bonds. They're easily available: In most cases your public library will carry them. Bonds of the highest quality are rated AAA by S&P and Fitch's; Aaa by Moody's. These are the best bonds—the issuer has an outstanding ability to repay. The next-highest grade is AA or Aa; then A— conservative retirement investors should stick with these bonds. Then comes BBB or Baa, where the issuer has an "adequate" ability to repay. Sometimes a plus or a minus is added to the rating for bonds slightly above or below the letter ratings. All these bonds are called investment-grade bonds; they carry the least risk.

Below these ratings bonds are much riskier; in fact, those with ratings of BB or Ba or lower are called junk bonds. The lower the rating, the riskier the bond—and in most cases, the higher the yield. Regardless of yield, most retirement investors should stick with high-grade bonds or bond funds, or invest in bond mutual funds that carefully monitor the types and levels of riskier debt.

With U.S. Treasury Bills, bonds, notes or Savings Bonds you don't have to worry as much, since they're backed by the full faith and credit of the U.S. government. They're rock-solid, AAA-plus investments.

▶ **Bonds carry other risks as well—a major concern is interest rate risk.**

Interest rates go up and they go down—but remember, when you buy a bond you buy a specified, locked-in interest rate. And that's where problems can occur.

For example, say you've bought a $1,000 bond at par (in other words, you paid the full price of $1,000) paying you 9% a year for 20 years. Each year you can sit back and collect $90. Now suppose interests rates rise—in other words, the government starts issuing bonds at 10% interest, and banks start charging more to lend money. Your bond is still worth $1,000—you'll get back the full amount at maturity—but try to sell it for $1,000 now. You won't be able to. Why should anyone pay $1,000 for a bond earning $90 a year when they can pay the same amount for another 10% bond earning $100 a year? What happens is simple—if you want to sell your bond now, you must sell it at a *discount,* or a value under par. For example, if you offer your bond at $950, you may get some takers; now they'll earn a higher equivalent interest rate of 10.55% ($90 a year from their investment of $950), and they'll get an extra $50 if they hold the bond to maturity. Naturally, the opposite can also occur—interest rates could fall and your bond could be worth more—it would then sell for a *premium,* or some amount over par.

▶ **Either way, when you buy a bond, you're betting on where interest rates will go.**

This is why it's usually better to stick with short- or intermediate-term bonds—it's harder to bet accurately farther into the future. This is also why it's better to plan on holding bonds for the income rather than trading them for capital gains (profits).

If you hold bonds to maturity and don't sell them, and just sit back and collect the income, you're fine—unless inflation kicks in dramatically. As an example, AAA bonds were paying around 5% 25 years ago. You wouldn't be too happy if you had bought 30-year bonds then and were still holding them now.

One final note, however: When interest rates get really high, consider buying at least some long-term bonds. The odds are good that no society, particularly our own, can sustain higher and higher interest rates forever. You could be locking in a 10% or 12% or 15% rate for a future in which high-yielding bonds are again paying 5%.

▶ **Avoid a major error bond-buyers often make—confusing nominal and current yield with yield to maturity. Buy and compare bonds on the basis of their yield to maturity.**

It's confusing—but pay attention; you could save money. Figuring your yield at first seems simple—it's the interest rate you're getting on your bond. But what if you paid more—or less—than par (face) value for the bond? In that case, your yield is less—or more—than the interest rate the bond is paying. For example, with the 9% $1000 bond we mentioned earlier, if you paid only $950, we said you'd actually be getting a yield of 10.55%. But it gets more complicated than that—since at maturity, you'd also get back the par value of the bond, which in our example is $1000. This means you'd not only get back the $950 you paid, but you'd get an extra $50 as well. So to really figure out what your yield is you should take this extra money into account too. *Yield to maturity* does all this— and to make it easier for you, bond tables (and your broker) can tell you the "YTM" for any bond you buy at any price. Why should you check? To avoid the mistake many buyers make—they buy a bond paying out interest of say, 15%—but buy it at such a high price (or premium) that their YTM might be a low 5%. It's the opposite of the example above—and it's surprisingly common. One final note: if your bond is "callable" (see below) after a certain date, ask your broker to figure out yield to call instead of yield to maturity, since the odds are good the bond will be called at that time.

▶ Some bonds carry another risk—callability.

One advantage of bonds is that you can lock in a high rate—unless the bond is callable. In this case, the issuer can buy back the bond on demand, paying you back your principal and a little extra, as specified by a (usually complicated) formula. Rest assured it's a good deal for the issuer and not a good deal for you: Usually high-yielding bonds are called when interest rates go down, though they're just the type of bond you want to keep. Often, as with many municipal bonds, bonds are callable after a certain period of time, say 10 years, from their date of issuance. Always check whether the bond you're buying is callable.

▶ The rest of this section lists the major types of bond investments for your portfolio.

Stick with safer bonds if you're just beginning—and if you've got a limited budget, check out bond *mutual funds* and *unit trusts*. These are collections of bonds that you can buy shares of for smaller amounts. They're described below under the specific type of bonds they hold. And when buying more complicated bonds, consider going to an expert, an experienced bond broker who can steer you in the right direction. Bond brokers can be found at major stock-brokerages—in many cases your stockbroker will be able to refer you or will be able to check with experts within the company. In addition, there are many regional firms that specialize in selling and buying bonds.

U.S. SAVINGS BONDS

▶ U.S. Savings Bonds are convenient and easy, particularly for small or beginning investors.

Everyone knows about U.S. Savings Bonds. What some don't realize is that they're not so bad an investment since the government improved yields.

What they are: U.S. Savings Bonds are bonds issued by the federal government. There are two main types—HH and EE bonds.

EE bonds, the most common, are available in denominations from $50 to $10,000. They are sold at a discount of 50%—to buy a $200 bond you put down $100, hold it, and at maturity, collect $200.

Interest is set at 85% of U.S. Treasury note rates for bonds held for more than five years. A new rate is set every six months. Interest is paid to you only at the bond's maturity—in the meantime it keeps accruing, adding to the value of your bond when you cash it. Depending on the interest rates, most bonds mature in about 10 to 12 years—but the government can issue bonds for up to 30 years. Of course, you can get your money back before that time.

Once you buy a bond, you can't cash it for six months, and if you hold it for less than five years, you don't get the maximum interest rate, but otherwise there are few problems and many advantages. EE bonds are state and local tax-free, and you don't have to pay federal taxes on the interest until you actually receive it at the bond's maturity.

HH bonds can only be bought by exchanging matured EE bonds for them—in which case the income earned from the EE bond is still tax-deferred. HH bonds mature in 10 years. Like other bonds, (and unlike EEs) they pay interest twice a year, and this interest is taxable when paid.

Pros: *Tax advantage.* Like other Treasury issues, EE Savings Bonds are free of state and local taxes (a definite advantage in high-tax states and cities like New York), and federal tax is deferred until you redeem the bonds or they mature. *Safety.* They are guaranteed by the U.S. government. *Good for planning.* You know what amount you'll get at maturity, making them easy for retirement planning. *Convenient.* They are easy to buy, available in bite-size amounts for small investors. *Yield.* For the safety and convenience, not a bad yield.

Cons: *Short-term illiquidity.* Bonds are not a good option if you might need the money before five years. *Yield.* Many other investments pay more.

Savings Bond Investment Strategy

▶ **U.S. Savings Bonds are particularly useful to small investors.**

Savings Bonds are an option for investors looking for safety, convenience, tax deferral, and certainty—along with a fairly good yield. But remember that many other investments offer higher yields as well as safety. Buy U.S. Savings Bonds to fill a conservative part of your portfolio, or as the starting point for your long-term savings. But match investments in Savings Bonds with higher-yielding investments in other areas.

▶ **Think of Savings Bonds as a sort of IRA.**

Savings Bonds are long-term investments that have the advantages of federal tax deferral (like an IRA) and state and local tax exemption. Therefore, they can be used as part of a long-term retirement savings program. And they have the nice feature that, as they are deeply discounted bonds, you put up only a little money for a lot later. (See zero-coupon bonds on page 242.) They're an easy way to build a small retirement nest egg. Also, you know ahead of time how much you'll have at certain times, which is a useful feature when looking to retirement.

▶ **Savings Bonds can also be used for a long-term education plan for your children or grandchildren, or possibly yourself, depending on Treasury interpretation of their rules.**

With certain restrictions, the Treasury Department has *exempted* (not just deferred) EE Savings Bonds from federal taxes provided they are used for education at colleges, universities, or certain technical schools. There are various requirements and changing income standards. (For details, contact the Office of Public Affairs, U.S. Saving Bond Division, Department of the Treasury, Washington, DC 20226.)

TAX TIP: Don't forget—don't put EE Savings Bonds in your IRA! They're already tax-deferred.

How to Buy U.S. Savings Bonds

▶ **U.S. Savings Bonds are easy to buy.**

U.S. Savings Bonds are offered for sale at most banks, savings and loan institutions, and credit unions, as well as through payroll savings plans at many corporations throughout the country.

When you purchase your bond, you are required to register your ownership. You can register as a single owner, a single owner with a named beneficiary, or as co-owners where the rights are shared.

TIP: If you register with a co-owner—be careful. *Either* co-owner can redeem the bond and collect the cash, *without* consent of the other.

▶ **Redeeming EE bonds is as easy as buying them.**

Simply go to any issuing bank, savings and loan, or credit union, sign the bond, wait for your signature to be verified, and collect the cash. Series HH bonds may also be turned in at your local bank, but here you'll have to wait a bit longer for your cash. Stolen or lost bonds are replaceable at no cost. Simply go to your issuing bank, ask for Form PD 1048 (or PD 1934 for partially destroyed bonds), fill it out, and wait for your replacement.

TIP: To find the current rate of U.S. Savings Bonds, call toll-free 800-USBONDS. To find the current market value of your Savings Bonds, write the Office of Public Affairs. U.S. Savings Bond Division, Department of the Treasury, Washington, DC 20226. Ask for Table PD 3600—this is a listing of the current market value of issued Savings Bonds.

SOURCE: For more information, write the above address for two free booklets. One is *The Savings Bond Question and Answer Book,* and the other covers educational uses for the bonds. Your local banker or financial advisor also may stock the booklets or be ready to answer questions.

U.S. TREASURY BONDS AND NOTES

▶ **Treasury Bonds and Notes are supersafe investments for retirement.**

"Treasuries" are the investment of choice for many who wish to fill the fixed-income bond portion of their portfolio.

Just remember, as with all bonds, if inflation heats up, bond values go down. And more important for retirees, the fixed income these bonds pay stays the same—but buys less.

What they are: U.S. Treasury Bonds and notes are debt of the U.S. government, guaranteed by its full faith and credit. Treasury

Bills, notes, and Bonds are "auctioned" by the government: Every week or month the Treasury determines how much money it needs and, in a giant computerized auction, goes out and sells them to banks, brokers, and individuals. Unlike U.S. Savings Bonds, but like other bonds, they can be also sold after issuance, on secondary markets (via your broker, for example). The interest is exempt from state and local tax. Treasuries are noncallable (to be technical: no Treasury Bonds or notes issued after November 1984 are callable; some others can be recalled five years before maturity only). U.S. Treasury *Bills,* you'll recall, are the shortest-term instruments, maturing in less than one year. Of the longer-term instruments, there are two types, bonds and notes (although both are generally called bonds).

U.S. Treasury notes are medium-term bonds. They mature in 1 to 10 years. Buyers get interest payments twice a year and the principal at maturity. The minimum denomination is $5,000 for notes with maturities of less than four years, $1,000 for over four years.

U.S. Treasury Bonds are long term—maturing in 10 to 30 years. Buyers get interest payments twice a year and the principal at maturity. Because interest rates change the most over the long term, the price of these bonds is the most volatile of the three types of Treasuries. This can be a problem for people who want to sell their bonds, but if you hold them to maturity, there is of course no loss. The minimum denomination is $1,000.

Refcorp Bonds, a new issue, are not Treasury Bonds, but are backed by Treasury Bonds. These bonds were created out of the savings and loan collapse, by the Resolution Funding Corporation, as authorized by Congress. Refcorp Bonds are backed by zero-coupon Treasury Bonds, with interest paid by the Federal Home Loan Bank (FHLB). But if the FHLB can't make those payments, the Treasury is directed by law to do so, which for all practical purposes makes these bonds as safe as Treasuries, according to experts. Key advantage: higher yields. And like Treasury bonds, they offer semiannual interest (or can be purchased as zero-coupon bonds), can't be called early, and are exempt from state and local taxes. They have maturities of 30 or 40 years.

Pros: *Safety.* U.S. Treasuries are as safe as you can get in terms of creditworthiness; relatively high yielding for their safety; and fairly liquid—long-term bonds and notes can be easily sold on the secondary market. *Noncallable.*

Cons: Corporate bonds and other types of bonds usually offer higher yields. As with other bonds, there is an interest rate risk.

SOURCE: *Treasury Securities: Making Money with Uncle Sam,* by Donald Nichols (Dearborn Trade, $24.95), describes and explains every U.S. Treasury issue sold, and the mutual funds that specialize in them.

Treasury Bond and Note Investment Strategy

▶ **U.S. Treasuries are excellent for most long-term retirement plans.**

Buy bonds for two basic reasons: for retirement income and to save money for your retirement date. They'll balance out other investments.

First, look at your target retirement date. You have two goals—to build principal up to that date and to have money coming due on and during retirement to meet your needs.

▶ **Try "laddering" your bond investments.**

Buy bonds with different maturities in a series extending into retirement. This is called "laddering" or "staggering." It assures you a steady supply of principal coming due, as different individual bonds mature over the years. Most important, laddering allows you to reinvest this money at higher rates, if rates have gone up. You don't get all your money locked in at lower rates. In effect, you're diversifying your bond investment over time.

Even if retirement is a long time off, if rates are very high, you may also want to buy some long-term notes.

▶ **In general, buy *medium*-term bonds—issues of around 10 years.**

Medium-term bonds have the most stable market values—the money from short-term T-Bills may have to be reinvested at much lower rates, while long-term bonds can be volatile. Yields on medium-term bonds tend to be high—at the time of writing, 10-year Treasury Bonds were paying 8.5%. They're relatively liquid and can easily be sold on the secondary markets. And you can of course reinvest either before maturity (by selling them) or after they come due.

▶ **Consider bond mutual funds.**

These pools of U.S. Treasury Bonds and notes and often other securities are managed by experts, but are accessible to investors with small amounts of money, and they save you the hassles of worrying about interest rate movements. Of course, you'll have to pay a small percentage management fee.

There's something else you need to understand about *all* bond mutual funds: Technically they're not fixed-income investments like bonds. Things work out differently when you buy them instead of an individual bond.

When you stop to think about it, it makes sense. When you buy a bond, you lend money to a corporation or the government—and in return, you get back a fixed amount of interest and, at maturity, you get back what you loaned (your principal). But when you buy a bond fund, you buy *shares* of a fund that owns bonds. Yes, in effect you get interest (in the form of income from the fund), but you won't get your principal back at a specified time—because you bought shares of a fund owning bonds, not the bonds themselves. The value of your shares fluctuates, as does your income. And the fund is perpetual; it doesn't have a maturity date.

This is important for one reason: If the bonds in a fund lose money, shareholders in the fund can lose money. Unlike bondholders, who can get their original investment back when their bond matures, fund shareholders can only cash in their shares.

Does this make bond mutual funds bad investments? Not at all—just different. It makes sense to pick your bond funds carefully; you want top-notch managers who keep your share values rising—and relatively stable.

▶ **As an alternative to a money market fund, consider a short-term bond fund.**

In general, the longer it is until your bond matures, the higher the rate you'll get (until you get to very long maturities). So short-term *bond* funds pay a bit more than much *shorter*-term money market funds, making them a good substitute—if you're willing to accept the slightly higher risk.

These funds invest in bonds with maturities of one to five years. Historically, two- to five-year securities have tended to outperform short-term T-Bills as well as long-term bonds, so you'll usually be earning a good yield. Recently, these funds paid 2% to 3% more than money market funds.

Unlike money market funds, short-term bond fund share prices rise or fall when interest rates go up or down—but unlike regular bond funds, the swings up and down are much smaller. Many short-term bond funds have unlimited checking as well as other perks to encourage investors to switch out of money market funds. They're also good investments for bond fund investors who prefer more conservative strategies. Some major short-term funds:

Benham Treasury Note, 800-472-3389.

Scudder Short Term Bond, 800-225-2470, Ext. 1447.

Vanguard Fixed Income—Short Term, 800-662-7447.

▶ **Look at zero-coupon Treasury Bonds for another source of assured money at retirement.**

These are bonds sold at a steep discount, with no interest payments until the day of maturity. (For more, see Zero-Coupon Bonds on page 242.)

▶ **In an inflationary environment, you may want or have to do some trading of some of your bonds.**

Either to make a profit (earn capital gains) or to reinvest in higher-yielding instruments, you may want to trade your bonds.

Bond trading is difficult, however, and success depends on your reading of where interest rates are heading and the bond yield curve. In general, bond prices go up when interest rates are going down, and vice versa. Best bet: Go to a trusted financial planner or broker for advice. Or better yet, buy bonds for income and security, and concentrate on stocks for growth.

How to Buy U.S. Treasury Notes or Bonds

▶ **In general, there are three ways to buy Treasuries: directly from the U.S. Treasury and Federal Reserve Banks, indirectly through a broker, and via a mutual fund or unit trust.**

For most people, buying individual bonds through a broker is most convenient. You can also sell bonds through your broker on the secondary market with no problem, and commissions are quite low—averaging about $50 per order, without regard to the number of bonds you buy or sell.

▶ **You can buy Treasury issues directly from the Treasury in Washington, or from one of the Federal Reserve Banks or offices across the country.**

Check the phone book of the major city nearest you for your area's Federal Reserve Bank or office, or call the U.S. Treasury at 202-287-4091.

When you buy Treasury issues from the Treasury, you're actually "bidding" for them at the government auction. You can choose to bid either competitively or noncompetitively. The best way is to take the *non*competitive bid. You'll then pay the average price for that Treasury auction. If you bid competitively you may pay too much, or if you've bid too low, your bid may be rejected and you'll have to bid at another auction.

Some problems: Bonds purchased directly from the Treasury (so-called "Treasury Direct") must be reregistered to commercial entry form if you wish to sell them on the secondary market before maturity. No Treasury issue bought directly from the Federal Reserve can be sold 20 days or fewer before maturity, or 20 days or fewer from your date of purchase.

Buying a Treasury Mutual Fund

Treasury mutual funds are portfolios of Treasury issues, managed by professionals who buy and sell depending on interest rate movements and their personal strategies. Before buying a Treasury mutual fund, read the prospectuses carefully. Note that many government funds invest in higher-yielding non-Treasury issues as well. Some tips:

- *Check historical performance of the fund.* Lipper's rating service rates funds (see page 210). Look at funds under U.S. government funds, as well as under GNMA funds, which often also invest partly in Treasury issues.

- *Buy a no-load fund with a low management fee.*

- *For conservative investing, look at funds with average maturities in the low to medium range of well under 10 years.* Risks and volatility tend to be lower, although gains can be less. More risk-oriented investors can invest in longer maturities.

- *Look carefully at the fund's portfolio.* Particularly if you're looking for capital gains, be very careful—many funds load up on Ginnie Maes (mortgage backed securities; see below), which are fine for high current yields or income, but your principal can fluctuate and eat into any gains you've made.

SOURCE: For free information about buying Treasuries at Federal Reserve Banks, send for *Buying Treasury Securities at Federal Reserve Banks* (Federal Reserve Bank of Richmond, Public Services Department, Box 27622, Richmond, VA 23261). Another free source offers *United States Treasury Securities: Basic Information.* Write: Federal Reserve Bank of Dallas, Public Affairs Department, Station K, Dallas TX 75222. And for the free booklet *Basic Information on Treasury Bills,* write: Federal Reserve Bank of New York, Public Information Department, 33 Liberty Street, New York, NY 10045.

For more (free) information about buying Treasuries from the Treasury Department, you can call the Division of Customer Services at 202-287-4113. Write for *Information About Treasury Notes and Bonds* and *Information About Treasury Bills.* Both are available from the Bureau of Public Debt, Department of the Treasury, Washington, DC 20239. Be prepared to wait—it may take six weeks or more for a reply.

GINNIE MAES, CMOs, AND OTHER NON-TREASURY U.S. GOVERNMENT SECURITIES

▶ **What is a Ginnie Mae?**

It's not a girl, it's the Wall Street term for a non-Treasury U.S. government security, issued by the Government National Mortgage Association, a U.S. government agency.

For many retirement investors, Ginnie Mae and her cousins are preferred investments that offer higher yields than Treasury Bonds. In fact, Ginnie Maes are currently the highest-yielding AAA taxable instruments in America. So there's a place in many portfolios for some higher-yielding government debt. Understanding them can be tricky, however, so read carefully.

What they are: *GNMAs,* or as they are commonly known, *Ginnie Maes,* are mortgage-backed securities—in effect, bonds made up of real estate mortgages. Investors like them because they pay 1% to

2% more than Treasury Bonds, and because, unlike bonds, they pay income each month.

How they work: Instead of a bank's holding mortgages, a bank sells large bundles of homeowner mortgages to the government or to other financial institutions, which chop them up into investor-size chunks and sell them to you as mortgage-backed securities. And like a bank holding a mortgage, each month you as an investor receive the interest due from the mortgage owners *as well as* bits of principal as individual mortgages are repaid. Unlike a bond, then, a Ginnie Mae pays back your principal gradually, over the years, rather than all at once the end.

Ginnie Maes are sold in minimum chunks of $25,000. However, if much of the interest and principal has already been paid off, you can buy them for less.

Ginnie Maes have a stated maturity of 15 or 30 years. However, their *average* life is shorter: They usually mature in about 12 years. Why? Over the years, interest rates rise and fall, and when they fall, many homeowners refinance their mortgages, and that means you as an investor holding a Ginnie Mae package will then be repaid principal earlier, before the stated maturity. This is sooner than you would have wanted: you will now have to reinvest the Ginnie Mae money at lower prevailing rates. That's the main problem with Ginnie Maes—you don't know how much and when you'll be repaid, and it often happens sooner rather than later.

Ginnie Maes are the most popular of the mortgage-backed securities, originally sold and guaranteed by the Government National Mortgage Association. Of course, you don't have to buy from this agency—you can get them from brokers.

There are other similar types of bonds: *Freddie Macs,* backed by the Federal Home Loan Mortgage Association, and *Fannie Maes,* backed by the Federal National Mortgage Association. Because these are only "quasi–government agencies" created by Congress, their bonds are not considered quite as safe as Ginnie Maes. One result: their yields are often slightly higher.

As always happens in finance, smart brokers and investment bankers got into the Ginnie Mae act and created a new type: *Collateralized Mortgage Obligations,* or CMOs. These are not government securities per se but a Wall Street attempt to remedy the problem of early repayment on the GNMA and similar securities. (A similar investment is a REMIC, or real estate mortgage investment conduit, which acts similarly.)

What the Wall Street brokers do is take Ginnie Maes and other mortgage-backed securities and sort them into 12 different groups (called tranches) according to different maturities. The idea is to regularize the cash flow from the mortgages, so that when home-owners do refinance, the principal repayments go first to the CMO tranche with the shortest maturity. When these CMO bonds have been repaid, the principal then goes to the next-shortest maturity. This makes the CMO more predictable, more under control. You have a better idea of when you'll get everything back. The tranche system allows your broker to calculate a "weighted average life." And this way you can buy a short-term CMO of 3 years, or a long-term one of 20 years, and so forth, with a better idea of when principal will start coming to you and when you will be completely repaid. (Of course, this doesn't *guarantee* that early payment won't occur.) As a result of all this, CMOs act much more like long-term corporate bonds with call features.

CMOs can be made up of Ginnie Maes, Freddie Macs, or other types of mortgage-backed security, including private ones. For retirement purposes, you're best off with those backed by government agencies only.

Pros: *High yields.* Ginnie Maes offer 1% to 2% over U.S. Treasuries. *Safety.* Ginnie Maes are AAA rated (but other types are less safe). *Liquidity.* Ginnie Maes are fairly easy to buy and sell. *Monthly income.* This is particularly good for retirees. CMOs offer the added advantage of more certainty about when your bond will mature.

Cons: *Uncertainty.* Early repayment of Ginnie Mae principal can jeopardize your investment plans—and the same thing can also occur with CMOs, although it is less likely to. The opposite can also occur: Repayment can take longer than you expected. Although very safe, Ginnie Maes are still classified as slightly less safe than U.S. Treasuries (and others are less safe than Ginnie Maes). Finally, GNMAs and others have high minimum investments (although older GNMA pools, which have been already partially paid off, are much cheaper, and moreover, investors can buy shares of unit trusts or funds for less).

Investment Strategy

▶ **Ginnie Maes and their CMO cousins are good investments for retirement.**

Buy Ginnie Maes and CMOs as part of the bond portion of your portfolio. Use them as:

- *Retirement income:* They're a good way of getting a monthly retirement check.

- *A bond investment:* To do this, you reinvest your Ginnie Mae income in another Ginnie Mae or bond.

▶ **Don't forget that Ginnie Maes work differently from other bonds—the principal isn't repaid at the end, but over the entire term.**

Remember that the income (called pass-throughs) from your Ginnie Mae includes bits of principal from all those mortgages as well as interest on the principal. This means that over time, the principal value of the Ginnie Mae gets smaller and smaller, as more and more mortgage holders pay off the principal. And, of course, since interest income is based on the size of the principal, interest income gets smaller too.

Many investors reinvest at least some of their income as soon as possible. At any rate, be aware that unlike a bond, a Ginnie Mae won't pay you anything at maturity. The principal has already been paid back.

▶ **Like other bonds, Ginnie Maes are traded on the financial markets.**

Ginnie Maes are *income securities,* and your best bet is to hold them to maturity. In general, retirees shouldn't plan on trading them for capital gains.

If you must, you can sell them relatively easily via your broker. However, Ginnie Maes trade a little differently from other fixed income securities. Bond prices generally rise when interest rates are falling. But Ginnie Mae prices may not rise as much, since falling interest rates usually prompt mortgage holders to refinance mortgages. This reduces your Ginnie Mae principal, and generally reduces the level of Ginnie Mae price appreciation.

▶ **Another way of investing in Ginnie Maes is through a mutual fund.**

Key advantages: You can easily invest sums considerably under $25,000. Expert managers are (one hopes) able to offset maturity problems. In a similar manner, unit trusts made of Ginnie Maes also exist, with minimum investments of $1,000.

How to Buy Ginnie Maes

▶ **Ginnie Maes and CMOs are available through most brokers.**

Prices are given as a percentage of par or face value, as with bonds. For example, a CMO with a quoted price of 99 means that for a $1,000 CMO, you'll pay $990. A $25,000 Ginnie Mae quoted at 90 sells for 90% of $25,000, or $22,500.

The rates on Ginnie Maes and CMOs vary widely, depending on what year they were issued and what the prevailing mortgage rates were at the time. But they're sold based on *current* rates—what the interest rate is now. So, like other bonds, Ginnie Maes with low rates sell as a large discount if interest rates are high, and vice versa. And, as with other bonds, the broker will charge a little as well to sell them to you. Some basic tips:

- *Buy current-value Ginnie Maes with yields close to Treasury yields for the same period, or with a small discount.* This is the best strategy for long-term income. These are the ones with the most stable value. That small discount is desirable because it can boost your yield so you're making a point or a point and a half over the comparable Treasury rate.

- *Avoid high-yielding Ginnie Maes.* Chances are you'll pay more for them, sometimes up to 15% or 20% over the face value. And chances are they won't be worth it—because the mortgages in that high-yielding Ginnie Mae package probably will be refinanced early.

- *If you have under $25,000 but want to buy Ginnie Maes,* invest in older Ginnie Maes with much of the principal already paid off. Or buy CMOs. Or invest in Ginnie Mae funds (see below).

Some special tips on buying CMOs:

- *Before buying a CMO be certain it has an underlying backing from Ginnie Mae,* or at least one of the other government agencies (Fannie Mae or Freddie Mac) listed above. Reason: CMOs may also be guaranteed by banks, financial institutions, even developers; these tend to be riskier; some are a lot riskier. Always ask about and double-check backing on your CMO and avoid non-U.S.-government-backed issues.

- *Ask your broker the weighted average life of your CMO*—how long it will be before you're completely repaid.

▶ Buying GNMA funds is easier.

Many smaller investors looking for higher yields sacrifice a small percentage and buy a Ginnie Mae mutual fund. Sure, you'll pay a few tenths of a percent to the fund managers, but you won't have to worry about repayment hassles.

Some funds are *specifically* devoted to GNMAs: These are called GNMA funds (or mortgage-backed securities funds). They are required to invest at least 65% of their assets in Ginnie Maes and the like.

However, other U.S. government funds purchase GNMAs to boost yields as well. They just may not buy as many. This is the strategy of the AARP's most popular fund:

AARP GNMA and U.S. Treasury Fund, 800-253-2277.

This fund divides its investment between GNMAs and Treasury Bonds. Its five-year return was recently at the very respectable rate of 52.67%.

To find other funds, check listings of mutual funds or ask your broker. The mutual fund rating service, Lipper, rates Ginnie Mae funds by quarterly, yearly, and five-year performance. Some leaders up to 1990 were:

Smith Barney Government Securities, 800-544-7835.

Vanguard Fixed Income GNMA, 800-662-7447.

Kemper U.S. Government Securities, 800-621-1048.

Merrill Federal Securities Trust, 609-282-2800.

They averaged a five-year approximate yield of 59% to 62%. But a better bet is to check the information for yourself. And read Mutual Funds (page 200) for tips on what to look for with costs.

TAX TIP: The interest you receive from GNMAs, CMOs, etc. is subject to federal and, generally, local tax as well. Return of principal is not—but remember that if you sell your GNMA, CMO, etc. for a capital gain, you are liable to tax. To avoid interest income taxation, you may consider placing these investments in your IRA—check with your broker or accountant.

ZERO-COUPON BONDS

▶ **Zero-coupon bonds are an easy way of setting up a retirement nest egg.**

They sound wonderful: Pay $14,200 now for a 10% zero-coupon bond maturing in 20 years, your planned date of retirement. Do nothing else—and on that day 20 years from now collect $100,000 cash. Of course, there are catches, and many factors to consider before buying one.

What they are: Zero-coupon bonds are bonds sold at a deep discount, with all interest payable at *maturity* instead of twice a year. Buy a zero-coupon now, and you won't get a penny back until the day the bond matures. But on that day of maturity, you'll get a lot back—the face value of the bond. You'll see how your initial small investment has grown to large proportions.

Zero-coupon bonds are bonds like any other except for the features of deep discounts and no current interest payments. They can be Treasury issues, or corporate bonds, or tax-free municipal bonds. But always, instead of interest going to you, it's building up in the borrower's ledger books.

For example, you can buy a $10,000 zero-coupon bond, maturing in 30 years and yielding 9% interest, for just $710. The difference between $10,000 and $710 is the discount—and as you can see, that's quite a discount. But it didn't come out of the blue. It came from the interest rate and the maturity date. The 9% interest on $710, compounded over and over again, will yield exactly $10,000 in exactly 30 years. So for your purposes, putting $710 in the bank at a guaranteed 9% compounded for 30 years is the same thing as buying this zero-coupon bond.

There's one major hitch—the IRS taxes that "phantom" interest piling up on your bond as if you're receiving it every year—even though you're not. This is why many people put zero-coupon bonds in their IRAs and avoid paying the tax.

Sometimes there's another hitch: Some zero-coupon bonds are *callable*—they can be bought back from you by the issuer at a predetermined price. In this case you lose your locked-in high interest rate.

There are various types of zero-coupon bonds, depending on whom you're lending your money to.

Treasury zeros are U.S. Treasury Bonds, notes, or other obligations with the interest payments "stripped" off to create, appropriately enough, a zero-coupon Treasury Bond. Key advantages: Treasury zeros are not callable before maturity, thus assuring that you can lock in the rates you want. You are exempt from state and local taxes, and you have the absolute safety of backing by the U.S. Treasury. You may hear your broker talking about CATs or TIGRs: these are U.S. Treasury zeros created by private brokerage houses. With these you will have to pay taxes on all levels, but the yields are higher on all levels. So on an after-tax basis, it amounts to the same thing—the yields are roughly equivalent.

"Refco" strips are zero-coupon bonds issued by the Resolution Funding Corporation (Refco) a quasi-government organization created to fund and rescue savings and loans. These are AAA-rated bonds, and offer high yields.

Corporate zeros work like other zero-coupon bonds, but of course, here it is a bond of a corporation that is "stripped."

Municipal zeros work like other zeros, but here the issuer is a municipality, and the interest is free from federal, state, or local taxes, depending on where you live. Problem: Some of these issues are of low quality, reflecting problems municipalities have. (And if you buy them, remember *not* to put them in an IRA or other tax-deferred account—they're already tax-free.)

Pros: *Good for planning.* You can calculate to the penny (unless your bond is called) what you'll be getting at maturity in 10, 20, or 30 years. *Double investment advantage.* Unlike other bonds, with zeros you not only lock in an interest rate, you lock in the right to *reinvest* your interest from the bond at the same rate (since you're not getting the interest; it's automatically accruing to your account). This is excellent if interest rates are heading down. You're getting a double advantage.

Cons: *Double investment disadvantage.* Because you are locking in rates, if you buy a new zero in a period of *lower* interest, you may be locking in or compounding lower interest (you must in effect reinvest that interest at the same lower rate). You're magnifying your loss. *Credit risk.* Because you get no money until maturity, if the zero-coupon bond issuer goes bankrupt before your bond matures, you may lose your entire investment (whereas with a regular bond you at least got your interest payments). *A tax disadvantage.* Even though you're not getting biannual interest payments, you are taxed as if you were receiving the interest as income (unless, of course, you buy a tax-free zero, or shelter a zero in an IRA or Keogh).

Investment Strategy

▶ **Buy zero-coupon bonds to assure yourself of a specific amount of money in the future—particularly at retirement.**

Use zeros as part of the conservative bond portion of your portfolio, making certain that you purchase high-grade zeros.

One strategy is to work backward when making plans to purchase these bonds—and buy them with due dates that match times when you'll need the money. (For example, on your targeted retirement date, or several years thence.) Or plan to reinvest at some future dates.

▶ **Put your zero-coupon bonds in IRAs or other tax-deferred retirement accounts or buy tax-exempt zero-coupon bonds.**

In this way, you don't have to pay tax on all that phantom interest piling up. No one wants to pay extra taxes, particularly on money you don't yet have. And in this way they're *easy* investments. You just buy them and leave them for 10, 20, or 30 years, lock in the yield regardless of the ups and downs of the financial markets—and forget about taxes until payday at retirement.

▶ **As with other bonds, zero-coupon bond prices fluctuate according to interest rates.**

If interest rates go up, a zero-coupon bond with a lower yield that's already been issued will have to be discounted more to match the market and find buyers. It will be sold for a lower price. And if you buy it, you're in effect locking in that new higher rate—about the same as if you bought a new zero-coupon bond.

By the same token, if you've got a high-yielding zero-coupon bond and interest rates fall, your bond is worth more. You can sell it for a profit, or a capital gain. Naturally, you'll now have to search for another investment that you think is worth more than the high interest you lost when you sold your bond. Best bet for retirees: Trade bonds only with the advice of experts.

▶ **Don't buy zero-coupons at the wrong time.**

No one wants to lock in low rates. So wait to buy zero-coupon bonds when interest rates are high, or beginning to go down. Predicting interest rate movements, however, is not easy. So read the financial papers, talk to experts, and get a rough idea before buying a zero-coupon bond or any bond.

▶ **Another investment option: Buy a zero-coupon mutual fund.**

Mutual funds exist that buy zero-coupon bonds of specific maturity—bonds maturing in 2000, 2005, and so forth.

Naturally, they're slightly lower yielding—a portion goes to the mutual fund managers. But in return you get easy liquidity, low minimum initial investments, and regular statements—in short, all the convenience of a mutual fund. Six no-load zero-coupon U.S. Treasury mutual funds are all offered by one fund family, with maturities ranging from 1995 to 2020:

Benham Maturities Trust, 800-472-3389.

How to Buy Zero-Coupon Bonds

▶ **As with many other bonds, the best way to buy zeros is through your broker or via a mutual fund.**

When buying zero-coupon bonds, look for:

- *Noncallable bonds:* Why pay to lock in a high rate only to have it taken away? Ask your broker about "call provisions" and buy noncallables. U.S. Treasury Bonds are noncallable.

- *High-quality borrowers:* Remember that you can lose everything if your borrower goes belly-up. Check that the corporation issuing your zero-coupon bond is highly rated by Standard & Poor's or Moody's (AA or higher) or buy U.S. Treasury zero-coupons. Many municipal zeros are insured—but a better bet is to make sure the municipal bond is of super-high quality; many are not.

CORPORATE BONDS

▶ **Corporate bonds offer higher yields than government bonds.**

Investors who want more yield should look at corporate bonds. Of course, they'll be taking on more risk. Many major U.S. corporations are as rock solid as ever; the chance that AT&T will default on its bonds is almost nil. But times have changed, and many once-solid corporations aren't as solid anymore. Many retirement investors will prefer sticking with government bonds.

What they are: Corporate bonds are corporate debt; in most cases interest is paid twice a year, principal at maturity. Yields of high-rated corporate bonds have averaged between 10% and 16% in recent years—some junk bonds have yielded more. Many corporate bonds can be "called," in which case the bondholder must surrender the bond in exchange for the return of principal and some additional interest. Corporate bonds are rated for safety by the major rating services.

There are several types of corporate debt—in most cases the differences depend on what kind of collateral the company is putting up to back the bonds. If it puts up something tangible, the bond is *secured.* Here are a few key types and terms.

Debentures are primarily issued by manufacturing corporations. These bonds are backed by the credit of the company and nothing else—so they are *unsecured* bonds. Usually, only companies with a strong financial background can sell them successfully.

Mortgage bonds are primarily issued by utilities. These are backed by mortgages on the land or the buildings the company owns.

Equipment trust bonds are backed by the capital assets of the corporation. They're usually issued by transportation companies; your collateral may be trucks, airplanes, or oil and gas drilling equipment.

Collateral trust bonds: In this case, the bond issuers put a portfolio of securities in trust (usually at a bank) as collateral for the bond.

Junk bonds are not a specific type of bond, just those bonds that are rated under BB (Ba); they are not necessarily issued by "junk companies." The problem: After the go-go years of the 1980s, many values plummeted. And even while junk bonds gave high yields (14% and up), most junk bond prices declined. (On the other hand, recently "high-rated" junk bonds rated BB or BB+ outperformed other bonds.)

High-yielding junk bond funds often didn't do better. For example, when factoring in depreciation, the real return of one junk bond fund went from 6.24% a year from 1985 to 1989 to a total return of *negative* 13.73% afterward. On the other hand, some funds may do well—by picking out the best junk bonds, diversifying risk, and offering high yield. And in 1991 certain junk bond funds beat other bond funds in performance.

Convertible bonds are bonds that convert into a corporation's common stock. These give investors the advantages of a bond (good in down markets) and the upside potential of a stock. The idea is to collect the bond interest income and wait for the corporate stock to start rising; when it does, convert to the more valuable stock. Convertibles usually sell at a price higher than the equivalent amount of common stock—this extra amount is called the premium.

Pros: Corporate bonds offer higher yields than many other bonds; some are noncallable issues.

Cons: There is greater risk, ranging from little to high; recently many bonds have been downgraded, and this will probably continue. Junk bonds and lower-rated bonds, which offer greater yields, have significantly higher risk.

SOURCE: *Understanding Corporate Bonds,* by Harold Kerzner (Liberty Press, $24.95), details corporate bonds, and has a (relatively) easy-to-use chapter on bond mathematics and the nuts and bolts of trading bonds or buying lower-rated issues.

Corporate Bond Investment Strategy

▶ **Best bet for retirement investors: Be conservative.**

Treat corporate bond investments as you would other bond investments—the basic strategies are the same and have already been covered. Plan to hold the bonds for income, not trade them for capital gains. Some basic tips:

- Buy high grades of corporate bonds—AA or better.
- Concentrate on intermediate maturities.
- Diversify among bonds.
- Try laddering your bonds, having some come due in different years.

▶ **Evaluate the risks and the rewards with corporate bonds.**

For very conservative investors, buying corporate bonds may not be worth it: The yields of the highest-rated corporate bonds recently have been as little as 0.5% higher than some Treasury issues. And corporate bonds face what is known as "event risk"—the risk that sudden corporate restructuring can change the financial stature of companies, and result in the downgrading of their debt. Another risk is callability: Many corporations reserve the right to call bonds paying high interest when rates fall.

There are some advantages, usually best explored with the help of an experienced broker. Corporate bonds do offer more yield, and there are strong corporate bonds in the market. Some corporate bonds offer downside protection against calls.

▶ **One good solution for investors: Consider bond mutual funds.**

Many corporate bond funds recently have been balancing their corporate bond holdings with U.S. government bonds and cash. This points to the key advantage of buying a corporate bond mutual fund—expert management.

How to Buy Corporate Bonds

▶ **Buy individual corporate bonds very carefully.**

In today's uncertain business climate, check ratings carefully and remember that ratings can change. Be prepared to do a little research of your own or seek the help of an expert. Some basic tips need repeating:

- *Buy high-grade bonds:* Stick with A or AA or higher.

- *Look for intermediate term:* The longer the maturity, the greater the volatility.

- *Diversify:* That a bond is highly rated doesn't mean nothing can threaten the financial stability of the corporation. Play it safe and spread your money among several bonds.

- *Avoid very high-interest bonds.* Chances are there's a reason for the high yields—more risk than you can afford to take.

▶ **Look at bond *fund* strategies carefully.**

For example, some funds boost yields by buying longer-term bonds. This can work—but it can be a risky strategy. For peace of mind, make certain you're comfortable with the fund's strategy. Read prospectuses carefully and read recommendations and articles in major magazines.

Be careful that you don't get taken in by the high yields of some bond funds. Check the underlying value of the funds. High yields are fine, but not if the value of the bonds is going down consistently. This is what happened to many people in junk bond funds. Many are still getting high 16% annual yields, but their original $50,000 investment, for example, may have shrunk in value to $10,000, because the value of the bonds in the fund's portfolio shrank. On the other hand, certain junk bond funds were doing quite well in 1991. If you wish to buy, buy well-run junk bond funds with BB or BB-plus issues, and do your research very carefully. (For general tips on buying mutual funds, see page 209.)

TIP: **The Bond Investor's Association monitors municipal and corporate bonds, notifying members when their bonds are to be called or when ratings change. Membership costs $35. For more information write: Bond Investors Association, 15327 NW 60th Avenue, Miami Lakes, FL 33014 (or call 800-852-0444).**

Tax-Free and Tax-Deferred Investments for Your Portfolio

▶ **There are two basic types of tax savings: tax exemption and tax deferral. The advantages of not paying taxes on investments are obvious, but the distinctions may not be.**

Tax-*exempt* investments are those investments on which the interest is tax-free. Now and forever. Tax-*deferred* investments are different—with these investments you defer your taxes until a later day when, one hopes, you will be in a lower tax bracket. Thus, it is important when considering tax-deferred investments to estimate where you will be in terms of taxes and income years from now. You may avoid lower taxes now—only to pay higher taxes later.

That said, it's always important to look at your total investment picture when considering tax-exempt or tax-deferred investments.

▶ **The critical question is simple: Which offers you higher *after-tax* income?**

For example, tax-exempt investments usually offer lower yields; but if you are in the right tax bracket, their tax-exempt status offsets those lower yields. If you're in the wrong bracket all you get is lower yields.

Also consider IRAs, Keoghs, and SEPs once more after reviewing these options. These give you the advantages of tax deferral, and you're free to pick almost any type of investment at all. And consider U.S. Savings Bonds and U.S. Treasury issues—these provide some tax advantages as well.

TAX-FREE MUNICIPAL BONDS

▶ **Municipal bonds—"Munis"—are excellent *tax-exempt* savings investment for persons in high income brackets.**

The key criterion: Are you in a high enough tax bracket? If you are, strongly consider putting these bonds to work for you.

What they are: Tax-free or tax-exempt municipal bonds are obligations of state and local governments and government agencies. The key advantage for investors: They are free (exempt) from federal tax, and from state and local tax if you are a resident of the same state. In other words, a New York City resident who buys a New York City municipal bond receives tax-free income from that bond. He or she pays no federal, state, or city tax on this bond income. A New Jersey resident buying the same bond pays no federal tax, but must pay New Jersey state tax on this income.

There are various types—the basic differences are in how the municipality plans to repay you as the bondholder. The two major types are general-obligation bonds and revenue bonds.

General-obligation bonds are issued by municipalities, which pledge to meet their debt obligations through their taxing power. These are generally considered the safest municipal bonds.

Revenue bonds are usually issued by an agency or a district of a municipality; the borrowed money is used to build such facilities as dams, highways, and sports stadiums. Revenue from these facilities is pledged to meet the debt obligations—but since revenue predictions may be wrong, these bonds are generally considered less safe.

Municipal bonds are usually issued in serial form: For example, a major issue of $200 million will be broken up into different staggered issues of $1 million each, with different maturities and different interest rates. This allows the municipality to pay down its debt gradually. Municipal bonds are rated by the major rating agencies.

Pros: They offer tax-free income—free of federal taxes, and free from state or city taxes for residents of the region in which they are issued. They are one of the few tax shelters left after the Tax Reform Act of 1986. They are convenient, as they are available through bond mutual funds and unit trusts, or as individual bonds.

Cons: Yields are lower than those of most other bonds, so they are definitely not an advantage for lower-income investors who do not need the tax savings. Not all municipal bonds are safe—defaults have occurred (although somewhat safer *insured* bonds are available). Some bonds are callable, meaning you can't lock in high interest rates, since the issuer can call them back—after paying you back your principal and a premium.

Investment Strategy

▶ **Use tax-free municipal bonds for tax-free income and savings—but be certain you need them.**

If you're in the 28% or 33% income tax bracket you probably need them—at current rates, the 7% that municipal bonds are earning is the equivalent of 10.5% in a non–tax-free bond.

The table below compares tax-exempt returns at various rates to the equivalent taxable rate.

TABLE 7.1

Your Tax Bracket	Tax-Exempt Returns of . . .								
	6.00%	6.50%	7.00%	7.50%	8.00%	8.50%	9.00%	9.50%	10.00%
	Equal Taxable Returns of . . .								
15%	7.06%	7.64%	8.23%	8.82%	9.41%	10.00%	10.59%	11.17%	11.76%
28%	8.33%	9.02%	9.72%	10.41%	11.11%	11.80%	12.50%	13.19%	13.89%
33%	8.96%	9.70%	10.45%	11.19%	11.94%	12.68%	13.43%	14.18%	14.93%
40%	10.00%	10.83%	11.67%	12.50%	13.33%	14.17%	15.00%	15.83%	16.67%
45%	10.90%	11.82%	12.73%	13.64%	14.55%	15.45%	16.36%	17.27%	18.18%
50%	12.00%	13.00%	14.00%	15.00%	16.00%	17.00%	18.00%	19.00%	20.00%

▶ **Hold tax-free municipal bonds for income and savings: Don't plan on trading them.**

You should buy tax-free bonds for the tax-free income they provide. You may choose to reinvest the income in other tax-free instruments, as part of a long-term retirement savings plan. Don't trade them for capital gains, betting on interest rate swings. These bonds don't trade very often, so the odds are the price offered will not be good anyway. Moreover, any gain you make will be taxable at capital gains rates. Only the interest is tax-free.

▶ **Buy only high-quality bonds.**

Municipal bonds are among the few tax shelters left since tax reform, and with their current high yields, they've become popular. The problem: Many people have been buying lower-grade bonds, exposing themselves to the risk of default.

Shop carefully for high quality—an AA or better from the major rating services of Moody's or Standard & Poor's. Only about one-third of all municipal bonds make that grade. However, don't stop there. Rating municipal issues is difficult—shop around and find an experienced bond broker (see below) and seek his or her advice.

▶ **In general, buy intermediate-term bonds.**

Intermediate-term bonds mature in 5 to 10 years. Longer-term bond prices are more volatile and are harder to assess.

▶ **As with other bonds, consider *laddering* your bond investments.**

Buy bonds with one- or two-year differences in maturity in a staggered fashion. For example, buy one bond maturing in five years, another in six years, and so forth. As each bond matures, you can take what you need from the principal of the bond and roll over or reinvest what you don't need into another. This way, you can reinvest at higher rates if rates go up. And if you need the money, you'll have a bond coming due each year.

▶ **Spread your risk among different municipal bonds.**

Always diversify your portfolio. Experts recommend buying at least five different bonds. Don't buy all five bonds from one state, even with the tax advantages for residents. If that state experiences fiscal difficulties, many issues could be affected at once. Since municipal bonds generally sell in $5,000 chunks, that means for individual bonds you'll have to spend at least $25,000.

▶ If you have less than $25,000 to invest, spread your money among municipal bond funds or unit trusts.

These buy a greater number of bonds but allow you to purchase shares for individual investments of as little as a few hundrd dollars.

They normally already offer a diversified portfolio—however, you must choose carefully, since some funds include more risky bonds than they should. There are many advantages to funds and unit trusts: It's harder to be well diversified with under $25,000 when buying individual bonds. For example, transaction costs are high for investors buying only a few bonds, and unless they have the services of a reliable broker, they must be careful to check such criteria as call provisions and relative risk. A good bond fund does all this for you. Of course, your yield may be lower, since you're paying management fees and perhaps an up-front commission for these services.

▶ *Unit trusts* are good investments if you plan to hold your municipal bonds to maturity.

Unit trusts buy and *hold* about 25 to 50 bonds in a portfolio until maturity. Unlike mutual funds, they don't continuously buy and sell bonds.

When you buy a unit trust you buy a slice of this fixed, diversified portfolio of different bonds. You get the advantages of owning bonds, you get your principal back in the end, and meanwhile you get tax-free interest income by the month or quarter. And if you hold a trust to maturity, you normally make more than with an equivalent municipal bond fund, because unit trust funds charge less annually than do mutual funds. The reason: A unit trust doesn't have high management costs—the bonds have all been purchased already, and all the trust managers do is perform such administrative chores as sending you your checks. Therefore, they charge less annually.

There can be drawbacks, however.

- *Smaller portfolios:* You must be sure the bonds in the portfolio are high grade, because with so few bonds, defaults can substantially affect your principal.

- *Commissions (load):* Up-front sales fees range from 2% to 5%. (However, if you hold a unit trust to maturity, this isn't so bad compared to the low annual fee.) Many mutual funds, on the other hand, have no sales fees (but higher annual fees).

- *Lack of active management:* If a bond is called or redeemed early, the bond is usually not replaced. And while your proportionate share of the principal will be returned, your monthly income will go down.

- *Resale value:* You can usually easily sell trusts if you need the money—the price will be higher or lower, depending on interest rates and hence the value of your bonds. But you won't make back the commission you paid.

And sometimes unit trusts offer:

- *Misleading rates:* The initial rates may be high. But the higher-yielding bonds may be called, leaving you with bonds yielding less.

- *Poor-quality bonds:* Some trusts include higher-risk bonds to increase the yield rate.

Don't get discouraged, however. There are high-quality trusts out there—and in the section on buying these bonds we'll show what to look for.

▶ *Municipal bond funds* **are good options for tax-free income, with the advantages of wide diversification and professional management.**

Municipal bond funds offer larger portfolios of tax-exempt bonds—usually up to around 300. As with other funds, you purchase shares of a fund, and in return receive a proportionate share of the income. And you can choose to reinvest this income in the fund.

There are hundreds of individual funds, and many different types: high-yield funds, insured funds, national funds (bonds from around the country, not exempted from state and local taxes), and state funds (which are unique to the buyer's state).

One advantage of funds is active management—fund managers buy and sell bonds, trying to better yields. Also, fund managers do the worrying for you on risk, defaults, and early calls on bonds.

However, that management carries a price—usually up to 1 percent of your holdings a year, which eats into your total return. And unlike a bond or a unit trust, funds have no maturity. So while you can always redeem your shares, you don't have the comfort of knowing you'll get your principal back. If share prices go down dramatically, you'll lose a lot of money with no cushion of principal.

Nevertheless, well-run bond funds provide reliable tax-free income.

TAX TIP: **Beware. You can *overbuy* tax-free investments if you're collecting Social Security. Social Security benefits (usually) become taxable if your adjusted gross income and your tax-free income and one-half of your Social Security benefits total over $25,000 for singles or $32,000 for couples. (See Social Security, page 65.)**

How to Buy Individual Tax-Free Municipal Bonds

▶ **Look to make a portfolio of five or more high-rated bonds with competitive yields.**

Tax-free municipal bonds are sold, like other bonds, at premiums or discounts. Prices are quoted as a percentage of the value of the bond. Most tax-free municipal bonds are sold in units of $5,000—but prices are quoted, as for other bonds, as a percentage of par value. So a bond quoted at 98¼ is selling for 98.25% of $5,000, or $4,912.50. Here are some general buying tips.

- *Shop around for a good bond broker*. With thousands of issues and countless municipalities, municipal bond buying is complex. You need a trustworthy broker to help. Look either to regional bond brokerages that specialize in the bonds of the area, or to major national brokerages that have specialists in the region.

- *Check bond ratings* with various bond-rating services, such as Moody's Investor's Service or Standard & Poor's. Buy bonds rated AAA or Aaa or AA (Aa)—the safest. *Never* buy an unrated municipal bond or a bond not rated by one of the *major* rating services.

- *Do a little research on your own*. Rating services are far from perfect: almost no one predicted the current downgradings of major city debt. Ask for bond prospectuses and read them. Read recommendations in major magazines.

- *Consider insured bonds.* If these default, the insurer will make up the difference. The price difference between insured and uninsured bonds in 1991 was very small—between 0.25% and 0.5%. Make sure the insurer is a major insurer; one recent scam has been to sell unrated bonds "insured" by uncreditworthy insurers. And in view of recent problems with some major insurers, don't over-rely on insurance. Check the underlying quality of the bond.

- *Search for noncallable issues.* Ask your broker about the call provisions of bonds you are interested in and try to buy noncallables. Never buy callable tax-free municipal zero-coupon bonds.

- *Shop around.* Prices for bonds (as a percentage of the total value) can vary widely. Average rates and fees in 1990 for individual bonds: Expect to pay your broker a commission of between 1% and 3%.

TIP: If you are a very conservative investor, ask your broker to buy you *escrow bonds*. These are guaranteed by the federal government. One drawback: slightly lower yields.

How to Buy Municipal Bond Unit Trusts

▶ **The best way to buy unit trusts is through brokers—they can steer you to new trusts sponsored by major insurers. Look for:**

- *High-grade bonds:* Look for bonds rated A or better. Check all bonds in the trust; make certain it doesn't include some much riskier issues to boost yields. Don't buy trusts with any bonds lower than BBB (Baa).

- *Insurance:* Many unit trusts are insured by giant life insurance companies, guaranteeing your interest payments and principal against default. Yields are only slightly lower. But again, don't over-rely on insurance—the underlying quality of the bond is more important.

- *Maturity:* Look for intermediate maturities of around 10 years; as a rule, don't buy older trusts maturing in a few years, since you may be paying a price based on the original holdings, and since then, higher-yielding bonds may have been called or sold.

- *Call provisions on the bonds:* High rates are nice, but they do you no good if the bonds are called shortly after you've bought the trust. Ask about bond call provisions, and calculate yields to the date the bonds are first callable, not to maturity.

- *Fees and commissions:* Expect to pay from 2% to 5% (usually around 3% or 4%) load or sales commission and annual fees of about 0.1% or 0.2% of your holdings.

How to Buy Municipal Bond Mutual Funds

▶ **One of the easiest ways to choose is to read major magazines like *Money* or *Kiplinger's Personal Finance Magazine*. Their experts can steer you to strong, well-managed, low-cost funds.**

In general, look for:

- *Total Return:* Look for a history of strong total returns (current yield—or annual interest divided by current market price; and market appreciation of the bonds).

- *Load (sales commission):* As with other mutual funds, in most cases you're best off with no-loads, which charge nothing.

- *Intermediate bond maturities:* Bonds that mature in 5 to 12 years tend to be the least volatile.

- *High-quality bonds:* Look for diversified portfolios with high-rated bonds. "High-yield" funds offer higher yields by investing in lower-rated or unrated bonds—particularly in recessions these may be riskier than the yields warrant.

- *Low management and other fees:* Look for fees around 0.8%. High fees mean the fund has to take more risks to offset the costs—something you definitely do not want.

A few well-regarded major funds:

USAA Tax Exempt–Intermediate, 800-531-8181.

Vanguard Municipal Bond—Intermediate, 800-662-7447.

Safeco Municipal Bond, 800-426-6730.

T. Rowe Price Tax Free, 800-638-5660.

Retirees may also consider AARP's two no-load tax-free funds:

Insured Tax Free Short Term Fund, 800-253-2277.

Insured Tax Free General Bond Fund, 800-253-2277.

Although *Money* magazine reported that their yields were lower than the average (5.8% versus 7.9% and 8% versus 11%), AARP funds offer special features specifically designed for older retirees.

TIP: **The Bond Investor's Association monitors municipal bonds, notifying members when their bonds are to be called or when ratings change. Membership costs $35; for more information, write: Bond Investor's Association, 15327 NW 60th Avenue, Miami Lakes, FL 33014 (or call 800-852-0444).**

ANNUITIES

▶ **Annuities often sound better than they turn out to be, but they can be useful—if you shop carefully.**

Don't be tempted by the attractive and seemingly simple ideas of paying now for a comfortable stream of retirement income in the future or of accumulating tax-deferred retirement nest eggs. First, understand the different types, weigh the advantages against the problems, and then make a decision.

What they are: Annuities are investments, usually sold by insurance companies, designed to give you a steady stream of income after you retire, or after a certain period of time. Of the many types and variations, there are three that especially concern retirees. One type, an *immediate annuity,* offers a stream of guaranteed income for retirement. Another, a *deferred variable annuity,* offers the chance to build a tax-deferred nest egg before (or during) retirement by investing in a variety of mutual funds. The last, a *deferred fixed-rate annuity,* is something like a tax-deferred CD. Now, for more specific details:

Immediate annuities offer the nice feature of a guaranteed income for life or for a specific period. They are principally designed for someone retiring now who wants an immediate income. Typically, you pay a lump sum (with a minimum of $5,000) called a "single premium" and are guaranteed a monthly income for your lifetime, and if specified, the life of your spouse. The amount is based on what you've invested, interest rate expectations, and actuarial tables on the average life spans of people your age. Many pension plans pay income in this manner—and many people take their IRA money and buy these annuities at retirement.

Deferred variable annuities. In most cases, this is mutual fund investing, with a key difference—the tax on your earnings is deferred until withdrawal. You invest either with a lump sum or over the years with a series of payments, and your money is invested in mutual funds (managed by an insurance company or a hired mutual fund). Unlike most funds, the deferred variable annuity accumulates interest, capital gains, and dividends free of tax until your retirement or age 59½. You may be able to specify how you want to allocate your money among the various portfolios.

At retirement, you have the *option* of "annuitizing" (which basically means you transform the investment into an immediate annuity based upon your life expectancy according to actuarial tables) and getting a monthly stream of income for the rest of your life or for a specified period. Or you can take the money as a lump sum and invest it elsewhere.

This deferred annuity is called "variable" because the size of your investment at the end—and the amount of your monthly payment—will depend on how well your money has been invested. In some cases, there is a guaranteed interest rate on your investment.

Deferred fixed-rate annuities work something like Certificates of Deposit (CDs). You usually make an initial investment of over $5,000, which pays a certain interest rate. The yields usually hover around those of one-year CDs. Very often this rate is guaranteed for a number of years—and after the guarantee period is over, a new rate is set.

Taxes: Annuities are tax-deferred investments, falling under IRS rules. In most cases you will have to pay a 10% IRS penalty on the income or taxable distribution portion of your annuity for withdrawals before age 59½. Exceptions include disability, death, and setting up a series of scheduled payments based upon life expectancy. Remember that many annuities also include insurance company penalties for early withdrawal. (For more, see Chapter 3, "Pension Plans.")

SOURCE: For a free booklet, *Is an Annuity In Your Future,* write: The National Association of Life Underwriters, 1922 F Street NW, Washington, DC 20006, or call 202-331-6031—but remember that the booklet is hardly unbiased. It's published by the professional association of people whose job it is to sell them.

Pros: *Tax deferral.* Annuities are one of the last tax shelters left after the tax reform in 1986. The investment earnings in deferred annuities are free of tax until you withdraw them—when you should be in a lower tax bracket. *Convenience.* Annuities take much of the hassle of investing and retirement planning out of your hands. *Income.* With immediate annuities, you have the prospect of a guaranteed income for life.

Cons: *Problems with deferred variable annuities* are high fees; early withdrawal penalties; possibly poor investment performance; some sponsoring insurance companies with financial problems; and problematic tax advantages. *Immediate annuities* have many of the same problems, plus their payouts may not keep up with inflation, and if you die early, your heirs may lose much of the investment. *Deferred fixed annuities* have no federal insurance, and there are tax penalties for early withdrawal and insurance problems.

Annuity Investment Strategy

▶ **Purchase an annuity only if you have certain definite needs that an annuity can fill.**

The best way to assess an annuity is to first assess what you want out of an investment. Then see if an annuity fills the bill. A major problem with annuities is the sheer number of them, with all sorts of bells and whistles that can confuse you when you're making the decision to buy or not to buy. Remember that there are other investments that do the same thing—usually with more control on your part.

Deferred varible annuities are obviously good vehicles for tax-deferred accumulation, while allowing you some investment flexibilty, but so are IRAs and Keoghs—and these are a lot more flexible.

Deferred fixed-rate annuities are also a useful way of accumulating a retirement nest egg with taxes deferred. But, again, so are IRAs and Keoghs.

Immediate annuities are a nice way of getting a monthly check for the rest of your life, without worrying too much about where and how it is coming. But then again, bonds can give you the same thing.

▶ *A deferred variable annuity* **allows you to build a retirement nest egg faster by deferring taxes.**

Buy a deferred variable annuity if you want to invest in a mutual fund with the advantages of tax deferral.

Note that the money you pay *into* an annuity is not tax-deferred (unlike an IRA, you can't deduct the amount to reduce your current taxes), but any increases in principal in the annuity and interest earned are. This creates a faster accumulation of money than would usually occur in another type of investment without these tax advantages. Unlike IRAs, with annuities there is no limitation on the amount of money you may contribute. (In addition, the money invested is not subject to the 15% excise tax on excess pension accumulations and distributions.)

▶ **Think about the disadvantages of deferred variable annuities.**

The basic problem with annuities is that charges and fees offset the advantages of tax-deferred buildup of your investment—unless you hold the annuity for a very long time.

Deferred variable annuities have a number of disadvantages.

High commissions or fees: Many funds have high commissions up front, or formidable surrender penalties—boiling down to lower total returns. Ask your insurance agent or broker about up-front fees. Get a written estimate and compare with other annuities. Typical fees include a 1% annual management fee, an insurance charge of 1.25%, and a maintenance charge of about $40 a year. Typically, fees amount to about double those for the typical mutual fund.

Withdrawal penalties. If you want to get your money out of an annuity once you've invested in one there is usually a penalty of anything from 1% to 10% of the cash value of the annuity if you withdraw money before a set period of time, usually 5 to 10 years. This is called a surrender charge.

IRS withdrawal penalties: As mentioned on page 101, if you withdraw before age 59½, you'll usually pay a 10% tax penalty on your taxable distribution (up to the total amount of investment income in the annuity), in addition to any surrender penalties the insurance company may have. Also, your distributions will be treated as taxable income and taxed at your tax rate.

Insurance company jitters: Many insurance companies are strong, but recently, some have been suffering financial problems.

Fund management: Annuity funds may be well managed or poorly managed. If they're poorly managed and you want to get out, you'll have to pay those high withdrawal penalties. If you stay, you may get a smaller stream of payments for retirement.

Is there a tax advantage at all? Remember, taxes are deferred, not eliminated. You may be in a *higher* tax bracket at retirement and have to pay tax on all those accumulated earnings. This is not as improbable as it may seem—remember that very recently, maximum tax rates reached 70%, before they were cut back. Increases could come again—and you might be worse off tax-wise.

Buy a deferred variable annuity if:

- You want tax deferral and are confident you won't need the money for *at least* 10 years. Usually it takes at least this long to offset the fees and withdrawal penalties in terms of the growth of your money.

- You have exhausted other tax-deferred options, such as IRAs, Keoghs, and SEPs.

▶ **After you reach retirement age, what should you do with your deferred variable annuity?**

You've got some options. You can take the lump sum and invest it elsewhere, you can transform it all into an immediate annuity to get a stream of income over the years, or you can do both, with a *split funded annuity,* which is a combination of the immediate and the deferred variable annuity. Part of it gives you an immediate income, the rest is a deferred annuity that keeps accumulating money for a later payout. Usually, the deferred annuity is designed to grow back to the amount of your original principal.

▶ **Be aware of the tax consequences of withdrawals from your annuity.**

To repeat, annuities are tax-*deferred,* not tax-*free.* This is obvious, but is sometimes forgotten. Remember the early withdrawal penalties. You must pay taxes and penalties if you redeem early and don't roll them over into another tax-deferred instrument.

Also, when you withdraw money from your annuity, the IRS

recognizes the income first. This means if you put in $50,000 and earn $60,000 in the annuity, the IRS would tax the first $60,000 of withdrawals as income.

▶ *Immediate annuities* **offer investors the comfort of income for life or for a specified period of time.**

Many people take their deferred annuity and transform it into an immediate annuity at retirement; others buy them direct.

It sounds enticing—income for the duration of your retirement. The guarantee of income for life removes worries and lets you enjoy retirement.

The *amount* of your yearly income depends on:

- The size of your investment.

- Your actuarially determined projected lifespan.

- The insurance company's expectation of interest rates.

Naturally, the younger you are, the less you'll get per year—since you'll probably live longer. But no matter what your age, you can benefit from immediate annuities by living a long time. With guaranteed income for life, if you outlive the actuarial projections you'll probably get more money than you would have if you had just invested it.

▶ **Your key concern with immediate annuities is that** *payouts are fixed; inflation is not.*

An annuity of $900 a month is nice, but if inflation erodes buying power 10 years from now, $900 may seem like a pittance. One solution: Put other money in growth-oriented investments to offset the hazards of inflation.

There are many varieties of immediate annuity payouts; here are two common ones:

- With a basic *single-life annuity,* if, for example, you are 65 and have made a $100,000 investment, an insurance company will currently guarantee you about $950 montly for as long as you live. If you live longer than average, you will probably end up beating the insurance company and making more than you paid in. If you die early, the insurance company gets the remainder—

unless you have included a spouse or some other survivors in the payout calculations. In this case, you will receive less monthly—in this example, probably about $200 less a month.

- Probably the most popular option is a *lifetime annuity with 10-year period certain,* which means you'll get a lifetime payout, but if you die before the 10 years are up, your beneficiaries will be guaranteed the same level of payout until the 10 years are up.

Think carefully about your own life expectancy and your own expectations of inflation, review the options with more than one insurer, compare costs and payouts—then decide.

▶ *Deferred fixed-rate annuities* **are like bank Certificates of Deposit (CDs) that are tax-deferred.**

Use them for the same reasons that you use bank CDs—for long-term savings, with the added advantage of tax deferral.

But of course there are disadvantages. First, unlike federally chartered bank CDs, fixed annuities are not federally insured. You'll have to carefully check the health of the insurance company offering them. Also, some companies guarantee a high interest rate on their fixed annuities for a year or a number of years—and after the period is over, slash the rate. Ask your insurance agent or broker how long the guaranteed interest period lasts. Check if there is a "bail-out" provision—this permits you to withdraw your money without penalty if interest rates drop more than a specified percentage.

Withdrawal penalties are common, and if you withdraw and don't put your money into another tax-deferred instrument, the IRS will assess penalties.

How to Buy an Annuity

▶ **Three rules: Proceed cautiously, research, and comparison shop.**

You can purchase an annuity directly through an insurance agent or through your broker. Some major mutual fund companies, including Scudder and Vanguard, also offer no-load annuities. Many brokerage houses offer them as well. Often they're not referred to as annuities—they may be called "private tax-deferred retirement accounts," or the like. Whenever your broker mentions something that sounds like it may be an annuity, ask if it is and compare it with other annuities.

Some basic considerations: Decide why you want an annuity and pick the basic option that seems to fit your needs. *Never sign an agreement without first researching your own needs, the insurance company, and the specific annuity.* Recently, some insurance agents have been exploiting bad news in the insurance industry to frighten investors into switching policies or annuities. In some cases, this is done merely to gain additional business. Always research before buying or switching. Check:

- *Quality and ranking of the issuer:* Read A. M. Best, Standard & Poor's, or Moody's ratings in your library. Look for a rating *no lower* than A-plus or the equivalent from two of the three. The average insurance company rating with Moody's is about Aa2 or Aa3. Also call your state insurance office for information on the company. Recently, some new, more rigorous rating companies have emerged; ask your librarian for specific names.

- *Does your state have a guarantee fund?* Check also whether your specific insurance investment is covered by the fund. Some funds, for example, do not guarantee GICs. Also be aware that some state funds may be weak—and may have trouble reimbursing you if your insurance company fails.

- *Sales commissions:* How high? Are they up front or deferred?

- *Other fees:* These can really reduce the value if they are yearly. For example, with a deferred annuity, a 3% fee a year can completely offset tax savings until the 24th year, assuming a $100,000 initial investment at a 9% return, and a 35% total tax rate—according to calculations by *Financial World.*

- *Withdrawal provisions:* What penalties are there for premature withdrawal? Penalties vary greatly: One firm may charge a flat 5% for five years, for example, while another starts at 7% and winds it down to nothing after eight years. Also ask about free partial withdrawal—10% per year is the industry norm. Some firms allow you to roll over any unused withdrawals—a valuable option.

SOURCE: *The Annuity Shopper* costs $10 and lists and describes hundreds of annuities. Call 800-872-6684.

And here are some buying tips specifically for deferred variable annuities:

- *Purchase one that allows you to switch among funds,* depending on where you see the economy heading. This preserves some control.

- *Is there telephone switching?* Some firms charge for this.

- *Assess fund performance, but beware:* Tracking variable annuities may not be all that useful. According to the Variable Annuities Research and Data Service (which tracks variable annuities and issues quarterly reports for $149), the top and bottom performers often switch places, depending on the economy. A better bet: Check with outside rating firms for safety and quality, look at the investment strategies of the funds, and invest where you feel comfortable.

Specifically for deferred fixed-rate annuities:

- *Does the firm offer a guaranteed fixed annuity rate?* If so, how long does this guarantee last? And does the insurance company have a history of slashing or cutting rates after the guarantee period is over? Many firms pay high up-front rates to attract new buyers, and once they've got you they let the rates drop. Don't just ask your agent if this is the case, check yourself. Ask for the company's listing of credited interest rates, and check these listings against market rates at the time. Or write for a copy of *Life Insurance Selling Magazine* (Commerce Publishing, St. Louis, Mo.): It puts out a listing of rates.

- *Be careful of annuities with very high rates*—this may be a tip-off that they are investing in high-yield, low-grade junk bonds.

Other Investments for Your Portfolio

REAL ESTATE (GENERAL INFORMATION)

▶ **This section deals primarily with different real estate *investments*—including REITs, RELPs, and rental real estate. (For information on your *personal* real estate, see page 359.)**

General Real Estate Investment Strategy

▶ **Whether you're buying a REIT, a RELP, rental property, or a real estate annuity, there's one thing to keep in mind: Real estate investments must always be approached with caution.**

Real estate is trickier than other investments. There is no central market that an investor can use to track prices and forecast trends. Real estate is highly local and highly differentiated. A 9.75% Treasury Bond sells for the same price in Seattle as in New York, but three-bedroom apartments sell for completely different prices.

Perhaps even more so than with other investments, you must research real estate investments very carefully. Read both general books and local magazines: Get a "feel" for the local market as well as a knowledge of the numbers and underlying values. If you buy a fund that invests in real estate, be even more careful about quality than you would normally, since it's harder to make judgments about performance.

REAL ESTATE INVESTMENT TRUSTS (REITS)

▶ **These were once the preferred real estate investments for retirees. In recent years, they declined in price and popularity, then in 1991 started turning back up again.**

What they are: REITs work something like a mutual fund, except that instead of stocks or bonds, the assets are real estate. Investors purchase shares in the REIT, which holds mortgages and operates property. Professional managers manage the property and collect rents and other income, which is passed on to the investors. This type of REIT income is called the dividend income and is usually quoted as a percentage, as in a 9.5 % yield. REITs can offer high yields, because they must pay out 95% of their operating profits to investors and because they are not subject to corporate tax. REITs can also pass on the proceeds of sale of real estate assets as capital gains, although REITs usually are constructed as perpetual investments—that is, money from sales is usually reinvested in new real estate. Because REITs are shares of an investment pool, they are like stocks and are often traded on stock exchanges. Shares of REITs usually sell at a discount from their asset value, called their net asset value.

Some basic types:

- *Equity REITs,* the most common type of REIT, buy income-producing properties, such as apartment buildings, office buildings, and shopping malls.

- *Mortgage REITs* are investment pools that lend money to real estate developers.

- *Hybrid REITs* are a combination of mortgage and equity REITs.

- *FREITs* are *F*inite REITs—there's a time limit on the investment, usually 7 to 10 years, after which the assets are sold and the proceeds distributed to the stockholders. One advantage of this is that the market price is probably closer to the underlying value (and it keeps getting closer as it nears the time limit), making it easier for you to evaluate your investment.

Pros: REITs trade on exchanges like stocks and so are relatively liquid. If you want out of a REIT, you can tell your broker to sell it for you. REITs can offer good yields because they don't pay corporate taxes. They are required by law to pass on 95% of their income to investors. And investors are able to defer taxes (until the REIT's shares are sold) on 40% of the REIT dividends. Finally, as a result of the real estate downturn, many REITs are selling at bargain-basement prices, many others made impressive gains in early 1991.

Cons: At the same time that real estate doldrums make REITs bargain buys, real estate problems also make them tricky investments. Which areas will recover fastest? Which REITs are good bargains and which will show poor performance for years more? Many REITs have shown poor performance in recent years—lower than average returns. In some senses, they face double volatility—they're affected by fluctuations of both the stock market and the real estate market.

REIT Investment and Buying Tips

▶ **REITs are available through many brokerages.**

Ask for and read prospectuses carefully. Carefully assess the trends both in the location and for the type of real estate owned. Also look into the REIT's track record to see how well it has performed and choose only those with a history of successes. Best bet: Have a trusted outside expert go over everything for you.

A few REIT specifics: Look for good dividend yields and growth (8% to 12% was good in 1990). If you find one with much higher yields steer clear: The odds are it is in risky markets or highly leveraged. Look also for a strong cash flow, and for REITs that are not highly leveraged (50% to 60% or less). There should be low yearly management fees—about 1% to 1.5% is currently the norm. And, of course, with equity REITs look for ownership in improving markets. Conservative investors should probably steer clear for now.

REAL ESTATE LIMITED PARTNERSHIPS (RELPS)

▶ **Real Estate Limited Partnerships (RELPs) were another investment once recommended for retirees, but the best advice now is to stay away.**

For more on how limited partnerships work and why to keep away, see Limited Partnerships (page 274).

What they are: Usually, RELP limited partners pool their money in a partnership that purchases properties that are to be sold within 10 years—and in meantime earn income from the rents collected on the property.

Pros: There may be some tax advantages (despite the changes in the tax code) for investors in RELPs involved in low-income housing and landmark and historic rehabilitation. Other pluses: They allow owners to avoid double taxation of profits and allow smaller investors to participate in ownership of large assets that they normally couldn't afford. Some RELPs are not as highly leveraged (debt-laden) as in the past. Nevertheless, no type of limited partnership, including RELPs, can really be recommended for retirees.

Cons: They are not as liquid as REITs. Most people holding RELPs recently have sold them at heavy losses. In the depressed real estate markets of 1990 and 1991, RELPs did particularly badly.

In addition, there are the problems inherent with all limited partnerships: high sales and management fees and fewer tax advantages than previously.

RELP Investment and Buying Tips

▶ **Shop very carefully—better yet, avoid.**

Try to see and monitor the property you're investing in, as opposed to investing blindly and being kept in the dark as to where your money is going. Follow the same general guidelines as with REITs.

REAL ESTATE ANNUITIES

▶ **Real estate annuities combine the advantages of an annuity with the advantages of real estate, but the best advice for retirees is to steer clear for now.**

What they are: Sold by insurance companies, these are variable annuities (see Annuities, page 258) that are invested in real estate, either through direct ownership of property or as a real estate mutual fund. As with other variable annuities, income and capital gains are tax-deferred until withdrawn.

Pros: They combine the tax advantages of tax-deferred annuities with the advantages of real estate investing, which once seemed immense in the booming markets of the 1980s. Also, some annuities may allow you to switch to stock or bond mutual funds if you wish, a nice extra in an uncertain real estate market. Withdrawal is relatively easy—but penalties are high (and if too many annuity holders wish to withdraw at once, you may be forced to wait).

Cons: The depressed state of the real estate market is a drawback now. You normally face large withdrawal penalties if you must liquidate your investment in the first five years, an extra 10% penalty by the IRS if you withdraw from a tax-deferred annuity before age 59½, usually high annual fees and poor performance in the past.

How to Buy Real Estate Annuities

Look for quality asset ownership. Look for management fees averaging 1% to 3%. However, in most cases, these investments are not recommended.

RENTAL REAL ESTATE

▶ **Rental property and personal speculative investing was fine in the go-go 1970s and 1980s, but for the 1990s the best advice is to be extremely cautious.**

What it is: Buying rental property as an investment was extremely popular in the 1980s, and all too frequently the topic of talk shows and "investment seminars"; interest declined somewhat in the 1990s as many markets turned down and some investors were left with high mortgages and unproductive real estate. In general, this option is not recommended for retirees. It may, however, prove profitable for young, motivated, energetic investors, with a detailed knowledge of real estate in general or a particular local real estate market, who are ready and willing to take advantage of some of the lower prices prevailing now.

Pros: This option gives you a great deal of control. You can choose the best real estate growth areas, based on your own knowledge or that of experts of your choosing—you're not relying on unseen REIT managers; you have financial control over your investment; you can extract the best income and tax advantages. You also have a degree of flexibility. You can choose when to sell.

Cons: There is the lack of liquidity. It's hard to resell houses in tough times. Real estate in 1991 was in the doldrums in much of the United States. Rental property involves hard work: managing, worrying about repairs and rents, and so forth. Also, there is the uncertainty—can you rent or sell your properties? And there are problems of freedom—unless you're very wealthy, owning real estate can trap you into years of working long hours to pay off mortgages on unsold or unprofitable properties.

How to Invest in Real Estate

▶ **It is crucial to *know* local real estate.**

Real estate markets are all local. Buy a property only after in-depth analysis of the region, the neighborhood, the street, the neighbors next door.

Be especially careful when reviewing information on the property—go over financial information carefully, have property value appraised by your own appraiser. Many investors are currently "bottom fishing"—looking at sectors that took hits in the real estate recession but look poised for a comeback. The problem here is usually not targeting the bargains, but deciding which areas will come back.

Finally, research through books and experts as well. Real estate, because it is expensive and not liquid, is not a casual investment. For a detailed and balanced exposition of real estate investment, see *J. K. Lasser's Real Estate Investment Guide*, by Gary Barr with Judith Headington McGee (J. K. Lasser Institute, $18.95).

REAL ESTATE MUTUAL FUNDS

▶ **Real estate mutual funds are yet another combined investment you should steer clear of.**

This is a very short section, for one reason. There is currently virtually no reason to buy these funds.

What they are: These are mutual funds that buy stocks of real estate corporations. Best advice: Avoid. Unlike most other real estate investments, there are no tax benefits. These funds haven't done very well. Also, many types of regular stock mutual funds will purchase real estate stocks if they're good buys (that is, if they're currently undervalued by the market), and you'll get your potential appreciation via these stock funds. If you want to purchase diversified portfolios of real estate stocks, check mutual funds that have real estate stocks as part of their investment portfolio.

GOLD

▶ **Gold is a valuable part of a diversified portfolio.**

Why buy gold? For one prime reason: *just in case.* Gold is recommended by many financial experts as a hedge against political or economic crises. As such, it should form a small part of a balanced, fairly large retirement portfolio.

What it is: Like the dollar, gold is recognized internationally as a medium of exchange. And more important, people tend to turn to it in times of crises—and the price tends to move up. In this way it is valuable as a hedge. Gold tends to do well when every other investment does poorly.

Gold Investment Strategy

▶ Don't buy gold to speculate.

First of all, gold doesn't pay dividends. Second, it *costs* you money (storage fees) to hold it. And third, gold hasn't been much of a speculative investment since it hit its all-time high of over $800 in 1980. Gold seems to have settled to a price of roughly 40% of its all-time high.

▶ Buy gold as a hedge.

If markets collapse you can use gold to buy bargain-priced stocks, or just possibly you may need it for living expenses. Either way, the cost of holding it will have been worth it.

How to Buy Gold

There are various ways to buy gold.

Bullion and coins: Gold can be purchased through large brokerage houses like Merrill Lynch. Depending on how much gold you're buying, you can buy 32-ounce bars, one-ounce coins, or various sizes in between. Coins are probably the most convenient way to buy gold. The American Gold Coin Exchange, operated by a subsidiary of the American Stock Exchange, sells coins at low prices close to the "spot price" (professional trader's price) plus a commission of about 2%. Coins can be stored in the firm's Delaware vault, and by doing so you can avoid your state sales taxes. Coins and bullion can also be stored and insured for you at major brokerage houses for about 0.5% of the value of your investment.

Gold accounts and certificates: Sold by brokerages and banks, these give you a proportionate interest in gold held by the institution. You get a certificate of ownership, or monthly statements. As with bullion, fees average about 0.5%.

Gold stocks and gold mutual funds: There are many companies in the United States, in Canada, and in South Africa that mine gold. Problem: Buying shares of these companies will not normally get you the same protection as owning gold. For one thing, in a major political disaster, to whom will you sell the shares? And in the more likely event of less severe crises, the prices of these shares tend to be more volatile than the price of gold. Gold mutual funds, because they invest in more than one company, are usually less volatile than individual gold stocks. Naturally, both may be purchased through a brokerage; some large fund families also include gold and precious metal funds.

Gold futures: This involves betting on the price of gold. Buying futures is speculative, and should not be part of a retirement strategy.

LIMITED PARTNERSHIPS

▶ **One word sums up limited partnerships as a part of a retirement investment package: Don't.**

Limited partnerships have a *limited* role even in nonretirement investment portfolios—they tend to be risky, they tend to be very illiquid, and there are a lot of bad investments out there (and of course, some good ones). Generally, limited partnerships are for the rich or the young—who can afford to take chances, and who are certain they won't need the money. Why? Because many investors lose their money.

What they are: Limited partnerships allow you as an investor to join in the profits of owning such large investments as real estate or TV franchises. Typically, individual investors purchase "units" of a partnership (usually at $5,000 each) and so become limited partners. This partnership has a predetermined purpose—to own and operate an oil well, for example. And it passes the profits, on a proportionate basis, back to the limited partners. Limited partners do *not* manage or even choose the partnership's investments beyond investing in the partnership. Naturally, someone must run the partnership: This person or group is termed the general partner, who usually invests only a nominal amount. Limited partnerships are in effect for a specified period of time, usually 8 to 12 years. After this period, the general partner liquidates the assets and turns the proceeds over to the limited partners.

Limited partnerships can be invested in real estate, oil and gas wells, film productions, cable and TV franchises, and so forth. Recent partnerships have stressed current income more than capital gains or tax benefits. Public limited partnerships are sold by stockbrokers and financial professionals, involve over 35 investors, are regulated by the Securities and Exchange Commission, and maintain minimum net worth requirements. Private offerings are less regulated and usually riskier. *Master limited partnerships* that are publicly traded, like stocks, are usually less risky.

Pros: They offer income and growth, if they are good investments. They allow smaller investors to participate in the ownership of large assets, such as office buildings, which they couldn't own otherwise. Unlike corporate investments, they allow owners or participants to avoid double taxation (stock owners are in effect taxed twice because the corporation is taxed and so are their dividends). They can offer tax deductions (depreciation) for those in high tax brackets. For the very rich, they can also be fun: Although most film production limited partnerships lose money, they are an enjoyable, partially tax deductible way to meet movie stars and hang around movie sets.

Cons: There are reduced tax benefits. Investors can now only deduct losses against "passive" income, which means income from other partnerships, as well as rents and the like. They are usually high risk. Well over 50% of limited partnerships in film, theater, agricultural equipment, agriculture, and oil and gas lose money, for example. Almost all limited partnerships are long term and not very liquid—once you've put your money in it's very tough getting it out. There are limited secondary markets. Finally, most are sold with high commissions tacked on—up to 8% of your money may go into the salesperson's pockets. Then there are the start-up fees and so forth. Many investors pay out 20% to 30% of their initial investments.

Limited Partnership Investment Strategy

▶ **If you do buy a limited partnership read the fine print very carefully.**

Some reputable brokers push these partnerships on people when they shouldn't—presumably to earn the fat commissions they carry. To be sure, some partnerships, usually real estate limited partnerships sold by reputable brokers, have sometimes proved to be reasonable investments. But even here, they suffer from problems of illiquidity that should turn off anyone looking for retirement investments—even if the partnerships are specifically tailored for retirees. One major estate and trusts lawyer recently reported selling a client's real estate limited partnerships—sold by a major brokerage—back to the same brokerage for 11 cents on the dollar. Caveat emptor.

▶ **How to sell one if you're convinced you should be out.**

Try the secondary market via your broker if you've purchased one through a brokerage. Ask your broker what the last unit traded brought, use that as a very rough guide to what yours will probably fetch, and decide if the amount is acceptable to you. But remember, partnerships are not often traded so the price can vary enormously between sales. *Master limited partnerships* are commonly traded on exchanges and are generally easier to sell.

You may try private listings. The National Partnership Exchange (NAPEX, Inc.) electronically lists and trades partnerships—for a fee. Call 800-356-2739. Also: Raymond James Limited Partnership Trading Desk, 800-237-7591. There are others: Check your library and do some research before you sign on with any exchange.

TAX TIP: **Caution: If you sell a limited partnership constructed to produce early tax writeoffs for investors, you may now be required to pay taxes on the proceeds from your sale. Check with your accountant or financial planner.**

"Don'ts" in Retirement Investing

▶ **Wealthy retirees are *conservative* retirees.**

Below is a list of "don'ts" in retirement investing. The reasons are simple. Either these investments are too risky, there are too many cheats, or there are far better alternatives. Be aware that many salespeople will deluge you with "examples" of why their specific investment isn't like the others. Usually they're overstating the facts or they're lying.

Some bad investments and ideas for retirees:

- *Limited partnerships* (see above, page 274).

- *Over-the-phone investing:* Never agree to invest over the phone and never give out credit card numbers. (Obviously, it's another thing once you have a relationship with a reputable broker.) Reputable brokers may solicit over the phone but why take chances? Penny stock scams and precious metals "deals" abound.

- *Commodities:* The Wall Street Journal, analyzing a Chicago commodities broker, found that 71% of its customers *lost* money. The average account closed in 11 months. The broker made money but most clients didn't. Another study found that *everyone* lost money at another firm. The average person doesn't have the knowledge, the time, or the money to bet on the price of pork bellies or other such commodities. Yes, some commodities funds have shown better averages. But these funds are also risky—and expensive, with high sales charges, very high annual fees, and very volatile performances. Don't be taken in by promises of big money.

- *Super-high-yielding investments:* If you receive a mail advertisement or prospectus, look at it closely. Notice that these ads very often promise yields of "up to" 20%, 50% or whatever. "Up to" can mean anything under that amount—like zero. Call your local better business bureau, reasearch the firm—and when it seems that it is almost too good to be true, it is.

- *Buying stocks on margin, shorting, and so forth:* Don't magnify your losses on the stock market by using leverage.

- *Collectibles:* If you like them, don't stop buying them—just don't bet on them for your retirement income. Collectibles, with some exceptions, are often very volatile in price, depending on the fad of the moment. Antique cars, for example, used to be touted as a good investment. Then the baby boom came along and post-1950s cars became the rage—and antique prices dropped substantially.

Some Advice on Investment Scams

▶ **Don't ever get pressured to make an immediate investment decision.**

The easiest giveaway for most cheats is a high-pressure phone solicitation during which the salesperson tries to get you to commit over the phone and wants you to give out a credit card number or to send a check immediately. Such salespeople may try to insult you into signing on ("You have to ask your *wife?* Hey, who's the *man* in your family?"), or play on your greed ("The investment's getting taken up as we talk—they'll be nothing left if you wait"). Another routine is to offer to have a messenger come over immediately to pick up your check. In such cases, hang up the phone. Pressure tactics and sound investment don't mix.

Even when you're sent a prospectus by one of these high-pressure phone sales people, look carefully. Odds are that the yields have been restated to look better or that *potential* returns are shown, not actual historical returns. Read the fine print, too. Another ploy is to vaguely state reasonable terms and conditions in big print, and then in fine print take all the good options away and add fees and requirements.

Always check with the authorities (A. M. Best for insurance, state agencies, and so forth) before buying anything. Resist the offers of easy money overnight. The airwaves are full of interviews with people who got conned and lost their retirement nest eggs.

And one final note: many investment or credit television ads ask you to call phone numbers beginning with 900. These are pay-per-call phone numbers, which are often expensive. In most cases you can get better advice and better service from credit agencies or investment companies that will not charge you for doing business with them.

SOURCE: A free booklet describing common investment scams, how to avoid them, and how to find a qualified financial planner is ***Avoiding Investment and Financial Scams: Seeking Full Disclosure Is the Key.*** Write: The Institute of Certified Financial Planners, 10065 East Harvard Ave., Suite 320, Denver, CO 80231 (or call 800-282-PLAN).

Estate Planning and Legal Considerations

▶

▶ PART II

Chapter 8

ESTATE PLANNING

INTRODUCTION

▶ **Successful estate planning allows you to live comfortably now, then pass on your assets to whomever you choose with the lowest possible taxes and the fewest possible administrative troubles.**

This is a straightforward proposition, but one that requires thought, planning, and usually professional assistance.

Do keep in mind that it is not only the wealthy who require estate planning. Estate planning is the only way you can ensure that your money and other assets go to the people you want—not to those determined by state law. It's the only assurance you have that a large portion of your estate won't get eaten up by taxes. And it's the only way you can be sure that your survivors get what is due them.

When you plan your estate well, you will have a plan that:

- *Maintains your assets for a comfortable life now.* You will manage your estate in the present so that you can live comfortably and provide for any dependents.

- *Determines the distribution of your estate to your heirs.* You will devise a way of dividing your estate among your survivors—through gifts, trusts, or direct inheritances—in such a way that they face the fewest possible legal hassles.

- *Minimizes the tax bite on your estate after your death.* You will prepare your estate in such a way that you can keep estate and inheritance taxes down for your survivors.

To do this, you should follow a simple process: First, determine what your assets are and what your goals are for your estate. Do you want to pass a large portion of your assets on to heirs? Or do you want to leave only a small amount and use the rest now?

Next, draw up a plan that meets your goals and takes into account the twin evils of *probate* (the lengthy legal process that ultimately settles your estate—but can result in mounting expenses) and *estate taxes* (the transfer taxes that can take a healthy chunk out of your heirs' inheritance). To minimize their effect, you should devise a strategy of passing on your estate through one or a combination of direct inheritance, gifts, and trusts.

And you should write a will—the legal document that assures that your estate is distributed in the way you have planned.

▶ **In general, you are best off getting the assistance of a professional, especially if you have a large or complicated estate, or if you're planning on setting up trusts.**

While the basic process of estate planning is simple, the individual elements can get complicated. This is why, in most cases, you should work with a professional—an estate lawyer or certified financial planner. Without a professional, there's a very good chance your estate will be whittled down more than necessary by taxes.

If you're not going in for anything but a straight will, you can make do on your own if you want—with a computer software program or guidebook—but this isn't recommended. It's easy to get lost in the complexities the legal system, federal taxation codes, and the like. You're best off spending a little more money to protect your estate. It may save money in the long run.

TIP: When choosing an estate lawyer, speak with at least three. Aside from listening to their plans, you should pay attention to your gut feelings. Do you like the person? Do you feel comfortable with him or her—comfortable enough to frankly discuss your finances and family with that person? Is the lawyer a good listener—or is he or she only interested in what he or she has to say?

▶ **Pull together some essential information to facilitate the estate-planning process.**

When you see the professional you have chosen to help you plan your estate, you should bring the following information:

- *Assets overview:* a list of your assets, including bank accounts, securities accounts, real estate, and death benefits from pension plans. This should be very detailed—in the case of accounts, list the account number and financial institution; with real estate, bring the deed.

- *Personal information sheet:* information on you and your spouse, including date of birth, Social Security numbers, and marriage date and place. Also include names, addresses, and ages of beneficiaries.

▶ **While a professional will take you step by step through the estate-planning process, it is a good idea to have a working knowledge of the components ahead of time.**

The following sections should give you a general idea of the different components in planning for the management and distribution of your estate: how to value your assets, probate and how to avoid high probate costs, estate and inheritance taxes and how to set up trusts that can ease their bite, and how to write a will that works.

DETERMINING YOUR ASSETS AND YOUR GOALS

▶ **To come up with a successful estate plan, you must first be aware of the real value of your estate.**

Estate planning begins with valuing your assets and subtracting any liabilities.

Your assets include real estate, savings and checking accounts,

WORKSHEET 4: ESTATE PLANNING

Step 1: Start by determining the gross value of your estate. Add up the following assets:

1. Securities (stocks and bonds) _____

2. Real estate _____

3. Cash (savings and checking accounts) _____

4. IRAs, pension plans, other retirement benefits _____

5. Life insurance (cash value of policy, annuities) _____

6. Valuables (furniture, collectibles, jewelry, etc.) _____

7. Properties held jointly _____

8. Properties in revocable trust _____

9. SUBTOTAL: _____

Step 2: Add up the following debts:

10. Mortgage balances _____

11. Outstanding loans and credit card balances _____

12. Income taxes _____

13. Property taxes _____

14. SUBTOTAL: _____

Step 3: Add up the following expenses:

15. Funeral expenses _____

16. Administration of your estate _____

17. SUBTOTAL: _____

Step 4: Add debts and expenses (lines 14 and 17) _____

Step 5: Subtract this total from subtotal of assets (line 9) _____

TOTAL (rough estimate of estate) _____

securities, insurance, motor vehicles, household effects, valuables (such as jewelry and coin collections), any death benefits that will be paid upon your death, even properties held jointly.

Liabilities include mortgages, outstanding loans (including credit card balances), and income and property taxes. Also subtract any costs that will be incurred after your death, such as funeral expenses and estate administration costs. (The typical funeral now runs between $3,000 and $5,000; and executor's fee and expenses might amount to between 2% and 5% of your estate.)

The amount you come up with is a rough estimate of the value of your estate—the assets you can pass along to heirs.

▶ **Once you have a general idea of the worth of your estate, start thinking about who you want to leave assets to and who you don't.**

This is a personal matter—only you know how you want your estate distributed.

A few points to keep in mind as you think about this matter: *It is difficult (and often impossible) to completely disinherit a spouse.* Many states require that your spouse get some of your estate, usually a third to a half. Similarly, it may be difficult to disinherit children. In Louisiana, it is against the law. In other states, it is difficult. If you want to disinherit a child, spell it out in your will—state clearly that you are making no provision for your son or daughter.

You should also start thinking about the assets you want to distribute and the form in which you want to distribute them. Many people automatically assume they should leave their estate. Remember—you earned your money yourself. If your children are financially well off, there's no reason for you to pass on a large sum. You may prefer to use your assets *now,* for *yourself.*

PROBATE: WHAT IT IS AND HOW TO AVOID PROBLEMS

▶ **A crucial part of estate planning is designing the distribution of your estate in such a way that you avoid probate problems.**

Probate is the legal process by which your estate is administered and distributed after your death. Your executor inventories your assets, values them, pays any debts, files taxes, and distributes the estate per your directions in your will. All this is usually done with the help of an attorney. The entire process is overseen by a probate judge.

So far, so good. But the problem is, probate is an often lengthy process that can tie up your estate for quite some time, leaving your heirs waiting for their share of your assets. And the costs of probate can add up—legal fees may take a sizable chunk of the estate you planned to pass on to heirs.

To keep probate problems at a minimum, follow these tips:

- *Have a will.* Wills help streamline the probate process. Because the court won't have to appoint a public administrator to settle your estate, you keep costs down.

- *Keep organized records.* This, too, speeds the process. Keep a list of assets covering everything you own, including real estate, savings and checking accounts, securities, insurance, any death benefits that will be paid upon your death, valuables, even properties held jointly (note: this list should be detailed—be sure to include names of financial institutions and account numbers). Include a personal information sheet, containing data on you and your spouse—birthdates, Social Security numbers, marriage date and location, beneficiaries' names and addresses, insurance policies, and so forth. Keep copies of these lists at home, with your attorney, in a safe deposit box, with a family member or friend.

- *Keep a portion your assets entirely out of probate.* This will ensure that your spouse or other survivors can get immediate cash for living. First, keep in mind that life insurance proceeds, IRAs, Keoghs, and other retirement plans will pass to the beneficiaries without probate. You also can deliberately set up methods of passing assets to beneficiaries without probate, such as living trusts, joint and survivorship ownership, and payable-on-death bank accounts.

▶ *Living trusts* go into effect while you are still alive.

Living trusts are one of the most popular ways of avoiding probate problems: Some people use them in place of a will. The big advantage of a living trust: Although you've placed assets in trust, you can name yourself as trustee and keep control over those assets, how they are invested, and so forth.

Lately, however, many lawyers claim that living trusts are a waste of money—probate expenses are less than the cost of setting up a living trust. Your best bet is to compare costs—ask what your lawyer will charge for setting up a living trust and find out what the average probate expenses are in your area by asking a friend or relative who has recently been through the probate process.

How it works: A living trust is a trust that you set up while you are alive to provide for your beneficiaries immediately upon your death. You transfer title of your assets—from bank acccounts to real estate to securities—to the trust. Setting up a living trust is the same as setting up any kind of trust—you (the grantor or donor) determine what you want in the trust, choose a beneficiary, and choose a trustee. Typically you will be the trustee, which means you can keep control of all assets in the trust. In this case, you also designate a successor trustee, who will take over upon your death or if you become incompetent or incapacitated. (This points to another use for living trusts: to ensure that your finances are taken care of should you become unable to take care of them yourself, without having to go through a competency hearing. To cover this possibility, you must state in the trust agreement that the successor is to take over if you are certified incompetent by a doctor.)

As with other types of trusts, living trusts can be either revocable (which means you can change the trust arrangement or cancel it) or irrevocable (which means that the trust can't be changed or canceled). With a revocable living trust, you, the grantor, are taxed on trust *income*. With an irrevocable living trust, you are taxed on income only: if you receive the income, if it is accumulated for you or your spouse, if it is used to support a legal dependent, if you use the income to pay your (or your spouse's) life insurance premiums, or to cover legal obligations, or if the trust's assets will revert to you or your spouse. Most people opt for revocable living trusts, so that they can keep the option to change the trust arrangement at any point during their lifetime. The costs of setting up a living trust cover a wide range—anywhere from $500 to $2,000. (For more information on setting up trusts, their provisions, and so forth, see page 290).

Pros: Beneficiaries immediately receive assets upon your death; living trusts are difficult to contest; cost is relatively low compared to probate. Another big advantage—if you become mentally or physically incapacitated and can't manage your assets, your successor trustee will manage them.

Cons: Transfer of assets into the trust can take a great deal of time. The cost of setting up a living trust can be higher than probate.

▶ **Even if you use a living trust to replace your will, you need a will.**

This sounds like a contradiction, but it's not. Although a living trust can encompass virtually all of your assets, you should still draw up a basic will. There are two important reasons. First, if you have children who are minors, a living trust won't provide instructions regarding guardianship. You need a will to specify this. Second, a will can ensure that any property you omitted from the trust will go into it. This is done by inclusion of a "pour over" clause, which states that any assets you overlooked and didn't include in your living trust should be placed there after your death. These assets will be subject to probate, since the transfer to trust occurs after your death.

▶ *Joint and survivorship ownership* (also called joint tenancy with right of survivorship) is another way of keeping your property out of probate.

This arrangement is especially common with married couples, who usually hold their home and bank accounts in joint tenancy with right of survivorship. An important note: don't make a common mistake and assume that *any* joint bank account will immediately pass to the co-owner upon death of the other owner. Unless the account is specifically set up as a J&S account or payable-on-death (see page 289), the assets in the account will be frozen until probate is completed.

How it works: With joint and survivorship ownership, you own assets with another person; your name and theirs appear jointly as owners on documents (for example, if you want to pass a house on to your child, the child's name and yours appear on the deed); and upon your death, your share automatically passes over to the co-owner. The transfer takes place with no will and no probate.

Pros: Assets completely avoid probate; J&S is a simple procedure.

Cons: J&S makes it difficult to divide your estate equally among a few people; co-owners have the right to control the assets (you'll need to get their approval on any actions you want to take regarding the assets); if you add a name to a deed, the new co-owner may be liable for a gift tax; the co-owner may be liable for capital gains tax after the transfer if an asset has appreciated and is sold.

Best for: Most married couples; people who want to pass a specific asset on to a specific individual.

TIP: **If you are married and live in a community property state, you may be better off without J&S. Because the state treats any assets acquired during a marriage as community property, the surviving spouse won't get hit with large capital gains taxes when the property is "stepped up" to market value and transferred.**

▶ **An option somewhat similar to joint and survivorship ownership, *payable-on-death accounts* (or trustee accounts) enable you to pass a bank account to your beneficiary upon your death.**

How it works: With a payable-on-death account, you name a beneficiary (or beneficiaries) who receives the cash in the account after your death—never before. Like irrevocable living trusts, payable-on-death accounts give you a degree of flexibility—you can add or change beneficiaries, add or remove funds in the account, or close the account. However, unlike living trusts, payable-on-death accounts don't allow you to put a range of assets into the account. Payable-on-death accounts are generally restricted to either straight bank accounts or U.S. Savings Bonds.

Setting up a payable-on-death account is usually a simple process—you can contact your bank for specifics; you don't need a lawyer.

Pros: Payable-on-death accounts are simple to set up; costs are low or nonexistent.

Cons: You lack flexibility in terms of what kind of assets are allowable.

▶ *Life insurance* **proceeds also stay out of probate, giving your survivors immediate cash while they are waiting for the will to be settled.**

Life insurance is a way of providing quick cash for your survivors. The proceeds of your policy go immediately to your beneficiary, without going through probate. (For information on annuities and other aspects of life insurance, see Annuities, page 258, and Life Insurance, page 121.)

TIP: If your estate is worth $600,000, or nearly, your life insurance may *cost* your survivors money. While life insurance proceeds aren't part of the probate process, they are counted as part of your estate for federal tax purposes. And estates worth $600,000 or more are subject to federal tax. So if your estate plus your life insurance add up to that figure, it's all taxable. The way around this? Set up a life insurance trust. (For information on how to do this, see page 297.)

ESTATE AND INHERITANCE TAXES, AND THE TRUSTS THAT CAN HELP REDUCE THEM

▶ **Another important aspect of estate planning is devising a way for your heirs to pay the lowest possible estate and inheritance taxes.**

First, a quick definition of *taxable estate:* It is every asset you pass on (or transfer) to your heirs, including property you own in your name, half of the property you own jointly, property over which you have the general power of appointment (which includes living trusts), and the face value of your life insurance.

Unlike probate, which only applies to property you own when you die, federal taxes apply to your entire estate. You may also face state estate taxes. These vary according to the size of your estate and the state in which you live. (For a list of states with low or no estate taxes, see page 375.)

If your estate is a small one, you have little to worry about. Federal estate taxes affect only estates worth over $600,000. However, it isn't difficult to reach that amount when you factor in real estate values, life insurance, and other assets.

A few facts:

- *You can pass on an unlimited amount tax-free to your spouse.* This is known as the "marital deduction," and it ensures that your spouse will not lose a large portion of the estate to taxes. But it *doesn't* mean that the estate will be passed on intact after your spouse's death. When your spouse dies, only $600,000 can be passed on tax-free to heirs.

- *You owe no estate taxes if your estate is less than $600,000.* In other words, you can pass on up to $600,000 tax-free to heirs other than your spouse. From then on, though, the tax bite mounts. If the estate is worth from $600,000 to $750,000, the tax bracket is 37%; from $750,001 to $1,000,000, 39%; for $1,000,001 to $1,250,000, 41%; from $1,250,001 to 1,500,000, 43%; and on up to 55%.

This means that a married couple can pass $1.2 million to their heirs tax-free (if the first to die passes $600,000 to the heirs: For specifics, see Family Trusts, page 296). Anything over that will be taxed. The bottom line? If you have a substantial estate—one worth more than $1.2 million—that you want to pass on to your heirs, you must come up with a strategy that will keep taxes from taking a sizable bite of the estate. If your estate is smaller, you may be better off without special trusts—the cost of setting up and maintaining the trust simply isn't worth it.

▶ **To minimize taxes and avoid probate costs, consider setting up certain trusts, making gifts, and making other provisions.**

If you have a large estate, setting up trusts can help preserve your estate for your heirs and prevent it from being diminished by probate costs or—more important—estate taxes. In addition, if you are concerned about the ability of your heir (or the guardian of an heir) to manage money, setting up a trust ensures that the estate won't go broke because of poor financial decisions.

Setting up a trust is a fairly straightforward procedure. You (the grantor or donor) lay out what you want done with the trust in a trust agreement. You choose the beneficiaries of the trust, and the trustee—the individual or institution who will *administer* the trust (that is, manage and distribute the assets you have placed in trust according to the trust agreement). Any competent adult can be a trustee, or you may appoint a professional trustee, usually a bank or trust company. The trustee is entitled to a fee for services, usually from 1% to 2% of the trust's assets each year. Often trustees who are friends or relatives will waive the fee.

A popular, and logical, choice for trustee is a family friend or relative, one with financial know-how and management ability. By choosing someone you know, you can be assured that your trust is in good hands and that your beneficiaries will be dealt with sensitively.

Appointing a professional trustee is a good option if you have a very large estate, need complex trusts, and want to be sure everything is properly administered. This option is usually open only to people setting up trusts in excess of $200,000. To be sure you are getting the best possible professional trustee, you should shop around. Check the investment performance of the institutions you are considering, paying special attention to the long-term yields. Also check how much trustee fees will be. As mentioned above, they usually will be from 1% to 2% of the assets annually.

TIP: **If you have an estate that warrants a professional, you may want to consider another popular option: Appoint cotrustees, one a professional, the other a friend or family member. In this way, you can have the best of both worlds—the professional expertise of the professional trustee and the personal touch of the friend or relative.**

Finally, in some cases (as with a living trust), *you* may elect to be trustee. In this situation, you must also name the recipient of the trust after your death and a successor trustee, who will succeed you after your death or if you become incapable of managing the trust. Depending upon the instructions you include in your trust document, this successor will either keep the trust intact upon your death or have the trust terminated and the assets in the trust distributed to your beneficiaries.

▶ **There are two very basic types of trusts—revocable and irrevocable.**

A *revocable* trust can be changed or canceled at any time by the creator (or donor) of the trust. If a revocable trust is canceled, the assets in the trust revert to the donor, become part of his or her estate again, and upon the donor's death, are subject to full estate taxes.

An *irrevocable* trust's donor can't change or cancel it. Similarly, he or she can't receive any benefit from the trust's principal or income. Because assets never revert to the donor, assets in an irrevocable trust are not liable to estate taxes. Why create an irrevocable trust? Certain types of trusts *must,* by law, be set up this way.

Whichever, type of trust you choose, you are getting several big plusses: Assets placed in trust are removed from probate; they're exempt from estate taxes; they're difficult to challenge; and they ensure that your heirs get the money you wanted them to get—and quickly.

Below are brief descriptions of the most common types of trusts, how they work, and when you may want to use them in your estate planning. Do keep in mind, however, that trusts are complicated devices. In all cases, you should consult a professional about whether to use them. The following material is intended only to serve as an introduction. For more information, speak with a specialist.

Gifts

▶ **Giving away some of your assets while you are still alive is a simple way of avoiding taxes—and is emotionally satisfying as well.**

How they work: Giving gifts is a way of passing assets on while you are still alive. Each year, you can give each person you choose up to $10,000—$20,000 if the gift is from a married couple—free of gift or estate taxes. Anything above this amount is taxable: You have to report any such taxable gifts to the IRS (on Form 709); the excess amount will also be deducted from your $600,000 exemption. (Note: As of 1990, Louisiana, New York, North Carolina, Oregon, Puerto Rico, South Carolina, Tennessee, and Wisconsin also impose *state* gift taxes.)

TIP: When making gifts to minors, remember the "Kiddie Tax." Minors until the age of 14 have to pay taxes on all interest, dividends, and other investment income over $1,000 at the donor's tax rate; minors over the age of 14 pay taxes on investment income over $500, but at their own rate (most often 15%). One suggestion: give *non-income-producing assets* to children under 14.

Pros: Gift giving is extremely simple. You don't have to do anything but give the gift, and you can see the results of your generosity when you give gifts—a very pleasant benefit.

Cons: Assets worth over $10,000 (such as houses, other real estate, businesses, and other non-liquid assets) can't be given as gifts without incurring the gift tax.

Minors' Trusts

▶ **To pass assets on to children or grandchildren, you may set up a minor's trust—either a 2503(c) minor's trust or a Crummey trust.**

Minors' trusts recently have lost some of their popularity, chiefly because of the previously mentioned Kiddie Tax. Because a child under 14 will pay tax at his or her parent's rate on any investment income over $1,000, the benefits of switching money to a minor's trust have diminished. But they still do offer several estate tax breaks and (if you split the trust's income between the trust and a child *over* 14) income tax breaks.

How they work: Briefly, a minor's trust provides income for a minor upon your death and removes assets from your estate, diminishing the amount that will be liable to estate taxes. One caveat: You'll need a lawyer to set up a minor's trust, and you'll need to file a federal income tax form each year for the trust. Because of this, most experts recommend setting up a minor's trust only for amounts over $50,000.

With a *2503(c) trust,* you set up an irrevocable trust. Your beneficiary doesn't receive either the income on the trust or the principal until he or she reaches 21. If he or she doesn't demand assets from the trust within 30 to 60 days of reaching 21, the trust continues for whatever length of time you have specified in the trust agreement. The tax break you get from this trust: Regardless of the beneficiary's age, the first $5,000 of income earned by the trust is taxed at 15%; anything above that at 28%.

A *Crummey trust* is a 2503(c) trust with a twist: While you get essentially the same estate and income tax breaks, the trust isn't susceptible to termination when the beneficiary reaches age 21. You can specify any age your want. One drawback, however: According to the IRS, if you are withholding trust assets from a beneficiary, those assets are considered "a gift of future interest," which isn't allowed under the $10,000 gift tax exemption. So you will face gift tax liability. To take advantage of the $10,000 gift tax exclusion, you can give your beneficiary "Crummey powers." With these, the beneficiary can withdraw a set amount of the principal each year: the annual gift tax exclusion ($10,000), the interest amount added to the trust that year, or 5% of the principal, whichever amount is lowest.

Pros: You can get income tax breaks while your children or grandchildren accumulate assets for such future expenses as college and housing. If you name yourself as trustee, you can continue to control the principal and income.

Cons: Costs are high. A lawyer will charge about $500 or more to set up a minor's trust; in addition, because you have to file an income tax form each year for the trust, you'll probably be paying an accountant.

▶ **You may also consider a** *generation-skipping trust.*

Generation-skipping trusts are just what they sound like. While the income of the trust can be used by your children, the principal of the trust passes on to your grandchildren. (Note: if you pass assets of more than $1 million to your grandchildren, they will be liable for a special estate tax.)

Custodial Accounts

▶ **You may set up** *custodial accounts* **for grandchildren or children under the Uniform Gift to Minors Act (UGMA), or the similar, but more flexible, Uniform Transfer to Minors Act (UTMA).**

These are popular with people who don't have the assets to set up a minor's trust, but who want to help children or grandchildren with such things as college expenses. Like minors' trusts, custodial accounts allow you to switch assets to your beneficiaries, removing them from your estate (and from estate taxes). In addition, if you time your gifts to the custodial account well, you can get income tax breaks. This can get very complicated. For information, talk to your accountant.

How they work: Under both acts, you set up a custodial account administered by a custodian with the grandchild or child as beneficiary. You can set up a no-fee custodial account at most financial institutions—at a bank, a brokerage or a mutual fund.

TIP: **Don't name yourself as custodian. If you do, and you die before your beneficiary reaches the age of majority, the property in the account will be included in your taxable estate.**

Under UGMA, the assets in the trust (only cash or securities) automatically go to the beneficiary on his or her 18th birthday—regardless of your wishes.

Under UTMA, you have more leeway as to what the gifts can be. In addition to cash or securities, you can give such assets as real estate or paintings. You also have more leeway as to distribution of the assets—distribution can be deferred until the beneficiary reaches the age of 21 (25 in California).

Pros: Setting these up at a bank or brokerage costs you nothing. If you plan carefully, you can have assets growing for your beneficiary and reap tax benefits.

Cons: You need to carefully plan your gifts (both the timing of deposits and what you are investing in) to get maximum tax benefits.

Family Trusts

▶ **Family trusts (also called bypass trusts) enable you to provide for your spouse upon your death, then have the amount in the trust pass tax-free to the trust's beneficiaries (usually your children) upon your spouse's death.**

Family trusts are often "testamentary trusts"—that is, they are set up in a will, and so go into effect upon the death of the donor. They are one of the most common types of trusts used to reduce estate taxes.

How they work: Upon your death, you can have assets up to $600,000 (within the exemption) go into trust. As with any trust, you will have appointed a trustee—a professional, family friend, or relative—to administer the trust. Your spouse can receive the income of the trust and, under what is called a "5 and 5 provision," can withdraw up to 5% or $5,000 from the principal each year—whichever is greater. If your spouse needs additional money, it is up to the trustee to decide whether to release it.

Upon your spouse's death, the assets in the trust pass on to the trust's beneficiaries—typically your children. (In addition, your spouse can pass on up to $600,000 tax-free to your heirs.)

TIP: The spouse is not required by law to take money from the trust—not even the income. By keeping as much in the trust as possible, you assume that the assets keep growing even faster, and beneficiaries get a substantial estate tax-free—up to $1.2 million.

Pros: You can pass on more of your estate tax-free; bypass trusts are easy to set up.

Cons: None.

Marital Trusts

▶ **As the name denotes, marital trusts are designed for married couples.**

How they work: With a marital trust, one spouse leaves his or her assets in trust with the remaining spouse as beneficiary. Because the assets become part of the remaining spouse's taxable estate, they qualify for the marital deduction—that is, no matter how much the assets are worth, they pass on to your spouse with no estate taxes. People often choose to set up a marital trust when a spouse is ill and often name a child as trustee.

There are two common types of marital trusts: general power of appointment and QTIP trusts.

General power of appointment trusts are designed so that your spouse can choose the beneficiary—that is, he or she has the power to appoint whomever he or she wants.

QTIP trusts (Qualified Terminable Interest Property trusts) are designed so that you—not your spouse—can choose the beneficiary. Usually you'll do this to ensure that your estate doesn't pass on to the new spouse of your husband or wife. Your spouse can get income from the trust over his or her lifetime; upon his or her death, the principal in the trust passes on to whomever you have chosen as the heir(s)—usually your children.

Since the principal of either type of marital trust is part of your spouse's estate, the heirs will face estate taxes.

Pros: Marital trusts enable you to be sure that your spouse is well provided for and doesn't run your estate into the ground—a big plus if your spouse is a poor money manager. QTIPs are good for those who have been married more than once and want to be sure children from previous marriages receive assets after the current spouse dies.

Cons: With a general power of appointment trust your assets may wind up with someone you don't want. No real cons for QTIPs.

Life Insurance Trusts

▶ **Life insurance trusts enable you to keep the proceeds of a life insurance policy free from estate taxes. This is a very big advantage, since many life insurance policies can be worth a large** sum of money—enough to push the value of an estate over $600,000.

How it works: With a life insurance trust, a third party—not yourself, not your beneficiaries—is the policy owner. You (the grantor) set up the trust, choose a trustee who will oversee the trust, and name beneficiaries. You fund the trust by making yearly gifts to it of $10,000 or less—untaxed because they fall within the legal gift tax exclusion amount. This will cover premiums, trustee fees (if any), and so forth.

You can either open a life insurance policy that is owned by a trust or transfer existing policies (even group policies sponsored by your employer) into a trust. One drawback, though, in the latter case, is that if you die within three years of the transfer, the trust is dissolved and the policy becomes part of your (taxable) estate.

A popular move for married people is to set up a life insurance trust with a second-to-die policy (in which the policy pays off only when the second spouse dies), with the children as beneficiaries. Why is this option so popular? Costs are very low. In addition, keep in mind that spouses can receive an unlimited amount of assets tax-free upon the death of their spouse, so they may not need the policy proceeds—while children will.

Pros: Proceeds are entirely free of estate taxes; life insurance trusts are easy to set up; the proceeds of a life insurance trust can be used to buy real estate or other nonliquid assets from the estate—which will enable the estate to cover taxes, and the real estate to stay in trust for the beneficiaries. (Note: This is an excellent way of preventing the sale of a family business.)

Cons: Life insurance trusts can be costly to maintain; because you're no longer the owner of your policy, you can't borrow against it.

TIP: For very prudent people—follow the advice given in Mary Rowland's *Your Own Account* column from *The New York Times.* Remember that when the trust is irrevocable you won't be able to change names if you divorce. So instead of designating your spouse as beneficiary by name, say "my current spouse," or "spouse at the time of my death." This way your former spouse won't be legally entitled to the proceeds.

GRITS (Grantor Retained Income Trusts) and Splits (Split Interest Purchases)

▶ **GRITs and splits are two other ways of avoiding high estate taxes. They are designed primarily for the very wealthy.**

With GRITs and splits, you lower your estate tax burden while getting the benefits of trust income while you live.

How they work: With GRITs, you put your assets into an irrevocable trust that is in effect for up to 10 years. You get all the income earned by the trust over those years. After 10 years or the length of the trust pass, the trust passes on to the beneficiaries you have named.

With splits, you split the purchase of an asset with another person—most often a child or grandchild. You buy a majority interest, the child the remaining amount. As with a GRIT, the trust is in effect for a predetermined time. Over that period, you receive all the income earned on the assets. After the trust ends, the assets transfer tax-free to the beneficiary. One drawback, however: The beneficiary needs to have the money to purchase his or her portion of the split—and it *can't* come from the person setting up the split.

Pros: The big plus with GRITs where your beneficiaries are concerned is that the IRS doesn't count your real contributions to the trust, but the actuarial value—called the remainder interest. With splits, beneficiaries get your assets for far less than the actual value.

Cons: If you die before the trust ends, the assets revert to your estate, and so are taxable. Setting up GRITs or splits can be very costly. Lawyer's fees of $1,000 are not uncommon.

Charitable Gifts and Charitable Remainder Trusts

▶ **By making gifts of assets to charities while you are alive, you get two tax benefits—an income tax deduction and a smaller estate for estate taxes. Or, if you want to remove more money, you may set up a charitable remainder annuity trust.**

How they work: Charitable remainder trusts allow you to contribute assets to a charity, yet have a beneficiary—or yourself—receive income on those assets. They are especially good ideas if you are going to receive a substantial capital gain. When you set up a charitable remainder annuity trust, the beneficiary you name receives a set income each year (usually 6% to 9%) from the trust's income. If you set up the trust so that you receive the income, you get two breaks—an income tax deduction and an annuity. (With a charitable *unitrust,* the yearly amount fluctuates. It is figured by multiplying a predetermined percentage, typically about 8 percent, by the current market value of the assets.) The nonprofit organization you are making the gift to has the use of the assets in the trust for the life of the trust. When the trust ends, it gets the assets outright. According to IRS rules, charitable trusts must be irrevocable.

Pros: You can contribute to a worthy cause and make money from it; you avoid capital gains taxes; your beneficiary can receive a yearly income.

Cons: It's not worth the bother unless you want to donate at least $25,000.

WILLS

Writing Your Will

▶ **When you've determined what you want to do with your assets—what (if anything) is going into trust and what you want to pass on to your heirs—it's time to write a will.**

Your will is one of the most important tools in estate planning, yet 7 out of 10 Americans die without writing a will—a very big mistake.

A will gives you the legal opportunity to determine where your property goes when you die—who gets what. It also allows you to be sure that, if necessary, your property will be managed for your survivors. If you die without a will (intestate), it's the state's choice—and you can't be sure the state will make the choices you think are best. The state will merely follow the laws of intestacy, which may mean that your property is divided in such a way that the person or people who need it most don't get what you want them to. For example, in most states, your children will get from 50% to 75% of your estate; your spouse the remaining amount. Perhaps you feel that your spouse should get the bulk of your estate. If you do not write a will, it won't make any difference what your wishes are.

Finally, a will ensures that your survivors get your assets—not unscrupulous lawyers, not the government.

TIP: **If you are a married woman with no property of your own and your husband has a will, you should still have your own will drawn up. Should you die before your husband or at the same time, you want to be sure to spell out your wishes regarding any minor children, jointly held property, and any assets you would receive under your husband's will.**

▶ **You have several options when it comes to the actual preparation of your will.**

In most cases, you are best off having an attorney or legal technician draws up a will for you. Why? Simple—in many cases, a self-written will creates open season for conflicts and problems. When you write your own will, there's more chance that it will be contested. Given that caveat, however, here are your options.

- An *attorney-drawn will* should be your automatic choice if you have a complicated estate, if you're planning to set up trusts and the like, or if you want legal advice on planning the distribution of your estate.

Costs vary according to the complexity of the estate, but you can expect to pay about $200 to $300 for a simple will drawn up by a private law firm; $80 to $100 at a chain lawyer.

Best for: People with complex estates, and good for almost everyone else—self-written wills are often contested.

- A *legal technician–prepared will* is another option. If your will is fairly simple, yet you prefer the peace of mind that having a professional write it will bring you, you can hire a legal technician. Legal technicians are paralegals who handle basic legal matters such as simple wills and uncontested divorces—and they charge less than attorneys. The average charge for a will is $60 to $75. Keep in mind, though, that legal technicians are prohibited from giving you legal advice.

Best for: People with uncomplicated wills who don't need legal advice but want to be sure that their will is properly and professionally done (as opposed to doing it themselves).

SOURCE: For a list of legal technicians in your area, contact: **National Association for Independent Paralegals** (or call 800-542-0034).

- *Do-it-yourself or statutory wills* are forms on which you simply fill in the blanks. They are currently recognized in several states, including California, Maine, Michigan, and Wisconsin. Check your state's regulations. One drawback of a statutory will is that, because it's a fill-in-the-blanks will, you can't customize it.

  Best for: Those with very simple estates or people who intend to see a lawyer in the future, but want the security of being covered by a will in the meantime.

- *Will writing how-to guides or kits* are legal guides, written so the layperson can understand the process easily, which give you step-by-step instructions on writing a will, general estate-planning guidance, rules for each state, and forms.

  Best for: Do-it-yourselfers who have fairly simple estates and who feel comfortable with technical subjects; and as above, for people who want to be covered by a basic will until they can write their "real" will.

SOURCE: A good will-writing guide is Nolo Press's **Nolo's Simple Will Book** ($14.95). It is available at most bookstores or you can order it by calling 800-992-6656.

- *Will-writing computer software programs* get the job done fairly easily and thoroughly. Often they come with step-by-step guidebooks to help you understand the estate-planning process. Costs vary, but average about $50 to $60.

  Best for: Do-it-yourselfers, as above, with simple estates.

TIP: For reviews of will-writing computer programs, check the indexes of major computer magazines such as *PC World, PC/Computing,* or *Personal Computing.* This way you can find out what a reviewer had to say about a particular product.

SOURCE: Some good programs are Nolo Press's **Willmaker,** Sybar's **Will Builder,** and Jacoby & Meyers's **Will Power.** Check your local computer store.

What Your Will Should Contain

▶ **In a nutshell, your will delineates how you want to distribute your assets.**

Your will should include:

- *Name and residence:* Your full legal name and your legal place of residence (especially important if you own property in more than one state).

- *Executor(s):* The individual(s) and/or institution that will manage and distribute your estate upon your death. If you don't include an executor in the will, the state will appoint one for you. (For information on choosing an executor, see page 304).

- *Beneficiaries, bequests, and legacies:* How you want your estate distributed—to whom, how much each person gets, and so forth. The individuals and institutions to whom you are leaving specific assets should be precisely delineated. Instead of actual dollar amounts, it's a good idea to state monetary amounts in percentages—you can't be sure of the exact amount of your assets once taxes and other expenses have been paid.

TIP: If you're planning to omit a child from your will, don't leave a way open for litigation. Instead of just not mentioning the child, state "I make no provision for my child (Name)." This makes it clear that the omission was deliberate and makes it difficult for the child to contest the will on grounds of mental incompetency. (Check your state's laws regarding disinheriting children. Louisiana prohibits it; other states make it difficult.)

TIP: Don't vent your spleen in your will—for example, by saying something like "I am making no provision for my brother, Arthur, the deadbeat." Your estate can be sued for libel.

TIP: If you're leaving money to an institution, it's a good idea to include the exact name and address to avoid confusion with other institutions with similar names or duties.

- *Contingent beneficiaries:* This covers you if your first choices for beneficiaries die, turn down the bequest, or can't be located within the right amount of time.

- *Provision for payment of estate taxes:* Explicitly state that estate taxes will be paid directly from the estate. Otherwise, beneficiaries will have to pay their shares themselves.

Choosing the Executor of Your Will

▶ **An executor is the person or institution you choose to oversee your estate and its distribution to your heirs upon your death. Choose your executor carefully.**

Choosing an executor sounds like a simple task, and it can be. Problem is, most people don't actually choose an executor. They just name someone (usually their eldest son or daughter, spouse, or a sibling) without thinking. By doing this, they may be causing problems later on.

TIP: **If you have more than one child, you may cause problems by choosing only one of them as executor. It may ruffle feathers and cause family problems—especially if conflicts concerning estate distribution arise. You may be better off choosing someone outside the immediate family—perhaps a close friend or a younger sibling.**

First, understand just what an executor will do for your estate. This can be a fairly complicated job. The executor of an estate is charged with pulling together all of the estate's assets, valuing those assets, filing federal income tax returns and inheritance and estate tax returns, paying any taxes owed, distributing the property to the heirs named in the will, and accounting for everything in the estate. Managing the estate may require a large degree of financial skill—for example, if assets need to be sold to pay debts or taxes, the executor decides which ones; if the estate includes a small business, the executor must keep it running, or if necessary, liquidate it.

▶ **Look for the right combination of skills in an executor—especially the ability to handle finances.**

Clearly, the financial side is the most important part of being an executor. Also look for management ability. The executor will have complete responsibility for the estate, so should be able to oversee it successfully. He or she should be well organized, good at record keeping, and able to deal with attorneys, accountants, and others involved in your estate. Having at least a rudimentary knowledge of bookkeeping is a big plus.

There's also the human side to think of. Because the executor of a will is dealing with people while they are grieving, he or she should possess good interpersonal skills; because problems with the division of your estate may arise, he or she should be a good mediator.

Finally, your executor should be easily accessible and available.

Remember, being executor does take time. You want to choose a person who will spend the time necessary to ensure the smooth distribution of your estate.

For serving as executor of your estate, the individual can receive an executor's fee—usually 2% to 5% of the estate—which is usually set by the state. Many individuals waive the fee; however, because the job is time-consuming, others accept the payment.

TIP: **Be sure to also choose an alternative executor, in the event your executor dies or turns down the appointment.**

TIP: **If you're naming a family member or friend as executor, it makes sense to choose one five years or more younger than you are.**

▶ **As for appointing a professional executor? Often it's not necessary.**

If your estate is small or straightforward (you name one beneficiary; you have no trusts or other complicated financial arrangements), you probably don't need a professional executor. A family member or friend—provided he or she has the basic skills needed—will serve more than adequately. If you have a large or complicated estate, choose a professional or (even better) consider joint executors—a professional and a friend or family member.

▶ **There are cases when a professional executor is highly recommended.**

Consider a professional executor if:
1. Your estate is large.
2. You own a business.
3. You have a number of trusts.

In these cases, the financial complexity of the estate demands a professional—such as a bank trust department. If you choose a specialist to serve as executor, you know that the estate will be handled properly and that your family need not be concerned about the smooth running of the estate.

When you choose an institution or other professional as executor, make sure you know exactly what services they will be providing. Ask them about how they operate and what fees they will charge. As mentioned earlier, executors' fees generally run to about 2% to 5% of the total estate. Often these fees are set on a descending scale as the estate size goes up—you will pay 5% on the first $100,000; 4% on the next $200,000; and so on.

TIP: **If a large portion of your estate is going into a trust, experts advise making the executor and the trustee one and the same. This way, the trustee has been involved in the will-making process, knows where the estate stands and what paperwork has been completed, and knows the beneficiaries.**

One drawback to having a professional as executor is lack of a "personal touch." Some families like the feeling that they know the executor and can talk easily with him or her. An institution may be too impersonal to handle these needs. If this concerns you, consider naming joint executors—a lawyer or bank trust specialist and a family member—which will give you the best of both worlds. You have a professional who knows the financial ins and outs of estates and a friend or family member who can add the personal dimension and represent the family's interests more closely.

Other Steps to Take

▶ **Once you've chosen an executor, write an instruction letter for the executor and for your heirs.**

An instruction letter makes things run more smoothly. Instead of having to pull together information on their own, your executor and heirs can have it all in one spot.

The instruction letter should include detailed information to help your executor keep track of your estate. Be sure to include the following:

- *A listing of all assets:* Everything, from real estate to art to securities to bank accounts. Be specific: Include financial institutions, addresses, phone numbers, account numbers. Also include assets *not* in your will, such as Social Security death benefits, pension death benefits, and insurance policies.

- *A listing of liabilities:* Debts, mortgages, etc.

- *Names and addresses of people to notify:* Both for professional and for personal reasons. List names and phone numbers of your lawyer, accountant, relatives, friends—anyone you want notified at your death.

- *The location of your will.*

- *The location of other important papers:* Birth certificate, marriage certificate, bankbook, other financial papers, tax records, etc.

- *Personal requests:* Information not included in your will, such as funeral arrangements.

Give copies of the letter to your executor, any heirs, your lawyer, and perhaps a family friend. Update the letter each year to reflect any changes.

▶ **File your will safely (with your attorney or in a fireproof box at home) and review it periodically.**

Also make several copies of your will and keep them in different places for safekeeping—at home, with a relative or friend, with the executor.

TIP: **Never keep the original of your will in a bank safe deposit box. In some states, your safe deposit box is locked immediately after you die—so your will won't be accessible to your family. If you want to keep a copy in a safe deposit box, though, fine.**

Every two years or so, review your will. You want to be sure it is kept as current as possible. Perhaps you have had a grandchild whom you want to give a bequest to, or you want to change executors or beneficiaries. If you've moved to a different state, be sure your will meets the legal guidelines of that state.

▶ **When you want to alter your will, you can add a codicil.**

Codicils are legal alterations or additions to your will. You can make them at any time and for any reason. Perhaps you want to change beneficiaries—someone has died, a grandchild or great-grandchild has been born, or someone has married and you want to include the new in-law. Or perhaps you want to change a bequest—someone's financial situation has changed and you want to give more or less than originally planned.

▶ **When you have your estate planned, your will drawn up, and an executor named, arrange a family meeting.**

A family meeting now may help prevent a court hearing later. Wills can often spawn misunderstandings, family rifts, and general confusion—which, in turn, often lead to contested wills and long, dragged-out court battles. You can ease matters by having a family meeting to explain the arrangements you have made and the distribution of your estate.

It's the perfect time to explain why you are dividing the estate the way you are. For example, if you are giving more to one child because he or she has more financial need, say so. Don't assume your heirs will understand your reasoning. Spell it out.

Along the same lines, be specific about who gets what objects. Saying "You'll each get half of the jewelry" can lead to squabbles later when it actually comes to dividing assets. Again, spell it out—one child gets the diamond necklace, the other the ruby earrings, and so on.

TIP: **Have your children bring their spouses. This way you can be sure everyone knows everything, no one will feel left out, and spouses will have heard exactly what your children have—again, lessening the chances of misunderstandings and eventual problems.**

Funeral Planning

▶ **Your letter to your executor should outline your last wishes—including your funeral arrangements. For this, and for other reasons, you should plan your funeral.**

Planning for your funeral pays dividends in peace of mind for yourself and ease later for your heirs. It's a taboo topic for some—but taking the time to make funeral arrangements now is a good idea, particularly because the costs are high and getting higher.

The typical funeral now costs between $3,000 and $5,000. Flowers, limos, and so forth can add more to the bill, as can more expensive caskets (usually costing about half the total funeral bill, they can range from $400 on up to many thousands), in-ground burial, and the like.

Some guidelines:

- *Shop around.* Prices may vary widely. Visit at least two funeral homes and compare prices and service. Check to see if those that you do visit are unaffiliated—recent mergers in the industry may mean that two seemingly independent funeral homes are actually owned by the same parent corporation and charge the same prices.

- *Know your rights.* By law (Federal Trade Commission funeral rule) funeral homes must give terms, conditions, and prices over the telephone.

- *Ask for an itemized price list.* Funeral homes must provide these for use in comparison shopping. This rule does not apply to cemeteries or crematoriums.

- *Review your payment plans with your accountant or lawyer.* Terms and conditions of *payment* are *not* regulated, so it makes sense to have a professional go over them.

- *Check with local government authorities and consumer agencies* about the reputation of the funeral home you are considering.

- *Don't be intimidated.* Many people are pushed into buying services they don't need or can't afford.

- You may what to contact a *nonprofit memorial society in your area.* There are hundreds throughout the United States, and for a low one-time fee (usually about $25), they'll help you find low prices through cooperating funeral homes in your area.

▶ **Be careful when considering "pre-need" funeral plans.**

You've probably seen the ads. Prepaid or "pre-need" funeral plans have become increasingly popular: More than 900,000 plans were sold last year. You can purchase funeral insurance, or pay or deposit money now, in exchange for a guarantee of services after your death. They make a lot of sense in terms of convenience, but there are different options to consider—and some pitfalls.

Prepaid funeral plans are often offered by *funeral homes* or individual companies. Be careful before you sign your check. A lot can happen before the funeral: The funeral home may be sold; the company may go bankrupt; and if you move, it may be difficult to transfer the arrangement. Some questions to ask:

- *Is the plan portable?* Can it move with you if you move to another area or state?

- *What kind of inflation protection is offered?* The longer you live after you make your pre-need arrangements, the more inflation protection you need. This can take several forms—for example, the funeral home may guarantee a single fixed price, no matter how much costs rise in the future.

- *If your money will be deposited in a fund, will it earn interest?* With some plans, it will not. Also check for the disposition of excess funds—do they go to the funeral director or to your heirs?

The best advice if you choose this option: Before signing anything, have the arrangements checked by your lawyer or accountant. And consider other options before signing up.

▶ **Prepaid funeral plans or funeral prearrangement insurance offered by *insurance companies* may be a better option—although here too problems may arise.**

These plans can be costly, and the coverage may be limited for the first few years. Before buying into a plan, check with your state insurance commissioner. The largest provider of prearrangement insurance is Houston's Service Corporation, International, which offers the Guardian Plan; another large insurer, operating in most states, is the Hillenbrand Group of Batesville, Indiana, which offers Forethought Life Insurance. With all plans, carefully compare costs and check for portability, inflation protection, and interest practices.

▶ **A *Totten Trust* is a good pre-need funeral option.**

This is a trust that serves as a prepaid funeral plan that *you control.* You deposit money in a fund at a bank or other financial institution and specify a funeral home as the beneficiary. Some advantages: You can pick the funeral home and the type of funeral arrangements, you can easily transfer funeral homes if you move (just change the beneficiary), and you avoid the middleman (the insurance company) and may end up saving money. As with other trusts, you can set this up with an attorney.

▶ **With all funeral arrangements: Check with your professional advisors (and perhaps the authorities) before signing anything.**

This can't be emphasized enough—check out your plans with your accountant and lawyer before you sign on the dotted line. The price and coverage of plans can vary considerably, and with a little forethought you can avoid such problems as inadequate coverage and excessive charges.

SOURCE: For more information, contact a consumer's organization: *The Association of Funeral and Memorial Societies,* 20001 S Street, Washington, DC 20009 (phone 202-745-0634).

Chapter 9

LEGAL CONSIDERATIONS FOR RETIREES

INTRODUCTION

▶ **There are legal matters other than estate planning that concern you as a potential or current retiree.**

Retirement and growing older often impose different legal needs on a person. Some common legal issues faced by the elderly are age discrimination, disputes concerning pension payouts and other retirement plans, and problems with nursing homes or long-term care providers.

Some helpful general sources:

SOURCE: **Legal Counsel for the Elderly,** 1909 K Street, NW, Washington, DC 20049 (phone 202-872-4700). Legal Counsel for the Elderly is an AARP-sponsored free legal support center based in Washington, D.C. Among their services is a telephone hotline. They also are a great place to turn to for information on legal issues, and they also put out an annual calendar and a resource listing of publications.

SOURCE: **Legal Services for the Elderly,** 132 East 43rd Street, 3rd Floor, New York, NY 10036 (phone 212-391-0120). Legal Services for the Elderly, an advisory center for lawyers who specialize in legal problems of senior citizens, puts out a number of publications that may be helpful to you. Among them are *A Survey of the Legal Problems of the Elderly* and *Savings for Seniors.* Contact them for a full list of publications.

SOURCE: *The Rights of Older Persons: A Basic Guide to the Legal Rights of Older Persons Under Current Law,* by Robert N. Brown with Legal Counsel for the Elderly (425 pages; $7.95). This book covers legal questions you may have on a range of subjects—Social Security, pensions, Medicare, nursing homes and much more. It also includes lists of resources—places where you can go for help. It is available at your local bookstore or from Southern Illinois University Press, P.O. Box 3697, Carbondale, IL 62901.

SOURCE: *Your Legal Rights in Later Life,* by John J. Regan with Legal Counsel for the Elderly, An AARP Book/Scott, Foresman & Company (321 pages; $13.95). This is one of the most comprehensive and thorough books on your legal rights when you get older. It is highly recommended.

CHOOSING A LAWYER

▶ **Most of you probably already have a lawyer. If you don't have a lawyer, you may need to get one.**

As a retiree, you will need a lawyer at different times—when you are drawing up a will or handling other matters of your estate; if you are suing an individual or an institution, such as a nursing home; if you are facing pension disputes; if you have run into Medicare fraud . . . the list goes on and on.

While certain situations may require a specialist, in most cases your legal needs can be handled by a generalist—a family lawyer. To find the right lawyer for you, follow these simple guidelines.

- *Ask friends, family, and other professionals for recommendations.* As when choosing any professional, getting referrals from others is one of the best methods of finding competent help. Friends who are also planning retirement may know of a lawyer who will be able to handle your needs; your financial planner or accountant may work with a lawyer who specializes in retirement planning.

- *If you need more names, check with your local bar association or other legal association.* These groups will give you the names of lawyers in your area.

- *Call the lawyers whom you are considering.* Screening candidates saves you time later. Find out now whether the lawyer handles the type of work you'll be wanting him or her for and, if so, how often. Ask about other clients—are they similar to you? Other retirees?

- *Finally, interview the lawyers to see which is best for you.* Ask about fees. How will you be charged? What is the billing rate? Will you pay an hourly rate? Or a flat fee? (Usually, you will pay both— an hourly rate for special situations, a flat fee for such routine transactions as drawing up a will.) Pay attention to how you *feel* with the lawyer: Comfortable and able to talk frankly? Is he or she a good listener? Do you think he or she will make a good advisor?

TIP: **If your needs are simple, you may want to use a legal technician (a specially trained paralegal) instead of an attorney. Legal technicians handle such routine matters as uncontested divorces and simple wills.**

TIP: **To save money: Consider legal clinics. Many communities offer low-cost legal advice for senior citizens. Check with your state agency on aging (listed in Appendix D on pages 518–22).**

SOURCE: For the booklet *The Directory of Legal Services for Older Adults,* contact: Brookdale Center on Aging, 425 East 25th Street, New York, NY 10010 (phone 212-481-4426).

▶ **An option for you to consider, especially if you are caring for a spouse or relative with long-term care needs: Hire a lawyer who specializes in *elder law*.**

Elder law—dealing with the legal problems of older adults—is a growing specialty among lawyers. Lawyers in this field typically handle such needs and problems as estate planning, benefits, age discrimination, long-term care issues, right to die, nursing home issues, and asset protection.

Typically, you'll find that elder law attorneys charge fees that are comparable to those of other attorneys in their region. However, while they don't charge more, they do offer services designed with their elder clientele in mind. For example, most elder law attorneys will pay home visits if needed; their offices are usually set up to allow easy access for disabled people; they provide easy-to-read, large-type legal forms and communications; they are skilled at communicating with the hard of hearing. As one elder law attorney quoted in *The New York Times* put it: "One thing that differentiates us from the usual trusts-and-estates attorney is that our practice involves a lot of social work."*

Should *you* hire a lawyer who specializes in elder law? It depends, of course, on your situation. However, if you or your spouse are going to require long-term care—which would entail nursing home stays or living at a long-term care facility—hiring an elder law attorney is probably a good move, because he or she will be well-versed in the specific problems that may arise. Similarly, if your spouse is afflicted by a debilitating illness, such as Alzheimer's, an elder law attorney will be able to help.

SOURCE: For information on lawyers specializing in elder law, contact: **National Academy of Elder Law Attorneys,** 665 N. Alvernon Way, Suite 108, Tucson, AZ 85711 (602-881-4005).

IMPORTANT LEGAL OPTIONS

▶ **There are certain legal arrangements that you may need to make up during your retirement years.**

Certain arrangements are more likely to be needed as you grow older—and as those around you also age. The following are the ones most commonly needed by people in their retirement years. In some cases, they become necessary when a person is ill and unable to manage his or her own affairs.

Power of Attorney

▶ **Power of attorney gives a person the legal right to act on another person's behalf.**

When you give a person power of attorney, you are giving him or her the right to take care of financial or legal matters for you—such as making investments, transferring funds from one account to another, or paying your bills. You might need this should you become ill—and therefore unable to take care of routine matters—or if you should be away from home for a period of time and need someone to look after your affairs.

How it works: Power of attorney is a written agreement in which one person (the donor) gives another person (often referred to as

*"Legal Needs of Elderly Give Rise to New Specialty," by Deborah Stead (*New York Times,* April 28, 1989).

the attorney-in-fact or the agent) the authority to act for him or her on legal or financial matters. With *general power of attorney,* the agent has the authority to handle all business in general; with *special power of attorney,* the agent handles only those matters specified in the agreement. The agent can be anyone you choose—typically a spouse, child, other relative, or close friend. By giving another person power of attorney, you can ensure that your interests will be looked after if you are incapable of doing so. Power of attorney agreements can be ended at any time, as long as the donor is legally competent, and they are automatically terminated upon the death of the donor.

There are three different types of power of attorney: standard, durable, and springing durable. A *standard power of attorney* is ended if the donor becomes incompetent. For a *durable power of attorney,* however, you specify in the agreement that the power of attorney is to remain in effect even given the donor's incompetence. This distinction is especially necessary when the power is designed to help an individual who has a progressive disease such as Alzheimer's.

The third type, *springing durable power of attorney,* currently recognized in 20 states, offers another option. With a springing power, the donor continues to act personally on his or her own behalf, until an event specified in the agreement—such as entry into a nursing home or loss of mental or physical competence—takes place. Many people choose this option to avoid assigning the power until absolutely necessary, but to make sure it will be assigned at that point. However, it is important to make sure that the power won't spring into effect too early. To avoid this, legal experts recommend specifying in the agreement that two doctors must certify incompetence.

If you want to set up a standard power of attorney, you can get standard power of attorney forms (or statutory short forms) at most office supply and stationery stores. In other cases, a lawyer or legal technician will draw up the agreement.

TIP: Many banks, brokerages, and other financial institutions won't recognize a general power of attorney and require that you fill out their own power of attorney forms. Check with the institutions you deal with to be sure of their rules.

Pros: Peace of mind. You can rest assured that your affairs will be taken care of when you are unable to take care of them yourself. In case of possible disability, you can *choose* whom you want to handle your affairs, rather than relying on a court to appoint a guardian.

Cons: There are no real drawbacks—as long as you choose someone you trust implicitly.

Best for: Virtually anyone who needs them, especially people with deteriorating health; sojourners or people leaving home for an extended period; or people entering a nursing home or long-term-care facility.

TIP: Another good use for a power of attorney is to have someone make medical decisions for you if you are unable to do so. You can assign "durable power of attorney for medical treatment" to a spouse, relative, or friend.

Guardians and Conservators

▶ **Like granting a power of attorney, appointing a guardian or conservator authorizes someone to manage a person's estate or take care of the person him- or herself.**

How it works: A court appoints a guardian or conservator when a person is unable to manage his or her affairs and when no one has been given power of attorney. The guardian or conservator may be charged with the care of a person's estate, the person him- or herself, or both.

The *guardian or conservator of the estate* handles all of the assets of an individual—property and money. He or she pays all bills, makes investments, receives payments—does anything and everything relating to the management of the estate.

The *guardian or conservator of the person* is charged with caring for the person—handling such things as medical care, living arrangements, and housing.

You can petition the court to be appointed guardian or conservator for a family member or friend. All you need to do is have a lawyer file the proper papers with the court. However, regulations vary from state to state as to what constitutes actual need for guardianship/conservatorship.

Pros: This guarantees an incompetent person's financial and physical welfare; if a person has deteriorated and can't take care of him- or herself, a guardian or conservator can step in.

Cons: None—although setting up power of attorney *before* a person is incapable may be simpler and permit more comfortable planning.

Best for: People with Alzheimer's or other debilitating illnesses and their spouses.

Representative Payee

▶ **A representative payee has less responsibility than a guardian or a conservator, or an individual with power of attorney.**

How it works: A representative payee receives a person's income (benefit payments, investment income, etc.), sets up a fund or account with this income, and uses the money to pay bills for the person. This arrangement is drawn up by a lawyer and signed by both individuals—it doesn't need court approval, and can be canceled at any time.

Pros: It is simple to set up—all you need is a lawyer. Because it is easy (and easily cancelable) it is a good test balloon for a power of attorney—the person can see if he or she feels comfortable with the payee before setting up a power of attorney.

Cons: It covers only bill paying, not other financial matters.

Best for: People who are somewhat incapacitated, who need assistance with simple financial matters, but who don't want to give up power of attorney. Usually best for spouses.

Living Wills

▶ **"Living wills" are documents that spell out explicitly what methods should be taken (and not taken) to keep a person alive.**

As more people worry about the extraordinary measures that could be taken to keep them alive—and about the potential loss of quality of life, the possibility of being kept alive in a permanent vegetative state, and the high cost to their families—living wills are becoming more common. According to the American Medical Association, about 15% to 20% of all Americans have a living will, and the number is growing rapidly.

How it works: A living will spells out what exactly a person wants done in the event he or she falls victim to an irreversible, incurable condition or becomes permanently unconscious. It specifies which treatments should be used and which should not be—and, to be effective, should be as explicit as possible. Different states require different things from a living will. Some allow a living will to appoint someone to make medical decisions for a person if he or she is unable to; others do not. However, in spite of the need for explicitness and the differences in state requirements, writing a living will isn't as difficult as it sounds. You can get forms that comply with each specific state's requirements and are easy to fill in. You may want to consult with your family and, for classification of medical terms and conditions, with your doctor.

TIP: **Give your doctor a copy of your living will to keep with your medical records. That way, it is immediately accessible. Also give dated copies to your spouse or child and your attorney.**

Pros: Living wills are simple to write—forms are easily available. There is no cost—you don't need a lawyer to write a living will. Living wills can be changed or canceled at any time. Making one can release your family from difficult legal or moral conflicts.

Cons: You must be very specific so there is no room for error in interpretation.

Best for: People who want to be sure their wishes are carried out if they become terminally ill or permanently comatose.

SOURCE: For assistance in writing a living will, including forms, check with your local senior center, or contact the **Society for the Right to Die,** which has forms for each state: Society for the Right to Die, 250 West 57th Street, New York, NY 10107.

PLANNING FOR CATASTROPHES

▶ **Perhaps the most important—and difficult—aspect of your legal responsibilities will be arranging to deal with catastrophic events, including debilitating illness and death.**

Planning for such catastrophic events clearly involves much more than legal issues. You will also be thinking of emotional needs, administrative tasks, and the like. It is not an easy aspect of life after retirement, but it is, unfortunately, a very real one. Knowing how to cope in these difficult situations will make them no less pleasant, but easier. Following are some suggestions on how to manage and where to go for help.

▶ **When a spouse or loved one gets a debilitating illness, such as Alzheimer's, there are several steps you can take to ease the burden.**

The emotional toll is great—as is the general burden on you. In many cases, you will have to take care of a number of administrative and legal matters at the same time that you are taking care of your loved one. When possible, you should make things easier on yourself by making arrangements as soon as possible. Many things are best done when a person is still competent and thus able to give you the permissions you need.

Some steps to consider:

- *Double-check health insurance policies.* Be sure you are covered in the ways you need to be. You don't want to be hit with a rude surprise.

- *Set up a durable power of attorney or other arrangement that will ensure that the financial affairs of your spouse will be taken care of.* A power of attorney will enable you to take care of the affairs of a person who is incapable of doing so him- or herself. The earlier you can do this, the better. This will enable you to take care of your spouse's financial affairs—bill paying, signing insurance forms, and the like. If necessary, you can petition the court to be appointed guardian or conservator.

- *If your loved one expresses certain wishes about medical treatment and the like, you can arrange to have these wishes carried out.* If he or she has a living will, be sure it is current, dated, and readily available. If there are any areas in the living will that are questionable or any illnesses or treatments not covered, your loved one can grant you durable power of attorney over medical treatment.

- *Arrange for Social Security benefits to be sent to you or another person.* This is especially wise if your spouse will be in a nursing home or hospital for an extended period. For specific instructions, contact your local Social Security office, or call their toll-free number: 800-234-5772.

- *Similarly, arrange for any pension benefits to be sent to you.* Call the human resources manager at the company from which the pension comes for information on pension benefits.

- *Ask your bank about special services.* Many banks offer services that will help you with financial matters. One popular service is a *custodian account*, in which the bank becomes the custodian of an estate and, as such, pays bills and income and property taxes and handles all other financial matters—collecting income and the like. In this case, you give the bank a limited power of attorney to sign your name when necessary. Be sure to ask about fees for this type of account. Monthly or annual costs may be high.

For related information, see Continuing Care Facilities, page 350; Day Care/Elder Care, page 447, Respite Care, page 453; and Nursing Homes, page 449.

▶ **In addition to coping with the present, you should take several steps to prepare for an impending death.**

While this is a difficult time, you shouldn't wait until the last minute. Putting off certain steps may cause problems later, especially if your spouse becomes incompetent.

A few steps to take:

- *Know where all important documents are*—insurance policies, will, real estate deeds, birth certificate (you'll need this for a death certificate), keys to a safe deposit box. In addition, if you haven't already become familiar with your and your spouse's financial situation, do so now. Know your assets, where they are, names and addresses of financial institutions, and the like.

- *Review your spouse's will and final letter of instruction to executors.* Be sure your spouse's will is up to date, in a safe location. If your spouse wants to make any changes, now is the time to make them. This is also a good time to review your own will. If the illness was unexpected, and you have not planned for the distribution of your estate, do it now. Don't wait a minute longer—contact a lawyer, draw up wills, and so forth.

- *Your spouse may want to take steps to reduce his or her estate by making gifts now to heirs.* By taking advantage of the $10,000 gift tax exemption, your spouse can reduce his or her estate—and estate taxes—and give heirs assets equaling $10,000 now, instead of through a will.

- *Review life insurance policies, if any.* Double-check beneficiaries—are they current?

- *Make funeral arrangements.*

- *Go over who gets your spouse's possessions—the ones not mentioned in the will.* Be sure you know who gets certain personal objects, mementoes, the things that aren't valuable but that your spouse wants given to family and friends.

- *Make certain you have credit in your own name.* Many women have credit in their husband's name, but not in their own. Upon their husband's death, they face real problems getting credit, as they have no credit history of their own. Get credit quickly. If you can open an account on your own, do so and start establishing your own credit record. Even if you have no income of your own, you often can get credit approval based upon your joint accounts with your husband.

SOURCE: An excellent general book on death and dying that may help you through the experiences is Elisabeth Kübler-Ross's **Living with Death and Dying** (Macmillan, 1990).

When Your Spouse Dies

▶ **The death of your spouse will affect you on a number of levels—emotionally, financially and legally.**

While you are coping emotionally with the loss, you will also have to take steps to cope with the many changes wrought in your life by your spouse's death. You will have administrative and legal responsibilities. You will have to be sure that your spouse's final wishes concerning his or her estate are fulfilled. And you will have to take steps to take care of your own future. One consolation: Sometimes taking care of business helps ease your emotional pain.

A few guidelines:

- *Pull together important documents*—your spouse's will and letter to executor; death certificate; life insurance policies; other financial documents (pension plan agreements and so forth).

- *See your lawyer regarding your spouse's will.* You need to get information on the will, the steps to take concerning probate and estate taxes, and so on. If you are executor of the will, you should discuss when to have a will reading and distribute assets. This is also a good time to review your own will. You may need to revise it to take into account your spouse's death.

- *Have all assets transferred into your name*—this includes bank accounts, securities, credit cards, real estate and all other property that you held jointly.

- *Take care of necessary administrative tasks,* or have someone do it for you. Among the little things that need to be taken care of: Get copies made of the death certificate. You'll need these for all legal work involving the estate. Notify friends and colleagues. Notify insurance companies.

- *Notify Social Security.* Call first—you may not need to go to the office in person.

- *Call the Veterans Administration if your spouse was a veteran.* If your spouse served on active duty, you should receive a lump sum death benefit of $250, a free plot in a national cemetery, or $150 toward burial elsewhere. Have your spouse's military identification number ready.

- *If you are executor, contact heirs and set up a timetable for reading the will and distributing assets.*

- *Be sure you are getting the benefits to which you are entitled from your spouse's company.* Call your spouse's company's human resources office—double-check about pension agreements, group life insurance policy payout, credit union account, and so forth.

- *If you need professional assistance in dealing with the estate—the assets your spouse has left you—look for help.* Ask friends, family, and your lawyer for referrals.

- *On the more personal side, this may be a good time to make a change in lifestyle.* You have already gone through a wrenching change. Perhaps one of the best moves you can make is to move on. Start doing something new, get a new hobby, travel—anything that helps you move into the future.

SOURCE: Displaced Homemaker Network, Suite 930, 1411 K Street, NW, Washington, DC 20005 (phone 202-628-6767). This group offers recently widowed women assistance, including employment counseling, training, "job clubs," and support services.

SOURCE: AARP, 1909 K Street, NW, Washington, DC 20049. AARP sponsors support groups for people who have lost their spouses. In addition, they put out a free booklet, ***On Being Alone.*** Contact them for information.

SOURCE: There are also a number of books that people in this situation may find helpful: *The Widow's Guide: How to Adjust,* by Ida Fisher and Byron Lane (Prentice-Hall); *Suddenly Alone: A Women's Guide to Widowhood,* by Philomene Gates (Harper & Row, 1990); *Beyond Loss,* by Lilly Singer, Margaret Sirot, and Susan Rodd (Dutton, 1988); *Survival Handbook for Widows,* by Ruth Jean Loewinsohn (Scott Foresman, 1984); *When Bad Things Happen to Good People,* by Harold Kushner (Schocken Books, 1981).

Retirement Lifestyles: Getting the Most Out of Your Retirement

PART III

Chapter 10

RETIREMENT HOUSING OPTIONS: WHERE TO SPEND YOUR RETIREMENT YEARS

INTRODUCTION

This part of the book takes you beyond the financial aspects of retirement and into the *lifestyle* aspects. Retirement planning is much more than figuring out how to save money to live comfortably. It's also deciding *where* to live comfortably, whether to stay in your current home or more into a new home, whether to follow the lead of thousands of other retirees and seek the sun, or whether to move abroad—the choices are many. And only you can be sure which is the right move to make.

This chapter and the following one take you through these different choices you'll be facing. They explore the different housing options you have and the different locales in which you may want to spend your retirement years.

▶ **When it comes to retirement housing, the options that are most popular with retirees are retiring at home (that is, in their current house or apartment); moving to a new house or apartment; retiring to their vacation or second home; and moving to a retirement community.**

Deciding among these options is only the first step in planning where you are going to spend your retirement years.

Next come the other choices you face: If you decide to move to a new house, should you buy or rent? If you think a retirement community is the way to go, what kind of retirement community? And so on.

This chapter looks at the different types of housing available to you and offers suggestions on how to decide which fits your retirement lifestyle and what to look for (and look out for) in each type of housing. (For the *financial* aspects of choosing whether to sell and trade down, sell and rent, or use your current home for income, see Financing Your New Home with Your Old, page 359.)

SOURCE: One of the best resources on senior housing is the free booklet ***Housing Options for Older Americans,*** offered by AARP. Write: D12063, AARP Fulfillment, 1909 K Street, NW, Washington, DC 20049.

KEEPING YOUR CURRENT HOME

Is Retiring at Home Right for You?

▶ **In a 1990 AARP study, a definite majority of the people surveyed—86%—said "they wanted to stay in their present home and never move."**

Retiring at home has always been a popular option, and it's becoming more so. If you're thinking about staying on at your home once you retire, you're certainly not alone, and for good reason. There are some very compelling advantages in keeping your current house or apartment. Perhaps you own it already (like 67% of retirees); or you like the location or the neighborhood; or you're close to your family and friends. And there's the most compelling factor of all: It's *home* already. You've lived your life within these four walls. Your children may have grown up here; you've seen a lot of milestones pass in this house.

▶ **Even so, you have to assess your current home with a clear head.**

It may be tough, but you have to separate sentimentality from your decision. While there are good reasons for staying in your current home, there may also be very good reasons for leaving it. You have to be as honest with yourself as possible and try to project your needs 10 or 20 years down the road. You will be getting older. Will your current house still be the right place for you? The answer could very well be yes. But it could also be no. The only way to be sure is to carefully think it over, weigh the pros and cons, and then decide.

Some points to consider:

- *Are the friends and family you want to stay close to now going to be here in a few years?* People move. Especially in today's transient world, children may pick up roots, be transferred. Friends may decide to leave, move down South or to a retirement community.

- *Is the neighborhood changing? Where do you think it will be headed in 5 years? In 10 years?* Even the best of neighborhoods sometimes slump. Be on the lookout for signs that your neighborhood is beginning to slide—a number of houses for sale, changes in demographics, dropping property values, a general lack of maintenance. Also check if your neighborhood is similar to others in your area that have changed.

- *Will the house feel too large? Too lonely?* Homes that once housed an entire family may feel oddly large when it's just you and your spouse, or you alone, should your spouse die.

- *Will you be able to handle upkeep of the house?* When you get older, your house and yard may be too much to maintain.

- *What about the climate?* Most people like to retire to climates with little fluctuation in temperature and little severe weather. If you live in an area of the country that gets the snow, sleet, and cold of winter or, on the other hand, excessive heat or humidity in summer, you might not be comfortable as you age.

Also consider the advantages:

- *Are family and friends nearby and unlikely to move?* Staying close to family and friends is the most popular reason for retiring at home.

- *Is the area going strong? Are property values either stable or rising?* If this is the case, your house may be a great place to stay, and it may be wise to keep it to pass on to children or grandchildren.

- *Is the location just right for you? Are you close to sources of entertainment, religious facilities, shopping, or your job? Do you like the climate?* Location is one of the most important aspects of retirement living. If you're already in a place you like, one with the right climate, the right sources of entertainment, and so on, you may be hard pressed to find a similar "fit" in another location.

- *Are you actively involved in community groups? In local recreational or cultural activities?* Once you retire, you'll probably have more free time. If you're already involved in activities that you enjoy near your home, it may make sense to stay put.

- *Have you paid off your mortgage? Are property taxes affordable?* If you have no mortgage payments to make and low or reasonable taxes to pay, staying at home may be less expensive than moving. Another advantage is that you know exactly what your expenses will be, which helps you make up a practical retirement funding plan.

The bottom line: If you're happy at home, if you can afford it, and if you can picture yourself living comfortably there in the future, making *no* move may be the best possible move for you.

How to Ready Your Home for Retirement

▶ **If you do decide to retire at home, now is the time to take a few simple steps to make it "senior-citizen friendly."**

What's perfectly comfortable to you now may not be quite as comfortable when you're older. It makes sense to make certain small renovations, additions, and adjustments to your home to make it better suited to your retirement life.

Among the steps to take:

- Change bathroom faucets from double hot-and-cold knobs to one easy-to-use lever.

- Install grab bars, nonslip bottom, seating ledge, and hand-held shower fixture in your tub. (Instead of a seating ledge, you could put a waterproof deck or lawn chair in the tub for the same results.)

- Get an automatic door-opener for the garage door.

- Make kitchen storage more accessible. Install lazy susans in cabinets, wire drawers in pantry, pull-out shelves—anything that streamlines storage and makes it easier for you to reach items.

- Change your lighting fixtures to work with dimmer switches. This way, when you get older, you can switch to higher-wattage, brighter bulbs—a real help to older eyes—but not always use the brightest setting.

- Install nonslip tiles in bathrooms and kitchen.

- If feasible, think about wall-to-wall carpeting. It keeps a house warm and helps prevent one from slipping on floors. If you have area and scatter rugs, be sure they're padded and not slippery.

- If you don't have handrails—on stairs leading to basements, outside stairs, and so forth—install them.

TIP: Look into the availability of lawn and yard maintenance services—neighborhood kids or professionals.

TIP: A compelling reason to make adjustments to your home: More than 22,000 people are killed each year because of home accidents; more than 3 million become permanently disabled. Each week, do a quick walk-through of your house to be sure rugs are secure and electrical cords out of the way, and that objects aren't left on the floor.

SOURCE: AARP puts out a free booklet, *The Doable, Renewable Home,* which can help you make modifications in your home. Write: Booklet #D12470, AARP Fulfillment, EE094, 1909 K Street, NW, Washington, DC 20049.

SOURCE: *Home Modification for the Elderly* is a free booklet designed for homeowners and remodelers, put out by the Research Center of the National Association of Home Builders. Write: NAHB Research Center, 400 Prince George's Blvd., Upper Marlboro, MD 20772.

▶ **In addition to your comfort, there's another big advantage to keeping your current house: finances.**

Your current home—if you've already paid off the mortgage—can give you money. For detailed information on how it can do this, see Chapter 11.

Special Situations

▶ **If you want to stay in your current home, but are concerned about money, see page 362 for a discussion of reverse mortgages and other financial options open to homeowners.**

▶ **Some retirees may want to consider** *renting rooms* **for additional income.**

We cannot wholeheartedly recommend this practice, because of the possibility of crime; however, many retirees do rent rooms or apartment space in their houses.

The biggest advantage is an obvious one: You receive rental income, which helps pay your monthly expenses.

If you do choose to let rooms in your house, be sure to screen rental candidates thoroughly. Ask for references and *check* those references. Many people don't bother, but you would be a fool not to.

TIP: Renting a room or apartment in your house works best if you live in a college town. Contact the Student Housing Office for information on listing your house with them. Another advantage—they usually screen students. Another possibility: If you live in a city or town near corporations, contact corporate headquarters or human resources. Speak to the person who handles relocation if possible. Young professionals often need places to live.

▶ **Another option—as a hobby or business venture—is setting your house up as a** *bed-and-breakfast.*

Bed-and-breakfasts are springing up all over the country, in everything from rural farmhouses to seaside Victorians to highrise city apartments.

If you turn your house into a bed-and-breakfast, you accept paying guests and provide them with a room, access to a bathroom and shower, and breakfast (although some offer other meals also). Usually you also offer conversation, information about the town or city in which you live, tips on activities—in short, tourist advice.

It's an option you might want to consider if you're a social person (or couple), if you're located in an area that gets tourists, and if you want a full-time occupation that doesn't take you out of the home.

There is a downside, however—the sheer amount of work. According to many owners, running a B&B can be a great deal of work, and usually the financial rewards aren't that great.

SOURCE: For information on setting up a bed and breakfast, contact: **The American Bed and Breakfast Association,** 16 Village Green, Suite 203, Crofton, MD 21114 (301-261-0180). For a membership fee, you receive a monthly newsletter. For an additional fee, you get a start-up kit.

MOVING TO A NEW HOME

▶ **If you're planning to move elsewhere rather than retire at home, you should begin planning a few years before you retire—three years ahead of time is best.**

Last-minute moves lead to hasty decision making—and potential disaster. Better to begin looking for a new home while you are planning other aspects of your retirement than to wait. You need the time to explore the options open to you and to make clearheaded, *educated* decisions. Do you want to buy or rent? What type of home do you want—a house? A condo? What about retirement communities? Clearly, the choices are many.

Buying Versus Renting

▶ **Your first decision is whether you want to buy or rent your new place.**

There are positive things to be said for either option. (Note: For information on the financial aspects of buying versus renting, also see Chapter 11.) When you buy a home, the biggest plus is financial—you get the tax benefits of homeownership. The biggest drawback is that you're tied down.

Pros: You can build up equity in your home. You can fix, change, and decorate your home however you want.

Cons: Initial out-of-pocket expenses are higher than renting. Maintenance is up to you. If you want to move, you have to rent your home or sell—which makes you dependent upon the ups and downs of the real estate market.

Best for: People who need a tax shelter (usually if you're in a tax bracket of 33% or more); those who want to establish a new "home base," who sold their old house to make money or to move to a new location, but who want the roots of home; those who want an "active" retirement.

As for *renting*, the big advantage is also financial—your initial out-of-pocket expense is low, as (usually) are monthly fees. The big drawback? If you don't intend to move for a long time, you're missing out on the long-term financial advantages of homeownership.

Pros: You can pick up and move elsewhere with little trouble; you don't have to worry about maintenance and repairs; you may not have to pay such monthly expenses as water or heat; and you can more easily anticipate your monthly expenses.

Cons: You don't get a tax break and you don't build up equity. In addition, you lack the complete independence of a homeowner— you have to abide by landlord's rules and regulations. Also, space is usually limited, you don't have a garden, you often can't keep pets. In some areas, there may be few or no controls on how much rents can rise.

Best for: People who don't intend to settle down for any length of time; those unable to afford the immediate costs of a down payment; those who don't want the responsibility of maintaining a house.

Buying Options: Houses Versus Condos Versus Co-ops

If you opt for buying a new retirement home, your next choice will be between the two most popular housing alternatives: a house or a condominium.

▶ **Houses offer you independence and all the financial benefits of homeownership.**

Usually when you buy a new house, you'll be buying a smaller one, and one that is less expensive than your current house. Actual costs, of course, vary greatly depending on location, size, and so forth.

Pros: You get the financial breaks of homeownership. You usually have more space than with an apartment. You may have a garden, patio, or deck.

Cons: You have all the worries of owning a house—maintenance, upkeep of interior and exterior, security. Plus you have to pay for all utilities and day-to-day upkeep.

Best for: Active retirees, those who want independence and privacy; people who can either afford a substantial down payment or (better) pay for the house in full.

▶ **Buying a condominium gives you some of the benefits of a house and some of an apartment.**

When you buy a condominium, you pay a price for the unit itself and a monthly maintenance fee. The monthly fee usually covers common costs—upkeep of the building and grounds and the like. If the condo building offers any recreation—health club, pool, tennis—your maintenance fees also pay for this. When special needs arise (for example, if your building needs a new furnace), the condo association sets the level of payments each condo owner will make to cover the cost. These are called "special assessments" and tend to occur more frequently in older buildings.

TIP: When shopping for a condo, ask about the number of special assessments in the past and how much they have cost. This will give you an idea of how much to budget in your living expenses. (It also may give you a clue that the building is falling apart!)

Costs vary widely for condos depending on location, size of the unit, special features, and so on. Maintenance fees also vary, and generally escalate over a period of time.

Pros: You get the financial benefits of homeowning—including tax advantages and the ability to build equity. Cost is lower than for a house. As when you rent an apartment, you have a degree of flexibility. For example, you can go off traveling with little preparation. If you decide to move elsewhere, you probably can rent a condo more easily than a house. Condo buildings or communities are good for socializing. You may also have the benefit of recreational facilities.

Cons: A condo is usually smaller than a house. You will have to abide by rules of the condo association. Also you have to be careful—

reports of substandard construction have followed the surge of condo building in the 1980s. You may lose money if you try to sell your condo.

Best for: People willing to be actively involved in the management of the condo building; people in a high tax bracket who need the tax break.

TIP: **Remember—technically you are going to be involved in real estate management—the management of your condo building. This is why you should always have a lawyer carefully go over the condo agreement before you sign. Make sure you understand everything in it.**

▶ **Buying a cooperative apartment is becoming a less popular option, but it still exists.**

Under a co-op arrangement, you don't buy a specific apartment, but a share in the building and grounds. As with a condo, you usually pay a monthly maintenance fee that covers cost of upkeep and any recreation facilities.

Pros: Again, you can easily go away for periods of time and not worry about security; costs may be low.

Cons: The co-op board can approve or disapprove your application; it usually prohibits you from renting your apartment to others; it sets rules and regulations that you have to follow. Another drawback—if any other member of the co-op defaults, you and the other members are financially responsible. Also, co-ops tend to be more difficult to sell than condos.

Rental Options: Apartments Versus Houses

▶ **Renting an apartment is a relatively low-cost, low-stress housing alternative.**

When you rent an apartment, you don't have to worry about making a large payment as you would when buying a home. Instead, you'll usually have to pay a security deposit (refundable with interest when you move) and, in some cases, an extra month's rent. Your lease may cover any period of time, although one- and two-year leases are the most common. Because most states have rent regulation laws, usually your rent can only increase by a small percentage each year. If your lease indicates the yearly rental increases, you can plan for your future living expenses.

Pros: This is the most flexible of living arrangements—you can easily move when your lease is up and not think twice about it. You don't have to be concerned with maintenance, security, and the like. Because you don't have to spend a lump sum as a down payment, you can invest that amount of money and use investment income for rent or other expenses.

Cons: You earn no equity and get no tax advantages. You may face problems should the building go condo or co-op. (Note: your rights as a tenant in this situation should be spelled out in the lease.)

Best for: Retirees who want few hassles; single retirees; people who want interim or short-term housing; people who are contemplating a move elsewhere, are waiting for entrance into a retirement community, and so forth.

▶ **Renting a house gives you more space, but more responsibilities.**

One of the best reasons for renting a house: You're thinking of buying the house or you're thinking of buying *another* house or condo in that area and want a real feel for the neighborhood.

Pros: You will probably have much more space than in an apartment; it's easier to keep a car; you will probably have more storage space; you have more independence.

Cons: You have to be concerned with maintenance and upkeep; since most house rentals are through individual landlords, you may feel constrained—uneasy about hanging pictures, gardening, or anything that "changes" the house.

Best for: People seeking interim housing or short-term housing; people considering buying the house or seeing how they like a certain area.

What to Look for in a New Home

▶ **Whether you're buying or renting, it is important that you carefully evaluate the house or apartment you're considering.**

You should give prospective homes a close going-over, both to be sure you'll be comfortable and because you want to avoid problems—and expenses—later on.

Comfort features to keep an eye out for: if there is more than one floor, a bathroom on each floor; ample storage, including at least one closet in each bedroom, entrance hall closet, and a linen closet near bathroom and bedrooms; large kitchen; large bathrooms; enough phone jacks.

Practical features to check: roof in good repair; working gutters; exhaust fan in kitchen; smoke detectors on each floor; enough electrical outlets; airtight windows.

And remember the little things: Are there storm windows? Are there screens? Is the neighborhood serviced by cable television? Is there any sign of mildew in basement or closets?

Check the grounds as well: Are trees and shrubs healthy? Remember, you may have to pay if they are infested or dying. Is the front sidewalk smooth and safe or is concrete broken or forced up by roots?

▶ **Look for features that are "senior-citizen friendly" to make your later life easier.**

If your new home has the following features, so much the better. (Not all of them are necessities; you may be physically active enough not to need certain modifications.) Look for:

- One level or, if more than one, stairs that are short and easily converted to a ramp

- Wide doorways (to accommodate wheelchairs)

- Banisters on all stairs or landings (Check the basement stairs— this is a spot where many home accidents happen.)

- Covered entryway

- Entryway that is unhidden, visible from street and house

- Automatic garage door opener

- Central heating, central air conditioning

- Ceiling fan (for energy-efficient room cooling)

- Modular phone jacks throughout house (in all bedrooms, bathroom, etc.)

- Electrical outlets at least 18 inches from floor (higher—24 inches—is better)

- Light switches low enough to reach from wheelchair

- Faucets operated by a single lever instead of two knobs

- Dishwasher, garbage disposal or compacter, freezer and other labor- and money-saving appliances

- Large bathrooms equipped with a tub you can step into, hand-held showerhead attachment, large medicine cabinets, and a toilet 18 inches or more high

TIP: If you're married or living with someone, think *two bedrooms or more* when you're considering a new house or apartment. This way, if one of you needs medical attention, you have the option of getting home health care instead of paying for more expensive nursing home care. If necessary, you can turn the second bedroom into a one-room nursing home for the person needing medical care.

▶ **If you're considering an apartment or condominium, there are other features to look for.**

The building should appear well-maintained, with clean, vacuumed halls and lobby and landscaped grounds. As for the apartment itself, always check closet space and test kitchen appliances and plumbing fixtures.

In addition, the following features are good for people in their retirement years:

- Well-lit entryway

- Elevators (two or more)

- Easily accessible laundry room (ideally on your floor)

- Doorman or security system

- On-premises superintendent or handyman

- Wide hallways

- Adequate-sized and well-lit parking garage or lot (Be sure the garage looks safe. Look for an elevator, or two, security cameras, and a card- or key-accessed safety gate.)

- Storage area—rooms or bins

TIP: **Try to get an idea of who your neighbors are. You don't want to rent or buy a unit and find out your neighbors play loud music, argue constantly, or have noisy parties.**

Sales Agreements: Making Sure You're Protected

▶ **Once you've made the decision to buy a house, condo, or co-op, your next job will be to carefully review the sales agreement you'll receive from the seller or seller's agent.**

You should, of course, have your attorney go over any contract. A few points you should make clear between you and the seller:

- *Deposit:* Specify the terms under which the deposit is returned.

- *Closing date:* Identify the date itself clearly, whether or not there is a grace period (for example, if the owner isn't ready to move out by the closing date or it takes longer than you planned to get your financing).

- *Repairs:* If any fundamental problems are discovered after the closing date, have you and the seller agreed to set up an escrow account to cover cost of repairs? If so, specify the amount of the account, the period of time covered by the account, and so forth.

TIP: **If you are on good terms with the seller, it makes sense to get the names of plumbers, contractors, electricians, and so forth from him or her.**

TIP: **It always makes sense to do a final walk-through of the house on the day of closing. It's your last chance to be sure everything is in move-in condition.**

▶ **When buying a condo or co-op, you will be presented with a fairly complicated contract. Be sure to review it closely and double-check all provisions.**

To a great extent, you should follow the same procedures as when buying a house. But when you're buying a condo or co-op, you face additional concerns. Again, you must remember that you aren't merely buying property, you are in effect becoming part of a real estate business. This translates into special clauses and provisions in your contract. Among the points that should be spelled out:

- *Maintenance and special fees:* What your monthly (or annual fees) are; what they cover; whether fees will escalate, and if so, when and under what formula; whether increases are subject to resident approval, and so forth.

- *Common areas (lobby, hallways, grounds):* Your responsibilities as a resident (for example, in many buildings, you are responsible for lighting your hallway).

- *Recreational facilities:* Hours you can use facilities; any additional charges for use; how facilities will be maintained.

- *Reselling or subletting:* Any restrictions and regulations that apply.

- *Your rights in bequeathing your unit:* Especially important if you're buying a co-op, since all prospective tenants are subject to board approval, including your heirs.

- *General rules and regulations:* Can cover a variety of issues—anything from pets to whether you need approval to hang a picture in the hallway.

Mobile Homes

▶ **They're not for everyone, but many retirees find that a mobile home is the answer to retirement housing.**

One key reason: cost. A mobile home (or manufactured home) is usually less expensive than an equivalent condo or house. The average mobile home costs about $34,000 (but prices do escalate depending upon size and features). Rental fees for sites are similarly low—on the average, you'll pay about $100 a month for lot in a mobile home park. At some mobile home parks, you can buy both mobile home and lot for one (usually low) price.

On the downside? Space—or rather lack of it. Mobile homes are smaller than most other residences, and mobile home park lots are on the small side too. In addition, you will face a certain amount of regimentation. Mobile home parks have regulations about a variety of things, from what you put in your yard to when and how you can put out your garbage.

One final point, which can be a positive or a negative, depending upon your point of view: Living in a mobile home park is similar to living in a retirement community. You often have on-site recreational facilities; you have a "campus" atmosphere; and you have neighbors with a range of ages.

▶ **Before you buy a mobile home, be sure you know what is included in the base price and what isn't, what (if any) financing arrangements you will be making, what (if any) service warranties will operate. And get it in writing!**

First of all, shop around. Remember, you're buying a *house*. That this house is not sitting on a foundation doesn't mean this isn't as large a decision. Visit different dealers, compare models and prices. Talk to other owners of mobile homes. Find out which features they consider important and which they don't consider important.

Then, when it comes time to make the actual purchase, check and recheck the sales contract. Among the points to be sure you have covered before you sign on the dotted line:

- *Transportation and set-up costs:* Under a good sales agreement, the basic purchase price of the mobile home includes transportation of the mobile home to your homesite, within a preset square-mile region, and initial set-up. This is a common feature in a sales contract; try to get it written into yours.

- *Cost of add-on features:* The base price usually doesn't cover the following (some of which are required by either state laws or mobile home park regulations): foundation skirting, anchoring, front door steps with handrails.

- *Financing:* Most retirees pay the full price for a mobile home. But if you choose to make a down payment and have the balance financed, be sure the financing agreement is clearly spelled out in the sales contract. Another option: Look into VA or FHA financing. You'll find the cost substantially less than if you were buying a regular house.

- *Service warranties:* Usually the manufacturer will cover certain aspects of service, the company that sold you the home others. Be sure you know who handles what, how long service warranties will cover you, where to go for problems, and the like.

▶ **It's a good idea to be on your toes when choosing a location for your mobile home.**

If you intend to live in a mobile home park, double-check site availability. Do this well ahead of moving time, since many parks have waiting lists.

To a great degree, choosing a mobile home park is the same as choosing any other residential area. Talk to other residents. Look for well-maintained grounds, well-kept houses, and so on. Advantages: recreational facilities, such as tennis courts and swimming pools. Be sure to ask about other features you may take for granted in a regular community, such as garbage pick-up, laundry facilities, and the availability of cable television hook-ups.

If you're not planning on living in a mobile home park, be sure the location you've chosen has zoning regulations that allow mobile homes. In some areas, you can put your mobile home only in certain sites; in other towns, mobile homes are prohibited. Make sure you know the restrictions ahead of time!

SOURCE: For information on mobile homes, contact: **Manufactured Housing Institute,** 1745 Jefferson Davis Highway, Arlington, VA 22202.

RETIRING IN A SECOND OR VACATION HOME

▶ **Some retirees choose to move into their vacation homes when they retire. If you're considering this, be sure you know what you're getting into.**

That your vacation home is a great spot to spend the summer or the winter doesn't automatically make it a great spot in which to spend all year. Yet many retirees assume that if it works for vacation, it will work for retirement living. In fact, many buy a second house shortly before retiring for the express purpose of moving into it full-time.

If you're shopping for a vacation home: Bear in mind the initial cost of buying the home and the continuing cost of insurance premiums. Your down payment on the vacation house can be as high as 30%, especially if you are reaching the limits on your debt load. This can be a large sum to part with if you're also beefing up your investments. And you'll be socked with higher insurance rates on a vacation home, chiefly because it *is* a vacation home, not a full-time residence. Premiums can be as much as 50% higher than for a regular home. If it's in a coastal area, you will have to buy additional flood insurance.

TIP: If you're thinking about buying a house in a beachfront area, check about erosion rates and water pollution. And look around—have neighbors built bulkheads or seawalls? If so, your beachfront land may be underwater in a few years.

TIP: **Think twice about renting out your vacation home—the rental money you make may not make up for the tax deduction you lose. As long as you don't rent it out, you can write off mortgage interest and real estate taxes.**

If you already own a vacation home: Don't assume that living in the home full-time will be the same as vacationing in it.

Either way, keep in mind the following pros and cons of retiring to your second home.

Pros: You are already comfortable in the house. You know the neighborhood, neighbors, shopping areas, and the like. You like the location. You enjoy the recreational aspects of the area.

Cons: Many vacation or resort areas aren't designed for year-round living—services are few, shopping areas close for part of the year, recreation may be limited. Fewer people may be around, which can make you feel isolated—and not very secure. In an isolated area, the cost for basics (including food) may be higher than average. It may be far from family. Medical services may be limited or distant.

▶ **If you're considering moving into your vacation home, first stay in it during the off-season.**

This is the best way to get a feel for what the area is like when the vacationers aren't there. You will be able to see firsthand what is still open and what isn't, how many people live in the area year-round.

Talk to the year-rounders while you're there. Ask them about the pleasures and drawbacks of life in the area. What is the lifestyle like? What do people do for entertainment when the beach is closed or the ski slopes thawed? What services are available? Also ask yourself if you think you'll fit in—these are the people you'll be spending most of the year with, not the vacationers you've met in past seasons.

This is also a good time to be sure the following are easily accessible or available:

Hospital and other health care services

Shopping

Restaurants

Banks

Public transportation

Post office

Recreational facilities (movie theaters, etc.)

▶ **A better idea that retiring to your vacation home: Use it as an interim home.**

Your vacation home may be the perfect spot for you to move to right after you've sold your primary residence and before you decide where to spend the bulk of your retirement years. This way you don't leap into an early decision, you don't spend money, and the money you make from your house sale can be invested and earn you more retirement funding.

This is an especially good choice if you are uncomfortable with rapid change. By breaking up your retirement move and first staying at a place that is familiar to you, you can more easily break with the past.

▶ **Another popular way to use your second home is as ... a second home. Many retirees split their time between two houses.**

This is called *sojourning*, and it's becoming a popular retirement lifestyle. (For detailed information, see Sojourning, page 394.)

RETIREMENT COMMUNITIES

▶ **A housing option for retirees that has been booming since the 1980s is communities designed for retirees or other older adults.**

The growing popularity of retirement communities—and the growing number of them—is a response to the graying of America. Where there used to be only a few retirement communities clustered in the Sunbelt, there are now hundreds across the United States. Recently, large hotel companies like Hyatt and Marriott have begun opening retirement residences.

One result of this boom is that you have more of a choice than ever before. You have a range of options now across the board—where you want to live, whether you want to rent or buy, if you want an apartment or a house, full service or no service, and so on.

▶ **There are different types of retirement communities—including standard communities that offer housing and recreation alone and service-oriented retirement communities that offer varying degrees of service ranging from housekeeping to long-term medical care.**

Clearly, each type of community serves a distinct purpose. And if you're considering a retirement community, you should be sure to understand the distinctions between the different types and think about where you would be the happiest.

When you're reading about the different communities, here or in other books and articles, keep trying to put yourself in the situation. Imagine yourself 5 or 10 years down the road—does what you're reading describe the surroundings you think you'll want?

The next section describes the different communities, what, if any, services they offer, the type of retiree each is best for, and finally, how to choose the right community for you—what to look for and what to look out for.

STANDARD RETIREMENT COMMUNITIES

▶ **The *standard retirement community* or adult community is a housing development geared solely to adults over a certain age—usually 45.**

This is the traditional type of retirement community—the sort of development that has sprung up in the retirement meccas of the United States, such as Scottsdale, Arizona; the Fort Lauderdale–Miami area of Florida; Palm Springs, California; and other spots in the Sunbelt.

How it works: The specific type of housing varies; different communities have one, all, or a combination of: garden apartments, single-family houses, co-ops, or condos. In most cases, you'll buy your home under a standard real estate arrangement. Prices will of course vary according to type of housing and location. You can pay anything from $25,000 to over $1 million. In addition, you'll pay annual maintenance fees (which cover upkeep of the grounds and so forth) and, often, recreation fees. Some communities allow you to rent your residence on either a short- or long-term basis.

TIP: Where maintenance and recreation fees are concerned, beware of "escalator clauses"—clauses that allow fees to increase. At some communities run by more unscrupulous developers, you may sign what appears to be a very reasonably priced agreement, only to find that the fees skyrocket the following year.

Pros: This type of community usually has recreation facilities—anything from clubhouses to pools, golf courses, tennis courts or more. They offer planned activities—you can enjoy any number of events. Housing is relatively inexpensive, especially when compared to the equivalent apartment or house in a regular community. You have a built-in group of friends—people in a similar age bracket, usually from similar backgrounds. You don't have to worry much about crime and security.

Cons: Due to their size and layout, communities are often located at a distance from cities. The above-mentioned advantages (the emphasis on recreational activities, the network of friends, and so forth) can lead to a lack of privacy. There is a "sameness" of surroundings. You'll have limited exposure to anyone but other retirees. Houses or apartments are often small. Some may have strict restrictions regarding children—a problem if you want grandchildren to visit.

Best for: Retirees who want low-maintenance housing plus the social benefits of living in a planned community of other retirees.

TIP: To find out about retirement communities in different cities and states, try contacting the local chamber of commerce. Most will have lists and more information on local retirement communities.

TIP: If you're considering buying into a retirement community, you're best off *not* buying property at a brand-new development. It usually takes a few years for a community to get its footing, get the kinks out, and begin settling into a routine. Moreover, it's often difficult to see *problems* until some time has passed. What looks pristine and perfect today may turn decrepit or shabby in a short time.

SOURCE: For a list of Florida retirement communities, including descriptions of what they offer, send $3.00 to: **Retirement Housing Council**, P.O. Box 12934, Tallahassee, FL 32317.

SERVICE-ORIENTED RETIREMENT COMMUNITIES

▶ **Service-oriented retirement communities take retirement living one step further than standard retirement communities by offering you services—ranging from basic housekeeping and meals to full-time medical care.**

Service-oriented retirement communities are designed to make life a little easier for their inhabitants. They are aimed primarily at middle- to upper-income retirees, and their costs vary according to the type of facility, its location, and the number of services.

There are three common types of service-oriented communities (with some overlap between them): independent living facilities, assisted living facilities, and continuing care (or life care) communities. (Note: There are always exceptions to the rule—some retirement communities might not offer all the services described here; sometimes the different names for communities are used interchangeably. The following should give you an idea, however, of the general types of communities and what they can provide for you.)

Independent Living Facilities

▶ **Independent living facilities are essentially hotels or condos designed specifically for retirees.**

How it works: This sort of retirement residence is at one end of the spectrum, offering little in the way of medical services (although some of these communities offer access to independent or affiliated nursing homes). On the whole, independent living facilities are geared for active retirees—those who don't want or need medical services as part of their living arrangement. Like a hotel, this type of facility offers certain day-to-day services, typically including meals, housekeeping, transportation, and emergency medical services. The specific services, however, do vary from facility to facility. Some residences will give you a continental breakfast and one other meal, others three full meals; some offer recreation facilities; some offer health monitoring, others no health services at all. Many facilities will charge you an entrance fee (sometimes called an admission fee or an endowment)—a one-time charge you pay upon signing up that entitles you to the housing and services. Depending upon the type of housing, the services, the location of the development, and so forth, entrance fees can be anything from $35,000 to $200,000. In addition, you will pay a monthly maintenance fee. Monthly fees can range anywhere from $250 on up to $4,000, although most generally fall in the $700 to $1,500 range.

Pros: Many independent living facilities offer a range of recreational activities and social programs; you can easily meet people; physical surroundings are usually attractive and well-maintained;

you don't have to worry about things like housekeeping or lawn mowing.

Cons: Cost can be high; because accommodations vary, you have to be careful and shop around for the best deal; many communities have waiting lists; in some cases, you have to qualify by showing a minimum net worth (typically about $150,000); as with other communities, the location may be far from towns; you may feel isolated.

Best for: People in good health, in the middle- and upper-income brackets, who want the stability of a planned community and the meals and housekeeping services.

Assisted Living Facilities

▶ **Assisted living facilities (also called personal care or board and care facilities) offer limited medical services to their residents.**

How it works: Assisted living facilities offer custodial care services—help in such daily activities as dressing, bathing, and eating. At many, a medical specialist, usually a nurse, is on call. Housekeeping and meals are usually included. Often at these facilities, you don't have the option of renting an apartment or detached residence. Instead, you have a room (semiprivate or private) and share living areas with other residents. As with other communities, costs for assisted living facilities vary. Average monthly costs range from about $1,000 for a semiprivate room to $2,500 for a private room.

Pros: The same as for other retirement communities (security, companionship, and so forth); this is a good bridge between nursing home living and nonservice living.

Cons: Also the same as for other retirement communities, but especially lack of privacy.

Best for: People who need some assistance, but not full-scale medical help; people with Alzheimer's—especially couples in which one person has Alzheimer's (this type of living arrangement allows the nonimpaired spouse some freedom and the knowledge that their spouse is being taken care of).

Continuing Care Retirement Communities

▶ **Continuing care retirement communities (CCRCs) technically are hybrids—the communities that offer a range of services, from independent living facilities on up to nursing care.**

Because of the flexibility of services, this is the most rapidly growing area of senior citizen housing. Hotel chains, such as the Marriott and the Hyatt, are moving aggressively into this area.

How they work: As the name denotes, continuing care communities are designed to care for you continuously—at different stages in your health. They usually combine independent living facilities with medical care and on-premises skilled nursing home facilities, as well as skilled staff members—nurses, social workers, and the like. For example, at one of Marriott's "catered living" residences, you can begin by renting an independent full-service apartment. As time goes on, you can shift into an assisted living apartment if you need it. Your monthly rent will change according to the changes in services you receive.

At most CCRCs, you can buy a condo or rent an apartment, from studios up to two bedrooms. Costs vary widely depending upon the specific service arrangement. Usually you'll run into one of three arrangements: all-inclusive service, modified continuing care, or a la carte services.

All-inclusive (or full) service: This type of CCRC offers the full range of services. This is the arrangement often called life care. You pay an entrance fee, which guarantees you living quarters for life. (In effect, while you don't own your residence, you own the right to live in it.) Entrance fees range from $35,000 for a studio to $200,000 for two-bedroom apartments, with the median fee falling at about $70,000. (Many communities will refund all or part of your entrance fee to you if you leave, or to your estate if you die. However, in these cases, the entrance fee may be substantially higher than fees at those CCRCs that require a nonrefundable entrance fee.) In addition to the entrance fee, you pay a monthly service fee, usually ranging from $700 to $2,000 per person. This service fee covers all services, including housekeeping, meals, utilities, custodial care (help bathing, dressing, and so forth), recreational facilities and social activities, and health care.

TIP: A relatively low percentage of residents (usually about 20%) go into permanent care. Unless your health background—including family health history—leads you to think that you'll probably need long-term care, you might be better off saving money and choosing another type of arrangement. A better choice might be one offering "a la carte" services (described below), which would allow you to take advantage of health care should you need it but not pay for it if you don't.

Modified continuing care: This type of CCRC is less costly because it offers less guaranteed medical service. Entrance fees typically range from $20,000 to $90,000; monthly fees from $600 to $1,200. This covers all housekeeping and meal services, but only some health care services. Common arrangements under modified continuing care contracts give you a percentage off nursing home rates. For example, one Hyatt CCRC offers residents insurance paying $40 a day toward nursing home care. Another common arrangement pays for a set period of nursing home care—usually about 60 days.

A la carte services (or fee for service): At this type of CCRC, you pay for services (both medical and personal) as you use them. Usually your fees are much lower—with entrance fees in the $10,000 to $60,000 range, and monthly fees in the $550 to $1,000 range.

Pros: You have easy access to medical services, guaranteed long-term care if you've signed up for it—and easy access even if you haven't. A big plus with these hybrid full-service developments: You have the security of knowing that, should you need the increased medical attention, you can get it *without* going to a nursing home or moving to another retirement home.

Cons: As with other retirement communities, you are faced with a lack of privacy, a "campus lifestyle"; CCRCs are often located at a distance from towns; you won't be with people from different age groups. A potential problem: Many CRCCs have been mismanaged; you have to be careful you don't wind up in a poor one. (For how to judge a retirement community, see pages 352–58.)

Best for: People with a middle to upper income concerned about long-term care needs; those who can't or don't want to move in with family members or don't want to worry about nursing home admittance in later years; couples who want the peace of mind of knowing that if one of them needs long-term care, they will still be together.

Federally Subsidized Congregate Housing

▶ **Federally subsidized congregate housing is essentially full-service retirement housing for people with less money.**

How it works: Like other unsubsidized retirement communities, many federally subsidized communities offer a range of options—from independent living apartments with little or no medical service to continuing care medical services. The difference? Cost. Because it's federally subsidized, this type of housing is less expensive. Often the entrance fee is either waived or negotiable, depending upon your particular financial circumstances. Monthly rents are substantially lower than the norm. For example, at one subsidized community, you and your spouse will be granted a subsidy if your annual income is $29,500 or less. You would pay 30 percent of the monthly rent of $485 for a one-bedroom apartment.

Pros: If you qualify financially and want to live in a service retirement community, federally subsidized housing can fit the bill; cost is low but services are still good.

Cons: It's still not cheap—even with the subsidy, costs may be higher than living independently.

Best for: People in low- to middle-income brackets who want the benefits of a service-oriented retirement community but can't afford the standard price.

CHOOSING A RETIREMENT COMMUNITY

▶ **If you're thinking about moving into a retirement community, start researching and planning a few years before you retire.**

It's wise to plan. Many developments—especially the newer ones—have waiting lists, some several years long. Keep this in mind and don't wait until the last minute.

▶ **The first step to take is the most basic. You have to decide which kind of retirement community is the right one for you.**

Once you've made the initial decision to spend your retirement years in a retirement community, you face more decisions.

Retirement communities today offer an array of choices. Some are full-service, others offer nothing but housing; some offer a range of recreational opportunities, others a limited amount. Some are nonprofit facilities run by sponsors, often with religious affiliations.

Others are privately owned for-profit ventures. The list goes on and on. So it's up to you to decide what kind of retirement community is right for you.

This is the point at which you have to determine just what you want and need from a retirement community. Part of this process is purely subjective: What makes you feel comfortable? What do you want in a living arrangement? The other part of your decision-making process should be more practical: What will you need—and what can you afford?

Consider how much or how little you may want or need in the way of services. What services are you willing to pay for and which are immaterial to you? To help you clarify your needs, rank the following services in order of importance:

Guaranteed health care

Nursing home facilities

Physical therapy facilities

Recreational facilities

Housekeeping service

Meals

Transportation services

TIP: **A study cited in the *Journal of Healthcare Management* found that the services most important to retirement community residents and potential residents were transportation, a library, and laundry facilities. Near the bottom were tennis, pets, and golf.**

▶ **Next it's a matter of assessing different communities to be sure they fit your needs.**

Assessing retirement communities is where legwork, research, and level-headed observation come in.

A few points to help you make the right decision:

• *Visit different retirement communities.* If you can see them in person, definitely do so. Brochures, articles, and phone calls can't compare to getting a firsthand look at a place. If you're thinking about getting meal service, ask if you can have a meal there; if you're interested in recreational activities, try some of them out.

Try to get a look at and a taste for everything that you would be involved in.

- *If possible, visit the communities that interest you more than once.* This is especially useful if you're considering a community in a resort area. An off-season visit will give you a better idea of what it's really like.

- *Check the retirement community's performance record.* Ask to see financial statements. You want to be sure that the community has met its financial obligations, that it is reasonably sound and won't go under. (Signs of strong financial performance include low debt, positive cash flow, consistent increase in income.)

- If the community is a new one and there is no track record to check, *ask about the developers or sponsors.* What other projects have they done? Have they been successful?

TIP: While the rule of thumb has long been that it's wise to choose a community run by developers or sponsors with experience in the retirement housing field, you can be a little more flexible these days. Hotel companies and other developers with experience *related* to retirement housing are good bets as well.

TIP: If you're thinking about a retirement community that is still in its planning stages, keep in mind the following rule of thumb: The developer shouldn't start building until *a minimum* of 50 percent of the residences are sold or leased. (Less than that shows poor planning—which could translate into poor financial stability later on.) Also, if building hasn't begun, ask if you can pay only a small refundable deposit instead of having a large sum tied up.

- *Make sure the community has the proper state licensing.*

- *Check that the community is accredited by the American Association of Homes for the Aging.* This industry group reviews retirement communities and awards accreditation to those that maintain certain standards of service and financial management. If the community you're considering holds their accreditation, it's a good sign. (See page 358 for address of the AAHA.)

- *Be sure you know what the financial arrangement is*—how much you're paying and what *exactly* you're getting for that money. Remember, you'll be paying quite a bit of money to live in the retirement community. You should understand what services you'll get, what services you won't.

- *Ask about refund arrangements.* Usually you should be able to get a refund of your entrance fee, but specific refund arrangements vary from community to community.

- *Be sure that staff members are experienced in their field and have the proper training*—either in gerontology or in retirement housing administration. And talk to them to find out if you like them and feel comfortable with them.

- *Find out if there is a residents' council or residents' board that has input into how the community is run.* It's usually a sign of a well-run community when residents are encouraged to get involved in its management.

- *Finally . . . don't ignore the intangibles*—the ineffable feeling you get about a place. After all, this is where you'll be spending many years. Intuition, gut feeling—whatever you call it, it matters. When you're picking a retirement community, *listen* to your feelings. Your subconscious may pick up signals that your conscious mind won't. What are the people here like? Do they seem to be people you'll like? People you'll enjoy spending time with?

TIP: **When possible, stay for a visit at the retirement community you're considering. A weekend visit will give you firsthand insights into how the community works, what the people are like—both residents and staff—what the routine is, and ultimately, whether or not you'll fit in.**

▶ **There are some danger signals that should tip you off that a community is poorly run.**

Some little clues speak volumes on how well a facility is run. Be on the lookout for maintenance problems—big and small. Notice how well the grounds are maintained. And check for the small signs of sloppy maintenance—dripping faucets, rusty toilets, stale or bad smells. Also pay attention to staff members. When a retirement community has troubles, the first areas to suffer are management and services.

▶ **When it comes time to sign a contract, first review the contract very carefully—and have a qualified professional review it also.**

Check and double-check the financial arrangements in particular. Nothing should be left to guesswork. Be sure the contract contains specific information on:

TABLE 10.1: QUESTIONS TO ASK ABOUT A RETIREMENT COMMUNITY

Clearly you're the only person who knows exactly what you're looking for in your place of residence. Only you know what is important to you. The following questions are designed to help you pinpoint the areas that concern you. By applying them to the communities you're considering, you can better decide whether a specific retirement community has the elements you want.

ABOUT LOCATION

1. Is it close enough to town? Shopping centers? Hospitals?

2. Do I like the climate?

3. Is it close or easily accessible (near airport) to family or friends?

4. Is it near a cultural center? A university or other educational facility?

5. If I plan to continue working or get a job, is the community near enough to an area that could offer me employment?

ABOUT RESIDENCES

6. Are they large enough? Well-built?

7. Do I have my own garden? Are there restrictions on what I can do with this garden?

8. Can I personalize my residence—bring in my own furniture, for example?

9. Can I have a patio? A terrace?

10. Are kitchens and bathrooms modern? Are facilities equipped for wheelchairs?

11. Is the residence close enough to the main dining areas? To recreation areas?

12. On the other hand, is the residence *too* close to common areas?

13. Are there rules about pets? About visitors?

ABOUT RECREATIONAL FACILITIES AND EVENTS

14. What recreational facilities are there? When can they be used?

15. Does the community offer enrichment courses? Cultural events?

16. Is there a library on premises?

17. Is there a religious facility? Or is it close to one?

ABOUT PERSONAL SERVICES

18. Does it offer housekeeping? Fresh linens?

19. Is there laundry service?

20. Is there a barber/beauty parlor on premises?

21. Is there a post office on premises? If not, is there regular mail pickup? When and where?

22. What about security services—are there police and fire departments?

ABOUT HEALTH SERVICES

23. Can I get health care in my home?

24. Is there a nursing home on site?

25. Are there physical therapy facilities?

26. Is there an on-premises pharmacy? What qualifications do staff members have?

27. Is there access to ambulance service?

ABOUT FINANCIAL ARRANGEMENTS

28. Can I sign up for a trial period before making a long-term commitment?

29. If so, and if I decide against the community, is my payment refundable?

30. What exactly do I get for my entrance, maintenance, and other fees?

31. Is any part of my entrance fee refundable? If so, under what arrangement?

32. How much can rent, maintenance, and other fees increase?

- *Refund arrangements:* You'll probably see one of two common arrangements. With a *high refund/high entrance fee combination,* you or your estate gets an 80% to 90% refund of your entrance fee when you leave or die—regardless of the length of your stay— but the entrance fee is correspondingly high. With a *traditional or declining percentage plan,* you get a full refund if you leave the community within a set, short period of time (usually 90 days). But for each extra month you stay, the amount of the refund decreases about 1% to 2%. In these cases, you can expect a lower entrance fee—and a lower refund amount after a number of years have passed. Which is best for you? It depends on how long you think you'll be staying at the facility. Generally speaking, the longer your stay, the better the traditional plan. You pay less, which means you keep more money. If you think your stay will be short, the high refund/high entrance fee plan is better.

- *Cost increases (rent or other fees):* The amount by which costs can increase each year should be limited to a set amount. Many contracts will tie increases to the Consumer Price Index or another inflation index. This is adequate. A better arrangement, if you can get it: cost increases of only 3% to 5% each year; proposed increases above this amount are subject to approval by residents.

- *Inability to pay monthly fees:* The contract should explain what would happen if you were unable to pay your monthly fees. Nonprofit communities will lose nonprofit status if they evict you, so at one of these, you are guaranteed lifetime housing regardless of your ability to pay. Often they have set up assistance funds to cover payment. However, privately run communities aren't bound by this constraint.

SOURCE: **The American Association of Homes for the Aging** is a professional organization of nursing homes, independent housing facilities, continuing care facilities, and community service agencies. They offer information on retirement housing, including *The National Continuing Care Directory.* For a free catalogue of the publications they have for the public, contact: The American Association of Homes for the Aging, Suite 400, 1129 20th Street NW, Washington, DC 20036-3489 (phone 202-296-5960).

SOURCE: *The Guide to Housing Alternatives for Senior Citizens,* by Margaret Gold, covers both the options open to you and financing arrangements. It's $12.95 (which include $3.00 postage and handling). Send a check to: Consumer Reports Books, 9180 LeSaint Drive, Fairfield, OH 54104. Ask for Ordering Code 2263P.

TIP: **Check with your state's Division on Aging for a list of licensed retirement communities in the state.**

Chapter 11

FINANCING YOUR
NEW HOME
WITH YOUR OLD

INTRODUCTION

▶ **Another part of preparing for your retirement is deciding what you will do with your current home. An important fact to be aware of: Your house may be a good source of retirement income.**

The first step is knowing something about the house you own—how much it's worth, how soft or strong your local real estate market is, and most important, if you want to stay in your house at all. Deciding what to do can be difficult. In Chapter 10 we dealt with the personal issues, here we focus on the financial aspects: How can you use your house to provide you retirement income?

▶ **There are four basic options: trading down, or selling and then buying a new, cheaper home; selling, then renting; taking a reverse mortgage; and arranging a sale-leaseback.**

The first two options are for retirees who want to move, and they offer important financial and tax advantages. The last two options are for retirees who want to stay in their current homes, but either can't afford to or want some current income out of their house. Fortunately for them, there are now ways to manage this.

OPTION 1: TRADING DOWN

▶ **Trading down can give you retirement income as well as substantial tax advantages.**

Trading down is the first choice of many retirees. Many people now approaching retirement age purchased homes in the 1950s, 1960s, or 1970s and have seen their home equity appreciate 10 or more times. Selling such a home and buying a cheaper one can leave a retiree with a substantial sum for investment.

How it works: The basic idea is simple. Sell your larger or more expensive house, collect the money, and buy a cheaper house. Put the rest of the money into a safe, income-producing investment. Key recommendations: *Plan* before you sell and trade down—you want to get the most for your house, and you should be well acquainted with the locale of your new house. Pay for your trade-down home in full—carrying a mortgage on a reduced retirement income is not advisable, even with mortgage interest deduction. Generally, you are taxed on the difference between the adjusted sale price of your old house and the cost of your new one. The adjusted sale price of your old house is the selling price of the house minus selling expenses (such as broker commissions, "points" you pay for the buyer, advertising costs, termite inspection costs, and other legal expenses) and minus IRS-qualified fix-up costs (such as painting or repairs necessary to make your house salable—done during a 90-day period ending when you sign the contract to sell your house and paid for within a month of the house sale). The cost of the new house is the purchase price (including mortgages you assume, if any), as well as buying expenses such as broker commissions, title search costs, and legal costs.

When you trade down, clearly there will be a difference between your old house's sale price and your new house's purchase price. Even so, you can defer paying a high capital gains tax and, if you or your spouse is 55 or older, you can avoid paying a capital gains tax entirely.

- *To defer capital gains tax on a trade-down:* Improvements made on your new "trade-down" house—such as adding a swimming pool, building an addition, or renovating an attic or garage—will increase the cost of your new house. This way, you can cut down or eliminate the difference between the selling price of your old home and the cost of the new. The result? You can defer all or part of the capital gains tax you would otherwise have to pay. To qualify for this, you must incur actual expenses and must spend the money on the improvements within two years of the sale of your old house.

- *To avoid capital gains taxes on a trade-down:* There is a special tax break for seniors called the $125,000 exclusion. This allows you an up to $125,000 one-time exclusion from capital gains tax for the sale of your house if you or your spouse are 55 years or older. Other requirements: You must have lived in the house or apartment for at least three of the past five years, or one of the past five years if the remaining four were spent in a hospital or nursing home. If your capital gain is $125,000 or less, subtract the amount from the total sale price of your house when determining your tax bill. If your gain is over $125,000 you can defer taxes on the amount over $125,000 by spending that money on a new primary residence.

TAX TIP: Unmarried joint owners selling a home are still eligible for the $125,000 exclusion. Also: if you're older singles considering remarriage, try to separately use your $125,000 exclusions *before* you join together—and turn two exclusions into only one.

TAX TIP: Regardless of your age any capital gains from your old house may be *tax-deferrable* if the price of your new house is as much as or more than the amount your old house was sold for, and if it is purchased within two years of the sale of your old house. (However, note that in this case it is not a trade-down house.)

Pros: *Higher income.* Put the money you save in bonds or mutual funds. *Lower expenses.* Your second home is apt to have lower property taxes and upkeep. *Greater convenience.* You can choose a second house that specifically meets your new needs as a retiree.

Cons: In a sluggish real estate area, it can be difficult to sell your home. Moreover, many people overestimate the value of their home. Many closings are delayed—and if you've already purchased your

THE ONLY RETIREMENT GUIDE YOU'LL EVER NEED

trade-down home you could face financial problems. Many people don't want to move. Fees mount—closing costs, moving costs, new home costs.

OPTION 2: SELLING, THEN RENTING

▶ **This is the "take the money and run" option. For some, the added flexibility is worth the price.**

Until recently, renting was more expensive than buying. The state of the real estate market may have changed things in some areas—and for those who want to see the country or the world, or who want to wait before buying, now may be the best time to take this option.

How it works: The only difference between this option and option 1 are that you are renting instead of buying another property, and that you face the possible loss of one tax advantage—the deferment option.

Pros: Income producing, if you put the money in safe investments; savings on property taxes and other home owners' expenses. Biggest advantage: flexibility—if you don't like your choice of a retirement home, you can move without the very real problems of selling another house (in today's soft markets, this is a very tangible advantage).

Cons: Rents eat up income without ownership advantages. A psychological problem for some: Renting gives them a feeling of impermanence.

OPTION 3: REVERSE MORTGAGES

▶ **For retirees who want to stay home, but can't afford to, reverse mortgages may be the answer.**

Maybe you face a dilemma. You want to stay in your house, but with property taxes, food bills, and the like, you simply can't afford to. Reverse mortgages may be a way out. They're a way of having your cake and eating it too—staying at home, but getting a monthly check from a bank with a reverse mortgage on your home. And because the money comes to you in the form of a loan and not income, the money won't be taxed as income, and you won't face a reduction of federal or possibly state benefits.

Of course, there are catches. In effect you're giving up equity—ownership—of all or part of your home, something you might not want to do. Also, you may be hesitant about taking out a loan. Being in debt is something prudent people often try to avoid as much as possible. These are not minor considerations. In fact, before considering getting a reverse mortgage, consider other methods of obtaining money. For example, you might take in tenants. Or you might consider trading down—selling your home and buying a smaller one.

Reverse mortgages aren't for everyone, and some types can be downright dangerous. But for many, this is an idea whose time has come.

How it works: A reverse mortgage is a type of home equity loan for homeowners with a mortgage-free home. You as a homeowner take out a home equity loan for a certain rate (usually tied to the prime rate, recently at 11.5%) and in return receive a monthly check for a specified amount, say, $500 or $800. Depending on the terms of your reverse mortgage, you'll receive that monthly check for as long as you live in your house, or, in some cases, for a specified number of years only. A key advantage: The money you receive is tax-free—it's only a loan, not income. And the money you receive won't affect your eligibility for various federal programs—and probably state programs as well.

At the term's end or when you move or die, the loan is to be repaid to the lender, usually by selling your home.

The payoff is simple: In return for your monthly check, you give the lender part or all of the value of your home, including a percentage of the price appreciation that occurs during the term of the reverse mortgage. As might be expected, the longer you live the better off you are, since your effective annual interest rate on the money you receive keeps going down.

If you die or decide to move soon after you sign your reverse mortgage, you or your heirs will have to repay the lender the total amount of monthly checks you've received, including interest, the appreciation of your house during this period, and all the initial costs of getting the loan. This can literally amount to 100% or more effective interest for that borrowed money—particularly since your house may have appreciated more in value than the amount you got over that short period.

On the other hand, you as a homeowner will probably benefit in declining or flat real estate markets—which currently exist in much of the country. In general, the longer you live (for a lifetime reverse mortgage), and the flatter the real estate market, the better off you'll be.

There is usually a loan ceiling with reverse mortgages, which depends on various factors, including your age. The older you are, typically the more monthly income you can receive.

American Homestead Mortgage Company is a pioneer and currently the largest lender in the reverse mortgage market. In return for monthly income, American Homestead usually receives from 20% to 100% of the appreciation of a home's value, although it won't take more than 15% in any one year. When you as a homeowner die or move, American Homestead reaps a maximum equity position of 94% in your house—the other 6% is left to pay real estate commissions.

There are various types of reverse mortgages, and various terms describing them (REMs or reverse equity mortgages, and IRMAs or individual reverse mortgage accounts), but the basics are similar. One key difference is the term of the loan—it can last for as long as you live in your home, or for a specified period of time.

FHA insured reverse mortgages are the newest type of reverse mortgages. The Federal Housing Administration (and recently the Federal National Mortgage Association) has now begun insuring reverse mortgages, in turn making them more attractive to lenders—and a good option for retirees, since federal guarantees assure that you'll get your money even if the mortgage lender goes bankrupt. The basics are the same—but the government is allowing for much flexibility with these reverse mortgages. The interest rate may be fixed or variable—and instead of monthly checks you may opt for a lump sum, or a line of credit which you may draw upon when you need the money. Moreover, the government plans to offer independent counseling to help you determine what type of reverse mortgage— if any—is best for you.

The federal government has set loan limits (the amount depends on the region; recently the highest limit was about $100,000), and has established terms of lending. Recently, homeowners paid an annual 0.5% fee on the principal balance of the loan, as well as 2% of either the house value or the maximum loan amount, whichever was less.

SOURCE: For lenders offering FHA insured mortgages, call the **Federal Housing Administration** at 800-245-2691.

Fixed-term reverse mortgage: Instead of receiving a check for life, in this case you as a homeowner receive a monthly check for a specified term, usually between 3 and 10 years. Sometimes the loan is renewable. The key problem is that you may be forced to sell your house at the term's end to pay off the loan—and you can wind up with nowhere to go. In most cases, you're best off avoiding this type of reverse mortgage. In general, fixed-term reverse mortgages are best for people with somewhere definite to go when the term of the loan is up; for example, someone planning to go to a nursing home after a certain number of years.

Pros: A guaranteed monthly income for life, or for a term that is tax-free. For many people, this means the difference between financial independence and imposing on others or being forced to move. (And that income can be very cheap: The longer the term of the loan, the greater the effective interest rate—you may wind up paying under 1% for your monthly income.) With FHA or Fannie Mae backed mortgages, there is the added safety of government guarantees.

TIP: **As nontaxable loan payments, reverse mortgage income will not affect your Social Security payments.**

Cons: Fixed-term mortgages may force you to sell your home to repay the loan. If your real estate is appreciating rapidly, you may lose all or much of the appreciation. A psychological burden: You may have worked years to pay off your mortgage—now you're going back into debt.

SOURCE: For a copy of *A Financial Guide to Reverse Mortgages,* send a self-addressed, stamped envelope to the National Center for Home Equity Conversion, Suite 300, 1210 East Collage, Marshall, MN 56258. This guide lists lenders nationwide who offer mortgages that guarantee the elderly monthly payments for equity in their homes.

SOURCE: AARP explains how to use your home for income in *Home Made Money.* Call 202-728-4300, or write: AARP HEIC, 1909 K Street, NW, Washington, DC 20049.

OPTION 4: SALE-LEASEBACKS

▶ **Sale-leasebacks are a way of selling your equity but retaining living rights in your home.**

How it works: Sale-leasebacks offer advantages to both buyers and sellers. Typically, as a seller, you offer your home to an investor—often for a price under the appraised value. You and the buyer agree to a mortgage, usually for 10 to 15 years, such that the buyer pays you a down payment of around 15% of the selling price and pays the balance over the term of the mortgage. The buyer is now responsible for property taxes, major maintenance, and insurance. You remain in the house, but now you are leasing it from the buyer, and you in turn pay the buyer rent—mutually agreed upon and with caps on yearly increases. Sale-leasebacks may be arranged with private investors, with your children or other relatives, or with such community organizations as churches, synagogues, or charities.

A key problem: What if you outlive the mortgage? One way to meet this problem is to buy a deferred annuity (or have the buyer pay the premium on a deferred annuity with you as the beneficiary). In this way, you will keep on getting an income to pay for rent.

Note: Terms and conditions vary, and as with most real estate transactions, it is best to hire expert legal help.

SOURCE: *Sale Leaseback Guide and Model Documents* is available for sale from the National Center for Home Equity Conversion, 110 East Main Street, Room 605, Madison, WI 53703.

Pros: Money up front when you need it; a stream of income in the future; and the advantage of maintaining residence in your home.

Cons: Private investors may be difficult to find; if you arrange a sale at a discount, you are obviously losing some potential money; the problems of outliving the terms of your lease; the psychological problems of no longer owning your own home.

Chapter 12

LOCALE: PICKING THE PERFECT RETIREMENT SPOT

INTRODUCTION

Deciding the type of home you're going to live in is only one aspect of planning your retirement lifestyle. Another aspect, perhaps even more important, is deciding *where* you want to spend your retirement years. Because retirement is a time of change, it's also a time when many people decide to move. Perhaps you've always dreamed of living overseas. Or maybe you've always wanted a home in a warmer climate. Now is your chance to make that dream come true.

That's why one of the most crucial aspects of retirement planning is seeking the right spot in which to retire—the location that will meet your needs and make your retirement years truly happy ones.

Of course, it's not a simple decision. You must weigh various considerations and research different spots before you find the perfect place for you. This chapter is designed to take you step by step through the decision-making process. In addition, it will give you brief sketches of the most popular retirement locales as well as lesser-known but recommended spots. It gives you pointers on what to look for and where to find the information you need to make your decision. Finally, because so many retirees decide to go abroad, this

367

chapter covers the pros and cons of retirement abroad, the special considerations you will have to make, and more.

HOW TO BEGIN YOUR SEARCH

▶ **Choosing a new place to live—or choosing to stay where you are—can be an enormous decision.**

Many people today decide to move. About 30% of all Americans move at some point after their 65th birthday, and about 4% move out of their home states. And those numbers are increasing.

How can you make a retirement move easier? Start early, and start at home by *thinking*.

What do you want out of retirement? Do you want to move or stay at home? Or do you want to do both—to maintain two addresses? Do you want to travel, and if so, how much? Does your spouse have different desires? Do you have any dream locations at the back of your mind? How much money will you have during retirement? Will you have to work? Do you want to work? What recreational activities do you plan?

At this stage, ask these questions and treat the answers holistically, that is, give yourself a *total* picture, not necessarily a detailed one, of what you want. Or of what you think you want.

▶ **Researching your new retirement home is probably the most enjoyable part of retirement planning.**

It can be enjoyable, wading through brochures, imagining yourself in hundreds of locales. It can also be daunting.

There is a wealth of information available telling you the best places to live, rating these places in terms of health care, climate, economy, cultural activities, and the like. However, nothing can beat going there. And then going back. The better you know an area, in the off-season as well as in the bright sunshine, the better you'll be able to evaluate it as a potential retirement spot.

Take a two-step approach to picking potential spots: Read about and narrow your choices; then visit them.

▶ **Start by reading books, magazines, and local newspapers.**

Shopping for the right retirement locale via books and magazines will give you an idea of what options you have, and most important, will help you decide what is important to you. Some of the best general sources for information on retirement places:

- *Retirement Places Rated,* by Richard Boyer and David Savageau (Prentice-Hall, $12.95), details and compares information on housing, taxes, health care, and costs for retirees. Includes a handy rating index of various key factors.

- *Retirement Edens Outside the Sunbelt* ($12.95), *Sunbelt Retirement* ($13.95), and *Travel and Retirement Edens Abroad* ($16.95), all by Peter Dickinson (the dean of retirement travel) all contain detailed recommendations on where to live in retirement—information on the health care, recreation, etc. Available from Phillips Publishing Company, 7811 Montrose Road, Potomac, MD 20854 (800-722-9000). For each book ordered add $2.25 shipping and handling.

- *The Rating Guide to Life in America's Small Cities* (Prometheus Books, $16.95), by G. Scott Thomas, details life and general conditions in 219 small cities, some of which look good for retirement.

- *Retirement Choices* (Gateway books, $10.95) is a chatty, enjoyable guide to retirement areas in the United States and abroad that emphasizes the "feel" of a place over statistics—although it does carry information on rents and so forth.

- *The Retirement Letter,* by Peter Dickinson, carries periodic timely recommendations and updates on retirement locales. Annual subscription is $87. Call or write: Phillips Publishing, Inc.; 7811 Montrose Road, Potomac, MD 20854 (301-424-3700).

- *Kiplinger's Personal Finance Magazine, Money,* and some newsmagazines publish yearly comparisons of various towns and areas across the United States, highlighting costs, housing, salaries, etc. This is a good way to get up-to-date, reliable comparative data.

- *Travel videos* (by various producers) are often useful; however, too often they show only the positive aspects from a tourist's perspective.

Don't forget to do your own research. Read and listen critically— often you'll hear about a good area long before the media write about it. Don't just rely on the experts to pass their observations on to you. Some suggestions:

- Write local chambers of commerce: Most have packets of information for newcomers.

- Read the real estate ads carefully—does it appear that prices are falling?

- Subscribe to regional magazines to get a feel for an area.

- Particularly if you have narrowed your search, an excellent tactic is to subscribe to a local newspaper. This can give you a feel for the intangibles, and an outlook on crime, on culture, on the mood of a city or an area that no book ever can.

SOURCE: A Florida retirement community industry association publishes a listing of retirement communities and their major features in Florida. Price: $3.00. Write: **The Retirement Housing Council,** P.O. Box 19234, Tallahassee, FL 32317.

▶ **Once you've come up with a few potential retirement spots, it's time to visit and judge them in person.**

Plan on making at least two visits to your potential retirement choices—including at least one visit during the off-season. Why? You want to see the area at its *worst:* Florida at its hottest, the mountains in the winter. Some tips:

- *Approach these visits as fact-finding trips, not vacations.* Even if one is a part of your vacation, take a few days off and get practical. Visit the chamber of commerce, read the local papers, check out area health care facilities, look at supermarkets as well as restaurants. Don't look at everything in that rosy vacation mood.

- *Think in the long term.* Remember you may be spending the rest of your life here—not two more weeks. Don't make the mistake of some retirees who sank their life savings into a dream home on a lovely vacation isle in the Caribbean. Even with such hobbies as fishing, boating, and diving, they forgot one thing: After a month or two island life can be *boring.*

- *Think practically.* You are what you are. You might change, but chances are that you won't—or that you won't change that much. If you don't swim, don't convince yourself that after you move to Florida you'll spend hours every day swimming. Select areas on the basis of what you already like to do, in addition to what you *might* like to do in the future.

- *Think critically.* Many people, particularly real estate salespeople, the local chamber of commerce, and association executives, have a vested interest in getting you to move to their area. Filter what they say.

- *Talk to people.* Don't depend on travel agents or community leaders or even your friends already living in an area—branch out and talk to others.

▶ **Instead of going on your own, consider joining a tour group for a special preretirement trip—without sales hype.**

It may be an idea whose time has come. It can be easier, more fun, and more comprehensive visiting retirement areas with an expert tour group. You can visit more areas, enjoy the company of others, and talk with bankers, realtors, and retirees living in the area. Tours usually include sightseeing trips as well. There are two major groups currently operating out of the United States—both try to eliminate hard-sell tactics in order to let you relax and get a feel of living in the area. One caution: A tour is just that, a tour, and things may look more attractive from the enjoyable perspective of a mini-vacation. There is no substitute for further in-depth research on your own. The two major tour groups are:

- *National Retirement Concepts,* which arranges "retirement rehearsal" tours to popular retirement areas in Florida, the Carolinas, Arizona, and Arkansas. There, you visit a number of retirement communities, talk with representatives from the communities, and chat with residents. Seminars present the practical aspects of retirement in the areas, and allow you to make contacts for further research on your own. For more information, contact: National Retirement Concepts, Box B, 1454 North Wieland Court, Chicago, IL 60610 (800-888-2312; 312-951-2866 in Illinois). Costs in 1991 averaged $700 per double, singles $850, not including air fare.

- *Lifestyles Explorations,* which arranges retirement tours to low-cost popular retirement areas abroad. Current destinations include Costa Rica, Spain, Portugal, Argentina, and Uruguay. Trips include seminars with government officials and bankers and visits to potential living areas. Tours last between 13 and 17 days. For 1991, the least expensive tour was $1,521, the most expensive $2,645; prices include air fare, local transportation, and hotels.

▶ Look at specific criteria on each trip you make.

What are you looking for? The right climate, good health care, low crime? Set out your basic criteria and rate each area on that basis. Many books, including some listed above, provide excellent ratings, but you're better off doing your own, even if informally. Why? You know best what you want. A mild sunny climate with low humidity may be perfect for most people—but for some, the rainy Northwest has everything they want.

Some criteria by which to judge:

Climate
Most people prefer mild average temperatures in the 70s, with good reason, since the body is most efficient at this temperature. In addition, most people prefer moderate humidity (about 50% average) and a sunny climate. Obviously, most people prefer to avoid or minimize such climatic extremes as hurricanes, tornados, and severe winter storms.

Geography
Many retirees prefer to live in small cities, or in small towns in reasonable proximity to larger cities. Many prefer to be near the shore, or lakes, or mountains, or some other distinct geographical feature.

TIP: **If you're thinking about a retirement home in a beach resort area, be sure to look into the local rate of erosion. Coastlines are eroding at a rapid rate, especially on the East Coast. A beachfront house today can be a bit *too* close to the beach tomorrow. Another important factor—will you have any trouble getting flood or other damage insurance?**

People
Most retirees prefer living in a community that includes a significant number of other retirees. Look also for areas that have a large number of newcomers or outsiders; it will be easier to adjust. Look at crime figures—many magazines publish annual crime rates with their ratings of cities. And check specific security measures in your immediate area.

Recreational and Cultural Facilities

Will it be fun to live here? That depends on your interests, of course. Look for the obvious—golf courses, playhouses, and so forth—but also look beyond. Look for local colleges that offer courses and produce plays, or community groups that involve senior citizens.

Housing

Look at the type of neighborhood and housing you plan (or hope) to be living in. Assess costs, availability, property taxes, costs of maintenance. Can you afford the kind of housing you want? Are property values moving up or down? Is the housing comfortable for senior citizens? How about access to shopping, places of worship, health care, recreation areas, and shopping? How is local security? If you don't want to buy, are short- and long-term rentals available?

SOURCE: **AARP** offers a free packet of housing literature. Write: AARP, H07 Program Department Correspondence Unit, 1909 K Street NW, Washington, DC 20049. AARP also offers a free booklet, *Housing Options for Older Americans.* Write: D12063, AARP Fulfillment, 1909 K Street NW, Washington, DC 20049.

TIP: **Always beware of fraud. Before buying, check with the local better business bureau.**

Health and Health Care

Look for good doctor-patient ratios (best is more than 1 per 750 residents), excellent hospitals, easy availability of health care, healthy climate and lifestyles.

TIP: **The healthiest states, according to a study by the Northwestern National Life Insurance Company, which ranked them by such criteria as life expectancy and availability of doctors, were clustered in the northern Midwest and the Rockies. The top five: Utah, North Dakota, Idaho, Minnesota, and Hawaii. The least healthy states were found in the Southeast and the Atlantic states.**

Travel

If you have family outside the general area and want to keep up contacts, this is a vital consideration. Can you visit, or can family visit you, relatively easily? Also: Can you get away easily, if and when you want to? Don't forget that even near-paradises may become boring.

Costs

Look for low food and energy costs. Are there special deals available for senior citizens? Check local property, income, and sales taxes. A key issue: Work at obtaining the *total* cost picture—avoid the mistake some make of assuming that if housing prices are low, or food prices are low, *everything* is. Check availability of part-time work. Look for the loopholes and problems. Call the state tax offices if necessary and talk to your accountant.

Taxes

Taxes can eat into your retirement income. Before moving, look into your tax liability in your present state: Some states, such as California, are strict and tax pensions derived from income earned in state, no matter where you retire to. Also look for low state income taxes (Florida has no income tax, California has a very high one) and check what income is taxed. Some states exempt Social Security payments, others exempt federal and state pensions, others also exempt private pensions. Look also at miscellaneous taxes (some states, such as Florida, levy a tax on the fair market value of stocks and bonds) and look for low property taxes (many states give tax credits or deferrals to senior citizens—check for this). In addition, look at gift and estate taxes, if you plan on leaving money or property to your heirs. Call your state Treasury Department, Office of Taxation, or general Public Information number to get tax information. Ask for current income tax, estate taxes, property taxes, and any special tax situations for senior citizens. Some examples of tax-friendly situations for retirees:

- *You pay no state income tax in:* Alaska, Connecticut (recently passed a temporary income tax), Florida, Nevada, North Dakota, South Dakota, Tennessee (taxes only income on stocks and bonds), Texas, Washington, and Wyoming.

- *Of the states with a personal income tax, you pay the least (5% or less) in:* Alabama (2% to 5% depending on income bracket), Colorado (5% for all income brackets), Illinois (2.5% for all income brackets), Indiana (3.4% for all income brackets), Maryland (2% to 5%, depending on income bracket), Michigan (4.6% for all income brackets), Mississippi (3% to 5%, depending on income bracket), New Hampshire (5% for all income brackets), New Jersey (2% to 3%, depending on income bracket), and Pennsylvania (2.1% for all income brackets).

- *You pay no increases in property taxes in:* Connecticut, South Dakota, and Texas.

- *You can defer property taxes in:* California, Colorado, Florida, Georgia, Illinois, Iowa, Massachusetts, Michigan, New Hampshire, North Dakota, Oregon, Tennessee, Texas, Utah, Virginia, Washington, and Wisconsin.

- *You pay no sales tax in:* Alaska, Delaware, New Hampshire, and Oregon.

- *You get a portion of your sales tax back in:* Idaho, Kansas, South Dakota, and Wyoming.

- *For estates going to your immediate family (spouse and children), you pay the lowest estate taxes in:* Connecticut (zero to 5%); Delaware (2% to 6%); Iowa (1% to 8%); Kansas (1% to 5%); Louisiana (2% to 3%); Maine,* Maryland† (applied to estates over $100,000 only); Michigan,* Minnesota,† Montana,* Nebraska,† New Hampshire,† New Jersey (for estates going to spouses, no estate tax; but for children, taxes range from zero to 16%); New Mexico,* Ohio (2% to 7%); Pennsylvania,† Rhode Island,‡ South Carolina (6% to 8%); and Vermont (equal to federal credit for state death taxes—prorated for nonresidents).

- *You pay no estate taxes in:* Nevada.

- *You pay no tax on income from municipal bond investments in:* District of Columbia, Indiana, Nebraska, New Mexico, Utah, and Vermont (the first $5,000 is exempt if you are 62 or older).

- *In states with a personal income tax, you pay no income taxes on all or a portion of private pension income in:* Arkansas, Colorado, Delaware, Georgia, Hawaii, Louisiana, Maryland, Michigan, Minnesota, Mississippi, Montana, New Jersey, New York, Pennsylvania, South Carolina, Utah, Virginia, and West Virginia.

(Note: The above information was prepared with 1990 data. Rates may have changed. For foreign tax considerations, see page 389.)

SOURCE: For free information, AARP publishes *Relocation Tax Guide: State Tax Information for Relocation Decisions* (D13400). It includes charts and a state-by-

*Equal to unused portion of the credit (allocated for nonresidents) that the federal estate tax allows for state taxes.
†Equal to unused portion of the credit that the federal estate tax allows for state taxes.
‡Maximum federal tax credit allowable for state death taxes.

state assessment of all tax considerations for older people and retirees. Send a postcard addressed to the above title and number to: AARP Fulfillment, EE175, 1909 K Street NW, Washington, DC 20049.

SOME OF THE BEST RETIREMENT AREAS

▶ **Listed below are the top retirement choices based on the major criteria, as recommended by a number of experts in the field.**

The Ozarks, in Arkansas and Missouri

The Ozarks, located primarily in northern Arkansas and southern Missouri, comprise about 50,000 square miles of low wooded mountains interspersed with glittering lakes. Once one of the poorest areas of the United States, with logged-out mountains and barren farms, the region was transformed by a massive electrification project in the 1940s, resulting in large-scale dam-building and a wealth of gleaming new lakes with a total shoreline of 9,000 miles, double that of Florida. Since then, a large number of retirees have moved into the area, creating a quiet dynamism of new retirement villages and golf courses set amidst quiet farms and woodland.

Other advantages of this area are low taxes, low crime, low costs, affordable housing (Bern Keating in *New Choices* reports new two-bedroom houses at $65,000, condos at $150,000; others report many low rentals and ample facilities for mobile homes), temperate climate (four seasons, but a short, cold winter), recreational opportunities—excellent fishing, golf, boating, hiking.

SOURCE: Four regional organizations offer free brochures for their regions: **Ozark Mountain Region,** P.O. Box 579, Flippin, AR 72634 (501-453-8563); **The Greers Ferry Lake and Little Red River Association,** Attn. Lou Evans, P.O. Box 1170, Fairfield Bay, AR 70288 (501-884-3333); **Ozark Gateway Tourist Council,** P.O. Box 4049, Batesville, AR 72503 (501-793-9316); **Northwest Arkansas Tourist Association,** P.O. Box 412, Eureka Springs, AR 72632 (501-253-8737).

Gulf Coast (Naples to St. Petersburg), Florida

This is a large area—and within that area virtually every retiree can find his or her ideal spot. In the south, Naples, lying at the western terminus of the Tamiami Trail, is a pristine, prosperous city that is particularly well-suited for wealthier retirees, with shopping, restaurants, and many activities—and of course fishing and boating are excellent. Fort Myers, a bit further north, is also beautiful—

streets are lined with incomparable and majestic royal palms. Many retirees choose to live in condos by well-kept golf courses. Sarasota is a regional cultural center that offers theatrical and other cultural events, in addition to golf, fishing, and swimming. Finally, St. Petersburg, which ushered in the retirement boom years ago (and then decided to match its success by attracting young professionals) offers a relatively low cost of living, many special services for senior citizens, and many cultural and recreational activities.

Some advantages: Many areas with major medical facilities and senior centers; plenty of company for retirees, sunny warm climate (average winter temperatures in the 60s, high summer temperatures in the upper 80s, tempered by nighttime Gulf breezes); and the total tax bill paid by Floridians averages the third-lowest in the nation.

Some disadvantages: Crime can be a problem in some areas, summer temperatures bother some, and housing costs can be high in some areas. One note: There are some indications that the Florida retirement population has peaked. The over-65 population is projected to grow by 26% in the 1990s, down from 44% in the 1980s and 71% in the 1970s.

SOURCE: **Naples Chamber of Commerce,** 1700 North Tamiami Trail, Naples, FL 33940; **Fort Myers Chamber of Commerce,** Fort Myers, FL 33902; **Sarasota Chamber of Commerce,** 1551 Second Street, Sarasota, FL 33577; **St. Petersburg Chamber of Commerce,** P.O. Box 1371, St. Petersburg, FL 33731.

Chapel Hill, North Carolina

Together with Durham and Raleigh, Chapel Hill encloses what is called Research Triangle, named for the significant research facilities and universities, which include Duke University, North Carolina State, nearby Wake Forest, and in Chapel Hill, the University of North Carolina. The countryside is beautiful wooded or rolling farmland, and Chapel Hill itself is a small (population 45,000) college town of Colonial-style buildings with a wealth of cultural attractions, art galleries, bookstores, easily audited college classes, and for some, the opportunity to teach. Sports are also big in the area—spectators enjoy college football or basketball, and participants enjoy the large number of golf courses; tennis and swimming are available to town residents as well. Medical facilities are among the best in the nation, with nearby Duke University a pioneer in cardiology. Winters are mildly cold, summers can be hot and humid.

SOURCE: **Chapel Hill Chamber of Commerce,** P.O. Box 2897, Chapel Hill, NC 27515.

Seattle, Washington

Not for sun worshipers, but Seattle and the island-studded Puget Sound area can be ideal for retirees looking for natural beauty, in a livable cosmopolitan city or on a peaceful island. Cool summers and cool, rainy winters make the area wonderfully lush, the Cascade Mountains tower in the west and the north and boating, fishing, hiking, and most outdoor sports are readily accessible. (Seattle has the highest number of boats per capita in the United States.) Seattle is a thriving city crammed with tea shops, restaurants, and bookstores (supposedly the highest concentration per capita in the United States). The Farmer's Market, filled with fresh vegetables and salmon and crab fresh from the cold Pacific, is a sight to behold. North along the coast are other wonderful spots for retiring, including La Conner, now transformed into a major art gallery center, and Birch Bay, near the famous Semiahmoo golf course, home to many retirees from Canada. Others prefer the Puget Sound islands, from Bainbridge near Seattle to Orcas farther up. Ferry service makes travel easy and picturesque. For those averse to rain, Sequim (pronounced "squim") on the Olympic peninsula gets only one-third the rain of Seattle, and more important, has many more blue-sky days. (People say, "Are the mountains out today?" Translation: "Is it clear?")

Other advantages: excellent medical facilities, excellent cultural life (ballet, symphony, theater), the world-class University of Washington and a host of other colleges, many parks. And for those who want to drive, Vancouver and Victoria are not that far away. Some problems: rising crime, rising real estate prices—and not all Washingtonians are happy with the new influx of out-of-staters.

Establishing Legal Domicile

▶ **When you finally move to your new retirement home, establish legal domicile.**

Where do you live? And where do you *legally* live? The two are not necessarily synonymous. Technically, legal domicile means that you have lived long enough in a state to show intent to make it your "true home," but for today's much-traveled, two-home retirees, it can be difficult to show or prove such intent. Establishing legal domicile is particularly important for tax purposes, or if you live overseas, but it also has ramifications at home—particularly when it comes to division of property after your death.

Among the steps to take:

- See if your retirement state allows you to declare domicile via an official form. Some states, such as Florida, do.

- File your federal income tax from the retirement address.

- Register to vote from this address.

- Get a driver's license from the state.

- Use the new address on your passport.

- Have this address listed on your financial accounts (bank accounts, brokerage accounts, etc.) and keep most of them in the state of your "official residence."

- Use the address on any contracts.

- Check with a local attorney to see if your will and other legal documents conform with local law.

- Change the titles and registration of cars.

TIP: For those who live in two states and try to avoid taxes by declaring to each that the other is the legal, taxable domicile, be aware that computerized cross-checking among states is becoming more common. The latest: Florida and New York.

RETIRING ABROAD

▶ **At one time or another we all dream of retiring abroad: Here's how to actually do it.**

Retiring abroad is a dream many have—and increasingly, many are fulfilling that dream. About 400,000 Social Security checks are sent abroad each month, making that the *minimum* number of Americans who have retired abroad. More undoubtedly have their checks mailed to U.S. bank accounts.

If so many have done it, it is obviously possible for you as well. However, retirement abroad carries special problems, disadvantages, and advantages, all of which you should consider *before* you decide to spend your retirement outside of the United States.

▶ **First of all, are you certain you want to live abroad at all?**

This question must be addressed very carefully. It can be difficult living abroad. You are no longer in your home country, you are no longer the same as everyone else, you are a foreigner—with all the psychological ramifications this implies. If you plan to move where English is not the native tongue, consider your fluency in the language, your language-learning ability, or your comfort with getting around without fluency. Consider how you will feel separated from family, old friends, familiar things that may not seem important now—whether the comforting openness of Americans on the street or something as simple as a good pizza, which no other country seems able to duplicate.

On the other hand, retiring abroad has its advantages. First of all, you may find special qualities of life—the civilized pace of London, the diversity of Mexico, the sophisticated city life of Vancouver, set in the unspoiled beauty of the Northwest. Second, in some cases, you may find life cheaper than in the United States. Third, you may be returning to your country of origin. Fourth and most important, you may enjoy the challenges and adventure of life abroad.

▶ **To choose your ideal retirement country: Start by reading and researching.**

Most people begin with areas they've visited or have ties with. By all means start from there and investigate the possibilities of retirement. You may also consider areas recommended by friends or magazines. You can read current books on retirement that recommend the best spots for retirees.

SOURCE: Some general books on retiring abroad: *Travel and Retirement Edens Abroad,* by Peter Dickinson (for details, see page 369); *The World's Top Retirement Havens,* edited by Marian Cooper (1989, Agora Books).

However, once you get past the general considerations it is essential to research in depth. We'll offer some guidelines here. The more aggressive strategies are most appropriate for countries that are less accessible. For example, you can easily obtain all the information you need about Great Britain without resorting much to U.S. government sources; on the other hand, if you're planning to retire to Ecuador, it's best to research in depth and use every resource you can. Always be careful of real estate salespeople, tour guides, even many writers. For various reasons, all may make overly glowing assessments of life abroad and gloss over the problems. The best way to make an educated, rational assessment is to get much of the information yourself. Here are some tips on how to get the facts you need.

In the United States:

- Write the U.S. commercial attaché at the U.S. embassy of your target retirement spot and ask about U.S. small business opportunities. These attachés are accustomed to sending out detailed information on their host country, and if you ask, you may also receive detailed housing information.

- Call or write the U.S. Government Printing Office and ask for the "Country Report" on your retirement spot. These are books of about 300 pages crammed with political, historical, and cultural information on virtually every nation on earth. Also ask to purchase the "Embassy Post Report" for your country. Post Reports are brief (40 or so pages) reports designed to inform new U.S. diplomats of the conditions of their new diplomatic posting. They're honest, practical, and full of tips on how to survive happily in the new country. They can be valuable in giving you an unvarnished feel of what it may be like for you as a retiree.

- If you're pushy, call the State Department and ask the State Department operator for the "Country Desk" of your target retirement spot. You'll be switched to the "desk officer"—the diplomat in charge of overseeing the policy paperwork on that nation—and if you're lucky, you may get a more detailed view of what's going on, or at least a referral to some books, articles, or local professors.

- Contact a local university's political science, geography, or related department. Arrange to speak with local experts on your country.

- Don't forget to do the easiest thing of all. Go to the library and look up what you need to know. Collect names and addresses and write to the relevant chambers of commerce, retirement organizations, newspapers, and newsletters. Often, local newsletters written by American retirees are invaluable—for information, as a source of other names and addresses, and for a feel of life as a retiree.

▶ **Never retire anywhere you haven't visited thoroughly first.**

What's "visiting thoroughly"? It's *not* visiting as a vacationer, but as an in-depth researcher. On pages 370–71 we offered general tips on how to visit a potential retirement spot, but in the case of foreign retirement, you must go far beyond this. Why? It's not as easy adequately assessing what you don't know well; and as a foreigner you may be unfamiliar with much about the country you're interested in. What may seem on the surface to be a happy populace and stable political situation may in fact be the calm before the storm; smiling friendly locals may in reality hate or resent Americans; cheap food prices may be more than offset by extremely expensive manufactured items.

Some guidelines:

- Before you go, particularly if you're going to travel in Third World countries, call the U.S. State Department Travel Advisory for information on dangerous situations.

- Go to the American embassy or consulate and ask to speak to the consular official who handles American affairs. The consul should be able to refer you to reputable local individuals or organizations who may be of help, as well as the local U.S. expatriate community. Ask about crime: Often a consul will tell you what others won't say.

- If possible, consider staying in an apartment or an efficiency instead of a hotel. This will give you an immediate feel for living in the area.

- Shop (don't just look) in the local markets or supermarkets. What are costs like? Don't just look at food—look at such dry goods as soap and toothpaste. If the familiar brands are high-priced, are there acceptable local substitutes?

- Go beyond what you've read about costs—see for yourself and explore all aspects of cost, including possible alternatives. If car, washing machine, and other costs are high, what about duty-free entry? What about repairs? What kind of electric current is available? If you're planning on bringing in items, can spare parts and knowledgeable repair people be found? If repairs will be difficult, how much does this matter to you?

- See if there is a local better business bureau—and ask for a list of reputable guides, real estate agents, and the like.

- Even if you're only visiting, go out with real estate agents and get a real feel for real estate prices and availability. Go out with more than one agent, comparison shop, and check the local paper.

- Read newspapers carefully. Do what CIA operatives do—read the classifieds, the marriage announcements, and so forth for a real look at the country. Headlines are ultimately alike all around the world. The classifieds and local news tell you what's really going on—what's valuable, how much it costs, whether housing costs are going up or down, what daily life is like.

▶ **Where do most Americans retire? Where other Americans already are.**

It makes sense—and eases the problems of living abroad. In many popular areas, Americans have well-established support groups and resources. These people can be valuable resources to tap when you visit; try to get them talking about the hassles and the frustrations, not just the joys of retirement abroad. If they're like most expatriates, they'll probably tell you more than you want to hear.

Many retirees want to see more than the same American faces they saw at home. When considering a specific country or area, carefully judge how easy it is to make contacts among the locals, and more important, try to assess how easy it will be for *you* to make these contacts. Everyone is different: While some people will tell you it is virtually impossible to make English friends as an American, perhaps they aren't as patient as you, perhaps not as "British" in attitude. On the other hand, many times smiling tour guides will assure you of how "friendly" the local population is toward Americans—and they are, as long as you remain in the hotel. By all means work to get behind the hype, and there is a lot of it around, on tours and in books and magazines.

Wherever you may go, be aware that some American has probably retired there before you. Estimates are that half of all retirees living abroad live in just four countries—Mexico, Canada, Italy, and the Philippines—but Americans can be found virtually everywhere. Following is a brief roundup of the most popular retirement choices of the 1990s.

Mexico

More than 150,000 U.S. citizens live in Mexico—and 100,000 of them are retirees. U.S. retirees are clustered in northern Baja, Guadalajara and nearby Lake Chapala, San Miguel de Allende, Mexico City, Acapulco, and the Pacific coast. There are relatively few U.S. citizens on the Atlantic coast and in the Yucatán.

Some advantages to Mexico: The country is rich in culture and natural beauty, the climate is generally warm and sunny, prices are low—not so low as the frequently touted $400-a-month figure, but perhaps close to the still-reasonable figure of $1,000, according to an authoritative newsletter on the area. Proximity to the United States is an advantage, particularly in regard to health care; pensions are exempt from Mexican income tax; retirees are able to import household goods free of customs duties in their first year; there is no inheritance tax. In many cities there are enough Americans to actually make a real expatriate community, an advantage for the occasionally homesick.

Of course there can be disadvantages as well: occasional hostility to North Americans, crime, poverty, currency problems.

There are a variety of modes of living in Mexico as a retiree. Near the border you may be satisfied with a nonimmigrant pensioner visa (which you must renew every six months), but most prefer obtaining *immigrante rentista* status, which entitles you to duty-free entry of household goods, property ownership, and easy departure and reentry. To qualify, retirees must be over 50 years old and have a guaranteed monthly income (currently about $1,000). For more information, write your local Mexican tourism office or consulate (in New York, Chicago, New Orleans, El Paso, San Antonio, Los Angeles, San Francisco) or the consular section of the Mexican embassy at 2829 16th Street NW, Washington, DC 20009 (202-293-1711.)

SOURCE: *AIM* is a very comprehensive bimonthly newsletter specializing in retirement and travel in Mexico. It includes detailed information on costs, apartment rentals and major retirement areas as well as alternatives off the beaten track. Annual subscriptions are $15. Write AIM, Apartado Postal 31-70, Guadalajara, 45050, Jalisco, Mexico.

SOURCE: *Choose Mexico,* by John Howells (1988, Gateway Books, 66 Cleary Court, Suite 1405, San Francisco, CA 94109) is a comprehensive, useful, popular book—although it tends to be *very* optimistic. Balance it with *AIM.*

Canada

While most Americans head for the sun, a substantial number head north to Canada. Retirees are clustered close to the U.S. border in Vancouver and Victoria in British Columbia, and some live in Toronto, Montreal, Nova Scotia, and Prince Edward Island.

Some advantages: Canada is quite varied, from cosmopolitan Vancouver, set in the lush Pacific Northwest, to the rugged beauty of Nova Scotia. Retirees in major cities like the large cultural base enlivened by recent immigration from India and Hong Kong (Vancouver is fast becoming the metropolis of the northern Pacific) coupled with the ready proximity to natural beauty. Canada enjoys a lower crime rate than the United States, surprisingly mild winters on the Pacific coast (average winter temperatures are above freezing), and cool, temperate summers in most areas. The way of life is (sometimes) more sedate—as in England, gardening is a cherished hobby. The culture is familiar enough to be unintimidating, but different enough to be interesting. Health care is good—and Blue Cross coverage is available.

Some disadvantages: Much of Canada is cold and winters are long; taxes are high; U.S. retirees can deduct about $3,500 from their taxes—but must still pay high federal and provincial taxes, which can top 50%.

Retirees wishing to settle in Canada must apply formally, pass a medical examination, and prove a minimum income. For details, contact the consular section of the Embassy of Canada, 1746 Massachusetts Avenue, NW, Washington, DC 20036 (202-785-1400). For more information on retiring in Vancouver or other parts of British Columbia, contact: Federated Legislative Council of Elderly Citizens Association of British Columbia, #410, 1755 West Broadway, Vancouver, BC V6J 4S5, Canada.

Europe

Once the dream of American retirees, retiring in Europe is becoming a financial nightmare for many. Why? High and still-rising costs, high taxes, including the ubiquitous "value-added tax" (a comprehensive sales tax that can add up to 35%), a generally falling dollar, and new laws and regulations that are often very stringent. For example, Britain has high financial requirements (minimum U.K. bank account of £150,000 or income of £15,000 per year), and requires a preadmission medical exam. In addition, you must have relatives in the country or have convincing reasons that your presence would benefit the United Kingdom. Moreover, as Western Europe unites economically and absorbs the impact of unification, further restrictions on foreigners are expected.

There are still some advantages to retirement in Europe: cultural attractions, natural and man-made beauty, excellent food, an unbeatable transportation system, the excitement of living in a melange of cultures. On the practical side: Most European nations have taxation agreements with the United States whereby U.S. retirees are not double-taxed on their income; most have excellent (and less expensive) health care—in many cases U.S. retirees are eligible for subsidized care after a suitable period of residency and passing a medical exam; otherwise, private insurance is available.

Cost-conscious retirees are probably better off now heading south to *Greece,* where costs are still relatively low. In Greece, many islands are still cheap, as is the northeast and the Peloponnese in the south. Potential immigrants to Greece must show a source of income that will sustain them during retirement, but beyond this requirements are minimal. Some problems: Greece can be frustrating. Phones, water, air-conditioning, and so forth often do not work as expected—but the food and lifestyle are wonderful. According to Abby Rand in *New Choices,* local Greek consulates in the United States have only limited information—so write Greek immigration authorities directly at: Aliens Bureau, 9 Halkondili Street, Athens.

Another way of having your cake and eating it too is *sojourning*— living in Europe for part of the year, spending the rest of the year home in the United States. In this way, you may avoid problems with health care and taxes, and can reduce expenses substantially. (For more on sojourning, see page 394.)

Philippines

The Philippines is a popular retirement spot, particularly for people with experience in the area, such as retired military personnel, as well as a number of Philippine-Americans. Advantages include a beautiful topography, historic Philippine-American friendship, widespread use of English, large numbers of Americans stationed in the country, and of course, a lush tropical setting and a rich cultural past. Many retirees choose to live in the suburbs of Manila. In recent years, however, retirement in the Philippines has become less desirable, because of significant political unrest. Best bet: Wait for the situation to stabilize. For more information, write: Philippine Center, 556 Fifth Avenue, New York, NY 10036 (212-575-7915) or the Philippine Embassy.

Costa Rica

Costa Rica is a popular retirement spot: Currently about 6,000 retirees from abroad live in Costa Rica, about half of them from the

United States or Canada. Costa Rica is a lush tropical Latin American country with a climate tempered by altitude in most areas. Unlike its neighbors, Costa Rica is a free and stable democracy that has enjoyed peace—it is one of the few nations in the world without a standing army. The capital, San José, is a small, temperate, cosmopolitan city set in a highland valley—many retirees live here or in neighboring suburbs; others, near the beaches and jungles of the Pacific coast. Under a liberal *pensionado* program, retirees are eligible for duty-free entry of household goods, including a car (up to a certain limit), no tax on pensions or income from abroad, and the right to set up a business (but not to be employed by others). To many, this has been a retirement paradise. Nevertheless, some retirees have left in recent years, principally due to an increasingly poor economic situation, a rising petty crime rate (though still nothing like that in the United States, and violent crime is rare), and unrest in neighboring countries. Note: According to the local *Tico Times*, Costa Rica has many con men who prey on newcomers with "bargain" rentals and investments. Beware—and contact the local American–Costa Rican Chamber of Commerce.

Some advantages: Costa Rica is a friendly, peaceful country. The countryside is lush and beautiful, houses and streets are filled with flowers, the people are warm and hospitable, cost of living is lower in terms of housing and food, health care is excellent (some say it ranks in the top 20 countries in the world) and inexpensive. Retirees can join the national health care system for a relatively low fee. Custodial care for the ailing elderly is also much less expensive. For fishing enthusiasts, Costa Rica offers some of the best fishing in the world. Its rain forests are world famous for their beauty. Costa Rica is one of the few nations that has shown a real commitment to environmental preservation—it has an extensive national park system.

Retirees are eligible to live in Costa Rica as permanent residents as *pensionados* (with a minimum pension of $600) or *rentistas* (investors of $75,000 in a Costa Rican bank, or those with proof of a nonpension income of $1,000 a month). For more information, write: Associación de Pensionados y Rentistas de Costa Rica, Edificio Anexo CCSS, a4, c5, San José, Costa Rica (506-23-17-33). Or write: The Embassy of Costa Rica, 2112 S Street NW, Washington, D.C. 20008 (202-234-2945).

SOURCE: *The New Key to Costa Rica,* by B. Blake and A. Becher (Publications in English, Apdo. 7-1230, 1000 San José, Costa Rica, 506-23-31-69) is an excellent guidebook to Costa Rica; it also offers some valuable advice to potential retirees.

SOURCE: *The Tico Times,* a weekly English-language newspaper, available via air mail. Along with news, this paper can give potential retirees a feel for life in Costa Rica. Write: The Tico Times, Apdo. 4632, San José, Costa Rica (22-8952 or 22-0040). *Costa Rica Report* is a small monthly newsletter, with helpful notes. Address and price as of 1989: P.O. Box 6283, San José, Costa Rica, $42.

SOURCE: For retirement in Costa Rica and other Latin American nations, see also: *Choose Latin America,* by John Howells (Gateway Books, 1750 Post St., Suite 111, San Francisco, CA 94115 (415-922-7299).

Money: How to Get It, and Keep It, While Living Abroad

▶ **The first problem you may face once you settle overseas is currency fluctuation or constantly changing financial rates.**

The change can be good: If you get your pensions in dollars and the local currency is low or falling, this means that fewer of your dollars can buy more of the local currency. Your living standard goes up. Cheap local currency made Europe a wonderful place for Americans in the post–World War II years.

Unfortunately, rates can change in the opposite direction—the dollar can decline in relation to the local currency so that your pension money is worth less. This is why it has become difficult for many American retirees to continue living in Europe.

What do do? Hedge against currency movements by investing some of your pension money in local currency. There are several ways:

- Buy money funds denominated in the local currency. For example, if you live in Britain buy a fund in British pounds. Many large brokerages have these funds.

- Buy one-country mutual funds of the country. Again, many brokerages maintain such funds.

- Buy multicountry mutual funds of the *region* as well. This may work with funds that are principally invested in several countries with currencies that move in tandem. Check with a qualified financial planner.

- Open a foreign currency interest-bearing deposit account in the United States before you move.

Be careful of where you invest. As an American, you are used to FDIC protection and other U.S. safeguards—but remember that other nations have different laws and regulations. To protect yourself against nationalization or bank failure, you may prefer to bank with reputable large multinational or U.S. banks with local branches.

▶ Look at your tax situation.

Unfortunately, you can't escape the IRS by living abroad. In fact, in recent years, the IRS has beefed up its international capabilities, in the hope of compiling a comprehensive profile of American taxpayers abroad—and then auditing and catching the cheats.

Here is a brief rundown on what to expect.

- *U.S. taxes:* Generally speaking, you will pay U.S. taxes on pension income earned in the United States—even if you give up U.S. citizenship. (There is a $70,000 tax exclusion for U.S. citizens, but this applies to income earned abroad.) One advantage: Depending on your state, you may not be liable for state taxes. Check your specific situation with your accountant.

- *Foreign taxes:* This depends on your retirement choice: The tax situation varies enormously, depending on where you choose to live. Call the IRS and get a copy of the tax treaty between the United States and the country where you will retire, if there is one.

   Look at countries with tax advantages for retirees. Some popular retirement destinations are:

   Costa Rica: No income tax on U.S. pensions, no inheritance taxes.

   Bahamas: No income or inheritance taxes.

   Guernsey: No income taxes.

   Grand Cayman Islands: No local taxes.

   Greece, France: Income tax credits for United States citizens.

   For more information, contact the embassies or consulates of nations that interest you.

   Ask about *inheritance taxes*—many countries have strict laws that specifically dictate how you may dispose of your assets on your death.

TIP: **One way of sheltering your pension from taxation, which may work in several countries that tax pension income: Take your pension as a lump sum and roll it over into an IRA. The foreign government *may* view the IRA as capital rather than** income, even if the money is drawn down for living expenses, and you may avoid foreign taxation—according to Steven Kates, of Ernst and Young, interviewed in *The New York Times.*

SOURCE: The **IRS** publishes a number of publications that can help you avoid problems. By dialing 800-829-FORM and specifying the appropriate publication number, you can get several valuable IRS publications for retirees living abroad: Publication 54, *Tax Guide for United States Citizens and Resident Aliens Abroad;* Publication 554, *Tax Information for Older Americans;* Publication 901, *United States Tax Treaties;* and maybe the most valuable, *Instruction for Form 2555,* which deals with the foreign income exclusion.

- *Social Security:* In most cases, the checks will keep coming.

    The exceptions are certain Communist countries—including North Korea—and the chances are most of these exceptions will be gone as communism disappears.

    Obviously, the most important thing is to keep the Social Security Administration informed of your address. Notify Social Security of your new address. Abroad, you may report to the nearest U.S. embassy or consulate. In Canada or Mexico, you may inform a local U.S. Social Security office, and in the Philippines, you may write to the Veterans Affairs Regional Office, SSA Division, 1131 Roxas Boulevard, Manila, Philippines. Or you may inform Social Security directly. (Write: Social Security Administration, P.O. Box 1756, Baltimore, MD 21203.) If your checks are being sent directly to a bank, you still must report address changes.

    If you are living abroad, you will periodically get questionnaires about your continued eligibility and status; fill these out and return them to the nearest U.S. embassy or consulate, or send them directly to the Social Security Administration.

    The Social Security Administration can withhold the monthly benefit for each month in which you, as a beneficiary under 70, work more than 45 hours outside the United States where the work is not subject to U.S. Social Security taxes. Check with Social Security for details. There are also different rules about your eligibility if you are not a United States citizen.

SOURCE: *Your Social Security Checks While You Are Outside the United States.* For this free booklet, and other information, write: Social Security Administration, P.O. Box 1756, Baltimore, MD 21203.

▶ **One problem with retiring abroad: Medicare coverage—or lack thereof.**

This is an important factor. Medicare generally doesn't cover your hospital or medical expenses outside the United States and certain United States territories. (It does pay for care at qualified Canadian and Mexican hospitals in certain situations, particularly when persons living in the United States find that either a Mexican or Canadian hospital is closer in an emergency.)

And for retirees returning to the United States, another potential problem is the medical insurance portion of Medicare coverage. This part of Medicare care, called Part B, pays for your doctor bills and other expenses, and is elective—if you want it, you pay the retiree rate of $28.60 a month. If you've been living abroad and haven't paid this premium when you turned 65, be aware that you'll pay a 10% surcharge for every year you delayed coverage. And you'll have to wait a few months for coverage to begin. You are eligible for the hospital insurance portion (Part A) of Medicare without any additional cost or delay once you return to the United States.

A final problem: Many employee health plans are coordinated with Medicare. Now that you've moved abroad, your employment health care plan may change. Employers may not cover you at all, may only cover you partially—or on the positive side, they may cover you completely. Check before you move.

▶ **Insuring yourself abroad is the normal option.**

Before even considering a move abroad, assess your and your spouse's health. Call your insurance company to find out if and what you're covered for abroad. In most cases, you'll want to insure yourself overseas.

Call the embassy or the local health officials of your planned retirement area and find out about health coverage there. You may be better off than you think. In Europe, most nations have national health insurance, which offers free coverage. Others may have cheap private insurance. Check with the embassy or health authorities to find out:

- What kind of national insurance (if any) is in effect.

- How comprehensive the insurance is.

- What the residency requirements are (they may range from six months to a year).

- If health exams are required (for example, in France, you must pass a medical exam given by approved doctors).

SOURCE: A subsidiary of Blue Cross/Blue Shield, called **Access America**, covers many medical expenses overseas. For more information, contact: **ACCESS AMERICA**, 600 Third Avenue, New York, NY 10163 (212-490-5345).

You'll probably be settling in an area which offers excellent health care, and now is the time to make certain you'll be getting what you need. One helpful source is the International Association for Medical Assistance to Travelers. Although they do not offer insurance information, they maintain a list of English-speaking doctors worldwide who offer standardized fees and provide up-to-date medical information and immunization requirements overseas. Contact: IAMAT, 417 Center Street, Lewiston, NY 14092 (716-754-4883).

How Will You Move—and Live—Abroad?

▶ **Moving abroad is very different from merely traveling abroad.**

And different nations have different procedures for emigration. Here are some guidelines.

- *Start planning early.* Take care of emigration procedures *completely* well before your target date—for many countries, applying for residency visas and permissions can take a very long time. Note: Before hiring legal help for emigration, contact the local better business bureau, chamber of commerce, or the U.S. embassy; be careful of frauds and incompetents—both find foreigners easy prey.

- *See if there is an organized American community.* In many areas, U.S. expatriates have organized community centers, which hold meetings, plan outings and activities—and welcome newcomers. Very often, by writing or calling, you'll get all the information you need.

- *Establish exactly what you will need in-country.* How? Write other retirees, write the local American community center (if there is one), check with the embassy and local authorities. Keep a list of what must be imported from the States, what is cheaper to buy in-country.

Also check:

Electrical standards.

U.S. washers/dryers, refrigerators: Are they necessary? Can your new house handle them? (U.S. durable goods are larger on average than those in Europe and Asia).

Cars: Should you buy in-country? Import from the U.S.? Or can you rely on mass transportation—certainly an option in European cities.

Medications, particularly prescription: Can you fill them in-country?

Small items: radios, TVs, VCRs. Check VCR standards, which are different in many foreign countries. A good bet: Buy a VCR with PAL/SECAM as well as NTSC standards. This way you'll cover most international bases and be able to watch local tapes.

Favorite small items: Some people crave a particular U.S. toothpaste, for example. Now is the time to check availability, and perhaps to stock up.

- *Check foreign requirements for duty-free entry of your goods.* Then establish what, if any, major extras you will take and pay duty on. Sell large durable goods, such as washers and furniture, well before you leave, or include them when you sell your house. Don't get stuck selling large items at a loss at the last minute.

- *Research shippers abroad.* Have a good idea of what you'd like to ship air freight or sea freight. Sea freight is cheaper, but takes months.

- *Prepare a detailed moving manifest.* It sounds obvious, but many people merely rely on the moving company. Prepare your own *before:* Know exactly what you are taking. Just before you leave, recheck. *Number* the boxes as you move.

- *Make temporary living arrangements abroad, if necessary.*

- *Check into a hotel while you move.* It's easier than living among boxes and packing crates.

SOURCE: Two useful government publications are *Tips for Americans Residing Abroad, Publication 9402;* and *Travel Tips for Senior Citizens,* Publication 8970. Both are free, available from: Department of State, Bureau of Consular Affairs, Washington, DC 20520.

SOJOURNING

▶ **One of the newest twists on retirement living is called "so-journing"—spending your retirement years in two different places.**

Sojourning is a growing trend among retirees who want to double their pleasure by spending part of the year at one home, the rest of the year at another.

Different people do it different ways. Some keep their current house and buy a second one, usually a vacation house or a condo in a resort area. Other people sell their current house and use the proceeds to buy two new places.

▶ **The advantages to a dual-address retirement are many. Most of the benefits are related, and stem from the fact that you are doubling your options.**

You can fulfill different needs. It's difficult to choose the "perfect" retirement lifestyle. Usually no one location or type of residence fulfills your every need. But with sojourning, you can live two different lifestyles. For example, you could split your time between a retirement community and your current house. In this way, you can enjoy the camaraderie of the retirement community part-time, become friendly with a large group of other retirees, and enjoy sharing activities with them. The rest of the year, you can enjoy the privacy of your own home, the comfort of your old routines.

You can explore different areas, both of the country and of yourself. Splitting your time in two allows you to get to really know two distinct locations. Instead of spending two weeks or one month in a vacation spot, either in the United States or abroad, you can spend months. You can talk to people, get into the rhythm of an area in a way that is impossible when you are just a visitor. Similarly, sojourning can enhance your personal growth. By living in two different places, you can explore different aspects of your personality. For example, one of your homes can be geared to the physical you—the one that loves golfing, or tennis, or biking. The other can be geared to the meditative you—the one that wants the time to sit and read, go for walks, observe nature. It's entirely up to you.

You double the number of your friends. Two homes give you two times as many opportunities to meet new and different people. If you keep your current house and buy a second one, you can keep your old friends and meet a group of new ones. If you get two new places, you can meet new people at both, people who share your enthusiasm for the location and probably some of your recreational interests.

You can take advantage of different climates. By splitting your time between two places, you can be assured of being in the right climate in the right season. You can summer where it's cool, winter where it's warm.

▶ **On the downside: While splitting your retirement years between two places can double the pleasure, it also can double the problems.**

There are distinct drawbacks to sojourning. Because you are living in two homes, you face difficulties that you usually wouldn't encounter if you were retiring to only one home. Among the concerns are the following:

Double your possessions: It sounds obvious, even simple, but many people don't realize just how many things will have to be multiplied by two to make life comfortable as a sojourner. With two residences, you will need two sets of everything that makes your home livable—including furniture, kitchen appliances, pots and pans, televisions, telephones, VCRs, clothing, even cars if one of your homes is on an island or overseas.

Security: You will be leaving one house unoccupied for a fairly long period of time. This may pave the way for break-ins. Another result—you may face higher insurance costs (sometimes premiums are up to 50% higher for part-time homes).

Complicated lifestyle: Having two residences means your life can get confusing—and messy. You have to keep on top of it to keep things running smoothly. Among the minor hassles: You'll be getting mail at two different addresses and will have to be sure you're receiving the important things at the home you're in at the moment.

Health care: You will need two sets of doctors and other specialists and access to hospitals at both residences. Your best bet: Keep one doctor as your primary doctor, but still get another doctor in your second location. Have doctor number two handle routine matters and check in with your primary doctor on larger matters, prescriptions, and so forth.

Cost: Most of the above cost money—furnishing two houses, buying an alarm system, paying higher insurance, and so on. When you're thinking about sojourning, you have to factor in the double costs of living. Another big cost factor: air fare. Depending upon where your two residences are, you may be flying back and forth many times a year—which can cost a sizable sum.

▶ **Is it worth it for you? Sojourning isn't for everyone. It takes a special kind of person to make it work.**

You need to have certain qualities to keep the double life from driving you crazy. Could it work for you? Ask yourself the following questions:

Are you well organized? If you aren't, you probably won't be able to manage the dual residences. You need to be on top of many things at once, juggle two homes, plan your moves twice a year, and so on.

Are you flexible, open to change? You have to be. With more than one home, you never can be quite sure what's coming next.

Do you have a high energy level? Sojourning isn't for those of you who envision retirement as a long, leisurely vacation. Remember: when you sojourn, you're going to be moving at least once a year. Yes, you're just moving to your own house, but it's still a move. And it still entails packing, closing up your first house, traveling to home number two, then unpacking, opening up your second house, and so on. If you're not energetic, it's simply not worth the effort.

▶ **To avoid getting hit with two state income taxes, choose an official residence. And choose it carefully.**

This is a common problem with sojourners who don't think ahead. Two different states consider them residents, so they are socked with two state income tax bills. This is why, if you choose to sojourn, you should pick one state as your official residence and establish legal domicile.

First, compare the two states in which you live. Which gives you the best break? Clearly, the one that either has no state income tax or has the lower tax is the one to choose.

Next, you should use your address in that state on as many legal and official documents as possible. (For the steps to take, see page 378.)

Healthstyles

PART IV

Chapter 13
MAINTAINING A
HEALTHY RETIREMENT

INTRODUCTION

▶ **When you're planning a successful retirement, you should be thinking about more than just the financial side of things.**

Yes, it's vital to be sure you have the funds you need for a comfortable retirement. But that's just part of the picture. To truly enjoy your retirement years, you need more than money to assure a comfortable lifestyle. You need your health.

Health is—or should be—a major concern for you when you retire and enter your older years. Whether you plan an active life traveling or working, or a peaceful, relaxing time, good health is directly related to how much you will enjoy yourself.

And just as you can take charge of your financial well-being through careful planning, you can do the same for your health. You don't have to leave your good health to chance or luck. There's a lot you can do to maintain, even improve, your physical well-being after retirement.

▶ **Because you're changing so much of your lifestyle when you retire, it's also a good time to change from bad health habits to good.**

Retirement is a time of changes. Maybe after years of commuting to a job, now you're not going to the office every day, or you're moving away from the hustle and bustle of the city to your dream house at the shore. Because so much is changing in your life, it's an excellent time to establish new routines, *healthy* routines.

You used to spend 45 minutes every morning on your commute to work by train? Now spend that same 45 minutes walking briskly to the store for the newspaper and back again. You used to begin each day with a fried egg sandwich from the deli? Now start with a whole grain cereal and skim milk.

Make health a habit.

TIP: **Laugh more. That's right. Try to indulge in a good laugh every now and then. Recent studies find different reasons why laughing is good for you. Some of them: 1) When you're laughing you're working your muscles. When you stop, they relax—which make laughter a great stress-reliever. 2) Laughter may help increase your production of immune cells, which help fight disease and decrease your production of cortisol, a hormone that depresses immune system activity (according to a study conducted by the Loma Linda University School, cited in *New Choices*). 3) Another study (conducted at Western New England College) shows that laughing increases your production of salivary immunoglobulin A—which helps you fight respiratory illness. The bottom line? You might as well laugh—it certainly can't hurt, and it may well help.**

▶ **Retiring healthy—and staying healthy—is a simple matter of eating right, exercising enough, and *relaxing*.**

It isn't difficult to pursue a healthy life. In fact, in many ways it is easier being healthy than not. If you practice good nutrition, follow a regular exercise regimen, and control the stress in your life, you'll have fewer problems. You'll have more energy, more stamina, and—in many cases—a stronger immune system.

The information and tips that follow are intended to give you an overview of the steps to a healthy retirement. For in-depth discussions of health and aging, nutrition and exercise, you should go to more specific sources. We've listed some of the most helpful sources after each subject. They might give you the detailed information you seek—and you may also want to discuss such matters with your doctor.

Following are some excellent general sources on your health in your retirement years. In addition, following each section is a source list.

SOURCE: *Conquest of Aging: The Definitive Home Medical Reference from a Panel of Distinguished Medical Authorities,* by Sigmund Stephen Miller et al. (Collier/Macmillan, 790 pages, $14.95). This book covers aging and typical diseases and disorders of older people. The authors have a holistic bent and emphasize the connection between body and mind, so that this book goes beyond the typical health book and offers advice on meditation, relaxation, and other aspects of healthy aging.

SOURCE: **Beverly Foundation,** Suite 750, 70 South Lake Avenue, Pasadena, CA 91101 (818-792-2292). A group interested in developing programs to provide opportunities for "creative aging," the Beverly Foundation offers a number of booklets to the public, including *Engaging in Aging.* Contact them for a list of publications.

SOURCE: **National Institute on Aging,** Public Information Office, Federal Building, Room 6C12, 9000 Rockville Pike, Bethesda, MD 20892 (301-496-1752). The National Institute on Aging researches the aging process and diseases and special problems older adults face. They're an excellent clearinghouse of information about aging, health problems, medical care, nutrition, and much more. Among their publications: *Answers About Aging, Age Pages* (a series of fact sheets on aging, medical care for older people, nutrition, etc.), *Health Resources for Older Women.* Contact them for any of these, or for a complete list of their publications.

SOURCE: *Successful Aging: A Sourcebook for Older People and Their Families,* by Anne C. Averyt with Edith Furst and Donna Dalton (Ballantine Books, 1987; 526 pages, $9.95). An excellent book packed with sources, cross-references and information ranging from health to medical care to coping with death. Highly recommended.

SOURCE: *Prevention,* Rodale Press, 33 East Minor Street, Emmaus, PA 18098 (215-967-5171). An excellent, no-nonsense health magazine. *Prevention* offers information on nutrition, health, and more.

SOURCE: *Longevity,* 1965 Broadway, New York, NY 10023 (212-496-6100). A magazine packed with tips on nutrition, vitamins, and other necessities for a healthy long life.

NUTRITION: EATING RIGHT FOR A HEALTHY RETIREMENT

▶ Eating healthily isn't complicated.

A good basic diet, according to experts, should include the following: five or more servings per day of fruit and vegetables; six or more servings of legumes, whole grains and other complex carbohydrates. (Note: These aren't the same nutritional guidelines you may have been taught in school. A lot of hard scientific research and many important statistical studies have led to the new guidelines.)

▶ Your dietary needs change somewhat as you age.

One of the most important changes: As you grow older, you lose the ability to absorb certain nutrients, nutrients that are essential for good health. So it's vital that you rearrange your diet to get the nutrients you need. At the same time, you should be cutting back unnecessary fats and calories.

What you're striving for is parity between what you eat and what you need. The bottom line, then: If you emphasize foods high in vitamins, minerals, and fiber and low in fat and calories, you can make up for the shift in your chemistry and eat what your body needs. There are six simple steps you can take to make your diet as nutritionally sound as possible.

▶ Step 1: Cut fat from your diet.

The reasons for keeping fat consumption down are compelling. Studies have shown that a diet low in fat is a diet that contributes to a longer life. A low-fat diet helps prevent certain diseases, such as heart disease, colon cancer, breast cancer, and prostate cancer. Eating low-fat foods helps you keep your weight down—which, in turn, helps you keep from falling prey to such diseases as hypertension, diabetes, and osteoarthritis. In addition, chances are that when you cut down on fat, you eat larger amounts of other foods, like those high in complex carbohydrates or nutrients—further strengthening your immune system.

Cutting down on the amount of fat you eat isn't as hard as you may think—and it doesn't mean your diet will suffer from lack of taste.

First, remember that you don't have to cut all forms of fat completely from your diet. What you should do is restrict your intake of *saturated* fat, the fat that increases your cholesterol level. The general rule: Have a maximum of one-third of your fat intake come from saturated fat (found in butter and red meats) and the rest from polyunsaturates (corn oil, safflower oil, and other vegetable oils) and monounsaturates (olive oil and canola oil).

Monounsaturated fat, in particular, can be an important part of a healthy diet. Recent studies have shown that monounsaturated fat lowers LDL-cholesterol (the "bad" cholesterol) and raises HDL—the cholesterol that helps against heart disease; others have shown that replacing saturated with monounsaturated fat helps prevent high blood pressure. Some guidelines:

- *Steer away from fried foods—especially deep-fried.* Fried foods are usually fat-laden foods. When possible, replace fried foods with baked or roasted foods. Instead of frying foods in butter, use nonstick pans.

- *Use meat as a condiment, not a main ingredient.* Switch to main-course dishes, such as pasta with a sauce, that contain a small amount of meat.

- *When you do eat red meat, pick lean cuts.* Get beef that has been graded Select. Or for even leaner beef that is 30% to 50% lower in calories, try the newer genetically lean-bred beefs (under different brand names at your supermarket or butcher). As for specific cuts of beef, your best bets are loin or round cuts.

- *Find low-fat replacements for high-fat favorites.* You would be surprised at how many high-fat foods can be replaced painlessly by "safe" foods. For example, replace sour cream with nonfat yogurt; make yogurt cheese from nonfat yogurt by letting it drain through a cheesecloth—it's a nice substitute for cream cheese. For other ideas and examples, skim through low-fat cookbooks and nutrition books.

- *Cook with olive oil and canola oil.* Olive oil is a great nutritional bet in three ways: It helps cut cholesterol, it is linked to lower blood pressure, and according to recent studies, it can help reduce your blood sugar level. Warning, though—do remember that olive oil is high in calories. As for canola oil, it's virtually tasteless—which makes it a good choice for baking and other cooking in which you want to avoid the stronger taste of olive oil. Another advantage of canola oil is that it contains a fatty acid that converts to EPA (eicosapentaenoic acid)—the fat found in fish oils that lowers blood serum triglycerides.

- *Go easy on processed and fast foods.* They're usually loaded with fat—even the most benign-sounding foods (many of the fast-food chicken sandwiches, for example). Processed foods are often prepared with saturated fats, such as palm, palm-kernel, and coconut oils, which have a long shelf life. And read labels to avoid "fat traps." Sometimes saturated fat is where you'd least expect it.

TIP: **Don't get sidetracked by food labels that trumpet "No Cholesterol." This doesn't make that particular food healthy. In fact, the food can still be loaded with fat. Many foods that contain no cholesterol are still fat-laden—such as potato chips and other snack foods. Better bet? Check the label for fat content as well as cholesterol content.**

▶ **Step 2: Don't overload on cholesterol-laden foods.**

High cholesterol has been linked to heart disease. The American Heart Association recommends that you keep your cholesterol intake to a maximum of 300 milligrams a day. To give you an idea of how easy it can be to reach this limit, a single egg gives you 213 milligrams of cholesterol.

- *Continue to eat eggs—but try to limit the amount to four egg yolks a week.* Again, aim for moderation. Don't cut eggs completely out of your diet, but don't get into the habit of two-egg breakfasts daily. When cooking, you may be able to replace whole eggs with egg whites.

- *Replace some high-cholesterol foods with low-cholesterol foods.* Replace ingredients in recipes—instead of lasagna with ground beef, make it with ground turkey, or better yet with vegetables.

- *Use butter sparingly.* Instead of cooking foods in butter, use a little canola or olive oil. Or, if you want the taste of butter, wipe a nonstick pan with the butter *wrapper* for a slight hint of butter flavor when you cook.

- *Switch from certain high-fat foods to low-fat.* You'll cut back on cholesterol if you switch to low-fat cottage cheese and other low-fat cheeses. Drink skim or 1% milk instead of whole or 2% milk; cut back on red meats, cold cuts, and the like.

- *Read labels.* What looks safe often isn't. A good example: microwaveable popcorn is often high in saturated fat.

▶ **Step 3: Make power-packed foods—those that are high in vitamins and other nutrients—the central part of your diet.**

When you emphasize foods that are nutrient-rich, you center your diet on foods that can *do* something for you, not just fill your stomach. One of the most compelling reasons is keeping your immune system strong.

Some of you may want to take vitamin and mineral supplements in addition to eating nutrient-rich foods. However, it's best not to use supplements as a *replacement* for eating properly.

Some guidelines on choosing power-packed foods:

- *Eat large amounts of food high in beta-carotene*—such as broccoli, greens, carrots, and kale. Also eat foods high in other types of carotene, such as tomatoes and melons.

- *Aim for two to three portions a day of calcium-rich foods*—milk and other dairy products, broccoli, kale, tofu, mustard and collard greens, canned sardines, and salmon.

TIP: Add nonfat dry milk *powder* to food when you're cooking. It mixes well into soups, stews, casseroles, and other main dishes and it's a painless way of getting extra calcium.

TIP: Spinach may prevent calcium absorption. A recent study conducted at the University of Wyoming showed that women eating a diet high in spinach were losing calcium from their systems. Best bet: Stick with a cup of spinach two or three times a week, but no more.

- *Usually you're best off with dark green vegetables over paler green ones.* Of course there are exceptions, but in general, the more richly colored vegetables signal higher nutrient value. For example, instead of pale green iceberg lettuce, eat dark green Romaine; instead of green beans, choose broccoli. You'll be getting more beta-carotene and Vitamin C.

TIP: **Drinking orange juice when you eat foods high in iron helps your body absorb about *four times as much* of the iron.**

- *Often the less you do to your vegetables the better.* In other words, don't overhandle or overchop your vegetables, don't cook them to death, and don't keep them standing. In many cases you're best off eating vegetables raw, lightly steamed, or stir-fried, since many vitamins are destroyed by excessive heat, air, or light, or lost in water when boiled. An important exception: If you're looking for beta-carotene, you are better off *cooking* most beta-carotene–rich vegetables. Cooking increases the availability of beta-carotene to your body.

▶ **Step 4: Make fiber an important part of your diet.**

Fiber does a number of positive things. It helps prevent colon cancer as well as other gastrointestinal problems such as diverticulosis; it helps keep your blood sugar levels stable; it helps keep blood cholesterol levels down.

For fiber, turn to fresh fruits, vegetables, and whole grains. The National Research Council recommends eating at least five one-half-cup servings of fresh fruits and vegetables, and at least six servings of whole-grain breads, cereals, and legumes. This should provide you with at least 20 to 35 grams of fiber each day, the recommended minimum.

Some tips to help you add fiber to your diet:

- *Look for whole-grain breads and cereals.* Whole grains are higher in fiber. Read labels—choose such breads as whole wheat, seven-grain, and oat bran; choose such cereals as oatmeal, muesli, and multigrains.

- *Opt for unbleached flours and rice.* Unbleached flour and rice are higher in fiber than their bleached counterparts. Opt for brown rice over white; grain breads over white breads; whole-wheat flour or unbleached all-purpose flour over traditional bleached white flour.

- *Choose high-fiber fruits and vegetables.* Some good choices are zucchini, raw cauliflower, brussels sprouts, corn, cranberries.

- *Bulk up on peas and beans and other legumes.* Legumes are an excellent source of fiber—and they're easily added to most meals.

Some good choices are pinto beans, lima beans, and lentils. Add them to your salads, eat hearty legume-based soups, such as split pea or lentil, make chili—you have a number of tasty options.

- *Make your snacks high-fiber ones.* Munch on air-popped or canola oil–popped popcorn, on dried fruits and chickpeas. Also eat dry cereals as a snack. Sprinkle dried cereal on nonfat yogurt.

▶ Step 5: Make your diet rich in complex carbohydrates.

Eating foods that are high in both fiber and complex carbohydrates will help you keep your energy level up, keep your weight down, and keep your heart healthy—all compelling reasons to change your eating habits.

Complex carbohydrates are found in many high-fiber foods, particularly breads and other starches.

- *Eat large amounts of starches—vegetables, whole grains, and bread products.* Some of the best choices are potatoes (which are also very high in potassium), pasta (try the whole-wheat variety), brown rice, oats, and breads.

- *Avoid the mistake of adding traditional high-fat toppings to foods high in complex carbohydrates.* It's a common problem—take a healthy baked potato and slather on the butter or the sour cream. Instead, use nonfat yogurt as a topping.

▶ Step 6: Take it easy with the salt.

Some studies have found that a diet high in salt can lead to hypertension; others disagree. Best bet? Moderation.

Generally, if you suffer from or have a family history of either high blood pressure or diabetes, it's best to play it safe and avoid salt and high-sodium foods. Otherwise, you can eat salt, but don't overdo.

To keep sodium intake down:

- *Watch out for processed foods and fast foods.* They're notoriously high in sodium. Many manufacturers have come out with low-sodium frozen and canned foods. But still be careful and read labels.

- *Use other flavor enhancers.* Salt isn't the only thing you can sprinkle on your food. Experiment with different herbs, chopped red or green peppers, horseradish. Squeeze lemon over foods. Another option: You can buy prepared nonsalt flavor enhancers that are combinations of dried herbs, or you can make your own.

▶ What about alcohol?

Experts disagree on this subject—some advocating strict abstinence, others saying that a glass or two of wine a day is actually better than nothing.

If you're a nondrinker, you don't have to change your ways. But if you're a heavy drinker, perhaps you should. Virtually all studies agree that excessive alcohol consumption (three or more drinks a day) increases your chances for heart attacks. In addition, many heavy drinkers are at higher risk for cancer.

The best rule, if you enjoy drinking, is moderation—*strict* moderation. One to two drinks a day. According to a recent study of drinking conducted in England, this amount of alcohol per day puts you at a low risk for heart disease.

SOURCE: **Food and Nutrition Information Center,** Room 304, National Agricultural Library Building, Beltsville, MD 20705 (301-344-3719). The center provides food and nutrition information to professionals and the general public. Their library is open weekdays from 8:00 A.M. to 4:30 P.M. You can contact them by phone or in writing for information on resource guides and bibliographies on such subjects as diet and nutrition for older Americans.

SOURCE: *Grocery Shopping Guide: A Consumer's Manual for Selecting Food Lower in Dietary Saturated Fat and Cholesterol,* by Nelder Mercer and Carl Orringer, M.D. (University of Michigan MedSport, 1989). If you're interested in comparing brand-name foods for saturated fat and cholesterol content, the *Grocery Shopping Guide* can help you. It contains dietary information (including fat, calories, sodium, fiber, and sugar) on more than 4,000 supermarket foods. It's available for $20.95 postpaid from: Ashford House, 1123 Broadway, New York, NY 10010.

SOURCE: *Jane Brody's Good Food Book: Living the High Carbohydrate Way,* by Jane Brody (W. W. Norton, 1985). This large book written by the *New York Times* "Personal Health" columnist is filled with information on healthy eating, the foods to choose, what different foods can do for you and more. Plus it has hundreds of great recipes—from appetizers to main dishes to healthy (and tasty) desserts.

EXERCISE: GETTING ACTIVE AND STAYING ACTIVE

▶ **It's never too late to begin exercising.**

If you haven't exercised in years (or haven't exercised at all), you're missing out. Take a look at some of the benefits of regular exercise.

Exercise can help you destress. It's a great way of ridding yourself of the tensions of daily life. Instead of sitting at home and stewing or venting your rage on your friends, family, or yourself, you can release your stress through physical activity. When you're moving, you'll start feeling better. It's also a biological fact. When you exercise, you release endorphins, the body's natural tranquilizer. It's endorphins that cause the so-called runner's high.

Exercise can improve your self-image. Exercise will make you look and move better, which in turn makes you feel better about yourself. Furthermore, when you exercise, you can see continual improvements in yourself. Each day you can win a small victory—you can walk a little further, feel yourself get more limber or stronger. A life filled with small victories makes you feel more positive about yourself. You're a winner!

Exercise can help you build lean muscle mass. As we grow older, we tend to lose muscle mass. Muscle mass is more metabolically active than fat—that is, it burns calories faster. So the more muscle you have, the more calories you burn, and the more easily you can control your weight.

Exercise can help you stay mentally sharp. This was the conclusion of a study conducted in 1990 at Scripps College in Claremont, California. Researchers tested a number of people ranging in age from 55 to 91. Half were physically active; the other half weren't. The results—those who were physically active scored higher in tests measuring memory, reasoning, and reaction time. Researchers speculate that exercise may improve blood circulation to the brain.

Exercise can help you increase your stamina. The more you exercise, the more your body becomes accustomed to expending energy. You'll find yourself becoming more energetic, more able to put up with physical tolls and stresses. You'll have more endurance—quite a plus.

▶ **If you haven't exercised in a while, there's a simple first step: Just start moving!**

You don't have to begin with anything strenuous, organized, or complicated. The best way to start exercising is to start small, start slow, but start. Don't go overboard with a strenuous program. You want to build up gradually to a higher level of fitness. By starting too aggressively, you run a very real risk of hurting yourself.

TIP: **Beginners often find it simpler to exercise if they do it with someone else, usually a friend who is also just beginning. Having someone to exercise with keeps you going—you're less inclined to skip a day if you know someone is expecting to meet you for your daily walk or tennis game. And it's more fun—more of a social event.**

Once you've begun exercising regularly, slowly begin increasing the amount you exercise and the intensity of your workouts. For example, if you begin with 20-minute walks three times a week, slip in one 30-minute walk. Swing your arms a little harder on the 20-minute walks. The trick is listening to your body. It will tell you when you're pushing too hard and when you're not pushing hard enough.

▶ **Make exercise part of your day-to-day routine.**

The simplest way to keep up with your exercising is to make it a regular part of your daily life. Remember that regular exercise doesn't necessarily mean formal activities. You can also incorporate exercise into your life by being active in small ways. Instead of taking an elevator, walk up a flight or two of stairs. Walk to the store instead of driving. Simple tasks like gardening, raking the leaves, even going for a stroll can—and should—be part of your fitness regimen.

Keep in mind that recent studies have shown that you don't need to opt for sustained, strenuous exercise to get many of the benefits. A little exercise can go a long way.

▶ **For total-body health, you should aim for a combination of aerobic, resistance, and flexibility training.**

Muscles are made up of two types of fiber: fast-twitch, which are used in resistance training, such as weightlifting, and grow in strength and bulk; and slow-twitch, which are used in aerobic activities, such as running, and don't gain in bulk, but in endurance.

For your body to be completely fit, you should work both types of muscles. You want to increase your strength and increase your endurance and—which is where flexibility training comes in—you want to keep your body supple and limber.

Some added benefits of doing a variety of exercises: Recent studies show that you increase your fat burning by 10% when you combine resistance training with aerobic activity. It's also a great way to keep from getting bored with your exercise routine.

Following are popular exercise options, the benefits of each, and who they may be best for. In all cases, be sure to check with your doctor before beginning any exercise program.

- *Aerobics:* High-impact aerobics—aerobic dancing in which you jump—works your cardiovascular system and is a great fat-burner. One problem, however, is that it also puts a great deal of stress on your joints. Low-impact aerobics, which are done with one foot staying on the ground, place less stress on knees, shins, and ankles, but are also less of a workout for people who are already in good shape. Adding handheld weights increases the efficacy of the cardiovascular workout. One of the newer forms of aerobics training is "step training," in which you step on and off a step or box, sometimes while carrying handheld weights. Like other forms of aerobics, it gets high marks for fat burning and cardiovascular workout. If you have knee problems, however, it's a no-no.

SOURCE: Those of you who would rather work out at home with a workout tape than work out at a health club can send for a free catalogue listing—and rating—nearly 200 exercise videotapes. Contact: *Video Exercise Catalog*, Department G, 5390 Main Street NE, Minneapolis, MN 55421.

- *Circuit training (weights):* A fairly new way of getting both a cardiovascular and a resistance workout. When you follow a weight-training circuit, you do a sequence of weight training with free weights or weight machines and aerobic activity (such as riding a stationary bike, running in place, using a rowing machine or step machine, jumping rope). Typically the circuit should take you about 30 minutes. It's not the best aerobic workout, because of the short amount of time you do the areobic portion of the circuit, but it's good for muscle endurance and strength. And it can fit into a busy day. You can do it at home or at a health club.

- *Cycling (outdoors):* Works the major muscles in the lower half of your body and gives you a cardiovascular workout. Even if you don't push hard and pedal slowly, you're getting benefits in your heart and lungs—and you can enjoy the outdoors.

- *Golf:* If you sit in a golf cart and drive from hole to hole, you might be having fun, but you're not getting much of a workout. Walk! Better yet, walk *and* carry your clubs.

- *Jogging or running:* Great aerobic workout, good for the large muscles in the lower part of your body, but it can place stress on knees, ankles, feet, and legs. Since running loads weight on your skeletal system, it can help prevent osteoporosis in women. A drawback: Running only works your lower body's muscles. For complete fitness, you should also do some simple upper-body exercises or weight training.

- *Martial arts:* Helps your cardiovascular system, your flexibility, and your muscular strength, depending upon the specific martial art. For example, tai chi is particularly good for flexibility and stress reduction; karate is better for muscular strength. An added benefit: most students of the martial arts report a rise in self-esteem.

- *Stationary bike:* Effectively works your cardiovascular system without putting as much strain on your lower legs as running. But, unless you have the dual-action bike that also simulates a rowing motion, it doesn't work your upper body at all. As with jogging and running, you should combine this with upper-body exercises or weight training or both.

TIP: If you find riding a stationary bike incredibly boring, try putting it in front of your television set. You can pedal while you watch your favorite shows or videotaped movies.

- *Swimming:* Gives you a great cardiovascular workout, increases your muscular endurance, and, a big plus, it puts no stress on your joints. However, some recent studies have shown that swimming isn't as effective a fat-burner as other aerobic activities, such as running or aerobics. Nevertheless, it's an excellent choice for people who want a fairly stress-free cardiovascular workout.

- *Tennis:* Gives you a fairly good cardiovascular workout, but the sudden stops and starts can be rough on your knees and ankles. One plus, however: Tennis is great recreation; because you play with other people, it can be a fun social activity.

- *Walking:* One of the most popular forms of exercise, chiefly because it's simple to do and fun to keep up with. Puts little stress on your joints and it's an efficient fat-burning cardiovascular exercise. If you walk briskly for only 20 minutes, you'll burn an average of 200 calories—half of them from fat. Walk for longer than 20 minutes and you'll increase the percentage of fat calories burned up to 70% more.

TIP: **To get the most out of walking, be sure to: 1) Walk briskly. While a stroll is relaxing, you'll get more benefit from a good, brisk stride. 2) Stride long, but don't overstride. 3) Bend your arms and pump them in natural rhythm with your stride. 4) Relax your upper body, instead of holding it stiff. Best bet—combine walking with some sort of upper-body workout, such as weight training.**

- *Weight training:* A good choice for building lean muscle mass—which helps you burn fat *after* you've exercised. You can work with free weights or weight machines. A very big advantage, especially for women: Weight training helps keep bones strong, which helps prevent osteoporosis.

TIP: **If you're starting weight training, begin by working out at a health club or Y instead of at home. You should have a trained instructor show you what to do. It's too easy to do weights incorrectly—in which case you may be getting little benefit from the activity, or may even injure yourself.**

- *Yoga:* One of the best activities for flexibility and stress reduction. Yoga works *with* your body and breathing, which makes it an enjoyable, natural-feeling activity. It can improve your posture and balance, make you more supple and limber, and relax you. It's especially good for people with back problems, or those seeking to manage their stress. An interesting note: A recent study showed that yoga helped coronary patients reverse their arterial blockages.

SOURCE: **National Association for Human Development,** 1424 16th Street, NW, Washington, DC 20036 (202-328-2191). This group distributes the fitness guidebook *Health and Fitness Program Manual;* a poster, "Join the Active People Over Sixty"; and exercise instructions.

SOURCE: **National Senior Sports Association,** Suite 205, 10560 Main Street, Fairfax, VA 22030 (703-385-7540). An organization designed to promote sports activities for older adults, the National Senior Sports Association organizes activities and sports competitions, sponsors trips, and publishes *Senior Sports News.* Contact them for information and an events schedule.

SOURCE: **President's Council on Physical Fitness and Sports,** Suite 7103, 450 Fifth Street, NW, Washington, DC 20001 (202-272-3430). Contact them for the publication *The Fitness Challenge in the Later Years,* which describes exercises and activities promoting cardiovascular fitness and flexibility, as well as their *Walking for Exercise and Pleasure.*

SOURCE: *Movement Is Life: A Holistic Approach to Exercise for Older Adults,* by Eva D. Garnett (Princeton Books).

SOURCE: *The Rockport Walking Program* (Prentice-Hall, $9.95). This book sets out a 30-day walking and diet regimen that helps you lose weight the healthy way. It includes sample menus and recipes.

A FEW WORDS ABOUT WEIGHT CONTROL

▶ **You can control your weight by following the basic rules of healthy eating and exercising.**

If you eat properly—sticking with high-fiber, high-carbohydrate, and high-nutrient food and steering away from high-fat food—and exercise even the minimum amount, you will get the added benefit of weight control.

Do keep in mind that controlling your weight is more than a cosmetic consideration. Keeping your weight at a proper level also affects your health. It's especially important if your weight collects primarily above your waist—in your waist and stomach, arms, neck, and shoulders. This makes you an "apple," and more prone to heart disease and, for women, breast cancer. Those of you who put weight on below your waist—chiefly in the hips, thighs, and buttocks—are "pears." Most women fall into this category. Healthwise, you probably face lesser risks than "apples," but weight should be a consideration for you too.

Excessive weight can cause or aggravate such things as arthritis, diabetes, high blood pressure, and heart disease. It also can take a toll on your self-esteem, your energy level, and your overall quality of life. But by following the simple precepts in this section, you can control your weight without struggling.

TIP: If you're thinking about resorting to one of the liquid diet supplements on the market, don't. Many of them contain sugar. All of them don't do one thing for you—educate you to eat properly. Instead of going for a liquid diet, change your eating habits. Eat properly and exercise a moderate amount, and you won't need to diet. Yes, it may take longer for the pounds to drop, but they will *stay* off. More important, you'll be training your body to live healthily.

TIP: Don't get caught in the "I should weigh what I did in my 20s" trap. Frankly, you probably shouldn't weigh what you did in your 20s.

Remember, you can—and should—make weight control a natural part of your life. Don't go for rapid weight loss diets or intensive quick-hit exercise programs. They may not do much—and they might take a toll on your health. Instead, opt for sound eating habits and regular exercise, which will give you results that last—and keep you healthy.

STRESSPROOFING YOUR RETIREMENT

▶ **The final—and very important—element in becoming and staying healthy is learning to reduce or deal with the amount of negative stress in your life.**

There's no doubt about it—stress can play a huge role in how healthy you are and feel. It affects you physically: It can raise your heart rate, increase your blood pressure, give you tension headaches. And it affects you mentally: Too much stress can make you nervous, depressed, anxious.

However, there's also no doubt that you will be faced with stressful situations in your retirement years. It's an inevitable part of being alive.

At the beginning of your retirement years, you may face the stresses of adjustment. You are changing your routines, moving, changing friends, leaving family, leaving your job. And you'll face other stresses as time goes on. You will have to cope with normal illness and the general stresses of aging. You will care for friends, relatives, or spouses, and may have to cope with the loss of those close to you. Plus there will be the positive stresses: the excitement of moving, the joy of seeing grandchildren and great-grandchildren.

Just as stress is caused by different events, so there are different types of stress: "fight or flight" stress, which causes the rush of adrenaline that pulls you out of a dangerous situation; "spice of life" stress, moderate amounts of stress that push you to try a little harder; and "chronic stress," the debilitating type of stress that keeps eating at you, draining you of energy and good health.

Because you can't escape stress, the key is learning to avoid or defuse those stresses that you can avoid, and learning to cope with those stresses that you can't.

▶ **Avoiding or defusing stressful situations when possible saves you mental and physical energy.**

The simplest way to stressproof your life is to avoid as many as you can of the little things that nag at you. Try to set up a routine that keeps you away from situations you know trigger stress for you. Some other thoughts on how to avoid or defuse stress:

- If it's a person causing you stress, *talk over the problem with that person.* Be honest. Perhaps that person is not aware that he or she is irritating you. The problem may be easily solved.

- *Decompress first, then deal with the source of the stress.* Particularly if it's a person, this makes sense. Before you confront the situation, force yourself to calm down. It's easier getting to the root of a problem when you're not supertense.

- *Speak up for yourself.* If you feel you are being taken advantage of, being ignored, or being taken for granted, perhaps you need a shot of assertiveness. Stand up for yourself. Let other people know what you think, instead of sitting back and letting them run the show. Often just stating your case will make you feel a lot better.

- *Physically remove yourself from the stressful situation.* If need be, leave.

- As a final option, you may want to *speak to a trained therapist,* especially one who specializes in situational therapy—that is, therapy aimed at helping you understand and cope with a specific problem.

▶ **When stress is unavoidable, you can help yourself by forcing yourself to wind down and relax.**

Often there's no getting around a stressful situation, but the following suggestions may help:

- *Sometimes the best way to deal with stress is to first acknowledge it.* Certain stressful situations won't go away. But denying that you are upset or tense may make a bad thing worse.

- *Unload your problems on a friend.* Talking out your tensions will help you decompress. A sympathetic listener gives you the opportunity to hear yourself vent.

- *Try to look on the bright side of life.* Obviously, this won't work in all cases. But it's a good idea not to dwell overly on negatives and "what ifs."

- *Take things one step at a time.* Often you are stressed by more than one thing. Instead of feeling overwhelmed by all your problems, deal with one at a time.

- *Meditate.* This is an excellent way of coping with regular stress. There are a number of meditation methods. The simplest is to sit in a darkened room, close your eyes, clear your mind, and focus on your breathing. Another simple way to meditate (and a great stress-reliever) is "mindful meditation." Every hour or so, take 10 to 30 seconds, close your eyes, and focus on your breathing. If your mind wanders, pull it back to your breathing. According to Dr. Jon Kabat Zinn, director of the stress-reduction and relaxation program at the University of Massachusetts, this method helps you develop concentration and mindfulness, which will enable you to respond thoughtfully to stressful events instead of merely reacting to them. In other words, you'll be in control of the situation, instead of vice versa.

- *Take breaks.* If you're faced with consistent stress—for example, if you're caring for an ill spouse or relative—taking a break can be a real lifesaver. Try to get away by yourself, away from the routine, and go shopping, to the movies, or out to lunch.

- *Keep yourself otherwise occupied.* If you can't avoid a particular situation that you find stressful, try to find something else to do at the same time to keep your mind off the irritation. For example, if you go crazy waiting in lines and have to spend the afternoon at the Motor Vehicle Department, bring a book, some needlepoint, or a friend.

- *Get a pet.* A variety of studies have shown that having a pet can help you destress, relax, and cope better.

- *Try yoga.* Yoga is a wonderful stress-reliever, because it forces you to pay attention to your body, breathe deeply, and let your tensions ooze out of you.

- *Take time for the little things in life that can relax you.* Go for a walk. Watch the waves crash onto the shore. Listen to a bird singing. In other words, let yourself stop and smell the flowers. It won't make your problems go away, but it will make you feel better.

SOURCE: *The Feeling Good Handbook: Using the New Mood Therapy in Everyday Life,* by David D. Burns, M.D. (William Morrow, 1989).

SOURCE: *Full Catastrophe Living: Using the Wisdom of Your Body and Mind to Face Stress, Pain and Illness,* by Jon Kabat-Zinn, Ph.D. (Delacorte Press, 1990).

COMMON AGE-RELATED DISEASES AND HEALTH PROBLEMS

▶ **Certain diseases and health problems are more common as we age.**

Following are brief discussions of some of the more common health problems and diseases that affect or concern people over the course of their retirement years.

SOURCE: *The Merck Manual of Geriatrics,* a general reference intended for physicians, may be useful. It is a $20 reference guide published by drug firm Merck & Co. that covers common health problems of the elderly.

Alzheimer's Disease

▶ **Over 2 million elderly people suffer from Alzheimer's disease.**

Alzheimer's is one of the most devastating diseases that affects the elderly—all the more because caring for an Alzheimer's patient takes a great toll on spouse, family, and friends.

The onset of Alzheimer's is usually characterized by growing confusion and disorientation; forgetfulness, even of such basic facts as what day it is, home address, and children's names; mood swings; and depression.

▶ **Keep in mind: While Alzheimer's is more prevalent in older adults, it is *not* an inescapable aspect of growing older.**

Aging doesn't automatically bring on Alzheimer's disease. Causes of Alzheimer's—and treatments—are still being researched. Heredity seems to play a role in whether you will get Alzheimer's. Some studies have found a link between the presence of aluminum in the body and the development of Alzheimer's, although evidence is as yet inconclusive. However, some medical experts suggest shying away from aluminum—cookware, antiperspirants with aluminum as an active ingredient—as a precaution.

Your best move, whether you fear you are at risk for Alzheimer's or not, is to maintain a healthy lifestyle—including good nutrition, moderate exercise, and as little stress as possible.

▶ **Many retirees will find themselves in a situation in which they have to care for an Alzheimer's patient.**

Because of longer life expectancies, more people in their retirement years are taking care of elderly patients—some of whom may be afflicted with Alzheimer's. Others are taking care of spouses with the disease. Whatever the specific situation, caring for a patient with Alzheimer's places a considerable emotional strain on the caregiver—to the degree that many call the caregiver the "second victim of Alzheimer's."

If you find yourself in this situation, joining a support group may help you cope with some of the stress. In addition, you may want to consider elder day care or respite care (described on pages 447, 453).

SOURCE: **Alzheimer's Association,** Suite 600, 70 East Lake Street, Chicago, IL 60601 (312-853-3060). A large voluntary organization with local chapters nationwide, the Alzheimer's Association runs a 24-hour toll-free hotline to help people get in touch with their local chapter, to answer questions about the disease, and to offer helpful suggestions and tips about daily living. The hotline number is 800-621-0379 (800-572-6037 for Illinois residents).

SOURCE: **Alzheimer's Disease Education and Referral Center,** Federal Building, Room 6C12, 9000 Rockville Pike, Bethesda, MD 20892 (301-496-1752). This center provides information on Alzheimer's disease, research, and services. You can contact them for a list of publications or get their bibliographical references on-line in the Combined Health Information Database (CHID) available through database vendor BRS Technologies.

SOURCE: **John Douglas French Foundation for Alzheimer's Disease,** 11620 Wilshire Blvd., Los Angeles, CA 90025 (213-470-5462; Information Service number 800-

537-3624). This group funds research to find a cure for Alzheimer's. In addition, it runs the John Douglas French Center in Los Alamitos, California, which offers long-term care exclusively for Alzheimer's patients, as well as day-care and respite-care programs. Similar centers are being planned in Massachusetts, Michigan, MInnesota, Ohio, Oregon, Pennsylvania, and Texas.

Arthritis

▶ **Arthritis is a term covering a wide range of illnesses—all characterized by pain and inflammation of the joints.**

In your retirement years, you probably will be contending with *osteoarthritis*—pain in one or a number of joints, such as your knuckles, hip, knee, shoulder, or back. Rheumatoid arthritis—a devastating form of arthritis characterized by symptoms including weakness, fever, severe pain in the joints—is less of a threat, as it tends to strike people in their 20s and early 30s.

Osteoarthritis occurs simply through excessive use (or abuse) of joints. For example, if you are overweight, you may be more prone to arthritis in the hip joint, because that joint has been stressed by bearing your weight. It is particularly common in joints that are regularly stressed when you work or exercise or joints that have been injured.

What helps? Weight-bearing exercise, aspirin, and other anti-inflammatory medications. Some nutritionists recommend shying away from certain types of foods, termed "nightshade foods," such as tomatoes.

Although your osteoarthritis may seem minor, it is still best to see your doctor. Some arthritis can be particularly debilitating and may eventually cripple you.

SOURCE: **Arthritis Foundation,** 1314 Spring Street, NW, Atlanta, GA 30309 (404-872-7100). This organization provides free publications on treatment options and arthritis, and also publishes such books as *Overcoming Rheumatoid Arthritis, Understanding Arthritis,* and the very helpful *Self-Help Manual for Patients with Arthritis.* Contact them for information on availability and prices. Look for chapters of the Arthritis Foundation in your area. Local chapters offer courses and health programs, including the Exercise Program, the Self-Help Course, and the Aquatics Program.

SOURCE: **National Arthritis and Musculoskeletal and Skin Diseases Information Clearinghouse,** P.O. Box AMS, Bethesda, MD 20892 (301-468-3235). This information service puts out such free catalogues as the *Directory of Information Resources,* and more.

SOURCE: **National Institute of Arthritis and Musculoskeletal and Skin Diseases,** Information Office, Building 31, Room B2B15, 9000 Rockville Pike, Bethesda, MD 20892 (301-496-8188). This, the federal government's principal agency for research on a range of diseases including osteoporosis, puts out a publication called *Osteoporosis: Cause, Treatment and Prevention.*

Cancer

▶ **The bad news: Each year, about 400,000 Americans die of cancer. The good news: The different forms of cancer are getting more curable every year.**

Over the past few years, breakthroughs in cancer detection and treatment are giving cancer researchers cause for cautious optimism. However, cancer is still a real threat. If you are over 65, you have a 10% higher chance of dying of cancer than those under 65.

However, cancer is not necessarily a death sentence. One thing that helps is early detection. Early detection of many cancers can often lead to completely successful treatment. In light of this, be aware of your body, of any changes in appearance or in how you feel. Periodically check for the American Cancer Society's early danger signs of cancer:

Unusual bleeding or discharge

Lump or thickening in the breast or elsewhere

Sore that refuses to heal

Change in bowel or bladder habits

Persistent cough or hoarseness

Indigestion or difficulty swallowing

Change in wart or mole

Treatment varies according to the specific type of cancer, the severity of the cancer, and other factors. Among the more traditional treatments are surgery, chemotherapy, radiotherapy, and immunotherapy.

▶ **While it is often difficult to pinpoint specific causes for certain cancers, there are certain simple preventative measures you may want to take.**

- *Get regular checkups.* Women should get yearly mammograms and Pap smears; in addition, they should be in the habit of monthly self-examination of their breasts. Both sexes should get proctoscopic exams every two years or so and annual physical exams.

- *Quit smoking* if you currently smoke. Nonsmokers, try to avoid secondhand smoke. Although studies differ in their assessment of the link between cancer and secondhand smoke, you're best off playing it safe.

- *Avoid unnecessary exposure to X-rays and ultraviolet radiation from the sun.* Always ask your doctor if an X-ray is really necessary. As for sunning, try to limit your exposure to the sun at its peak hours—from 11:00 A.M. to 3:00 P.M. Wear sunscreen with a sun protection factor of 15 or higher and reapply throughout the day.

- *When possible, avoid exposure to carcinogens, such as asbestos, nitrites and nitrates in foods, pesticides, and polluted air.* Cut down on your consumption of cured and smoked meats (bacon, hot dogs, salami, bologna, ham and other cold cuts, smoked salmon, etc.). Consider buying organic or pesticide-free produce (available at many supermarkets and at health food stores). Try to steer clear of highly industrialized areas, as factories and plants (especially chemical, plastics, and petroleum producers) emit noxious fumes. Similarly, avoid tap water if you live near a highly industrialized area (or perhaps even if you don't). Play it safe and use bottled water.

SOURCE: **American Cancer Society,** 1599 Clifton Road, NE, Atlanta, GA 30329 (404-320-3333). One of the best-known health organizations, the American Cancer Society has local chapters nationwide. These chapters offer services to cancer patients and their families (such as self-help groups and transportation programs) and organize the helpful "I Can Cope" and "Can Surmount" support groups. Look in your local yellow pages for the number of the chapter nearest you, or contact the national headquarters.

SOURCE: **National Cancer Institute,** Office of Cancer Communications, Building 31, Room 10A24, 9000 Rockville Pike, Bethesda, MD 20892 (301-496-5583; Cancer

Information Service, call 800-4-CANCER; in Hawaii, on Oahu, call 524-1234; call collect from neighboring islands). The NCI maintains a computerized system for doctors called PDQ (Physician Data Query) that contains information on treatment studies currently accepting patients, state-of-the-art treatment information, and a directory of doctors and institutions experienced in cancer treatment. (While PDQ is for doctors' use, you may want to ask your own doctor about it.) NCI also puts out a number of publications and maintains a toll-free Cancer Information Service, which provides information on cancer and cancer-related resources in local areas.

Dental Problems

▶ **The biggest dental problem for people past the age 50 is periodontal disease.**

If your gums are puffy and tender, if they bleed easily when you brush or floss, and if they look as if they are pulling back from your teeth, you have gingivitis. If it is left unchecked, you could begin losing some of your teeth.

Briefly, here's what happens: Plaque forms on your teeth. When it isn't removed, it hardens into calculus—which serves as an incubator for bacteria. This causes your gums to become swollen and tender. At this point, you have gingivitis. Your gums will begin pulling back from your teeth and the bacteria will move to fill in the empty spaces created. Your teeth begin getting shaky as the roots become weakened. And, eventually, your teeth must be pulled. In some cases, your gums have become so infected that you will also need surgery to drain them of bacteria-laden pus.

But this doesn't have to happen. It's easy to avoid this worst-case scenario.

▶ **Simple, basic care of your teeth and gums can prevent most dental problems.**

To help prevent gum or teeth problems:

- *Brush and floss regularly.* Everything you were told as a child by your dentist is true—brush after every meal; use a soft toothbrush; place bristles at a 45-degree angle to your gumline. Floss at least once a day with dental floss.

- *Replace your toothbrush regularly.* An old toothbrush harbors bacteria and doesn't clean your teeth well.

- *Make a mouthwash of baking soda and hydrogen peroxide.* This is one of the most effective ways of killing bacteria and killing unpleasant mouth odors. (Note—do *not* swallow this mixture.)

- *Get your teeth cleaned twice a year.* This way, you can remove the plaque in your mouth before it hardens into calculus—home to bacteria and the gingivitis-promoter.

- *Have dental check-ups at least once a year.*

SOURCE: **American Dental Association,** 211 East Chicago Avenue, Chicago, IL 60611 (312-440-2860). The ADA puts out a range of information, including information on planning a dental health program for older people. In addition, you may want to contact your state chapter of the ADA for information on special programs or services, as many provide free or low-cost services for older people and assistance in finding a dentist.

SOURCE: **American Society for Geriatric Dentistry,** Suite 1616, 211 East Chicago Avenue, Chicago, IL 60611 (312-440-2660). This is a professional association of dentists who specialize in providing care for older people.

Depression

▶ **Depression, in some form or another, strikes a number of retirees—often because of the adjustments they must make in their lives.**

People in their retirement years may find themselves caught in a downward spiral of depression because of the dramatic changes in lifestyle. Where once their lives were filled with routine, whether from a job or from the familiar neighborhood activities, now there is empty time. Some people feel they have outlived their usefulness, others feel unfulfilled and unchallenged. Many retirees suffer from boredom. After a full life, they feel they are stagnating.

The most common form of depression in older adults is termed "reactive" depression. People suffering from this type of depression often feel isolation, anxiety, and loneliness.

▶ **Some of the most useful treatments for minor depression are self-help treatments—simple and effective things you can do immediately.**

Of course, it depends upon the specific circumstances, but generally you can help yourself out of depression—or can help prevent yourself from getting worse.

One of the most important things you can do is *talk*—talk to your spouse, your friends, your family. Share your feelings. Be honest about your fears and anxieties. Other actions you can take: If you feel lonely and unconnected, join a group, consider doing volunteer work or getting a part-time job. Pets are often a big help in combating depression—especially if you are alone. A pet gives you something to care for as well as offering companionship. Start establishing new routines for yourself. Begin an exercise program—exercise is a great way of keeping busy, doing something beneficial and beating the blues.

▶ **Those of you who find yourself—or your spouse or a close relative or friend—slipping into a depression that doesn't lift should seek professional help.**

Some danger signs: a depression that lasts for two weeks or more; excessive desire to sleep or escape, increasing confusion or disorientation. When a person exhibits one or more of these signs, it's best to seek professional help.

SOURCE: **American Association for Geriatric Psychiatry,** P.O. Box 376-A, Greenbelt, MD 20770 (301-220-0952). This is an organization of psychiatrists specializing in the care of older adults. Contact them if you are interested in locating a geriatric psychiatrist in your area.

SOURCE: **American Psychiatric Association,** 1400 K Street, NW, Washington, DC 20005 (202-682-6239). To locate a psychiatrist for consultation, contact the association.

SOURCE: **American Psychological Association,** 1200 17th Street, NW, Washington, DC 20036 (202-955-7600). For help locating a psychologist in your area, contact a state chapter of the APA.

Diabetes

▶ **As you get older, your chances of getting diabetes increase.**

If you are also overweight, you have an even greater chance.

When you have diabetes, your body is incapable of properly processing glucose. Your pancreas may be underproducing insulin, or the insulin you are producing may not be breaking down glucose properly. Diabetes is especially common in people over 40 who are overweight. Left undetected and allowed to worsen, diabetes can affect your eyesight and your heart as well.

▶ **Certain danger signs may signal that you have diabetes.**

These signs are excessive thirst, frequent urination, frequent sweating, unusual fatigue, slow healing, skin rashes, and, for women, itching around the genital area; for men, impotence. Keep in mind that if you have one or more of these symptoms, you don't necessarily have diabetes. However, you should see your doctor.

Treatment for diabetes depends upon your specific case. Your doctor may suggest a special diet—one low in refined sugar, fat, and animal protein and high in complex carbohydrates and fiber. In addition, you may have to take insulin—either through injections or orally.

SOURCE: **The American Diabetes Association,** 1660 Duke Street, Alexandria, VA 22314 (703-549-1500). This national group offers a wealth of information to the public—from a toll-free telephone service that will give you general information and resources to pamphlets and cookbooks. Contact them for a list of their publications. Their toll-free Information Service number is 800-232-3472.

SOURCE: **National Diabetes Information Clearinghouse,** Box NDIC, Bethesda, MD 20892 (301-468-2162). In addition to putting out a number of publications on diabetes and related topics, this group also publishes a newsletter, **Diabetes Dateline,** and a list of activities and programs on diabetes education. You can contact them at the above address, or via computer on the Combined Health Information Database (CHID), which you can access through the database vendor BRS.

Eye Problems (Including Cataracts and Glaucoma)

▶ **As we age, our eyesight tends to worsen. However most eye ailments, while annoying, are not as severe as they seem.**

It is not uncommon for older eyes to suffer from a range of slight problems, such as periods of blurriness, "floaters" (moving spots in front of your eyes), shimmying images, and a halo effect around objects. If you have any of these symptoms, you should see an eye doctor. You may need a new prescription, if you already wear glasses or contact lenses; you may need to change your reading habits (use brighter lights and rest your eyes more often); or you may be suffering from overuse of a computer.

Beyond these irritations, the two most common eye problems affecting older people are glaucoma and cataracts.

▶ **With *glaucoma*, pressure builds up in the eye, affecting the optic nerve and eventually causing blindness.**

Glaucoma affects about 2% of the population over the age of 40. You have no warning of glaucoma because, at the beginning, it develops with no symptoms. However, a doctor can measure pressure in your eye and so catch it in its earliest stages. It is vital that you see an eye doctor for regular glaucoma tests as, left unchecked, it will cause blindness. Caught in time, however, glaucoma may be checked from advancing much further. Most doctors prescribe eyedrops to alleviate discomfort and reduce pressure.

▶ ***Cataracts*—which cause cloudy vision and, if left unchecked, will block light from the retina—are formed by the degeneration of protein molecules in the lens.**

Another very common eye ailment with older people, cataracts are also very curable. Cataract surgery is usually a fairly simple, in-office procedure, in which the doctor inserts a small needle into the eye to remove the portion of protein that has degenerated. In some cases, if the cataracts warrant it, the lens itself will be removed and replaced by a plastic lens. Surgery is nearly foolproof—over 95% of cataract operations are successful.

An important note: If you are over 65 and don't have a regular ophthalmologist or haven't had a checkup in at least three years, you may want to call the National Eye Care Project Helpline set up by the American Academy of Ophthalmologists. The hotline is open weekdays from 8:00 A.M. to 5:00 P.M. Pacific time. Call 800-222-EYES to get in touch with an ophthalmologist in your area, and you can set up an appointment for a free or reduced-cost eye exam.

SOURCE: The Better Vision Institute, Suite 1310, 1800 North Kent Street, Rosslyn, VA 22209 (709-243-1528). The Better Vision Institute offers information on the prevention, detection, and treatment of eye diseases. Contact them for a list of their materials.

SOURCE: American Association for the Blind, 15 West 16th Street, New York, NY 10011 (212-620-2147; the Information hotline, 800-232-5463, is open weekdays from 8:30 A.M. to 4:30 P.M.). In addition to developing programs and offering services for blind and sight-impaired people, this group also puts out a number of free pamphlets, including *Aging and Vision* and *Living with Glaucoma.* Call for a free catalogue of other publications.

SOURCE: **National Society to Prevent Blindness,** 500 East Remington Road, Schaumburg, IL 60173 (312-843-2020; Information service, 800-221-3004). This society puts out a range of publications on eye care, glaucoma, eye exams, and more. Call them for a free publication list. The group also offers a number of educational programs for the public, including *LIFESIGHT: Growing Older with Good Vision.* You also may call them to find out about local chapters that sponsor self-help groups for people with glaucoma.

Hearing Loss

▶ **Hearing loss is common as people age. The specific causes, however, vary widely, from nerve damage to excessive wax buildup.**

The good news is that, in most cases, hearing loss can be treated with a high rate of effectiveness.

Among the more frequent causes of hearing loss are excessive wax, eardrum diseases, and otosclerosis, in which a bony spur blocks the opening to the inner ear—all of which are usually easily treated by an otologist (ear doctor), who can usually eliminate the problem. Hearing loss caused by damage to the auditory nerve brought on by such factors as severe falls, prolonged exposure to excessive noise, or disease is less likely to be completely eliminated, but can be treated—usually by surgery or use of a hearing aid.

▶ **The key, of course, is detecting hearing problems as early as possible and getting treatment.**

If you are experiencing difficulty hearing, if you find yourself turning the volume up on the television, if people seem to be speaking too quietly, and if other people tell you you are speaking too loudly, you may be suffering from hearing loss.

Similarly, if your spouse is either mumbling or speaking too loudly, gets easily irritated or confused, and seems to be going through erratic personality changes, he or she may be suffering from hearing loss.

In either case, the first step is to see a doctor. The doctor will then either treat your problem, send you to an otologist, or if necessary, refer you to a hearing specialist for a hearing aid.

> ▶ **There are different types of hearing aids—in-the-canal, in-the-ear, and behind-the-ear aids. Many are now taking advantage of digital technology.**

In-the-canal aids—a tiny computerized hearing aid you wear in your ear canal—are the newest form of hearing aid. The problem—they are so small that some people (especially those with arthritis) may have problems with the controls. However, these are a good choice if you value appearance highly, as they are nearly undetectable. Average costs for these are about $800 to $1,000.

In-the-ear aids are the most common form of hearing aid. About the size of a quarter, these aids tend to last longer than in-the-canal aids. Cost runs about $600 to $800 for in-the-ear aids, $550 to $700 for behind-the-ear.

The newest wrinkle in hearing aids is the use of digitalization—or computer programmability. With digital aids, you can program your aids to block out background noise or pick up high-frequency sounds (typically the first ones that drop out of your hearing). Because the technology is so new, digital hearing aids are more costly. A single aid can cost $2,000.

TIP: **When buying a hearing aid, be sure to get a 30-day trial period. This will allow you to get a feel for the aid and how it works in your daily life. Keep in mind, though, that under many trial arrangements, you will have to pay for certain services (fitting, for example). Know the costs ahead of time.**

SOURCE: **National Hearing Aid Society,** 20361 Middlebelt Street, Livonia, MI 48152 (313-478-2610). This group publishes such booklets as *Facts About Hearing Aids.* In addition, their toll-free Hearing Aid Helpline offers information on hearing loss, hearing aids, and how to locate a qualified hearing aid specialist, and takes consumer complaints on hearing aids. The hotline operates weekdays from 9:00 A.M. to 5:00 P.M. Call 800-521-5247.

SOURCE: **Self-Help for Hard of Hearing People,** 7800 Wisconsin Avenue, Bethesda, MD 20814 (301-657-2248 [voice] or 301-657-2249 [TDD]). This group has local chapters nationwide. They offer support and encouragement to people with hearing problems and hold special programs to help people cope with hearing problems and hearing aids, and to communicate effectively. Contact them for information on publications they offer, as well as to check about groups in your area.

SOURCE: **National Information Center on Deafness,** Gallaudet University, Washington, DC 20002 (202-651-5051 [voice] or 202-651-5052 [TDD]). For information on organizations that provide services to deaf and hearing-impaired people, as well as fact sheets and pamphlets, such as *Aging and Hearing Loss: Some Commonly Asked Questions,* call the information service of the National Information Center on Deafness at 800-672-6720 or contact them at the above address and numbers.

SOURCE: **National Institute on Deafness and Other Communication Disorders,** Information Office, 9000 Rockville Pike, Bethesda, MD 20892 (301-496-5751). Contact them for a list of free publications on deafness and loss of hearing in older people.

Heart Attacks

▶ **Heart attacks are clearly not limited to retirees. Yet they are, unfortunately, not uncommon.**

A heart attack is any sudden instance of heart failure, including the formation of a clot or obstruction in one of the coronary arteries. Some signs that you may be experiencing a heart attack are:

Severe chest pain

Shortness of breath

Pain radiating from your chest to your arm, back, or jaw

Unusual or irregular heartbeat

Loss of consciousness

If you have any of these signs, get medical help immediately. Keep in mind, though, that there still is a very good chance you are *not* having a heart attack. Many times hyperventilation brought on by a panic or anxiety attack mimics a heart attack. But this is no time to wait until you are sure.

Don't dismiss minor chest pain either. Often the pain you experience when having a heart attack feels like simple indigestion or heartburn. Heart attack sufferers also describe an attack as a feeling of intense pressure, as if a heavy weight is on their chest.

Depending upon the severity of the heart attack, heart attack patients may be treated through medication, a controlled diet and exercise program, surgery—or a combination of these options.

▶ **The trick is to *prevent* a heart attack. How to do this? A good diet, moderate exercise, and a sensible outlook on health can make a difference.**

Here are a few simple preventative measures you can take—but, as always, it's wise to check with your doctor:

- *Diet:* Eat a balanced, healthy diet, and take it easy on salt and unsaturated fats.

- *Exercise:* Recent studies have come up with varying conclusions concerning the link between exercise (even cardiovascular exercise) and a healthy heart. Your best bet, then? If you already exercise, keep it up. If you don't, opt for a moderate exercise program—walking, in particular, is a good choice.

- *Smoking:* If you smoke, quit! If you don't smoke, try to stay away from secondhand smoke. While studies still differ as to the effect of secondhand smoke on adults, you're best off erring on the conservative side.

- *Weight control:* If you're overweight, it would be wise to lose weight—but in a slow, controlled way, by combining a balanced diet with moderate exercise.

- *Stress reduction:* Don't forget the mental side to health. Learn to relax. Try to eliminate stress from your life. Focus on the positive—friends, leisure activities.

SOURCE: **American Heart Association,** 7320 Greenville Avenue, Dallas, TX 75231 (214-750-5397). This organization offers a range of printed material, such as ***An Older Person's Guide to Cardiovascular Health.*** In addition, they sponsor public education programs to help people reduce their chances of heart attacks and other heart diseases.

High Blood Pressure and Stroke

▶ **High blood pressure—or pressure greater than 140 (systolic) over 85 (diastolic)—can cause heart attack or stroke.**

It's often a silent killer because many—some say up to 50%—of the people with high blood pressure are unaware of their condition. This is why you should get periodic blood pressure checkups by a qualified doctor or technician. Don't trust the "vending" machines that test your blood pressure or the people who do blood pressure tests at the mall or on the street.

To prevent or reduce high blood pressure, you can follow the preventative measures for heart disease. In addition:

- *Cut caffeine consumption.* Keep track of the caffeine in your diet. If you have high blood pressure, cut caffeine out entirely. If your blood pressure isn't high (and if your doctor agrees), you probably still can enjoy caffeine periodically, but it's best to keep consumption low.

- *Reduce stress in your life.* Perhaps it's easier said than done, but reducing stress will keep you healthier. Try to relax more. Meditate. Go for walks.

Treatment for high blood pressure varies according to the severity of the situation. Often high blood pressure can be treated through diet and exercise. In some cases, treatment requires medication—which may have side effects, including mood changes and a decrease in sexual desire. If you are told you need medication, be sure to get a second opinion. Often blood pressure medication is too quickly prescribed, when dietary changes—and time—would have sufficed.

▶ **A stroke occurs when a blood vessel to your brain breaks or is blocked.**

Warning signs of a stroke include:

Severe headache (especially above the eyebrow, at the base of the skull)

Vision disorders

Paralysis

Vomiting

Disorientation

Coma

If you, or someone with you, suffers from any of these warning signs, seek medical help immediately. Stroke victims may suffer from paralysis or slurred speech. In these cases, they typically go through a period of rehabilitative therapy.

SOURCE: **American Heart Association,** 7320 Greenville Avenue, Dallas, TX 75231 (214-750-5397). This group puts out a number of useful publications, including *Strike Back at Stroke* and *Stroke: A Guide for the Family.* Check your local telephone directory for the number of a local office, or call the headquarters. In addition, local chapters sponsor support groups called ''Stroke Clubs'' designed to assist people recovering from a stroke and their families.

SOURCE: **National High Blood Pressure Information Center,** 4733 Bethesda Avenue, Bethesda, MD 20814 (301-951-3260). This center distributes information on high blood pressure, its causes, and its treatments, as well as on programs on hypertension. Call for information, or you can access their bibliographical references in the Combined Health Information Database, available through database vendor BRS Information Technologies.

SOURCE: **National Stroke Association,** Suite 240, 300 East Hampden Avenue, Englewood, CO 80110 (303-762-9922). This group provides information about strokes, such as *Stroke, What Is It, What Causes It, Proper Diet After Stroke, What Every Family Should Know About Strokes, The Road Ahead: A Stroke Recovery Guide,* as well as supporting self-help groups, stroke clubs, and support groups for people recovering from a stroke and their families.

Incontinence

▶ **This problem afflicts a fairly large number of people in their later years—about 30% of those who live at home, and 50% of those in nursing homes. But the good news is that incontinence can be either significantly reduced or completely cured almost 90% of the time.**

Incontinence is clinically defined as uncontrollable urinary leakage occurring at least six times a year. There are different causes for incontinence. Women may become incontinent after a hysterectomy or other pelvic surgery, after childbirth, or conversely, if they have never delivered a child. Men may become incontinent after surgery for prostate enlargement or prostate cancer.

There are different types of incontinence, but the most common are *stress incontinence*, in which urine leaks out when you cough, sneeze, laugh, exercise, or the like, and *urge incontinence*, in which you feel an intense urge to urinate.

Treatment varies according to the specific reason for the incontinence and the severity of the problem. Among them: pelvic exercises, Kegel exercises, use of vaginal weights, surgery, collagen injections, biofeedback, and medication.

▶ **The biggest hurdle in curing incontinence is embarrassment.**

According to surveys, only about 10% of the people suffering from incontinence seek help for their problem. In fact, reticence about incontinence also makes it difficult to pinpoint the exact number of Americans with the condition—estimates range from 10 million to 30 million.

However, if incontinence is a problem, it makes sense to discuss it with a doctor. Chances are, the incontinence can be treated, if not completely cured.

Speaking with others who suffer from incontinence may help. In many areas, you can join a support group of patients and health professionals. Check with your hospital or doctor for information on local support groups.

Several national groups (many of which have local chapters) offer assistance, information, and support for people with an incontinence problem. Among them are the following sources.

SOURCE: **Help for Incontinent People (HIP),** P.O. Box 544, Union, SC 29379 (803-579-7900). Among their publications are *Resource Guide of Continence Aids and Services; Pelvic Floor Exercises for Men and Women;* and *Loss of Bladder Control: Your Guide to Treatment Options.* In addition, you can call them with specific questions and receive personal answers from HIP staff members.

SOURCE: **National Kidney and Urologic Diseases Information Clearinghouse,** Box NKUDIC, Bethesda, MD 20892 (301-468-6345). They put out a number of helpful free publications, such as *When Your Kidneys Fail . . . A Handbook for Patients and Their Families.* Call for a free list. In addition, you can see a listing of their material on the Combined Health Information Database (CHID), a computer database that you can access through database vendor BRS.

SOURCE: **Simon Foundation,** Box 835, Wilmette, IL 60091 (312-864-3913). This group distributes information on incontinence and offers assistance and support to incontinence sufferers and their families. They put out a number of publications, including a newsletter, **The Informer.** For information, call their toll-free Information Service at 800-237-4666.

SOURCE: **Staying Dry: A Practical Guide to Bladder Control,** by Dr. Kathryn L. Burgio, K. Lynette Pearce, and Dr. Angelo J. Lucco (Johns Hopkins Press, $12.95). This is an excellent book covering different types of incontinence, treatments, and more.

Menopause

▶ **Women typically experience menopause in their 40s or early 50s.**

Most women have been through menopause by the time they reach the age of 55. (Note: Women who experience late menopause—that is, onset later than age 55—may face an increased chance of cancer.)

The usual signs of menopause are:

Hot flashes and sweating

Tingling sensations in different parts of the body

Headaches

Fatigue

Upset stomach

Nervousness or depression

Changes in genital area

Changes in elasticity of the vagina

Treatment varies from nothing to nonprescription remedies to medication. In some cases, a gynecologist may prescribe estrogen supplements to alleviate some of the symptoms of menopause, such as drying of the mucous membranes, which can cause painful intercourse. However, in many cases, K-Y Jelly or other lubricants can ease the problem without side effects. In a minority of cases, a doctor may prescribe sedatives, tranquilizers or antidepressants for women suffering from particularly severe mood swings and behavioral discomfort.

SOURCE: **American College of Obstetricians and Gynecologists,** 409 12th Street, SW, Washington, DC 20024 (202-638-5577). This professional society of doctors specializing in women's health care puts out *The Menopause Years and Estrogen Use.* You can contact them for a free list of their publications and can call or write their Resource Center with inquiries on women's health topics. Contact the ACOG if you need assistance locating a qualified ob-gyn in your area.

SOURCE: **Consumer Information Center,** P.O. Box 100, Pueblo, CO 81109. Write them for the free booklet *The Menopause Time of Life.*

Osteoporosis

▶ **Osteoporosis, a condition marked by a loss of bone density, develops most often in older women.**

Some 25 million Americans—80% of them women—suffer from osteoporosis, a condition in which they suffer a progressive loss of bone density. This decrease of bone mass causes the entire skeleton to grow weaker, which is why people with osteoporosis suffer more easily from fractures, especially of the spine and hip. The problem is compounded by the fact that falls and other accidents are more common among the elderly.

Among the contributors to osteoporosis are low-calcium diets, smoking, little or no weight-bearing exercise, and low intake of such minerals as fluoride and phosphorus.

▶ **To help prevent osteoporosis, women should increase their intake of calcium.**

With renewed research in the field, experts agree that calcium supplements can help postpone or prevent bone loss. How much calcium? Recommended amounts vary, but the consensus is that women should have between 1,000 and 1,500 milligrams daily— which can be found in three to five 8-ounce glasses of milk.

Recent studies have determined that even after menopause, women can guard against osteoporosis by increasing calcium in their diets.

According to most studies, women past menopause who take estrogen generally need less calcium than other women. However, only about 20% of all postmenopausal women take estrogen, so chances are, even if you have passed menopause, you should be taking a calcium supplement.

▶ **The type of calcium you take is important.**

According to recent research conducted at the Agriculture Department's Human Nutrition Research Center on Aging at Tufts University, *calcium carbonate*, the most common calcium supplement, helps prevent bone loss in the hips and wrists. *Calcium citrate malate* (found in fortified orange juice) also helps prevent bone loss in the spine.

Beyond taking supplements, you can eat at least three servings a day of calcium-rich food. These include milk and dairy products, such as cheese, yogurt, cottage cheese, as well as broccoli, kale, tofu, mustard and collard greens, canned sardines, and salmon.

SOURCE: **American College of Obstetricians and Gynecologists,** 409 12th Street, SW, Washington, DC 20024 (202-638-5577). This professional society of doctors specializing in women's issues puts out free pamphlets, including *Preventing Osteoporosis.*

SOURCE: **National Osteoporosis Foundation,** Suite 822, 1625 I Street, NW, Washington, DC 20006 (202-223-2226). This health agency funds research, offers educational programs, and provides information—including a quarterly newsletter, and a guide, *Osteoporosis: A Women's Guide.* Contact them for a complete list of materials.

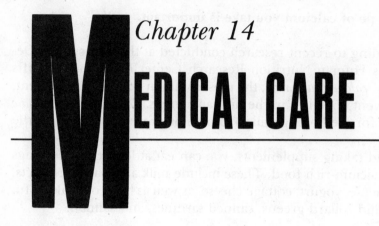

Chapter 14

MEDICAL CARE

INTRODUCTION

▶ **Part of retiring successfully is retiring healthily—which means you will need to be sure you have adequate medical care.**

Most of you probably already have doctors—both general internists and specialists. However, if you are planning to move upon your retirement, you will have to find a new doctor. In this case, here are some guidelines:

- In general, you are best off choosing a primary care physician for your everyday medical care. Primary care physicians usually charge less than specialists; they can handle a range of ailments; and, usually, they can refer you to a specialist when you need special care.

- To get the names of doctors, ask friends and neighbors for referrals. Often they will be your best source because they have firsthand knowledge of particular doctors.

- If you are moving to a nonmedical retirement community, ask other residents or administrators for the names of doctors in the area.

- Call the local chapter of the AMA and ask them for a listing of doctors who specialize in geriatrics.

- Get a list of staff physicians from the local hospital (again, you may want to ask for those who specialize in geriatrics).

- Once you have the names of several doctors, call their offices. Ask them if they treat people like you; talk briefly about your needs. Do they accept Medicare? What are their fees? Are they associated with a hospital or medical school? If so, what is its reputation? If they are part of a group practice, will you see other doctors or only this one?

- Make an appointment with the doctor you choose. This gives you the chance to assess his or her office, staff, and manner. Some things to look for: convenient office location, access to public transportation, parking close to office, convenient office hours. Also notice: Is the office crowded? Is it *too* crowded—do you have a long wait before seeing the doctor? What types of patients are waiting? As for the doctor, be sure you feel comfortable with him or her—does he or she ask questions? Is the doctor a good listener? Do you "click"? If not, keep looking. It's important that you and your doctor work well together.

Do remember another option you have besides getting a physician—you can join a health maintenance organization. Depending upon your needs, this may be the best choice of all.

HEALTH MAINTENANCE ORGANIZATIONS: A LOWER-COST ALTERNATIVE TO TRADITIONAL MEDICAL CARE

▶ **Health maintenance organizations (HMOs) are often a good choice for retired people interested in lower-cost health care.**

Since their appearance in the late 1970s, HMOs, which offer an alternative to traditional medical care, have been growing by leaps and bounds. More than 50 million people belong to either HMOs or the related PPOs (Preferred Provider Organizations—described on page 443).

How they work: Essentially, HMOs are designed to offer total (or near-total) health care services for one set fee—paid in either annual or monthly premiums. Services covered range from office visits to hospitalization to surgery. In addition, some HMOs pay for prescriptions, eyeglasses, and other special health services. However, even though flat-fee coverage has been the norm, some HMOs have been changing their practice and are beginning to charge for such things as prescriptions and office visits.

There are different types of HMOs, as well. Among the more common types are staffed HMOs, IPAs, and open HMOs.

In *staffed HMOs,* doctors work at one location and send patients to a restricted list of HMO-network hospitals (sometimes only one hospital).

In *IPAs* (individual practice associations), there is no specific HMO location or clinic. Instead you choose doctors from a list of HMO members (this includes generalists and specialists) and consult them in their offices. When necessary, you are sent to the HMO network hospital(s).

If you belong to an *open HMO,* which is more flexible than either a staffed HMO or IPA, you can seek treatment outside the HMO network, but you pay more for this flexibility—on average 13% more in premiums than with other HMOs. Plus you pay a deductible if you go outside the network of hospitals or doctors, while those treated by HMO members pay no deductible.

Costs vary according to region, the type of HMO you elect, and whether you're joining as an individual or through a group. Group costs are generally lower; individuals can expect to pay about $800 to $1,000 a year.

As for Medicare, about 50% of all HMOs are Medicare-approved.

Pros: You have access to a wide range of services for either a flat fee or a lower cost than if you went to independent doctors.

Cons: With traditional HMOs, you have less choice in doctors or hospitals; with modified HMOs, you do have a greater choice, but pay for the privilege. Many times, you face long waiting periods for appointments with HMO doctors. Services may be limited—you have to choose your HMO carefully. Finally, many HMOs went through financial rough times in the 1980s (due to such things as mismanagement); some went bankrupt. While the worst seems to be over, you still must be careful to choose a well-funded, well-managed HMO.

TIP: **If you want to check on the financial stability of an HMO, call your state regulatory office.**

▶ **Perhaps the best reason for a retired person to join an HMO is to *prevent* illness.**

Studies have shown that, because most HMO members don't pay for each office visit, they are more inclined to visit a doctor when they have a complaint rather than postpone a visit until symptoms get worse. The bottom line: HMO patients have more chance to detect many illnesses and diseases early, and so receive early treatment.

The trick, of course, is getting into a good HMO.

▶ **One of the best ways to choose an HMO is to get referrals from friends and colleagues.**

As always, getting recommendations from people you trust is one of the best ways of finding what you need. Ask them about their HMO. Are they satisfied with the treatment they've received? With the doctors and hospitals? Do they face long waits for appointments, or are they taken care of quickly?

Another way of seeking an HMO is to check if any HMOs in your area offer open houses. Many do in an effort to draw new members.

When you visit an HMO, check if there is ample parking, if it is accessible to public transportation, if it is easy to get to. Talk to staff members and observe them interacting with patients. Are they friendly? Do they answer questions? Do they make people feel comfortable? Do they treat patients like people, not numbers?

TIP: **Check whether the HMO offers any special services especially of interest to senior citizens, such as programs for Alzheimer's patients.**

▶ **If you're concerned about the financial stability of an HMO, there are a few guidelines that should help you.**

You'll probably have little to worry about if the HMO you sign with has:

- Been operating for three years or more, or is backed by a large insurance company.

- Doctors and other medical specialists as board members or founders.

- A low percentage (under 30%) of member dropouts.

- More than 60% of the HMO doctors certified or pending certification in their specialties.

In addition, know your rights as an HMO subscriber in the event of an HMO bankruptcy. If your HMO goes bankrupt, you are entitled to continued coverage for one month if you don't get Medicare, six months if you do get Medicare. Medicare-approved HMOs also have to cover the cost of any treatment in progress as well as outstanding bills.

TABLE 14.1: QUESTIONS TO ASK WHEN CHOOSING AN HMO

SERVICES

1. Is it Medicare-approved? (Does it cover all Medicare treatments and services?)

2. Does it cover eye care? Dental care? Podiatric care? Chiropractic care? Eyeglasses, hearing, aids and other medical appliances?

3. Does it pay for prescription drugs? If so, are there any limits?

4. What are the limitations on mental health care?

5. Can I get home care when necessary?

6. Does it offer special services, such as programs in nutrition for the elderly, Alzheimer's, and other health subjects?

DOCTORS AND OTHER STAFF MEMBERS

7. Can I choose my doctor or is my doctor determined by availability?

8. Can I see doctors outside the HMO network? If so, what charges will I pay?

9. Will it cover assistance from outside agencies (such as Visiting Nurses)?

10. What percentage of the staff are certified specialists?

11. What percentage of the staff have geriatric training?

HOSPITALIZATION

12. What are the affiliated hospitals?

13. Are they located conveniently for me?

14. May I stay at hospitals outside the HMO network? If so, what deductible will I pay?

15. Is there any limit on length of hospital stay covered? If so, what is it?

EMERGENCY CARE

16. Where do I go for emergency care?

17. Is there an HMO doctor on call 24 hours a day?

18. In emergencies, can I get care from non-HMO doctors and hospitals?

NOTE: Whenever possible, get printed material on the HMOs you are considering—directories of doctors and hospitals you can choose from, explanations of services, etc.

▶ **Another health care option, which is not strictly an HMO but is similar, is a *Preferred Provider Organization* (or PPO).**

How they work: PPOs are plans usually offered by such groups as unions, insurance companies, and employers. The PPO has a network of doctors and hospitals that provide discounted health care services to members. You usually pay a 10% copayment of costs if you go to the contracted or "preferred" doctors. If you go to other doctors or hospitals, the copayment goes up to 20% to 30%.

Pros: Cost is lower than with standard health care.

Cons: You have a limited choice of doctors and hospitals; you have to be sure you like the "preferred" medical practitioners. If you have access to an open HMO, it may serve your purposes better.

HOME HEALTH CARE

▶ **At some point during your retirement years, you may wish to use *home health care.***

When would you need home health care?

- If you are taking care of an elderly parent, a spouse, or other relative with a debilitating disease such as Alzheimer's, home care can offer you a much-needed break.

- If you are released from a hospital and still need nursing care or help in daily activities, home care will enable you to convalesce in the comfort of your home.

- If you or your spouse is terminally ill, home care can allow you to spend precious time at home instead of in the hospital or nursing home.

- If you are a widow or widower, frail and lonely, home care can provide you with companionship and general housekeeping assistance.

With home health care, your medical or custodial needs are taken care of at home. This is becoming an especially important element of retirement health care, especially as life expectancies increase.

How it works: There are different levels of home health care. *Housekeeper/companions* provide companionship, simple housekeeping, and the most basic custodial care. *Home health aides* provide custodial care. *Licensed practical nurses* provide general nursing care. *Registered nurses* provide skilled nursing care. In addition, *physical therapists* often provide home health care. Another type of home care is offered by a *private care manager,* a person who oversees a range of duties for a home care patient—such as signing the patient up for community programs (for example, meals-on-wheels), monitoring the patient's health, supervising other home health workers, and arranging doctor's appointments and transportation.

Costs vary depending upon the region of the country in which you live and the level of skill your home care worker has. Prices tend to be higher in the Northeast and on the West Coast and lower in the Midwest and South. Some hourly averages: companion, $4 to $10; home health aide, $5 to $15; licensed practical nurse, $15 to $25; registered nurse, $25 to $40; private care manager, $50 to $150.

Medicare will cover some costs of home care, but only if you are under the care of a home health care agency certified by the Health Care Financing Administration and only if you need skilled nursing care. Medigap insurance usually covers costs of skilled nursing care and other medical costs such as IV therapy, but usually doesn't cover personal services such as housekeeping.

Another way of reducing the cost of home health care: check with your state Department of Aging about financial aid. Many states will help you meet home health payments if you can demonstrate financial need.

Pros: You get the psychological advantages of being in your own home. You can see friends and family, feel more comfortable and less isolated. Another big plus: Home health care, while not inexpensive, is usually much less expensive than nursing home care or hospital care.

Cons: Costs can mount for long-term home care. You must screen home care workers carefully—even if using a reputable agency.

Best for: People who want to convalesce at home rather than in a hospital or nursing home, for both psychological and financial reasons; those over 80 who are frail or who lack companionship; terminally ill patients who need custodial care but want the comforts of home; people who want a break from caring for a terminally ill or Alzheimer's patient.

▶ **Choosing a home health agency is like choosing any other health-related facility or provider.**

Your best bet for finding a reliable home health care agency is to get the names of agencies from friends and relatives who have used one. They will have firsthand information about how good a particular agency was. Your next best bet is to ask your doctor or hospital for recommendations. You can also call national groups, such as the Catholic Charities or your local chapter of the Visiting Nurse Service, for information on home health care in your area, or call your state Area Agency on Aging for the names of agencies.

When you're actually choosing an agency, you should do some background research. How long has the agency been in service? What is its record? Is it licensed by the state? (This applies only to agencies in the states that require licensing.)

Some other guidelines:

- You are best off with an agency that is accredited by a group such as the Foundation for Hospice and Home Care, or the National League for Nursing.

- Make sure you know exactly what services will be performed, the cost for basic services, and any extra charges. And, to avoid any problems, get it in writing.

- Employees of the home health agency should *always* be bonded and insured. In addition, ask about security checks run on employees and required training.

- The agency should have a skilled staff member on 24-hour call in event of emergencies.

- If you have special needs, double-check whether the staff is qualified to meet them and whether there will be additional charges.

TIP: When interviewing home health attendants, it's a good idea to have a friend or family member sit in on the interview. Another good idea: Prepare a list of the specific tasks you'll need the attendant to do and give the attendant a copy to review during the interview.

SOURCE: An excellent source of information about home care in general is the **National Association for Home Care,** which develops standards and offers continuing education programs for home health care workers. For information on their free publications, contact: National Association for Home Care, 519 C Street, NE, Washington, DC 20002 (202-547-7424). For the *Directory of Accredited Approved Homemaker-Home Health Aide Services* or the free *All About Homecare,* and more, contact the **Foundation for Hospice and Home Care** at the same address and phone number.

▶ **A related service designed for retirees who don't want to move into a retirement community, but who are concerned about long-term health care, is the "life care at home" plan.**

This is a sort of home health care insurance—you pay now for services you may (or may not) need in the future.

How it works: Life care at home (LCAH) plans both insure you against the cost of long-term care and manage and provide you with medical services when you need them. With a life care at home plan, you pay an initial entry fee plus monthly fees. These payments guarantee you access to medical services. The specific arrangement—where you go for medical services or who provides them—depends upon the specific plan you're under and who is sponsoring it. Sponsors of LCAH plans include continuing care retirement communities, health maintenance organizations (HMOs), and hospitals. Costs for the plans vary. Average costs are entry fees of about $7,500 and monthly fees from $200 to $250.

Pros: You get the benefits of living in a life care community without leaving home. Since long-term care insurance often doesn't provide for home care, subscribing to an LCAH plan fills the gap.

Cons: Costs are relatively high and can mount up. These plans are still relatively new, so they may be difficult to find. Also because they are new, regulations as to insurance coverage are still vague.

DAY CARE/ELDER CARE

▶ **As more retirees find themselves taking care of elderly parents, "elder care" or assistance in the care of the elderly is becoming a growing concern.**

If you find yourself in this situation, look into the wide variety of support groups and senior citizen assistance programs that may help you. Many areas offer a range of services for senior citizens, such as meals programs and transportation. Check with your local hospital, state Agency on Aging, and area religious groups.

▶ **A growing trend is day-care centers for the elderly.**

How they work: Day-care centers for the elderly (also called elder-care centers) are similar to those for children. Elderly people can spend the day at the center, allowing their caregivers the time to take care of other matters (work, home, shopping, and so forth). They are often used for the care of Alzheimer's patients.

Pros: Elder-care centers give caregivers a break from nonstop care of the patient; they are an alternative to expensive nursing homes and long-term care; day-care clients can socialize with others.

Cons: Still relatively rare, elder-care centers can be difficult to locate.

SOURCE: **Children of Aging Parents,** 2761 Trenton Road, Levittown, PA 19056 (215-945-6900). This nonprofit self-help group offers a wide range of information and emotional support for caregivers, including a newsletter and such brochures as *Caring for the Alzheimer's Disease Patient.* Contact them for a list of publications. In addition, you can contact their information/referral service for information on resources in your area.

PRESCRIPTION DRUGS

▶ **Here are a few ways to save money on the high costs of prescription drugs and other medications.**

Shop around and compare costs. The simplest way of saving money, but effective. Prices vary from store to store. Don't be shy about asking what a store will charge to fill your prescription.

Consider buying generics. Generics cost substantially less, because you aren't picking up the manufacturers' costs of advertising and marketing. Because generics are the same as their higher-priced, better-known cousins, you are gaining a price break. What about the speculation that generics are unsafe or less effective? Recent tests run by the Food and Drug Administration concluded that only 1.6% of the generic drug samples tested were deficient—a percentage in line with normal industry standards.

Consider buying medication through discount mail order houses. Mail-order companies often sell medications at lower costs because of lower overhead. One good source for discount prescriptions: the AARP mail-order pharmacy service, which offers low-cost medications to members. Regional offices are in California, Connecticut, Florida, Indiana, Missouri, Nevada, New York, Oregon, Pennsylvania, Virginia, and Washington, D.C. (For more information, contact AARP, 1909 K Street, NW, Washington, DC 20049; 202-872-4700.)

Buy large amounts whenever possible. Often it costs less for you to get a bulk amount of a drug at one time, rather than getting the same amount over a number of refills. Ask your doctor if he or she can prescribe larger amounts of your medication.

Always ask your pharmacy about special rates or plans. Many pharmacies offer special programs for senior citizens and special customers.

When applicable, get free samples from your doctor. Drug companies give free samples of drugs to doctors.

SOURCE: An excellent book covering prescription drugs and medications and possible side effects, geared to the person 50 years old and over, is *50+: The Graedon's People's Pharmacy for Older Adults.*

NURSING HOMES

▶ **Chances are that at some point in your retirement years, either you or a loved one will need nursing home care.**

It's a fact of life—and a source of concern—for many people past the age of 65. When you're 65 or older, you have a 44% chance of having to enter a nursing home. The older you are, the more likely you'll need a period of nursing home care. For example, only about 2% of all people aged 65 to 74 are in nursing homes; the percentage increases to 6% for people 75 to 84. As for those 85 and older (often called "old olds") the percentage skyrockets to 23%.

Because the need to enter a nursing home generally arises suddenly, it is important to know about them ahead of time. A little knowledge can help save time and energy in an already stressful situation.

How they work: There are three levels of nursing home care: *skilled care,* intended for people who need round-the-clock supervision by a registered nurse: *intermediate care,* for people who need a limited amount of nursing care; and *custodial care,* for those who don't need actual skilled nursing care, but need help with daily activities such as eating, dressing and bathing.

Costs for nursing home care are high—nearly $40,000 a year. But keep in mind that most nursing home patients are in for a much briefer stay.

Pros: Nursing homes offer an ill person the care they need, without the need to manage and evaluate home health care.

Cons: Costs can mount quickly—in fact, according to statistics, about 50% of the middle-class people over age 75 who enter a private nursing home will be bankrupt in just four months.

▶ **There are certain steps to take when searching for a good nursing home.**

You can get a list of local nursing homes from your state Agency on Aging, or national organizations such as the American Association of Homes for the Aging and United Way. It's also a good idea to ask your doctor or local hospital for recommendations. Another good source—friends or relatives. They can give you a more personal perspective on individual nursing homes.

Your next step is to do some research on the nursing homes you are considering. Check:

- *The owners/administrators:* Who owns and runs the facility? What other facilities (if any) have they run? What is the history of this facility?

- *Call your state Department of Health* to find out about the nursing home's licensing status and inspection reports.

- *Costs:* What are the daily costs and what services do they cover; what are the costs of special treatments and services? Also be sure to find out if the costs are guaranteed for a set period of time.

- *Services:* What basic services are offered? Find out about the availability of special services, including physical therapy, podiatric care, and personal care—such as hairdressing.

- *Staff:* What is the staff-patient ratio? Check and double-check night staffing in particular, as this is an area some nursing homes skimp on. Also ask if there is a doctor on call for emergencies or a licensed practical nurse on premises.

- *Location:* Is it easily accessible to you or other family members and friends? Near to the patient's doctor and hospital?

▶ **Schedule a visit to the nursing homes you are considering.**

You should always get a firsthand look at any nursing home to be sure it meets your needs.

Look for signs that the nursing home is well maintained inside and out. Grounds should be landscaped nicely, lawn mowed, shrubs trimmed. Inside, look for clean, well-kept hallways and rooms. And look for the little signs: cheerful, bright color schemes, bright lighting in hallways, no rust stains in toilets or sinks.

Observe the nursing home residents. Notice the little things—are they well dressed? Are the men shaved? Is their hair trimmed? Is the women's hair done? Do they seem happy? Cheerful? Well taken care of? Are they kept busy and interested in life? Talk to residents too, if possible. They can tell you their impressions of the place. Plus you can get an idea if you'll fit in.

Get a feel for the daily rhythms of the nursing home. Look for a nursing home that has some activity—visitors coming and going, residents walking in the halls or on the grounds, staff members at their posts. A nursing home with no activity is depressing—and possibly dangerous. By the same token, a nursing home with *too* much frantic activity may be poorly managed.

TIP: **Go back for a second *unannounced* visit to see how the home is when you aren't expected.**

TABLE 14.2: NURSING HOME QUALITIES TO LOOK FOR

When you visit a nursing home, ask the following questions.

PHYSICAL APPEARANCE

1. Are the grounds well maintained?

2. Is the facility itself well maintained? Are hallways clean? Well lit? Are rooms cheerful? Are bathrooms clean? Are there any signs of disrepair?

RULES AND REGULATIONS

3. When are visiting hours? Are they convenient to friends and family?

4. Can patients keep personal mementos, small furnishings from home, or other items in their rooms?

5. Is there a patients' bill of rights?

EMERGENCY PREPAREDNESS

6. Are there regularly held fire drills?

7. Is there a physician on call 24 hours a day?

HEALTH CARE

8. Is there a physical therapy facility?

9. Can my own doctor visit me? Or must I see only staff doctors?

10. What hospital is the nursing home associated with?

11. Is there a pharmacy on premises? If not, are drugs available on-site?

OTHER SERVICES

12. How is the food service? Is food properly prepared and handled? Is it kept hot or cold as needed? Is it prepared under the supervision of a licensed dietitian? Can patients receive special menus?

13. Do patients have access to a hairdresser or barber?

RECREATION AND RELIGION

14. Does it celebrate holidays? Birthdays?

15. Are religious activities, facilities, and personnel available?

Respite Care

▶ **Respite care—short-term stays at a nursing home—bridges the gap between home care and lengthy nursing home stays.**

According to the American Association of Homes for the Aging, only about 30% of its members provide respite care. But this number should be increasing as the need grows.

How it works: Respite care is simply short-term nursing home care. If a person under home health care needs special treatment, he or she may opt for respite care, staying at a nursing home for the necessary time, then returning home. Respite care also gives caregivers (usually family members) of ill people a chance to recharge their batteries, take a vacation, and so forth. The length of the stay can vary, but generally ranges from a few days to several weeks. Costs vary according to the type of nursing home and the level of care required. The average cost is about $100 a day.

Pros: Respite care is a good way for caregivers to get a break; it can also allow a patient the chance to test a nursing home.

Cons: Respite care is not available at many nursing homes; Medicare usually does not cover respite care; you often have to arrange for respite care well in advance.

Best for: People who need short-term nursing home care for special medical needs that can't be taken care of at home; people who have gotten surgery at an out-of-town hospital, are discharged, and want to convalesce; people with debilitating long-term diseases (such as Alzheimer's) who are being taken care of at home.

▶ **You should choose a nursing home for respite care as you would any nursing home.**

Although the stay is a short-term one, respite care demands the same high standards as regular nursing home care. Follow the guidelines on pages 450–51.

SOURCE: **American Association of Homes for the Aging,** 1129 20th Street, NW, Washington, DC 20036 (202-296-5960). For lists of nursing homes that offer respite care, send $8.00 to the above address.

SOURCE: **Brookdale Center on Aging,** 425 East 25th Street, New York, NY 10010 (212-481-4426). The Brookdale Center on Aging runs a hotline specifically for people seeking respite care for Alzheimer's patients. Call 800-648-2673.

Active Retirement for the 1990s: Retiring to a New Job, Retiring to a New Life

PART V

Chapter 15

WORKING AFTER RETIREMENT

INTRODUCTION

▶ **More retirees than ever are working—or want to be working.**

Retirement used to mean stopping work, taking it easy, and enjoying newfound leisure. But more and more modern retirees don't want to take it *that* easy. They want to remain active, they want to stay involved. In short, they want to continue (or start) working. Take a look at a few facts about working after retirement:

- Nearly 25% of all retirees hold jobs—about half for the financial rewards, the other half for the emotional rewards. About 33% of the 30 million AARP members work full- or part-time—and another 33% say they would like to be working.

- A recent study commissioned by the Commonwealth Fund, a philanthropic organization, determined that nearly 2 million retired Americans 50 to 64 years old would rather be working.

- According to a study by Drake Beam Morin, Inc., which does retirement counseling, of a group of 4,100 executives about to retire, 49% became consultants or worked part-time, 13% took full-time jobs; 12% went into business for themselves—and only 25% actually retired.

- Some people continue working for purely financial reasons. According to an AARP survey, nearly 37% of the respondents said they worked because they have no private pension. Others work for medical benefits.

▶ **The bottom line? Some people just shouldn't retire the old-fashioned way.**

You may be one of them.

If you're like thousands of other retirees or soon-to-be retirees, you are probably happier working than not working. Work means more than earning money to you. It is a way of life, a self-defining act. It is something that keeps you active, happy, *alive.*

If you feel this way, perhaps you should view retirement not as a time to stop work, but as a time to work on *your* terms. This can mean taking the plunge and doing something you've always wanted to do, such as starting a business in your home, or traveling to developing countries as a consultant.

You have several options. Among them:

- *"Retiring" to a job at your current company:* Retirement can mean staying where you are today—with modifications. You might arrange a part-time or temporary work schedule with your employer.

- *Using retirement as a launching pad into a new career:* Maybe you've always wondered about different careers, different occupations. Now can be the time to try something different—you can look into the low-paying, but emotionally satisfying field that always attracted you, or simply opt for a new experience.

- *Putting your skills to work as a volunteer:* If you don't need the extra income, volunteer work may be the path for you. You can volunteer at hundreds of different organizations, in a wide range of positions.

- *Becoming a retirement entrepreneur:* This may be the perfect time to start your own business. You have years of experience behind you; you have more free time than you used to. And you can take advantage of special programs set up to help older adults.

- *Making your avocation your vocation:* Maybe you've always made handcrafted items that people admire, or you've restored antiques every weekend. Now that you have the time to devote to it, you can take your hobby one step further and make it a moneymaking venture.

- *Buying a franchise:* A sort of half-step between going the entrepreneurial route and working for someone else, franchising is a popular retirement choice.

Following is a look at each of these options, plus sources that can give you a hand in achieving what you want.

CHOOSING WHAT TO DO

▶ **The big question, of course, is which option is right for you.**

Only you know for sure, naturally. This is why, if possible, you should start planning your postretirement career *before* you retire. Experts recommend starting to think about the different postretirement work options about five years before you actually retire. As with most other steps of retirement planning, getting a head start can pay off. Before you retire, start thinking about how you want to spend your time after you leave your current job. Assess yourself, your needs, your situation.

Are you going to need an income? If your retirement nest egg, your pensions, and your Social Security benefits won't meet your financial needs, you'll need to keep working—possibly whether you want to or not. The options to consider are keeping your current job if possible; staying at your current company on a part-time or temporary basis; getting a new job (which may or may not entail career changing). If you need a job, start looking as soon as possible—the sooner you line up a job, the sooner you'll know your financial situation is settled. (See pages 464–71 for job-hunting tips, pages 472–77 for a listing of companies with reputations for hiring older workers.)

Are you interested in emotional stimulation more than financial reward? If this is the case, you have more options open to you—volunteering may fulfill your needs. (See pages 462–64 on choosing a second career; page 478 for volunteering information and organizations; page 482 on starting a business at home.)

▶ **When you're thinking about working after retirement, keep in mind that, while working may satisfy your emotional needs, it may damage your financial picture.**

Two factors can make earning an income a problem: Social Security and taxes.

Briefly, where Social Security is concerned, earning an income above a certain amount can cause you to lose your benefits. For example, in 1990, if you were 62 to 64, you could only earn $6,840 a year without losing benefits; if you were 65 to 69, $9,360. Once you go over the exempt amount, you lose one dollar in benefits for every two dollars of earnings if you're under 65; one dollar for every three dollars if you're over. Only when you're past the age of 70 can you earn any amount without penalty. (For more information, see Social Security, page 64.)

Add to this the fact that you'll be paying FICA taxes out of your earnings (even if you're receiving Social Security benefits). And then there's the possibility that your employment income combined with your retirement investment income and benefits will put you in a higher tax bracket.

What this means, in a nutshell, is that making an income can cost you money. You could easily wind up paying three-quarters of your employment income in taxes.

Your best bet is to sit down and assess the situation carefully. Go over your financial picture with an accountant or financial planner to see what income you can make without paying through your nose. One alternative: If you think you can earn a decent income, consider postponing your claim for Social Security benefits—and earn increases in future benefits.

STAYING ON WHERE YOU NOW WORK

▶ **If you're interested in keeping the job you have or taking another full-time job at your company, start working toward this as soon as possible.**

For some of you, the best move to make is no move at all. If you're comfortable at your current job, thoroughly fulfilled, and none too anxious to leave, you should stay.

The problem? Keeping your current job is often difficult, especially in these tough economic times. More companies are offering "golden handshakes"—early retirement packages that are difficult to refuse. With companies concerned about rising benefits costs and pension shortfalls, encouraging people like you to leave has (unfortunately) made sense. In these cases, no matter how much you want to remain working full-time, you may be better off compromising.

▶ **One of the best compromises: arrange a part-time, temporary or flexible work schedule with your company (or another).**

This gives you the best of both worlds in many ways—you are still working, but you also have the leisure time commonly associated with retirement. In addition, it's often easier to land a part-time job than a full-time job—especially in tough economic times. The final and most compelling reason: With part-time work, you can earn an income, but not so much that you lose Social Security benefits and jump into a higher tax bracket.

Part-time work is a very popular option for older adults. According to the Bureau of Labor Statistics, 50% more men aged 62 to 64 are working part-time today than 10 years ago.

Many companies have set up programs to accommodate their retiring employees. The most famous example is the program set up by The Travelers Corporation, an insurance company based in Hartford, Connecticut. They sponsor the Retirees Job Bank, a computerized job bank of over 700 retired workers (from Travelers and other insurance companies). These retirees fill in on a temporary or part-time basis, in clerical, word-processing, data-entry, and administrative positions. They can put in up to 1,000 hours a year—which equals about six months—without affecting their pensions.

Similarly, retired engineers, mechanics, and other high-tech professionals from Honeywell and Grumman Corporation step into temporary positions when they are needed.

▶ **Also consider transitional positions—jobs that you'll keep for a limited time.**

Some companies are beginning to offer transitional positions—jobs that help retirees adjust to retirement. For example, Mutual Benefit Life Insurance Company has set up a program called Second Start, which provides temporary, transitional work for retirees who don't want to stop working or who have second thoughts about their early retirement.

Programs like this are designed to help employees, particularly workaholics, make the move from full-time work to retirement. Usually you'll get a new job—still full-time, but less of a pressure cooker than your old one. You often get lower pay as befits your new job. You can put in the long hours but not feel the stress quite as much. This is a great way to start easing out of work without the stresses of stopping suddenly. Retirees who have held transitional jobs cite the added benefit of being able to "pay back the company"—to give the company the benefit of their expertise without the requisite high paycheck.

Check whether your company has a program like this. If not, look into the possibility of its planning one.

▶ **You should also explore doing consulting work for your company—or for firms that do business with your company.**

Doing consulting work for your current company is a lot like doing temporary work—you'll work on a per-project basis, you'll be removed from the daily stress of your old job, but you'll be able to use your skills.

You may also want to take it one step further and consult for other companies in your field, companies that are suppliers or clients of your current company. It's a logical extension of your background and a great way to use your experience.

Think creatively. Talk to people at firms that do business with yours. Explain that you can offer expertise and perspective from the other side—and supply information that can help a company better market its products and meet the needs of its clients.

RETIRING TO A NEW CAREER OR NEW JOB

Career Changing: Deciding What to Do with the Rest of Your Life

▶ **If you're considering a career change, you have to think carefully about what you want in this, your second career.**

It's different this time around. In the past you may have based your career choices on practical or financial considerations, now you can figure out what it is you *really* want to do. Give yourself free rein. Do a little soul-searching to determine what it is you want to do.

Start broad and gradually narrow your focus—you never know what is out there. Why narrow your options at the very beginning? Do some blue-sky brainstorming!

Some suggestions on how to direct yourself at this stage of the game:

- *Sit down and make a list of where and when you felt most satisfied.* Are there any common elements? Were you usually with people? Alone? Doing analytical work or dealing with the public? When did you feel most productive?

- *List your personality attributes.* Describe yourself on paper in short phrases. Be objective.

- *List the attributes of the "perfect job."* Again, be honest. Don't pull punches and write what you think you should, what is practical, or what you've always done. This is a dream sheet—you're trying to determine what makes a job compelling to you.

SOURCE: A book that can help you get started: *Wishcraft,* by Barbara Sher with Ann Gottleib (Ballantine Books). It's available at most bookstores.

- *If you want—or if it's readily available—try career counseling.* Sometimes counseling can help you pinpoint an area of interest and zero in on what it is you really want to do. Many companies offer outplacement and preretirement counseling to retirees. If yours is one of these, take advantage of it. In many cases, this counseling includes assistance in finding a new career. One noteworthy example is IBM, which has a unique program designed to help retiring or retired IBM employees change careers. It offers retiring employees $5,000 toward education that will train them for new careers, even hobbies. It also offers the Technical Academic Career Program, which provides training to retiring employees who will switch to academic careers. As part of the program, employees receive full benefits and a percentage of their salary for two years after retirement.

▶ **When you've got an idea of the careers that intrigue you, do a little background research on them.**

- *Research the jobs and careers that interest you.* Go to the library and read up on the different careers you're considering. Check the trade publications for an industry and read up on different companies, trends, forecasts, where an industry is heading, what types of opportunities there are.

- *Flip through a college, continuing education, or community school catalogue* to get ideas on what careers to pursue. Pay attention to the courses you stop to read about, the ones that grab your attention.

- *Talk to people in the fields or even the organizations you're considering.* As always, a firsthand impression is one of the most valuable. Get an idea of what it's really like in the field that interests you. Ask about hours, responsibilities, even frustrations. You want to get as clear and honest a picture as possible, not a glamorized view. By the same token, ask for an honest opinion of your chances—would you have problems getting hired? Do you need special preparation? Is there an "insider's way" around requirements?

- *Take courses.* Sometimes the best way of discovering if a career is for you is learning more about it. Night school courses taught by professionals can give you an idea of different positions, different responsibilities, and different aspects of an industry or career. In addition, taking a course can help you make contacts (the teacher and special lecturers are often helpful in job hunts).

- *Try volunteering as a test run on different areas.* It's a great way of getting an inside view of the careers or areas that interest you. You get experience in a new field and you can make the right contacts—the people who might be able to hire you for an actual nonvolunteer job.

TIP: Don't get caught in a status trap. At this point in your life, there's no need to let others dictate what you should do and what you shouldn't. Pick whatever moves you. Don't turn your nose up at lower-level jobs. If you're interested in having a job to keep busy, to make new friends, and to keep contact with the public, a lower-level job might just fit the bill. A big plus—they're usually easy to find.

Landing a Job: Tricks, Hints, and Strategies that Work for Older Job Hunters

▶ **When you know what you're looking for—or when you know that you need a job—you have to plunge into your job hunt.**

Problem is, you think, you have a double whammy against you— the job market is tight and you're competing with hundreds of other (younger) job candidates.

So why bother, right?

Wrong.

You *can* get a job after retirement. No one is saying you're going to be a shoo-in for the perfect job, but no one is saying it's impossible either.

While many companies are pushing early retirement as a cost-cutting measure, others are hiring older workers. One reason for this: The demographic shift in the labor market means the number of available younger workers is getting smaller and smaller. In other words, older workers are becoming more important and being hired more often than before.

Granted, many of the jobs available are part-time, temporary, or lower-level jobs. But others aren't—you can find part-time and temporary positions for professionals from engineers to lawyers to managers, and full-time positions in a range of fields.

The bottom line, then, is that you can get a job—even in the worst economic times. It won't necessarily be easy, but it can be done. The key, as always, is presenting yourself in the right way. And as an older worker, that means presenting yourself in such a way that your skills are noticed more than your age.

SOURCE: If you have reason to believe you're being discriminated against because of your age, call the **Equal Employment Opportunity Commission** for information and to file a complaint. You can call the toll-free information service or your local field office. Their headquarters: Equal Employment Opportunity Commission, 1801 L Street, NW, Washington, DC 20507 (202-634-6036; information service, 800-872-3362).

SOURCE: Women experiencing age discrimination may want to contact: **Women's Equity Action League,** 1205 I Street, NW, Suite 305, Washington, DC 20005 (202-898-1588). This group also offers information on career counseling programs, skill-training programs, and other information on job-training programs for women.

▶ **The first step is having the right attitude.**

It's simple: You're not going to get a job if you think you're too old. If you think of yourself as over the hill, you will communicate that attitude—and you probably won't get the job you want.

Recognize that most of the negatives you feel about your age are based upon misconceptions about older workers. Some of these common myths: Older workers cost a company money in medical benefits and sick leave. Their ability deteriorates with age. They can't be counted on.

The realities show almost the exact opposite: Older workers tend to cost *less* in benefits. They take fewer sick leaves, quit jobs less often, and are highly dependable. As for their ability? The following example says it all.

When the vice-president of aerospace company Grumman Corporation Donald E. Knowles, was addressing a National Council on Aging seminar in 1990, he explained that Grumman's workforce has always been older than average—which proves that a younger workforce isn't necessarily better. "When we put a man on the moon 20 years ago, we made the lunar module," he said. "Our past president told me, 'It wasn't a bunch of kids who put a man on the moon. It was a bunch of middle-aged and older workers.' That wasn't a put-down of kids. It was just a positive statement acknowledging the long services of the older guys, and that all that service and smarts make the place tick."*

Absolutely.

So when you're preparing for your job hunt, keep in mind the very real, very true *assets* you have going for you—assets that many employers are finding more and more attractive.

You have three impressive qualities to offer an employer:

1. *Expertise:* You have expertise gained from years of experience that far outweighs the expertise of younger job candidates. As many recruiters are beginning to realize, an academic background is no equivalent for actual on-the-job experience. Plus you won't be as concerned with chasing after promotions or praise. You can be a mentor to other employees.

2. *Dependability:* You can be counted on. Older workers are statistically more dependable than their younger colleagues. Companies report that older workers have better attendance records, take fewer sick days, and are more punctual than younger workers.

3. *Stability:* You're less inclined than a younger person to pack up and leave a company. Studies show that older workers usually stay with a company longer than younger workers. For example, Days Inn reports that corporate headquarters loses on average

*"Industry in Age Flip-Flop as Labor Market Shrinks," *Newark Star Ledger,* April 10, 1990.

about 40% of its reservation agents each year. The turnover rate of its older employees? Only 1%.

So your first order of business is recognizing that being past a certain age doesn't mean you're "too old." It does mean, however, that you're experienced, dependable, and stable. In other words, you're a great job candidate. Remember—people like you put a man on the moon.

▶ **Once you have yourself psyched, your next move is to begin job hunting in earnest.**

Job hunting after you pass 50 or 60 or even 70 is still job hunting. Age doesn't change the basic steps that constitute a well-thought-out job hunt. You will have to set a job objective, put together a resume, network for job leads, interview, follow up with letters, and ultimately, negotiate for what you want.

But there are some changes in *how* you act in each of these steps— and there are certain tricks and strategies that will give you, the older job hunter, some help.

▶ **First, try to get as far as you can *without* your resume.**

That's right—avoid using your resume until it's absolutely necessary. Your resume can be one of the most dangerous pieces of paper in your job hunt. In black and white, it lets people know how old you are, something you're trying to avoid doing. So make every effort to get job leads and interviews without your resume.

- *Get job leads from friends and colleagues.* Personal referrals are still the best way of landing a job. Talk to people, tell them you're looking for a job—and what you're looking for. Be as specific as possible. People can't help if you don't give them information. And don't be shy. Talk to anyone and everyone, friends and acquaintances, your next-door neighbor, and your spouse's jogging partner. Remember—you never know who knows who, or who knows what.

- *Keep up membership in professional associations or organizations.* It's a way of keeping abreast of industry developments, of knowing which companies are expanding, which are cutting back. In addition to talking with people you know, listen to conversations around you. You might overhear something useful—even what sounds like cocktail party chatter may hold a lead. People tend to talk about how things affect them personally. If you read between the lines, though, you may come up with something interesting.

- *Hobbyist clubs, night-school classes, health clubs, and other nonprofessional groups* are also good places to hear about job leads. In fact, sometimes they're better than job-related groups because you share an interest with the other people there.

- *Send detailed, targeted sales letters instead of the usual resume and cover letter.* Use a letter in place of a resume when you contact a company by mail. Because a letter is a more flexible document, you can leave out information that you would include in a resume— such as your age. Instead, include only the information that sells you. Make the body of your letter a sales pitch: Outline the qualifications that make you right for a job at the company; list specific accomplishments; use bullets to set off information. A strong, well-written letter can get you an interview.

▶ **Ageproof your resume.**

Chances are that at some point you will need to use a resume. This being the case, do everything you can to make your resume work for you, not against you.

To do this, try the following:

- *Remove anything that emphasizes your age.* You can do this by omitting or playing down dates. Dates draw attention to your age— you want to emphasize your skills and accomplishments. Be aware of all references to age in your resume: dates you attended school, dates you held jobs, military service.

TIP: If you list activities, make sure none of them are "old" activities—those that make the person reading your resume immediately picture you as a gray-haired senior citizen.

TIP: While it's not recommended, some people will lie about their age. If you're one of them, be careful—and be consistent! Take into account your spouse's age, your children's ages, how old you were when you graduated, and important dates in your life. One man was convinced he had completely snowed his interviewer—

he had dyed his hair, knew his new (more recent) date of birth, knew the revised date of his college graduation—but the interviewer looked a bit askance at him when he inadvertently blurted out the *real* year of his wedding. Given his new age, he had apparently gotten married at the tender age of 14!

- *Use the right resume format.* You're best off with a "combination" resume format, rather than a "chronological" format. A chronological resume is the type most commonly used, in which you list employment experience in reverse chronological order—including dates you held each job. This style draws too much attention to the dates. Instead, use a combination style, in which you organize your background under skill headings, then give a list of job titles, companies, and dates at the end. This format plays up your skills; you can emphasize specific accomplishments; you can tailor your resume easily to meet the specific needs of the employer.

- *Be specific in your descriptions.* Don't rely on vague generalizations and pat phrases. Being older means you have expertise on your side—let it come across in your resume. Cite concrete examples and specific accomplishments. For example, you "reversed long-term profit decline and loss to profit. Decreased expenses $256,000 by cutting warehouses from 5 to 2 with no decrease in customer service. Increased sales from 18,000 to 32,000 units— a 34% market share and 36% rise in profit contribution."

TIP: Always a good idea—use numbers in your resume. Statistics stand out and make the information you're presenting seem more precise. And don't write the figures out—numbers jump off the page.

TIP: Use bullets in the body of your resume, under each heading. They set off each piece of information.

- *Consolidate jobs.* If you worked at one company for a number of years and, over the course of those years, you received several promotions, compress them into fewer jobs. For example, instead of listing your path up from assistant vice-president to vice-president to senior vice-president, eliminate mention of the earlier position. Focus on the more recent work you did.

- *Cut early employment information.* Eliminate mention of your earliest jobs. There's no point in advertising the number of jobs you've held, nor the number of years you've been working. Moreover, the jobs you held in the distant past have little bearing on your marketable skills now.

▶ **When you get to the interview stage, remember to interview on the offensive, not the defensive.**

Your interview is make or break time—it's up to you to prove to the interviewer that you are right for the job. The real key at this point is maintaining your winning edge, your belief in yourself. If you believe in yourself, you can present yourself in the best possible way—as the person the interviewer should hire.

- *Keep yourself psyched up.* Even if you've been through a series of "nos," think of yourself as a winner. Read uplifting books before an interview. Review the high points in your life. Interviewing is salesmanship. Confident, aggressive people sell best. Remember that you're a winner, that the company could use someone like you. If you believe it, you can communicate it.

- *Make the right impression from the very start.* In the first five minutes, you set the tone for the rest of the interview. Be sure to look and act the part of a successful, polished professional, not a has-been. Don't give the interviewer any reason to think of you as old. Pay special attention to your appearance—present a neat, well-taken-care-of image. And remember the small touches—well-polished shoes, trimmed hair, well-groomed hands and fingernails. When you first walk in, shake hands firmly, look the interviewer directly in the eye, smile pleasantly, and maintain an upright posture. Speak in a strong but not overbearing voice.

- *Don't apologize.* This is one of the most common mistakes older job hunters make—they walk into the interviewer's office and apologize. "I know you ordinarily hire someone younger . . ." or "I realize that you may think someone 65 is older than the norm . . ." Instead, start out positively. Say why you're good and stick with it. If you think the interviewer has objections about your age, demonstrate to him or her that those objections are unfounded. Communicate the *advantages* of hiring someone your age and with your level of expertise.

- *Avoid giving the interviewer your resume until the last possible moment.* As mentioned earlier, a resume can hurt you by pointing out your age. When possible, keep your resume in your briefcase.

Sell the interviewer with your conversation. Explain why you have the right background, the unique combination of expertise for the job. Then, after you've already sold him or her, hand over the resume.

- *Emphasize specific accomplishments.* The hottest sales point you have going for you is your experience. Play it up—know what you've done and bring it up in the interview. As when you write your resume, use the details of your background to your advantage. Spell out what you've done: "In 1986, I was responsible for a sales staff of 10. My team increased sales by 35%, which was 15% above the average storewide increase." To help you with this, sit down and go through your background. Jot down at least ten specific accomplishments on notecards. Study these notes periodically so you are prepared to rattle off detailed information. This makes it seem that your memory is razor-sharp (which will help to quiet a biased interviewer's fears about your age).

SOURCE: For general job hunting information, read our *The Only Job Hunting Guide You'll Ever Need* (Poseidon Press, 1989). It takes you step by step through a job hunt, from choosing the right career to resume writing to researching a job hunt to networking to negotiating the best job offer possible.

Industries and Companies with a Reputation for Hiring the Older Worker

▶ **Certain industries—especially the retail, hotel, and restaurant industries—have specifically targeted the older worker.**

You've seen the ads on television—the smiling retiree manning the counter at a fast-food restaurant. The message is clear: Jobs once held by teens are now going to the teens' grandparents.

As the number of available teen-aged employees shrinks, many of the companies with jobs traditionally filled by teens are now seeking older workers, and in many cases, they're doing so aggressively.

McDonald's offers special training to older workers, with a four-week training program called McMasters. Kentucky Fried Chicken often offers higher wages to its older workers, citing their life and business experience.

And this is true not only of fast-food restaurants. With a resurgence of attention to customer service, retailers are eagerly pursuing older workers as sales staffers—and, as an added incentive, some of these are switching even part-time workers to a commission basis.

Do keep in mind that not all the jobs in these industries are low-level, minimum-wage positions. Hotels, in particular, are bullish on hiring older workers—not only for "meet and greet" front desk positions, but for back office duties as well.

A job-hunting lead: Elaine Grossinger Etess, president of the American Hotel & Motel Association, has established a job-finding service for "nontraditional" employees—which includes older workers. In the *Cornell Hotel and Restaurant Administration Quarterly*, she said that "If you're over 50 you may well have a definite advantage in getting a job in the lodging business. Life experience can count as much as, or even more than, an academic degree in an industry where service to the guest is key." Job opportunities in the field range from part-time to full-time to flex-time; positions also cover a wide range. You can send your resume and cover letter, or a letter outlining your skills, to her personally. The address is: Elaine Grossinger Etess, American Hotel & Motel Association, 1201 New York Avenue, NW, Washington, DC 20005-3917.

▶ **A number of individual companies have made efforts to attract older workers.**

Some have set up special programs for retraining older workers, or have arranged special flexible schedules. Others actively recruit older workers.

The following companies have a reputation for hiring older workers or maintain special programs aimed at older workers. This list is by no means complete—it is just a sampling.

Aetna Life & Casualty
151 Farmington Avenue
Hartford, CT 06156
203-273-0123
—insurance

American Airlines
4200 American Blvd.
Fort Worth, TX 76155
817-963-1234
—airline

American Express
World Financial Center
Tower C
New York, NY 10285
212-640-2000
—financial services

Atlantic Richfield Company
515 South Flower Street
Los Angeles, CA 90071
213-486-3511
—oil and petroleum

**Bankers Life & Casualty
Company**
4444 West Lawrence Avenue
Chicago, IL 60630
312-777-7000
—insurance

Bell Laboratories
295 Maple Avenue
Basking Ridge, NJ 07920
201-221-2000
—telecommunications, high
tech

Black & Decker Corp.
701 East Joppa Road
Towson, MD 21204
301-583-3900
—appliance manufacturing

Borg-Warner Corporation
200 South Michigan Avenue
Chicago, IL 60604
312-322-8500
—motor vehicle parts and ac-
cessories

Bullock's Department Stores
800 South Hope Street
Los Angeles, CA 90017
213-612-5000
—retailing

Citicorp
399 Park Avenue
New York, NY 10043
212-559-1000
—commercial banking, financial services

**Connecticut General Life
Insurance Company**
900 Cottage Grove
Bloomfield, CT 06002
293-762-6000
—life insurance

Control Data Corporation
8100 34th Avenue South
Minneapolis, MN 55420
612-853-8100
—computer products and
electronic components

Corning Glass Works
Houghton Park
Corning, NY 14831
607-974-9000
—manufacturing

Days Inn of America, Inc.
2751 Buford Highway NE
Atlanta, GA 30324
404-329-7466
—hotels and motels

Du Pont
1007 Market Street
Wilmington, DE 19898
302-774-1000
—chemicals, manufacturing,
environmental services, etc.

Duncan Enterprises
5673 Shields Avenue East
Fresno, CA 93747
209-291-4444
—paints

**Equitable Life Assurance
  Society**
787 Seventh Avenue
New York, NY 10019
212-554-1234
—life insurance

Exxon
1251 Avenue of the Americas
New York, NY 10020
212-333-1000
—petroleum

Fieldcrest Cannon, Inc.
326 East Stadium Drive
Eden, NC 27288
919-627-3000
—household furnishings
  (sheets, bedspreads, rugs,
  etc.)

**Firestone Tire & Rubber
  Company**
1200 Firestone Parkway
Akron, OH 44317
216-379-7000

Ford Motor Company
The American Road
Dearborn, MI 48121
313-322-3000
—auto manufacturer

General Dynamics
Pierre Laclede Center
St. Louis, MO 63105
314-889-8200

General Electric
3135 Easton Turnpike
Fairfield, CT 06431
203-373-2211
—multi-industry, including
  electronics, appliances, aerospace

General Motors
3044 West Grand Blvd.
Detroit, MI 48202
313-556-5000
—auto manufacturer

Grumman Aerospace
1101 Stewart Avenue
Bethpage, NY 11714
516-575-0574
—aerospace

Hewlett-Packard
300 Hanover Street
Palo Alto, CA 94304
415-857-1501
—computers

Honeywell
2701 Fourth Avenue South
Minneapolis, MN 55408
612-870-5200
—electronics

IBM
Old Orchard Road
Armonk, NY 10504
914-765-1900
—computers

Illinois Bell
225 West Randolph Street
Chicago, IL 60606
312-727-9411
—telephone services

S. C. Johnson & Son, Inc.
1525 Howe Street
Racine, WI 53403
414-631-2000
—household products, personal care products, etc.

Kaiser Cement Corp.
300 Lakeside Drive
Oakland, CA 94612
415-271-2000
—cement, building materials

Levi Strauss & Co.
1155 Battery Street
San Francisco, CA 94111
415-544-600
—clothing

Lockheed Company
4500 Park Granada
Calabasas, CA 91399
818-712-2000
—aerospace

Mack Trucks, Inc.
2100 Mack Blvd.
Allentown, PA 18105
215-439-3011
—trucks, motor coaches, components

R. H. Macy & Co.
151 West 34th Street
New York, NY 10001
212-560-3600
—retailing

McDonald's Corp.
One McDonald's Plaza
Oak Brook, IL 60521
708-575-3000
—chain restaurants

Mead Corporation
Courthouse Plaza NE
Dayton, OH 45463
513-222-6323
—paper products

Medtronic, Inc.
7000 Central Avenue NE
Minneapolis, MN 55402
612-574-4000
—medical equipment

Merck & Company
P.O. Box 2000
Rahway, NJ 07065
201-574-4000
—pharmaceuticals

Metropolitan Life Insurance
1 Madison Avenue
New York, NY 10010
212-578-2211
—life insurance

Morgan Guaranty Trust Company
23 Wall Street
New York, NY 10015
212-483-2323
—banking

Motorola
1303 East Algonquin Road
Schaumburg, IL 60196
312-397-5000
—electronics

Mutual of Omaha
Mutual of Omaha Plaza
Omaha, NE 68175
402-342-7600
—insurance

**New England Mutual Life
  Insurance Company**
501 Boylston Street
Boston, MA 02117
617-578-2000
—life insurance

Northrop Corp.
1840 Century Park East
Los Angeles, CA 90067
213-553-6262
—aerospace

**Northwestern Mutual Life
  Insurance**
720 East Wisconsin
Milwaukee, WI 53202
414-271-1444
—life insurance

Oscar Mayer
P.O. Box 7188
Madison, WI 53707
608-241-3311
—food

Pfizer
235 East 42nd Street
New York, NY 10017
212-573-2323
—pharmaceuticals

Philip Morris, Inc.
120 Park Avenue
New York, NY 10017
212-880-5000
—multi-industry, including
  food, tobacco

Polaroid Corp.
549 Technology Square
Cambridge, MA 02139
617-577-2000
—photographic equipment
  and supplies

Shell Oil Company
900 Louisiana
Houston, TX 77002
713-241-6161
—petroleum

Sherwin-Williams Co.
101 Prospect Avenue
Cleveland, OH 45202
513-977-3000
—paints

The Toro Company
8111 Lyndale Avenue South
Minneapolis, MN 55420
612-888-8801
—lawn and garden equipment

**Towle Manufacturing
  Company**
260 Merrimac Street
Newburyport, MA 01950
617-229-1919
—silverware

Travelers Insurance Companies
One Tower Square
Hartford, CT 06183
203-277-0111
—insurance

Wells Fargo & Company
420 Montgomery Street
San Francisco, CA 94163
415-396-0123
—banking

Wm. Wrigley Jr. Co.
410 North Michigan Avenue
Chicago, IL 60611
312-644-2121
—gum

Wilson Foods
4545 Lincoln Blvd.
Oklahoma City, OK 73105
405-525-4545
—foods

Xerox Corp.
800 Long Ridge Road
Stamford, CT 06904
203-329-8700
—office machinery

**Woodward & Lothrop
  Department Stores**
11th & F Streets
Washington, DC 20013
202-347-5300
—retailing

SOURCE: **AARP Works.** This AARP program is a series of job-hunting and career development workshops that cover everything from identifying your assets to planning your job hunt to job-hunting tactics. It's offered in 13 cities across the country and is recommended for people planning to begin job hunting. For information, write: Work Force Education Section, AARP Worker Equity Initiative, 1909 K Street, NW, Washington, DC 20049.

SOURCE: **Forty Plus Clubs.** Forty Plus Clubs are part of a nonprofit cooperative organization in many major metropolitan areas. They offer extensive aid to job hunters aged 40 and up—counseling, resume-writing assistance, workshops on job-hunting techniques, and more. Highly recommended.

SOURCE: **Older Women's League,** Suite 300, 730 11th Street, NW, Washington, DC 20001 (202-783-6686). An excellent organization for older women interested in staying in the workforce is the Older Women's League. Contact them for information on the different services and resources they offer.

SOURCE: **Operation ABLE.** Operation ABLE offers assistance to older job hunters in Arkansas, California, Massachusetts, Michigan, Nebraska, New York, and Vermont. For information, write: Dorothy Miaso, Operation ABLE, 36 South Wabash Street, Suite 1133, Chicago, IL 60603.

SOURCE: **Senior Career Planning & Placement Service (SCPP),** 257 Park Avenue South, New York, NY 10010 (212-529-6660). This is a group specializing in finding jobs for retired executives. An excellent resource.

SOURCE: **The Senior Community Service Employment Program,** Department of Labor, Consumer Affairs, Room S1032, 200 Constitution Avenue, NW, Washington, DC 20210 (202-523-6060). This program helps low-income people over age 55 to land a part-time job.

SOURCE: A book that may help is ***Finding Jobs for Older Workers,*** National Association of State Units on Aging, Suite 304, 2033 K Street, NW, Washington, DC 20006 (202-785-0707).

SOURCE: ***Happily Ever After: Making the Most of Your Retirement,*** by Edward Scissons (Dembner Books, 1987, $16.95). This book helps you determine what you want from your job and retirement.

SOURCE: ***Making More Money: 55 Special Job-hunting Strategies for Retirees,*** by Joyce Slayton Mitchell (Prentice-Hall, 1987).

VOLUNTEER WORK

▶ **Volunteer work is another option to consider if you want to keep busy, want to help others—and don't need (or want) the money.**

Volunteering can give you all the benefits of holding a regular, paying job—you stay involved, you meet new people, you can use your skills and talents—and you have the added bonus of knowing you're helping others. It's a potent combination, and one that is attracting more retirees each year.

According to a 1988 Gallup poll, nearly half of all respondents—47.1%—aged 55 to 64 did volunteer work, and 40% of those were aged 65 to 74.

It's a great way of putting your years of experience in the labor market to work. And it's by no means dull. There are as many ways to start volunteering as there are volunteer opportunities. Volunteers do everything from crisis counseling for troubled teens to taking care of AIDS-infected babies; from assisting a small nonprofit opera company to helping struggling entrepreneurs write a cohesive business plan. It's simply a matter of deciding what you are interested in and where you think you can help.

▶ **If you are interested in volunteering but don't know where to begin, often the best way is to start asking.**

It sounds simple, and it is. More often than not, organizations are eager to find volunteers and they'll be more than pleased that you approached them.

Here are some specific ways of finding volunteer work.

- *Contact your area volunteer referral center.* Most areas have one—a central office that refers volunteers to organizations that need them. Check your telephone directory. If you have trouble locating a referral center, the National Center for volunteers will give you the names of referral agencies in your area. Write VOLUNTEER—The National Center, 111 North 19th Street, Suite 500, Arlington, VA 22209.

- *Call the specific organizations that interest you.* If it's a national organization, try the local offices first. If you can't reach anyone there, try national headquarters. There's no harm in asking—and most organizations will be more than glad to help you speak to the person or department in charge of volunteers.

- *Also talk to local groups—hospitals, area nursing homes, and the like.* Often it's the smaller groups that can use your help the most. Again, just approach them. Speak to administrators or public affairs staffers.

- *Sign up with the AARP Talent Bank.* It's another way of being hooked up with an organization you can do volunteer work for. When you register, you fill out a questionnaire detailing your skills, interests, and so forth. Then the Talent Bank puts you together with groups (both AARP programs and groups and other organizations) that need someone with your qualifications and meet your interests. An important note: You don't need to be an AARP member to take advantage of the Talent Bank. For the registration information and forms, send a postcard request to: VTB Registration Packet (D910), AARP Fulfillment (EE104), 1909 K Street, NW, Washington, DC 20049.

- *Contact ACTION, the federal government agency that sponsors a number of volunteer programs for older adults.* Among them: The Foster Grandparent Program, in which volunteers act as foster grandparents to children who are physically, emotionally, or mentally disabled; the Retired Senior Volunteer Program (RSVP), in which volunteers work in schools, courts, libraries, day-care centers, hospitals, and other community service centers; the Senior Companion Program, in which volunteers help other older people with special health, education, or other needs in their homes, hospitals, or other settings. There are regional ACTION offices in Atlanta, Boston, Chicago, Dallas, Denver, New York City, Philadelphia, San Francisco, and Seattle. If you live in or near any of these cities, you can find the regional office address and number in the local telephone directory. Otherwise, you can contact the national headquarters at: ACTION, 1100 Vermont Avenue, NW, Washington, DC 20525 (202-634-9380).

▶ **A popular option is doing volunteer work to help the elderly.**

Volunteering for such programs as the Senior Companion Program mentioned above is becoming more popular among retirees, as senior citizens find it particularly rewarding to help others older or frailer than themselves.

One example: The AARP-sponsored Legal Counsel for the Elderly has begun a project that checks on how well court-appointed guardians are taking care of the elderly people who are their wards. To do this, they are recruiting AARP members as volunteers. Volunteers go through a training course, then visit those people who are under guardianship, and ultimately report back to the court on what the care picture looks like.

SOURCE: For more information, contact: **Legal Counsel for the Elderly,** AARP, 1909 K Street, NW, Washington, DC 20049 (202-833-6720).

SOURCE: Three other noteworthy national groups concerned with helping the elderly are: 1) **National Association of Meal Programs,** 204 E Street, NE, Washington, DC 20002 (202-547-6340). This organization is an association of professionals and volunteers who provide home-delivered meals to people who are housebound. 2) **National Caucus and Center on Black Aged,** Suite 500, 1424 K Street, NW, Washington, DC 20005 (202-637-8400). A nonprofit organization that works to improve the quality of life for older black Americans, the Caucus encourages the participation of older black volunteers. 3) **Volunteers of America,** 3813 North Causeway Blvd., Metairie, LA 70002 (504-837-2652). This organization provides assistance of many varieties, including sponsoring foster grandparent and senior volunteer programs and offering adult day care.

▶ Volunteer work can also be a fulfilling move for the retired executive.

If you're not interested in the money but want to put your business expertise to work, you may want to do what many other retired executives do—volunteer as a consultant. It's a rewarding way of keeping busy, staying involved in the business world, and sharing your knowledge with those who need it. Sometimes this type of volunteer work is similar to holding a regular job again—you're often doing what you know best, or giving business advice based on your specific experience.

See below for some recommended organizations to contact—call or send a letter or resume or both, outlining your background, special expertise, and qualifications:

SOURCE: **International Executive Service Corps (IESC),** P.O. Box 1005, Stamford, CT 06904 (203-967-6000). A great choice if you are interested in or have experience in international business. More than 9,000 executives and managers are IESC volunteers, consulting on projects in more than 90 developing countries. Volunteers go abroad to do consulting on-site—projects last from three to five months—and their spouses are encouraged to go along. The IESC picks up travel and living expenses.

SOURCE: **National Executive Search Corps (NESC),** 257 Park Avenue South, New York, NY 10010 (212-529-6660). Volunteers with this group do consulting work for nonprofit organizations in such areas as fund raising, marketing, and planning.

SOURCE: **Service Corps of Retired Executives (SCORE),** 1825 Connecticut Avenue, NW, Suite 503, Washington, DC 20009 (202-653-6279). This Small Business Administration program offers counseling to small business owners. Retired executives offer advice and information on a range of subjects, such as accounting, finance, writing a business plan, managing staff. There are 387 chapters nationwide. You can check your local telephone directory for the one in your area, or contact national headquarters at the above address and number.

GOING OUT ON YOUR OWN: RETIREE ENTREPRENEURSHIP

▶ **Many retirees use retirement as the time to finally start the business they've dreamed of.**

It seems like the perfect time to branch out on your own. You've left the corporate womb, the confining nine-to-five schedule, and the old routines. Why not take the plunge and start something new, a business that's all yours?

Why not indeed?

The ticket to success (or even to breaking even), however, is careful planning. You must be sure that you are suited for an entrepreneurial lifestyle. And you must be sure that your business idea is a sound one.

▶ **Before you take the plunge, think hard—are you *really* an entrepreneur? Or would you be happier working for someone else?**

It sounds like a tautology: Most successful entrepreneurs have always been entrepreneurs. If you're worked for a large company for decades, you may not be a natural entrepreneur. The dream of going out on your own may be just that—a dream. Ask yourself the following questions.

- Will you be comfortable with a lack of stability?

- Are you ready to spend long hours on your business? What about your spouse?

- Are you willing to spend those hours working with no guarantee of how much you'll make?

- Have you ever worked in a business like the one you're considering starting?

- Have you ever worked for yourself?

▶ **If you're convinced that the entrepreneurial lifestyle is the one for you, your next step is to research your business thoroughly.**

More than half of all small businesses bite the dust within five years of their opening. The problem? Lack of planning.

To avoid this worst-case scenario, *plan*. Know exactly what you're getting into. Research the marketplace to determine the feasibility of your business idea, and be sure you know how much money you'll need to fund your business. Lack of funds is a key reason for small business failure.

Some questions to ask yourself:

- Do you have the money you need for initial capitalization and to keep the business afloat for at least one year?

- How much money can you put in? How much do you need? Do you know where you can borrow any additional money you'll need?

- Do you know how much credit you can get from suppliers?

- What is the net income you can expect from the business?

- Can you financially manage to put all or some of your salary or income back into the business?

Also research other businesses similar to yours—and, when possible, businesses in the same area you're planning to open in, or in a similar one. Use them to get an idea of the amount of business you can expect, the competition you'll be up against, and the like. Think about the feasibility of your business. Is there a need for it? Do you have a customer profile in mind? Do you have plans on how to reach these customers?

Set up a business plan before you take the plunge. Be sure you know the bookkeeping system you'll use to track income and expenses; the taxes you'll be required to pay and their impact on your retirement nest egg; the suppliers you'll be using (if any); the inventory systems, and so forth.

The final piece of advice: No matter how much you think you know, be sure to get the assistance and input of professionals—an accountant, a lawyer, and a banker. Getting assistance before you begin a business can help get your business off the ground and keep it going.

For information and assistance setting up and running a small or home-based business, try the following sources.

SOURCE: American Home Business Association, 60 Arch Street, Greenwich, CT 06830 (203-661-0105 or 800-433-6361).

SOURCE: Center for Home-Based Businesses, Truman College, 1145 West Wilson, Chicago, IL 60640 (312-989-6112). This is a clearinghouse of information for home-based businesses. Contact them for information on resources they offer.

SOURCE: Service Corps of Retired Executives (SCORE), 1825 Connecticut Avenue, NW, Suite 503, Washington, DC 20009 (202-653-6279). The SBA-sponsored SCORE has volunteer retired executives who will give you advice on every facet of running a small business, from writing a business plan, to advertising, to financing your business. Check your local telephone directory for one in your area, or contact national headquarters at the above address and number. A highly recommended resource.

SOURCE: Small Business Administration, 1441 L Street, NW, Washington, DC 20416 (800-368-5855; 202-653-7561 in Washington, D.C.). The SBA Answer Desk is a great place to call for answers to questions and for leads to other resources. Call them weekdays from 9:00 to 5:00.

SOURCE: *Going into Business for Yourself (After Age 50),* AARP Books, Scott, Foresman, 1865 Miner Street, Des Plaines, IL 60016 (800-627-6565). A practical book that offers advice on starting a business, preparing a business plan, financing your business, and getting the business afloat. Includes a useful appendix of sources.

SOURCE: *Homemade Money: The Definitive Guide to Success in a Home Business,* by Barbara Brabec (Betterway Publications, $14.95). Gives advice ranging from choosing a business, getting started, and financial planning to marketing and expanding.

SOURCE: *How to Start, Finance, and Manage Your Own Small Business* and ***Mancuso's Small Business Resource Guide,*** by Joseph R. Mancuso (Prentice-Hall, $19.95). These two books cover every step of starting and running a small business, and the resources that can help you each step of the way.

SOURCE: *Starting a Mini-Business: A Guidebook for Seniors,* by Nancy Olsen, Fair Oaks Publishing, 941 Populus Point, Sunnyvale, CA 94086 (price: $8.95 plus $1.50 shipping). An excellent book that explains the steps to start a business—includes case studies and example. The author is a former director of a job-counseling business who now runs her own store.

SOURCE: *Starting and Managing a Business from Your Home,* Department 146-R, Consumer Information Center, Pueblo, CO 81009. This Small Business Association publication contains information on setting up a home-based business, financial information, and more. Send $1.75 to the above address for a copy.

Turning a Hobby into a Business

▶ **Often the best entrepreneurial move you can make, in terms of self-fulfillment, is to make an avocation your vocation.**

If you've enjoyed a hobby for years, retirement may be the time to turn the hobby into a moneymaker. Now that you have more free time to devote to your hobby, why not try making money at it also? Selling your arts and crafts can bring you additional income, as well as being a pleasant way of spending your time.

You can market your wares in a number of ways.

- *Through advertising and direct mail:* Put an ad in your local papers or in magazines. Even a small-print ad can generate interest. Also consider a direct mail campaign—sending flyers out describing your wares. Another excellent option: Send photographs of your work and a brief letter to catalogue companies that specialize in gift items.

- *At stores:* Contact gift shops in your area. Either send a letter with a photograph of your work or, better, make a series of sales calls. Go in person with samples of your work. Ask if the store is interested in buying some of your work. (You may also look into consignment arrangements—but this isn't recommended.) Don't be discouraged if you get a series of rejections. You may have to get through the "nos" to reach a "yes."

- *At craft fairs, flea markets, bazaars:* Buy a table or booth at craft fairs and other sales events. It's a great way for people to see your works. Keep an eye on the classified section of your paper—it often runs ads seeking vendors for upcoming events.

TIP: Contact the promotion or publicity department of area malls. They often hold craft and antique shows—especially around the holiday seasons. For a vendor's fee, you can set up a booth or table and sell your wares. The pluses: It's a safe location, it's comfortable, and you're guaranteed floor traffic.

SOURCE: *The Craft Report,* 700 Orange Street, P.O. Box 1992, Wilmington, DE 19899 (302-656-2209). This publication gives you information on running a crafts business from your home.

SOURCE: **Elder Craftsmen,** 135 East 65th Street, New York, NY 10021 (212-861-5260). This nonprofit group is designed to help older adults make and sell handcrafted items. They help teach crafts (such as woodcarving and needlework), manage a retail shop in New York City where handcrafted items are sold on consignment, and operate a training studio. If you're just beginning or thinking about selling your handicrafts, this organization may be a good place to start.

SOURCE: *Creative Cash,* by Barbara Brabec (Aames-Allen, 1986; $12.95). A very popular book that explains different ways of earning money through crafts.

SOURCE: *How to Sell at Arts and Crafts Shows,* by Kathleen D. and Robert L. Schultz, Sanddune Press, P.O. Box 58, Mosca, CO 81146 ($10.00). A handy how-to guide that will give you insights on selling the items you make.

SOURCE: *The Craft Fair Guide,* P.O. Box 5062, Mill Valley, CA 94942. This quarterly publication ($25.00) contains information on upcoming shows as well as reviews. May be useful if you are planning to get space at craft fairs to sell your work.

Franchises

▶ **Franchising gives you the opportunity to run your own business with a smaller initial financial outlay.**

It's the relatively smaller initial investment that makes buying a franchise a popular option with retirees. In addition, you have the security of dealing with a larger company, which can offer you business guidance, marketing muscle, and an established brand name.

In brief, when you enter into a franchising agreement, you make a capital investment in the franchise, agree to operate your franchise according to the conditions set by the franchiser (the company offering the business), and agree to buy all your products from the franchiser. In return, the franchiser helps out with site location, financing, marketing and promotion, record keeping, management training. A big advantage if you have never run a similar business: Buying a franchise provides you with an already established operating procedure. In effect, you are buying their experience.

But there are drawbacks to franchising: While you don't necessarily need the amount of capital you would to open a similar business on your own, you still need a fairly healthy amount of money in most cases to cover the franchise fee and products, your share of advertising, marketing and promotion fees, and more. In addition, there have been some franchise frauds and reports of poor business dealings. Finally, you should be sure that you really want to be involved in franchising—with possible long hours, financial uncertainty, and the like.

▶ If you are interested in franchising, do some background work.

Research the field, look carefully into the franchises that interest you, and do your homework. Compare franchises that are in the same business—which offers you the most services? What are the differences in costs, if any?

Once you have the names of a few franchises that interest you, contact them for information. Get a disclosure statement from the franchiser. This lists such information as the names and addresses of other franchisees, franchiser's business experience, any lawsuits against the franchiser, and the franchise fee.

Talk to some of the other franchisees listed in the disclosure statement. They can give you an honest appraisal of the franchiser and can tell you things that aren't written in the statement. Ask them about their business—have they gotten the support from the franchiser that they were promised? Is the product or service they offer successful? How does it stack up to a competitor's similar product or service?

TIP: When you interview other franchisees, make sure they have been in business at least one year—less that that, and they will not yet have gotten a realistic picture of the business. But do ask them about their first years—after all, if you buy a franchise, you may well be going through similar experiences.

Look closely at any financial statements the franchiser gives you. Go over them carefully. If they contain any projections of earnings, ask for written substantiation.

Finally, before you sign any agreement, always have your lawyer go over any contracts, agreements, or other paperwork.

One of the most useful and highly recommended sources to help you is the *Franchise Opportunities Handbook*. This guide, put out by the Department of Commerce, includes a list of franchise businesses, plus very helpful tips on what to look for, what steps to take, and how to assess a franchise. You can get it at your area Government Printing Office bookstore, or from the main U.S. Government Printing Office. Call 202-783-3238 for price and ordering information.

SOURCE: International Franchise Association, 1350 New York Avenue, Suite 900, Washington, DC 20005 (202-628-8000). This industry association puts out a number of information sources and publications, including the quarterly *Franchising World*.

SOURCE: *Franchise Magazine,* PG Communications, 747 Third Avenue, New York, NY 10017 (212-319-2200). A magazine devoted to franchising.

Chapter 16

TRAVEL AND LEISURE

INTRODUCTION

▶ **One of the things most people look forward to in retirement is finally having _time_.**

Having time . . . it's the aspect of retirement that virtually everyone can appreciate. Having time to do the things you've never been able to do before—travel, learn a different language. Having time to devote to your hobbies, your garden. Having time to simply relax and read a good book.

Many options for your leisure time are covered in other parts of the book, but there are certain activities that offer special bargains and arrangements specifically for the older adult. Following are brief discussions of some of these popular activities for retirees, plus sources and resources.

SOURCE: For information on special senior citizen programs and activities—including such things as who gives special hotel room rates, car insurance discounts, and airline ticket reductions—take a look at _**Unbelievably Good Deals & Great Adventures That You Absolutely Can't Get Unless You're Over 50**_ (Contemporary

Books; $6.95), by Joan Rattner Heilman. Its nearly 250 pages are packed with helpful sources.

TRAVEL

▶ **Travel is, hands down, the most popular leisure activity among retirees.**

Most retirees take advantage of their newfound leisure time to travel. They may return to the same vacation home time after time, take to the roads in an RV and camp their way across the country, enjoy a cruise through the Caribbean or fly to their ancestral home.

It's no wonder traveling is so popular: You can see new sights, meet new people and learn new things. It's a way of opening up your life—a wonderful choice for the active (or even the not-so-active) retiree.

SOURCE: *The Mature Traveler* is a newsletter filled with information on travel for people over 49, including discounts and special travel packages. The cost—$23.50 a year. Write: *The Mature Traveler,* Box 50820, Reno, NV 89513.

SOURCE: Also recommended is the book *Get Up and Go: A Guide for the Mature Traveller.* It's available for $12.70 from: P.O. Box 50820, Dept. 6, Reno, NV 89513-9905.

SOURCE: Don't let poor health keep you homebound. If you want to travel, but are chronically ill, handicapped or otherwise frail and need the custodial services of a nurse, there's a new company that may be able to help you out. **Langlois Medical Escort Service** provides registered nurses to travel with you. They talk to your doctor, discuss your case to be sure you are able to travel, and call ahead to your vacation spot to check accessibility to the handicapped and the like. The cost—$295 daily, plus travel and board. For more information, contact: Langlois Medical Escort Service, P.O. Box 51418, Durham, NC 27717 (800-628-2828).

▶ **When you reach retirement age, a number of leisure companies—tour operators, airlines, hotels, and more—vie for your attention and your money. What's in it for you? Discounts galore.**

It's one of the perks of reaching retirement age. You have more leisure time and (often) more disposable income than most other age groups, so companies try to appeal to you. One of the most common ways of trying to win your business is through offering a battery of discounts.

TIP: **Whenever you are making travel plans, always be sure to mention your age. Even if a company offers a senior citizen discount, they might not mention it unless you bring it up first.**

TIP: **A good way of getting discounts: Wait until the last minute. By making travel arrangements as late as possible, you can take advantage of last-minute price reductions offered by tour operators, cruise lines, airlines, and other travel companies. You can get as much as a 65% reduction in price.**

Here are some examples of the discounts you can expect, as well as hints on how to get the most for your money. (Note: Check with the travel provider for complete details on any discount offers, as prices and availability can change.)

Airlines

▶ **Most airlines offer special programs for senior citizens. The most common discount is 10% off all fares, often for both you and a companion (who doesn't have to be a senior citizen).**

Another common practice is to offer coupons for senior citizens. You buy a book of coupons for a set price and use the coupons for travel—typically you'll use one coupon for a one-way trip anywhere in the continental United States, two coupons for a round trip flight or for one-way to Hawaii or Alaska. Again, most airlines allow a companion of any age to travel with your coupons.

Here are some examples of other offers. (Note: All prices listed are from 1990—call for exact prices and availability.)

American offers coupon books for people over 62—a book of four for $420, a book of eight for $704. Reservations are required. Another opportunity: If you're an AARP member (and you can join at age 50), you and your spouse get a 10% discount on fares if you buy your tickets 30 days in advance. Destinations covered are the continental United States, Puerto Rico, Hawaii, Mexico, and various spots in the Caribbean. For more information, call 800-433-7300.

Continental offers 10% discounts to people over 62 and a companion. They also offer "freedom passports," which means you pay a set price ($1,599 in 1990) for a year's domestic travel in coach.

Certain restrictions apply, such as flight times, the number of flights, and blackout days. If you want to travel abroad to Europe, the Caribbean, Mexico, Hawaii, and other Pacific spots, you can buy add-ons—some are as low as $150 for a round trip. For information on any Continental discount program, call 800-441-1135.

Delta offers a 10% discount, plus books of four and eight coupons, valid a year from purchase. (Prices in 1990 were $420 for four coupons, $704 for eight.) Reservations have to be made at least 14 days in advance, and seating for couponholders is limited, but the coupons are valid any day of the week. For details, call 800-221-1212.

Northwest also offers books of four and eight coupons ($384 for four, $640 for eight in 1990) and 10% discounts for people over 62. An advantage of their coupon program: You can make reservations up to flight time. Their number is 800-225-2525.

TWA offers 10% off to seniors, and a coupon book—$379 for four coupons, good for the continental United States and the Caribbean. A plus: when you buy the coupon book, you also get a certificate allowing you to buy a round-trip ticket to Europe for $449 or $649 (price depends on the season). For information, call 800-221-2000.

United offers the standard 10% off, and coupons—four for $420, $704 for eight. One difference: You can use one coupon for a trip to Hawaii or to Alaska, as long as the distance is 2,000 miles or less. More than 2,000, it's two coupons. United also gives senior citizens 10% to 50% off on selected hotels and car rentals. For information, call 800-633-6563.

USAir offers 10% off published fares if you're 62 or over—destinations covered include the United States, Canada, Bermuda, and Puerto Rico. In addition, you can buy coupon books—$420 for four, $704 for eight. For more information, call 800-428-4322.

▶ *Foreign airlines* **don't offer as many senior citizen programs.**

But you can find some airlines that will offer you deals. *British Airways* offers the Privileged Traveller Card to people 60 and over—it gives you 10% off airfare, as well as 10% off certain hotels and package trips. Another plus: seniors pay no pretrip cancellation penalty. *Finnair* gives people over 65 a special fare of $496 on round-trip flights between New York and Helsinki, available any day all year.

Your best bet—ask your travel agent or check with different airlines.

Cruises

▶ **Over half of all cruise passengers are over 50, so cruise lines are less inclined than other leisure and travel companies to offer deals to older travelers.**

However, some lines do offer discounts to senior citizens, among them Bermuda Star Line, Discovery Cruises, Dolphin Cruise Lines, Premier Cruise Lines, and Sitmar Cruises. AARP members get discounts from a number of cruise lines, including Princess Cruises and Holland America.

In addition to discounts, often you can save money on cruises by making your reservations far in advance—sometimes as much as a year before sailing. Check with your travel agent or call the different cruise lines directly and ask about this feature.

Trains and Buses

▶ **Traveling by rail or bus is cheaper if you're a senior citizen.**

If you're 65 or older, you can get 25% off a regular one-way fare and any accommodations charges from Amtrak. The provisions: You must buy the ticket in advance and have legal proof of age (driver's license, passport, and so forth). However, the offer doesn't apply to the popular Florida Auto Train, or the Northeast Corridor's Metroliner. Canadian railroad ViaRail gives seniors a 30% discount.

As for buses—Greyhound sells special 7-day, 14-day, and 30-day unlimited passages for travel anywhere in the United States. You can get on or off on any of its routes. A big plus: These passes are good on more than 40 other bus lines in the country. For more information, call your local Greyhound operator.

Hotels and Motels

▶ **Many lodging chains and individual hotels and motels offer senior citizens' discounts.**

When making reservations, ask about special discounts offered to senior citizens. Many of the larger chains offer 10% discounts with special provisions—for example, Comfort, Quality, and Clarion Hotels offer a 10% discount, but you must make reservations at least 30 days in advance. For information, call 800-228-5150. Hyatt hotels in North America and the Caribbean offer 25% off regular room rates for people 62 or older, but the rate is subject to availability and must be requested when you make reservations. Call 800-228-9000 for information. Others have different arrangements.

Among the other chains offering discounts: Best Western (800-687-3383); Budget (800-835-7427); Days Inn (800-325-2525); Downtowner/Passport Motor Inns (800-238-6161); Econo Lodges (800-446-6900); Friendship Inns (800-453-4511); Independent Motels of America (800-341-8000); Journey's End (800-668-4200); Motel 6 (214-386-6161); Prime Rate Motels (800-356-3004); Red Carpet Inns, Scottish Inns, and Master Host Inns (800-251-1962); Relax Inns (800-661-9563); Super 8 Motels (800-843-1991); Susse Chalet (800-258-1980). For specific information, either call the different hotels or ask your travel agent.

TIP: **You can also seek our lower-cost budget motels when traveling domestically. These motels offer the basics (television, full baths, air-conditioning), but for substantially less than other motels. One reason—often there is no on-premises restaurant or lounge. If that's not a necessity for you, the price is most certainly right.**

▶ **Another way of saving money on travel: Join groups.**

Many senior citizens' organizations offer their members substantial discounts on travel. For the price of membership, you have access to special discounts as well as special programs and travel plans. The following sources are three of the best-known.

SOURCE: **AARP,** 1909 K Street, NW, Washington, DC 20049. AARP offers its members a range of price breaks—discounts on car rentals, hotels and motels, and cruises.

SOURCE: **National Alliance of Senior Citizens,** 2525 Wilson Blvd., Arlington, VA 22201 (703-528-4380). Members of the alliance receive discounts on car rental and lodging.

SOURCE: **National Council of Senior Citizens,** 925 15th NW, Washington, DC 20005 (202-347-8800). Members receive discount travel services.

SOURCE: Consider joining special travel groups designed to give information on discounts. One of these is **Moment's Notice.** For a $45 membership fee, you can call their telephone hotline for information on available discounts and receive a quarterly newsletter listing different opportunities. For information, contact: Moment's Notice, 40 East 49th Street, New York, NY 10017 (212-486-0503).

Special Travel Options: Tours, Packages, Adventures, and More

▶ **There are a growing number of special agencies and package deals that are aimed straight at you, the retiree.**

With more Americans growing older, more travel agencies are designing special tours and packages for senior citizens.

These agencies take into account some of the special needs of older travelers by providing such things as hotel rooms equipped for senior citizens—with brighter lights, and such safety features as tub grip bars, and on-call emergency medical care. Some arrange for you to travel only with other people your own age; others have trips for grandparents and their grandchildren. Some agencies offer "adventures"—physically challenging trips that are specially geared to seniors.

The following are some of the agencies that cater to older travelers:

Grand Circle Travel is an agency that, for many years, has specialized in tours for people 55 and over. Their philosophy, according to a vice-president, is to "slow down the pace of the trip. This gives a good balance between free time and traveling."* They offer a range of packages and tours, including cruises, escorted tours, and "multi-center tours" (a combination group travel/live abroad package). For more information, contact: Grand Circle Travel, 347 Congress Street, Boston, MA 02210 (800-221-2610).

SCI National Retirees of America offers a range of tours for seniors, from one-day excursions to cruises. Prices vary according to the specific package. For more informaiton, contact: SCI National Retirees of America, 134 Franklin Street, Hempstead, NY 11550 (800-645-3382).

AARP Travel Services offers about 250 tours for members and their families. You can take a trip in the United States or go abroad.

*"For the Older Voyager, Custom-Made Tours," by Leonard Sloane, *New York Times,* July 8, 1989.

A plus: You're asked to fill out a questionnaire on health topics—this way, the agents can be sure you're physically up to whatever package you choose. If you're not, they'll suggest alternatives. For more information, contact: AARP Travel Services. For land and air tours, call 800-927-0111. For cruises, 800-745-4567.

▶ **A growing trend in tours is "intergenerational travel," or grandparents traveling with their grandchilden.**

This is becoming a very common mode of traveling, ideally suited to our times. With the prevalence of two-income families in which both mother and father work, parents are often unable to spend vacation time with their children. At the same time, the grandparents are usually active and independent—and more than happy to travel with the grandchildren. It's a great way for grandparents to spend time with grandchildren, share happy times, and see different parts of the country—or other countries.

Here are some sources:

Grandtravel is one of the first agencies offering intergenerational vacations. Their programs are designed for children—usually between 7 and 14—and their grandparents, although other relatives or friends are also welcome. Destinations and tour offerings vary from season to season—you may be able to tour a national park, Washington, D.C., or Kenya! Prices are inclusive, covering meals, tips, taxes, and parties for the children. They start at $1,695 per person, double occupancy, for domestic trips and rise much higher for international trips. For information, contact: Grandtravel, 6900 Wisconsin Avenue, Suite 706, Chevy Chase, MD 20815 (800-247-7651).

Similarly, **Vistatours** offers bus coach tours to historical sites, national parks, and other points of interest in the United States. Itineraries are specially planned for each generation to spend time together as well as in solo activities. Some examples of recent packages offered: a weeklong "South Dakota Adventure" touring the Badlands, Mount Rushmore, and other spots, costing $649 per person double occupancy, $586 triple occupancy; the seven-day "Florida Adventure," including three days at Disney World, for $924 per person double occupancy, $780 triple. For more information, contact: Vistatours, 1923 North Carson Street, Suite 105, Carson City, NV 89710 (800-647-0800; 800-648-0912 in Arizona, California, Idaho, Oregon, and Utah).

Saga Holidays, a travel agency that has specialized in vacations for people over 60, offers several packages for grandparents and grandchildren. A recent offering was a five-day "Disney World Winter Break." Costs for their packages include airfare, and prices vary according to the time of year and the location from which you depart. For more information, contact: Saga Holidays, 120 Boylston Street, Boston, MA 02116 (800-343-0273).

▶ **Another special travel option for seniors is "adventure" tours.**

These are exciting options for active people. If you're interested in hiking, mountain climbing, trekking, or canoeing, consider an adventure tour.

For example, **Mount Robson Adventure Holidays** offers hiking and camping trips designed for seniors. You will hike, canoe, and so forth at a slower pace than that set by mixed groups. For more information, contact: Mount Robson Adventure Holidays, Box 146, Valemount, British Columbia VOE, 2Z0 Canada (604-566-4351).

Walking the World is a travel company that specializes in outdoor adventure trips for active people over 50. On some trips, participants camp in a tent; on others, they stay in cabins or bed and breakfasts in addition to or in place of camping out. Most programs, however, involve on-foot travel and outdoor skills, such as using a map or compass, fording streams, cooking outdoors, and fire building. Some programs offer instruction in such things as landscape painting, sketching, and bead working. Two experts, with training in CPR, first aid, and wilderness skills, accompany each trip. Among the specific trips offered recently: 12-day trips to Southwest Ireland, with daily walks and nightly stays at local B-and-Bs; a walking tour of Hawaii; llama treks in Colorado and Wyoming. For more information, contact: Walking the World, P.O. Box 1186, Fort Collins, CO 80522 (303-224-0449).

A slightly different offering that will also appeal to nature-lovers is a camp for senior citizens. For example, the *Vacations and Senior Centers Association* offers special senior citizen camp sessions at 16 camps in the New York, New Jersey, and Pennsylvania area. Camp activities include drama clubs, nature walks, and horseback riding. There are special camps for the visually impaired and for the disabled. For more information, contact: Vacations and Senior Centers Association, 275 Seventh Avenue, New York, NY 10001 (212-645-6590).

International Travel

▶ **For many older adults, retirement means time to go abroad.**

Seeing other countries is one of the big benefits of retirement. You can take certain steps to make your trip more enjoyable. Here are some brief guidelines.

1. *Research your trip carefully ahead of time.*

- Do background research on the countries you're planning to visit. Check the local library for books and magazine articles; call foreign tourist bureaus or travel agents.

SOURCE: You can send for pamphlets on different areas from the government. Among the titles: *Tips for Travelers to Sub-Saharan Africa . . . to the Caribbean . . . to Central and South America . . . to the People's Republic of China . . . to Cuba . . . to Eastern Europe . . . to Mexico . . . to the Middle East and North Africa . . . to South Asia . . . to the USSR.* Send $1.00 for each pamphlet ordered to: Superintendent of Documents, U.S. Government Printing Office, Washington, DC 20402 (202-783-3238). Another good source of information on different countries, also available from the U.S. GPO, is *Background Notes,* which are booklets on 17 different countries.

Send $1.00 for each pamphlet ordered to the previous address, or check with your local Government Printing Office (listed in the phone book).

- Check whether there are any travel advisories posted by the U.S. Department of State for the area to which you're planning to travel. These advisories are issued when there are serious health or security conditions that might affect U.S. citizens. For information, contact a U.S. passport agency, or call the State Department's Citizens Emergency Center at 202-647-5225.

- If you're planning to take a charter flight, double-check the contract: Make sure that the company will guarantee to deliver the services promised—charter companies can go out of business in the middle of your trip, leaving you with useless tickets.

SOURCE: To double-check the reliability of a charter company and to learn if there is a complaint record against it, check with the consumer affairs division of: **American Society of Travel Agents,** 1101 King Street, Alexandria, VA 22314 (703-739-2782).

2. *Take care of administrative tasks (passports, insurance, and so forth) before your trip.*

- Apply for your passport as soon as possible—ideally, three months before your departure date.

- Consider purchasing trip insurance, which will protect you if you are forced to postpone or cancel your trip. Shop around for the best policy. Some good bets—your credit card or traveler's check companies.

- Since Medicare won't cover your hospital or medical care outside the United States in most cases, go over your medigap insurance policy to see if it will cover you. If it doesn't, look into buying short-term insurance or emergency assistance policies—called "medical assistance programs"—to cover you while you're abroad. These will cover medical evacuation and emergency consultation by telephone, as well as hospitalization and medical care. If you have health insurance, you can buy coverage of just the evacuation and consultation for as little as $25 for two weeks; for the entire package, the cost is about $49.

- In certain countries, you will need immunizations. For information, ask your doctor or contact the local health department or U.S. Public Health Service.

3. *Make certain personal preparations before you leave.*

- Stock up on medication before your trip begins and pack an adequate quantity *in its original containers* (important for customs). It is a good idea to bring copies of your prescription with you, especially if it is a narcotic. Also bring along the generic name of your medication in the event you have to renew your prescription overseas. (Drug brand names may vary.)

- Bring an extra pair of eyeglasses. Pack medication and glasses in your *carry-on luggage*. This way, if your luggage is lost or delayed, you have what you need.

- As a just-in-case measure, pack a "passport emergency kit," which will enable you to get a replacement passport if yours is lost. In it, include a photocopy of the first page of your passport, the addresses of U.S. embassies and consulates in each country you're visiting, and two passport-sized photos. And, of course, keep this kit in a different place from your passport!

- Leave a detailed itinerary of your trip with a family member or friend. Include names, addresses, and telephone numbers of where you'll be staying (hotels or individuals); your flight numbers, departure times, arrival times, ticket numbers; your passport number, and the date and place it was issued; the numbers of any credit cards and traveler's checks you'll be bringing. Keep a copy of this information for yourself—away from your purse or wallet, in the event they are lost or stolen.

- Bring only one credit card. Most countries accept a number of them—you won't need to use more than one. If you're concerned about overcharging on one, you can also bring your bank ATM card. Most ATM consortiums—such as CIRRUS and Plus—operate cash machines in most European and many other countries. Ask your bank for more information.

- Don't let fears of inadequate health care keep you from traveling overseas. There are agencies and resources designed to help Americans with medical care overseas. For example, if you are planning to travel overseas and want information on medical assistance once you're there, contact the International Association for Medical Assistance. They put out a directory of English-speaking doctors in 120 countries. Write: International Association for Medical Assistance, 417 Center Street, Lewiston, NY 14092.

On the Road: RVs and Automobiles

▶ **A popular vacation choice for many retirees is traveling in an RV.**

People over 50 account for more than 70% of all RV trips, according to *Modern Maturity*. It's easy to see why—it's a relatively low-cost way of seeing the country; you can travel when and where you want; you can camp out, enjoy nature, and travel to a number of different places.

If you're renting an RV, shop around for the best deal. Many companies will give you a senior discount, ranging anywhere from 10 to 25%. Be sure to ask for quotes giving as specific information as possible, including the specific model of RV, the length of time for which you want it, and pick-up and return locations. Usually your price will include a set maximum number of miles—you'll pay extra for additional miles. It usually will not include insurance, prep charges, kitchenware, linens and other housewares, generator fees, and fuel. Costs for an RV trip are reasonable when compared to other forms of travel—expect to pay about $20 to $25 per night for your campground site (which includes water and electricity hook-ups).

If you're buying an RV, also shop around. You can expect to pay anything from $45,000 to $300,000, depending upon the vehicle you choose. A good idea if you're planning to buy: Rent a few models first to get a feel for how they drive—and how comfortable they are for living. If you own an RV, you can estimate costs of about $1,250 to $2,000 a month—including $300 a month for campsites; $400 or more monthly for gasoline and propane, $200 and up for insurance, and $150 to $200 for general maintenance.

▶ **An important note: Older drivers should take extra precautions.**

First the bad news: After age 65 you are twice as likely to be in a driving accident; after age 75 you are three and one half times as likely to be killed in one.

But by taking a few extra precautions and learning a few tips, you can make an enormous difference in your driving safety.

As you get older, there are two major changes that affect your driving: Your vision gets worse and your reaction time gets slower. Experts therefore recommend maintaining a greater distance between yourself and other cars on the road, making certain to maintain your speed (neither too fast nor too slow), and equipping your car with a few extras: an airbag (this makes an enormous difference during an accident), an antilock braking system (this can counteract your slower reaction time and let you brake effectively), and a special seat with headrest and back support.

SOURCE: For more information on what to buy and what to look for, write: **55 Alive,** AARP, 1909 K Street, NW, Washington, DC 20045.

SOURCE: Two helpful booklets for drivers are *Safe over Sixty* ($7.95), which contains driving tips and safety advice for senior citizens, *The Over 50 Buying Guide* ($9.95), which contains information on car buying and leasing for senior citizens, with recommendations of the best cars to drive, how they handle, and so forth. For either of these, send a check or money order and the name of the publication you want to: John A. Russell Associates, 650 Seventh Street, Hoboken, NJ 07030.

EDUCATION

▶ **You may want to spend some of your leisure time learning—taking courses in different subjects, even getting a college or postgraduate degree.**

Retirement gives you the time to pursue knowledge as never before—and for its own sake. Here are some of your options:

Adult community schools: Most communities offer night school courses on a range of subjects—from cooking to accounting to race-walking. For general information on educational opportunities for adults, contact: Adult Education Association of the United States, 810 18th Street, NW, Washington, DC 20036.

Local universities, colleges, and community colleges: The opportunity to take courses at local schools is one of the main reasons retirees choose to move to college towns. If you live near a school, contact them for their catalogue of continuing education classes. Many schools offer discounts, or even free classes, to people over 60 or 65. For a listing of the colleges in your area that offer free or reduced tuition, write the AARP-sponsored group: The Institute of Lifetime Learning, AARP, 1909 K Street, NW, Washington, DC 20049.

▶ **An extremely popular option combines learning with travel.**

This is the best of both worlds—you get the opportunity to travel and see something of the world, and you can learn something new and exciting at the same time.

One of the most famous programs is **Elderhostel,** a travel-study program that offers courses to people 60 and over at more than 1,000 colleges and universities nationwide and in more than 30 foreign countries. Domestic programs last one week; international programs one to three weeks. Usually it's a real taste of student life: You do everything on campus. You live in a college dorm, eat in a cafeteria, and attend classes. Course studies vary greatly—ranging across the humanities and sciences. Costs are fairly low: In the United States, you can expect to pay about $200 for the week; abroad, including air fare, travel, and room and board, it's about $1,500 on average in Europe; over double that for Asia or Australia. Write for the *Elderhostel Catalogue* of course descriptions: Elderhostel, 75 Federal Street, Third Floor, Boston, MA 02110 (617-426-8056).

Interhostel offers international travel and study programs for people over 50. Programs include stays at foreign colleges and universities, plus cultural events and sightseeing. Many also include special seminars by guest academics and experts. For more information, including a catalogue of their programs, contact: Interhostel, University of New Hampshire, Division of Continuing Education, 6 Garrison Avenue, Durham, NH 03824 (603-862-1147).

Another highly recommended program, especially exciting for people interested in the sciences, is **CEDAM** (Conservation, Education, Diving, Archaeology, Museums). This not-for-profit group arranges expeditions. You may work on an archaeological dig, do nature observancy, scuba dive—whatever it is you do, you can be sure it will be exciting and educational. With the resurgence of interest in the environment, this group has been growing in popularity. For more information, contact: CEDAM, Fox Road, Croton-on-Hudson, NY 10520 (914-271-5365).

Saga Holidays also has introduced lecture tours. One exciting development—they've begun working with the Smithsonian Institution to offer educational tours and cruises. Contact Saga Holidays at the address listed on page 497 or contact: Smithsonian National Associates, Smithsonian Institution, 1100 Jefferson Drive, SW, Room 304S, Washington, DC 20560 (202-357-4700).

SOURCE: If you're interested in adult study-vacation programs, *The Guide to Academic Travel* (240 pages; price, $16.95) is a great one-stop resource, listing hundreds of programs at colleges and universities, museums, and other organizations. Write: Shaw Associates, 625 Biltmore Way, Coral Gables, FL 33134 (305-446-8888).

▶ **You can join the computer revolution and learn how to use a computer, then connect with other retirees via modem.**

You don't have to be computer literate to get involved in high-tech. There's a program designed specifically for adults over age 55. It's called **SeniorNet,** and more than 3,000 older Americans are members.

SeniorNet is a nonprofit organization that trains older adults to use a computer. For a $10 membership, you get an 8-week course taught in person, a newsletter, and the ability to apply for a network account, which then allows you to communicate through your computer with thousands of other retirees.

You can use your computer to hook into the network and hold teleconferencing conversations with other people across the country. It's called "billboarding" and it allows you to type messages onto your screen, which are then transmitted over the telephone lines to other people at their computer terminals—and they'll type a message back. SeniorNet is available through Delphi, the General Videotex Corporation computer network. Costs average about $12.60 an hour. For more information, contact: SeniorNet, University of San Francisco, San Francisco, CA 94117 (415-666-6505).

SPORTS AND FITNESS

▶ **Many sporting organizations have "Masters" clubs and functions for the older athlete.**

As seniors become more active than ever, more sports and fitness activities are being tailormade for the older adult. There are exercise videos for people over 50, special classes for the older athlete, Senior Olympics, races, sporting leagues, "mall walking clubs," and more— all designed for older athletes. (We've covered several activities in the Exercise section on page 409.)

SOURCE: A handy source: The **National Senior Sports Association,** which organizes and conducts recreational activities and competitive events in golf, tennis, and bowling. They also put out the monthly publication *Senior Sports News* and print a schedule of events. For more information, contact: National Senior Sports Association, Suite 205, 10560 Main Street, Fairfax, VA 22030 (703-385-7540).

Appendix A. Early Retirement: When You Decide to Bail Out Early

▶ **Early retirement is tempting to most working people but should be explored carefully.**

The principal reason for careful research is obvious: By taking early retirement, you *could* lose out substantially with pensions and Social Security. In other cases, the loss might be small or nonexistent. Some problems: Particularly with pensions, weighing the financial pros and cons can be a grueling exercise in number crunching. This is one time when a knowledgeable financial planner or your CPA can be very helpful. And on the emotional side of things, it can be difficult deciding whether to leave a job or career.

For many people, however, the decision is easy—all they want is some assurance that it is possible. According to a recent survey by Lehigh University, of 115 early retirees questioned, 68% were satisfied with their decision. According to another survey reported in *The Wall Street Journal,* of the total number of employees offered early retirement at major corporations in the 1980s, 60% took it. But some experts see something else on the horizon. As companies face tougher competition, some are choosing layoffs rather than early retirement sweeteners as a way of reducing payroll costs. Moral: If you want to retire early, think about it early.

Emotional factors: The emotional rewards and problems of retiring early are all too often overlooked. People often idealize early retirement and fail to take major emotional factors into account. Key: Approach the decision calmly and honestly. Ask yourself some questions.

Do I really want to? Disregard the financial for a moment and concentrate on the psychological. What will you do in your time off? According to surveys, the happiest early retirees are those with hobbies and other interests or even new careers they want to pursue. Others became bored. In fact, upward of 50% of all retirees end up in some sort of organized work—part-time as well as full-time, volunteer as well as paid.

Am I ready for the change? Retiring involves a change in your psychological makeup. In the United States, for the most part, we are what we *do;* now others may identify you as a retiree. The psychological consequences of this can be difficult, particularly for younger retirees with friends still absorbed in their careers. One option is to start a new career. But this requires stamina and determination.

Do I really have to? Some people retire early involuntarily, or because they are "strongly encouraged" to. Health is a common reason for early retirement (in a recent survey 30% of a group of early retirees cited health as a primary reason); other reasons include the retirement of a spouse and other family reasons. Others are forced out by management before their time. Before deciding to take the plunge, analyze options. For example, can you switch locales and continue to work if your spouse is ready to retire and you are not? Can you work part-time or at home if your health no longer allows full-time work in the office? Is another corporation interested in your expertise? Don't assume you *must* retire early if you don't want to; very often there are alternatives if you search hard enough.

Is there a second career waiting for me? Retirement can be a time to do it over again without the responsibilities of children and the social pressures of "getting ahead." Some use early retirement to switch to something more fun, like the former banker who became a craftsman working in wood. One couple, formerly with a private accounting practice, took early retirement to become dance instructors for the elderly. They now take several (paid) cruises a year, are working on a video and a book, teach dance to numerous students, teach dance as volunteers at a local hospital, and feel their new career caps their working life. Some retirees find new and more meaningful careers, like those who work in hospices or hospitals, or as low-paid officials of charity organizations, ecology groups, or human rights organizations. Very often business skills are particularly transferable to the nonprofit sector, as with a former banker who retired into a job as the assistant director of a major metropolitan zoo.

Financial factors: Your pension is the heart of the matter for most. Can you afford to retire early? Will your pension cover enough? Problem: Pension rules vary. Below, we'll deal first with early re-

tirement sweeteners offered by corporations (or suggested by you)—
what to look for and what to look out for. Then we'll move to health
and other benefits, then to Social Security, and finally we'll briefly
cover your other sources of retirement income, your savings and
investments. If your pension won't cover early retirement, maybe
you can make up for it with investing or savings. (Also, read Chapter
3, on pensions, particularly page 89, for details on pensions before
59½ and how to reduce taxes.)

Pensions. First, a brief recap of how a typical company pension
plan works, how and why it is lower for early retirees, and how they
or you can sweeten the pot.

Remember: Your pension should replace 50% to 75% of your
current annual salary. And normally, your pension is determined
as a percentage of your final pay, multiplied by your years working
at the company. (Another mode concerns *average* pay, in which case,
early retirement also penalizes you.) A good plan is from 1% to 1.5%
of your last salary multiplied by the number of years you have
worked. Often a company will have a rule whereby a certain combination of years worked and employee age entitle the employee to
full benefits. If you retire early, your pension may be lower because:

- You have fewer years with the company and are younger.

- Your final or average salary, used as a basis for calculation, will
  probably be lower than it would be if you kept on working,
  assuming you would receive raises at least keeping up with inflation.

- Your company may have cut-off points for premature retirement.

The net result: A company usually reduces your percentage benefits by 4% to 5% on average for each year you are beneath the
official full-benefits retirement date. This date varies from company
to company. According to a survey by Hewitt Associates, as reported
in *The Wall Street Journal,* 36% of all companies started full benefits
at 62, another 21% began at 60, and 12% began at 55. A few (3%)
allowed full benefits under 55. If you retire early, these cut-off ages
can cut deeply into your pension. For example, a 60-year-old early
retiree at a firm with a full benefit age of 65 may lose 25% of his or
her pension up front. What can you do?

The first thing is to be lucky. In the 1980s, many companies, in
an effort to reduce high costs, began offering their employees special

"windows" for early retirement. Typically, during these 30- to 90-day periods, selected employees are given sweeteners to make early retirement more attractive. These deals will continue at selected corporations, but recently, the number of offers has dropped. One reason: Many people have already availed themselves of this option. Another: More companies are laying workers off.

How can you analyze an early retirement plan to decide if it's good for you?

- *Getting outside expert advice:* First, go to a well-qualified financial planner. Expect to pay from $75 to $200 an hour for several hours of professional analysis. What you want to do is compare various options: What your retirement salary will be if you choose not to retire early, what it will be if you choose early retirement under the offered plan, what it will be if the deal is sweetened. The next step is to examine alternatives, such as lump sum distributions you may receive. But search carefully for *objective* advice. (Review the section on Financial Planners, page 38.)

- *Negotiate:* You probably negotiated a better deal for yourself when you were first employed—now do the same as you retire. A company offer may not be written in stone: In many cases employees have gotten better deals for themselves by negotiating, or just by asking.

- *Look for pension sweeteners:* A good plan reduces (or eliminates or sweetens) the benefit reduction if you are under full benefit age. Typically, a company will add years of service and years of tenure to make you eligible for more pension benefits up front. What's the norm? It depends. One firm recently added five years to the age and five years to the years of service: The key, of course, is what this means in terms of actual benefits, something you must deduce by looking at your firm's pension schedules. A suggestion: Use their initial offer as a basis for negotiation, maybe adding a year or more to the equation.

- *Look for a Social Security supplement:* A good plan should add a Social Security supplement to tide you over until Social Security begins at 62. For the average middle manager, this is about $10,000 a year. It can be given as a monthly amount or in one large lump sum.

- *Check health insurance:* Unfortunately, you can't expect too much. By law, your employer must provide you your company coverage (at your expense but at company rates) for at least 18 months after retirement, whatever your age. As an early retirement incentive, many companies pay for this coverage until 65. In the past, many companies continued coverage throughout retirement, but this is usually no longer the case. The new financial climate has companies scrambling to trim health benefits any way they can. This can create problems for the early retiree, who is too young to qualify for Medicare, under which the average cost of health coverage drops 50%. Try to negotiate for coverage for as long as you can, a lump sum health care payment, and partial or full payment for another health plan, such as that offered by the American Association of Retired Persons. Also: Get your teeth fixed *before* you retire, since dental coverage is almost never included.

- *Check life insurance:* It's not usually continued. Some very generous companies continue coverage at group rates, others offer you the option of converting from the company group rate to an individual policy. But it is usually cheaper to buy your own new policy.

- *Ask about the extras:* First of all, ask about assistance in evaluating the retirement offer. Some companies offer in-house assistance, others will reimburse you for reasonable planning fees. Some companies pay a lump sum severance payment at retirement based on years of work, some offer discounted products at company stores. In terms of facilities, the U.S. military is probably the most generous, offering overseas PX privileges and MAAC flights around the world.

- *Ask about waivers:* Some companies have included a waiver or a release as part of an early retirement package. The idea is simple: What if an ex-employee who has accepted early retirement decides a few years later that he or she was the victim of age discrimination and decides to sue? A waiver or release protects the company by relinquishing your right to sue it on this or perhaps other issues.

    Naturally, waivers or releases have produced some controversy. However, courts have upheld them so far, providing they were not coercive. What should you do in the (unlikely) event you are asked to sign one? Best bet: Don't sign immediately. Seek the advice of a lawyer who can advise you on current implications.

Appendix B. Late Starters' Retirement: When You've Put Off Planning to the Last Minute

▶ **If you're starting your retirement plan late, here is one comforting thought: You're far from alone.**

For various reasons, many people put off planning for retirement—and then they discover that their pension plan is inadequate, their savings far too low. If you fit this profile, or if your savings level has been so low that it seems impossible to catch up, take heart. In most cases, there is a reasonable way out of your dilemma. Here are some suggestions.

Remember you may be living in your retirement nest egg. Your house may generate a sizable amount of retirement income. There are a number of options you can explore that will enable you to use your house as the prime source of your retirement funds. (See Chapter 11.)

Immediately rev up your savings rate. How? There are various ways:

- *Cut back on expenses and invest the savings.* Start with the fat: Reduce or cut vacations, restaurant expenditures, and your use of pre-prepared food; keep your old car longer, buy a used car if you need a car, fix things yourself, reduce your clothing budget. Encourage children to apply for scholarships. Go further if necessary. It's tough, but in many cases, it *is* possible to squeeze blood from a stone.

- *Cut back on interest expenses.* When you can, pay in cash, and reduce high-cost debt. Prime culprit: credit card expense with interest rates of 18% or more.

- *Cut back on unnecessary financial service expenses:* For example, get rid of high annual fee credit cards (some charge $60 to $80 a year. Look for no-fee checking from a bank. If you can't avoid credit card debt, at least use low-rate cards.

- *Cut back on temptations:* Stop carrying your bank access card (automated teller machines are a prime culprit in low savings rates), carry only one credit card, budget your expenses and bank the rest.

- *If you can, use pretax dollars in the form of FSAs (Flexible Spending Account for dependents) for medical expenses of your children or spouse.* This is a tax break, found mostly in large companies, where you are allowed to pay for up to $5,000 of these expenses with money deducted from your pay—before taxes. Restrictions abound, so check with your company for details.

Maximize the power of deferred tax savings. The more money you save from taxation, the more you have working (and compounding) for you, and the more you'll have later. In most cases, it's to your advantage to shelter as much income as possible from taxation for this reason. An example: $2,000 a year for 10 years (compounded at 8%) grows to $22,530—if you pay yearly taxes on it at 28%. If you shelter it, you'll have $31,291; a substantial savings. Some suggestions:

- *Maximize use of your company savings plan, if it offers one.* Most of these plans offer tax-deferred savings, and in many cases, your company kicks in a matching share.

- *Open an IRA and shelter income-producing investments in it.* You'll reap full advantages if you make a lower income and are not covered by another pension plan, but others can still reap partial advantages. (For more, see IRAs on page 94.)

- *If you're self-employed, supercharge your savings rate by opening a de-fined-*benefit *Keogh (versus the normal defined-*contribution *Keogh).* The difference? This type of savings plan lets you pick the income you want during retirement, then salt away as much in a tax-deferred account as necessary to produce the amount you need. Of course, there are various restrictions (for more, see Keogh Plans, page 105).

- *You might consider a tax-deferred annuity.* Key: Look for safety and shop carefully. (For more, see Annuities, page 258.)

Examine your investment strategy. Don't go wild, but maybe taking on some risk may give you substantially greater rewards. An extra 2% yield per year adds up. In all cases, however, maintain an emergency reserve in a federally insured savings account and remember to keep money you may need soon in fairly liquid investments.

- *Go for more growth stocks:* You might take some money out of fixed-income or money market funds. In almost every five-year period, stocks outperform every other major investment. Best bet: Shelter these money producers in a tax-deferred account. (For more, see Stocks, page 213.)

- *Look at more growth-oriented mutual funds:* If you've bought balanced funds, for example, consider switching some of your money into growth and income funds. But always spread your risk—invest in several different funds. Reinvest dividends. And here, too, shelter the money if possible. (For more, see Mutual Funds, page 200.)

- *Switch some of your money market fund to a short-term bond fund.* Short-term bond funds have longer maturities, which means more yield. Although these are riskier, by checking ratings, you should be able to find a safe fund.

Work now and into retirement. It's getting easier (but it's still not easy) to continue working during retirement. (For suggestions, see page 457.)

Working a second job now can pay off. It doesn't have to be onerous—all you need is a marginal income to increase your savings rate. One advantage of working now, rather than later, is that the sooner you put money into investments, the sooner it can go to work for you and the more you'll have later. And working a second job *can* be a way of socializing or putting your hobby to work. One opportunity is seasonal part-time work: For example, many department stores are extremely short of sales help during holiday seasons.

Appendix C. General Reference Sources

Associations

American Association of Retired Persons (AARP)
1909 K Street, NW
Washington, DC 20049
(202-872-4700)
Perhaps the best-known group for retirees, with over 32 million members age 50 and over, AARP offers a wealth of services and programs for retirees. Among them: a mail-order pharmacy service, travel services, tour groups, group health insurance programs, investment programs, the AARP VISA card, and a wide range of free consumer guide books. They also serve as a political lobbying group protecting the rights of older people. It is highly recommended that you join this group. Annual membership dues are low—$5.00, which includes a subscription to the AARP News Bulletin and the bimonthly magazine *Modern Maturity.*

National Alliance of Senior Citizens
2525 Wilson Blvd.
Arlington, VA 22201
(703-528-4380)
This consumer group lobbies for policies and programs on behalf of senior citizens. Members of the group are eligible for special services and benefits, including prescription drug discounts, special rates on health insurance, and discounts on car rental and lodging. They put out the monthly *Senior Guardian,* and the bimonthly *Our Age.*

National Council of Senior Citizens
925 15th Street, NW
Washington, DC 20005
(202-347-8800)

A nonprofit association of clubs, councils, and other groups, this group distributes information on federal programs for older people, Medicare, Social Security, and employment programs for senior citizens. Members are eligible for benefits such as discounted prescription drugs, discount travel services, and medigap insurance. They publish the monthly *Senior Citizen News*.

National Council on the Aging
West Wing 100
600 Maryland Avenue, SW
Washington, DC 20024
(202-479-1200)
This is a nonprofit organization that develops programs for the aging and provides a national information and consultation center. It holds conferences, puts out information on training programs for older people, sponsors senior centers, and maintains a library. Among their publications: *Older Workers News, Senior Housing News, Aging and Work.* For a complete list of publications, contact them.

Older Women's League
730 11th Street, NW, Suite 300
Washington, DC 20001
(202-783-6686)
This group works with problems and issues concerning older women. In addition to working to influence public policy, they put out a number of publications, such as *The OWL Observer, Questions Women Should Ask for a Healthy Future, Gray Papers,* and *Health Care in Retirement.* There are a number of local OWL chapters (check your telephone directory) that offer special services for older women.

Magazines

Business Week
1221 Avenue of the Americas
New York, NY 10020
(212-997-3608)
A weekly magazine that covers the business world, finance, and investment, *Business Week* gives you background information on your investments, the financial climate, and more.

Forbes
60 Fifth Avenue
New York, NY 10011
(212-620-2200)

This weekly covers business, finance, and investing. It is excellent reading for savvy investors.

Kiplinger's Personal Finance Magazine
1729 H Street, NW
Washington, DC 20006
(202-887-6400
800-544-0155 for subscription information)
One of the best financial magazines around, this monthly offers easy-to-use, hard-hitting financial advice, covering a range of subjects from investing to retirement planning to boosting the resale value of your home. Extremely helpful in preretirement planning and postretirement maintenance.

Modern Maturity
3200 East Carson Street
Lakewood, CA 90712
A subscription to this magazine is available free to members of AARP. With membership dues to AARP costing only $5.00 a year, that's quite a bargain for a magazine filled with useful information. It contains articles on a variety of topics of interest to retirees—money management, insurance, and federal programs, and much more. Recommended reading.

Money
Time & Life Building
1271 Avenue of the Americas
New York, NY 10020
(212-522-1212; for subscriptions, 800-621-8000)
A monthly magazine that offers wide-ranging coverage of a variety of financial issues. Very helpful investment information and hints.

New Choices
850 Third Avenue
New York, NY 10022
(212-715-2600)
This monthly magazine is designed for people age 50 and over. Articles cover monetary topics, hints, jobs after retirement, travel and leisure, and more. Recommended reading.

Smart Money, Real Estate Tips, etc.
Ken and Doria Dolan, noted financial experts, have a series of books and audiocassettes that are extremely useful—and, better yet, enjoyable. All are available at your local bookstore.

Appendix D. Government Agencies

ACTION
1101 Vermont Avenue, NW
Washington, DC 20525
(202-634-9380)
This is a federal agency that sponsors volunteer programs conducted by older adults. They put out a number of booklets on their programs and maintain regional offices in Atlanta, Boston, Chicago, Dallas, Denver, New York City, Philadelphia, San Francisco, and Seattle.

Administration on Aging
330 Independence Avenue, SW
Washington, DC 20201
(202-245-0641)
This federal agency is part of the Department of Health and Human Services. It develops programs for older adults, puts out *Aging Magazine,* and the free booklets *Where to Turn for Help for Older Persons* and *Nationwide Network of State and Area Agencies on Aging.*

National Institute on Aging
Public Information Office
Federal Building, Room 6C12
9000 Rockville Pike
Bethesda, MD 20892
(301-496-1752)
This agency conducts and supports research related to aging. You can contact them for information on physical and mental health programs in aging.

Social Security Administration
Office of Public Inquiries
6401 Security Blvd.
Baltimore, MD 21235
(301-594-1234)
The Social Security Administration puts out a number of booklets on your Social Security benefits, Medicare, and Supplemental Security Income. Check your telephone directory (under Social Security Administration or U.S. Government) for the number and address of your local Social Security office.

TOLL-FREE NUMBERS for Social Security and Medicare:
Social Security Administration: 800-234-5772 (for general information, forms, and so forth).
Medicare Part B: 800-462-9306 (for information on Part B claims).
Medicare Fraud and Abuse: 800-368-5779 (to report suspected Medicare fraud).

State Agencies on Aging

These state offices coordinate services and offer programs for older Americans. You may want to contact them for information on nursing homes, health insurance, special meal programs, transportation programs, and so forth. Offices are listed alphabetically by state.

Alabama
Commission on Aging
136 Catoma Street
Montgomery, AL 36130
800-243-5463 (in state)
205-242-5743

Alaska
Older Alaskans Commission
P.O. Box C, MS 0209
Juneau, AK 99811
907-465-3250

Arizona
Department of Economic Se-
    curity
Aging and Adult Administration
1400 West Washington Street
Phoenix, AZ 85007
602-542-4446

Arkansas
Division of Aging and Adult
    Services
Donaghey Plaza South
Suite 1417
7th and Main Streets
P.O. Box 1417/Slot 1412
Little Rock, AR 72203-1437

California
Department of Aging
1600 K Street
Sacramento, CA 95814
916-322-3887

Colorado
Aging and Adult Services
Department of Social Services
15775 Sherman Street, 10th
    Floor
Denver, CO 80203-1714
303-866-3851

Connecticut
Department on Aging
175 Main Street
Hartford, CT 06106
800-443-9946 (in state)
203-566-7772

Delaware
Division of Aging
Department of Health and So-
    cial Services
1901 N. DuPont Highway
New Castle, DE 19720
302-421-6791

District of Columbia
Office on Aging
Executive Office of the Mayor
1424 K Street, NW
2nd Floor
Washington, DC 20005
202-724-5626
202-724-5622

Florida
Office of Aging and Adult
    Services
1317 Winewood Blvd.
Tallahassee, FL 32301
804-488-8922

Georgia
Office of Aging
Department of Human Re-
    sources
878 Peachtree Street, NE
Room 632
Atlanta, GA 30309
404-894-5333

Guam
Division of Senior Citizens
Department of Public Health
  and Social Services
P.O. Box 2816
Agana, GU 96910
011-671-734-2942

Hawaii
Executive Office on Aging
335 Merchant Street, Room
  241
Honolulu, HI 96813
808-548-2593

Idaho
Office on Aging
Statehouse, Room 114
Boise, ID 83720
208-334-3833

Illinois
Department on Aging
421 E. Capitol Avenue
Springfield, IL 62701
217-785-2870

Indiana
Department of Human Ser-
  vices
251 North Illinois
P.O. Box 7083
Indianapolis, IN 46207-7083
317-232-7020

Iowa
Department of Elder Affairs
Suite 236, Jewett Building
914 Grand Avenue
Des Moines, IA 50319
515-281-5187

Kansas
Department on Aging
122-S, Docking State Office
  Building
915 SW Harrison
Topeka, KS 66612-1500
913-296-4986

Kentucky
Division for Aging Services
Department for Social Services
275 E. Main Street
Frankfort, KY 40621
502-564-6930

Louisiana
Governor's Office of Elderly
  Affairs
P.O. Box 80374
Baton Rouge, LA 70989-0374
504-925-1700

Maine
Maine Committee of Aging
State House, Station 127
Augusta, ME 04333
207-289-3658

Maryland
State Agency on Aging
301 West Preston Street
Baltimore, MD 21201
301-225-1102

Massachusetts
Executive Office of Elder Affairs
38 Chauncy Street
Boston, MA 02111
800-882-2003 (in state)
617-727-7750

Michigan
Office of Services to the Aging
P.O. Box 30026
Lansing, MI 48909
517-373-8230

Minnesota
Minnesota Board on Aging
Human Services Building
4th Floor
444 Lafayette Road
St. Paul, MN 55155-3843
612-296-2770

Mississippi
Council on Aging
301 W. Pearl Street
Jackson, MS 39203-3092
800-222-7622 (in state)
601-949-2070

Missouri
Division of Insurance
Truman Building 630
P.O. Box 690
Jefferson, MO 65102-0690
800-235-5503 (in state)

Montana
Department of Family Services
P.O. Box 8005
Helena, MT 59604
406-444-5900

Nebraska
Department on Aging
Legal Services Developer
State Office Building
301 Centennial Mall South
Lincoln, NE 68509
402-471-2306

Nevada
Department of Human Re-
sources
Division for Aging Services
505 E. King Street
Room 101
Carson City, NV 89701
702-885-4210

New Hampshire
Department of Health and
Human Services
Division of Elderly and Adult
Services
6 Hazen Drive
Concord, NH 03301
603-271-4394

New Jersey
Department of Community
Affairs
Division on Aging
S. Broad and Front Sts.
CN 807
Trenton, NJ 08625-0807
609-292-0920

New Mexico
Agency on Aging
La Villa Rivera Building
4th Floor
224 E. Palace Avenue
Santa Fe, NM 87501
800-432-2080 (in state)
505-827-7640

New York
State Office for the Aging
Agency Building
2 Empire State Plaza
Albany, NY 12223-0001
800-342-9871 (in state)
518-474-5731

North Carolina
Department of Human Resources
Division of Aging
1985 Umstead Drive
Raleigh, NC 27603
919-733-3983

North Dakota
Department of Human Services
Aging Services Division
State Capitol Building
Bismarck, ND 58505
701-224-2577

Ohio
Department of Aging
50 West Broad Street
8th Floor
Columbus, OH 43266-0501
614-466-1221

Oklahoma
Department of Human Services
Aging Services Division
P.O. Box 25352
Oklahoma City, OK 73125
405-521-2327

Oregon
Department of Human Resources
Senior Services Division
313 Public Service Building
Salem, OR 97310
800-232-3020 (in state)
503-378-4636

Pennsylvania
Department of Aging
231 State Street
Barto Building
Harrisburg, PA 17101
717-783-1550

Puerto Rico
Governor's Office of Elderly
   Affairs
Gericulture Commission
Box 11398
Santurce, PR 00910
809-722-2429
809-722-0225

Rhode Island
Department of Elderly Affairs
160 Pine Street
Providence, RI 02903
401-277-2858

South Carolina
Commission on Aging
400 Arbor Lake Drive
Suite B-500
Columbia, SC 29223
803-735-0210

South Dakota
Agency on Aging
Adult Services and Aging
Richard F. Kneip Building
700 Governors Drive
Pierre, SD 57501-2291
605-773-3656

Tennessee
Commission on Aging
706 Church Street
Suite 201
Nashville, TN 37219-5573
615-741-2056

Texas
Department on Aging
P.O. Box 12786
Capitol Station
Austin, TX 78711
512-444-2727

Utah
Division of Aging & Adult
  Services
120 North 200 West
P.O. Box 45500
Salt Lake City, UT 84145-
  0500
801-538-3910

Vermont
Office on Aging
Waterbury Complex
103 South Main Street
Waterbury, VT 05676
802-241-2400

Virgin Islands
Department of Human Ser-
  vices
Barbel Plaza South
Charlotte Amalie
St. Thomas, VI 00802
809-774-0930

Virginia
Department for the Aging
700 Centre, 10th Floor
700 East Franklin Street
Richmond, VA 23219-2327
800-552-4464 (in state)
804-225-2271

Washington
Aging and Adult Services
  Administration
Department of Social and
  Health Services
Mall Stop OB-44-A
Olympia, WA 98504
206-586-3768

West Virginia
Commission on Aging
State Capitol Complex
Holly Grove
Charleston, WV 25305
800-642-3671 (in state)
304-348-3317

Wisconsin
Bureau on Aging
Department of Health and So-
  cial Services
P.O. Box 7851
Madison, WI 53707
800-242-1060 (in state)
608-266-2536

Wyoming
Commission on Aging
Hathaway Building, 1st Floor
Cheyenne, WY 82002
800-442-2766 (in state)
307-777-7986

State Insurance Departments

These state offices are responsible for enforcing state laws and regulations on insurance, as well as providing information on insurance. You may want to contact your state insurance department for information on medigap insurance or to complain about any problems you are having with your insurance company or agent. Offices are listed alphabetically by state.

Alabama Insurance Department
136 South Union Street
Montgomery, AL 36130-3401
205-269-3550

Alaska Insurance Department
3601 C Street, Suite 740
Anchorage, AK 99503
907-562-3626

Arizona Insurance Department
3030 North Third Street
Phoenix, AZ 85012
602-255-4783

Arkansas Insurance Department
400 University Tower Bldg.
12th & University Streets
Little Rock, AR 72204
501-371-1813

California Insurance Department
3450 Wilshire Blvd.
Los Angeles, CA 90010
800-233-9045

Colorado Insurance Division
303 West Colfax Avenue—5th Fl.
Denver, CO 80204
303-620-4300

Connecticut Insurance Department
165 Capitol Avenue
State Office Building
Hartford, CT 06106
203-297-3800

Delaware Insurance Department
841 Silver Lake Blvd.
Dover, DE 19901
302-736-4251

District of Columbia Insurance
613 G Street, NW—Room 619
P.O. Box 37200
Washington, DC 20001-7200
202-727-8017

Florida Department of Insurance
State Capitol
Plaza Level Eleven
Tallahassee, FL 32399-0300
800-342-2762
904-488-0030

Georgia Insurance Department
2 Martin Luther King, Jr., Dr.
Room 716 West Tower
Atlanta, GA 30334
404-656-2056

Guam Insurance Department
855 W. Marine Drive
P.O. Box 2796
Agana, Guam 96910
011-671-477-1040

Hawaii Department of Commerce and Consumer Affairs
Insurance Division
P.O. Box 3614
Honolulu, HI 96811
808-548-5450

Idaho Insurance Department
500 S. 10th Street
Boise, ID 83720
208-334-3102

Illinois Insurance Department
320 West Washington Street
Springfield, IL 62767
217-782-4515

Indiana Insurance Department
311 W. Washington Street
Suite 300
Indianapolis, IN 46204
317-232-2395

Iowa Insurance Division
Lucas State Office Bldg.
East 12th & Grand Sts.
Des Moines, IA 50319
515-281-5705

Kansas Insurance Department
420 S.W. 9th Street
Topeka, KS 66612
913-296-3071

Kentucky Insurance Department
229 West Main Street
P.O. Box 517
Frankfort, KY 40602
502-564-3630

Louisiana Insurance Department
P.O. Box 94214
Baton Rouge, LA 70804-9214
504-342-5900

Maine Bureau of Insurance
State House, Station 34
Augusta, ME 04333
207-582-8707

Maryland Insurance Department
501 St. Paul Place
Baltimore, MD 21202-2272
301-333-2792

Massachusetts Insurance Division
280 Friend Street
Boston, MA 02114
617-727-7189

Michigan Insurance Department
P.O. Box 30220
Lansing, MI 48909
517-373-0220

Minnesota Insurance Department
133 East 7th Street
St. Paul, MN 55101
612-296-4026

Mississippi Insurance Department
P.O. Box 79
Jackson, MS 39205
601-359-3569

Missouri Division of Insurance
P.O. Box 690
Jefferson City, MO 65102-0690
314-751-2640

Montana Insurance Department
126 N. Sanders
Mitchell Building
P.O. Box 4009, Rm. 270
Helena, MT 59604
800-332-6148 (in state)
406-444-2040

Nebraska Insurance Department
Terminal Building
941 O Street, Suite 400
Lincoln, NE 68508
402-471-2201

Nevada Department of Commerce
Insurance Division
1665 Hot Springs Road
Capitol Complex
Carson City, NV 89701
702-687-4279

New Hampshire Insurance Department
169 Manchester Street
Concord, NH 03301
603-271-2261

New Jersey Insurance Department
20 W. State Street
Roebling Building
Trenton, NJ 08625
609-292-4757

New Mexico Insurance Department
P.O. Box 1269
Santa Fe, NM 87504-1269
505-827-4500

New York Insurance Department
160 West Broadway
New York, NY 10013
800-342-3736 (in state, outside of NYC)
212-602-0203 (in NYC and out of state)

North Carolina Insurance Department
Dobbs Building
P.O. Box 26387
Raleigh, NC 27611
919-733-2004

North Dakota Insurance Department
Capitol Building—5th Floor
Bismarck, ND 58505
701-224-2440

Ohio Insurance Department
2100 Stella Court
Columbus, OH 43266-0566
614-644-2673

Oklahoma Insurance Department
P.O. Box 53408
Oklahoma, OK 73152-3408
405-521-2628

Oregon Department of Insurance and Finance
21 Labor and Industry Building
Salem, OR 97310
503-378-4484

Pennsylvania Insurance Department
1326 Strawberry Square
Harrisburg, PA 17120
717-787-2317

Puerto Rico Insurance Department
Fernandez Juncos Station
P.O. Box 8330
Santurce, PR 00910
809-722-8686

Rhode Island Insurance Division
223 Richmond Street
Suite 233
Providence, RI 02903-4233
401-277-2223

South Carolina Insurance Department
P.O. Box 100105
Columbia, SC 29202-3105
803-737-6140

South Dakota Insurance Department
910 East Sioux Avenue
Pierre, SD 57501-3940
605-773-3563

Tennessee Department of Commerce and Insurance
500 James Robertson Parkway, 4th Fl.
Nashville, TN 37219
800-342-4029 (in state)
615-741-4955

Texas Board of Insurance
1110 San Jacinto Blvd.
Austin, TX 78701-1998
512-463-6501

Utah Insurance Department
3110 State Office Bldg.
Salt Lake City, UT 84114
801-530-6400

Vermont Department of Banking and Insurance
120 State Street
Montpelier, VT 05602
802-828-3301

Virgin Islands Insurance Department
Kongers Garde No. 18
St. Thomas, VI 00802
809-774-2991

Virginia Insurance Department
700 Jefferson Building
P.O. Box 1157
Richmond, VA 23209
804-786-7691

Washington Insurance Department
Insurance Building AQ21
Olympia, WA 98504-0321
800-562-6900 (in state)
206-753-7300

West Virginia Insurance Department
2019 Washington Street, E
Charleston, WV 25305
304-348-3386

Wisconsin Insurance Department
P.O. Box 7873
Madison, WI 53707
608-266-0103

Wyoming Insurance Department
Herschler Building
122 West 25th Street
Cheyenne, WY 82002
307-777-7401

INDEX